MAKING MUSIC AND
ENRICHING LIVES

Making Music
and
Enriching Lives

A Guide for All Music Teachers

BONNIE BLANCHARD
WITH CYNTHIA BLANCHARD ACREE

Indiana University Press
Bloomington & Indianapolis

This book is a publication of

Indiana University Press
601 North Morton Street
Bloomington, IN 47404-3797 USA

http://iupress.indiana.edu

Telephone orders   800-842-6796
Fax orders   812-855-7931
Orders by e-mail   iuorder@indiana.edu

The paper used in this publication meets the minimum requirements of
American National Standard for Information Sciences—Permanence of
Paper for Printed Library Materials, ANSI Z39.48-1984.

Manufactured in the United States of America

Library of Congress Cataloging-in-Publication Data

Blanchard, Bonnie.
  Making music and enriching lives : a guide for all music teachers /
Bonnie Blanchard ; with Cynthia Blanchard Acree.
     p. cm.
  Includes bibliographical references and index.
  ISBN: 978-0-253-34915-6 (cloth : alk. paper)—
  ISBN: 978-0-253-21917-6 (pbk. : alk. paper) 1. Music—Instruction
and study. 2. Music—Economic aspects. I. Acree, Cynthia Blanchard.
II. Title.
  MT1.B652 2007
  780.71—dc22
                                        2006038225

3 4 5 12 11 10

Music is the bridge from one heart to another.
—Unknown

CONTENTS

ACKNOWLEDGMENTS

Making Music and Enriching Lives was born of a one-hour speech to the National Flute Association. Over the years, teachers had often approached me saying, "Please write a book so we can share your techniques." I had envisioned writing a mentoring book for teachers. It wasn't until Karen Iglitzin, a fine violinist and youth chamber music program director suggested, "With handouts, your speech could be a book," that I turned my vision into action. Several years and challenges later, I'm grateful for the impetus she gave me to undertake such a demanding yet rewarding project.

Once I started writing, the natural person to turn to was my sister, Cynthia Acree, a writing consultant and author of *The Gulf between Us*. She helped me to find my writing voice while working tirelessly to organize and edit my writing, and add her own ideas. Most importantly, Cindy was my partner every step of the way. Without her patience, skill, and computer tutoring, I would have given up years ago. I'm indebted to her husband, Cliff, and boys, Stephen and Mark, for sharing her for so long.

Cindy introduced me to her remarkable literary agent, Jim Sutton. I felt flattered and grateful when Jim, a mainstream professional publishing executive, saw the value of the project, even in the early stages. With his guidance, I found the ideal publisher to share my vision. At Indiana University Press, I have had the good fortune to work with Assistant Music Editor Donna Wilson, who chose the book; copyeditor Carrie Jadud, who did an insightful job of editing; and Managing Editor Miki Bird, who enthusiastically oversaw the whole project. With their skill and support, my vision became reality.

Many talented music friends offered formative suggestions and encouraged me. It's impossible to name them all on this page. I sincerely appreciate Sir James Galway for his kind words and his brilliant performances that inspire me. I especially wish to thank my dear friend Melinda Bargreen, Classical Music Critic for the *Seattle Times*. My unfailing anchor and advocate, her invaluable advice and perpetual enthusiasm energized me and the book. Mary Kay Wilson, my talented accompanist, read every version of the manuscript and used her top notch grammar skills to spot even the most esoteric of errors. Hal Ott, Professor of Flute at Central Washington University, tested my ideas against reality and continually supported me.

I also wish to thank my teachers and colleagues who instilled in me a lifelong love of music and the skills to share it. They include my flute teacher, the late Dorothy Bjarnason, my college choir director, Rodney Eichenberger, and my viola teacher, Eileen Swanson. I became a better player and teacher by attending master classes from Amy Porter, Brad Garner, Tim Day, Michel DeBost, Patricia George, and Jill Felber. And I can't forget my students and their parents who allowed me to experiment with them and test my ideas. I'm privileged to be your teacher and your friend.

My cherished mom, Emily, instilled in her girls the tenacity to work fourteen-hour days, and shared my housekeeping to allow me precious time to write. My sons, Scott and Kyle, suffered while I hogged the computer for five years. Don, my tone-deaf yet supportive husband, helped me to keep my priorities straight and was always ready with a big hug. I am so lucky! And finally, a word of warning to my dear friends who cheered my progress in writing this book: I'm already hard at work on the second volume!

Part 1

ENRICHING LIVES

ONE

Transform Your Teaching Style: *The* Music for Life *Method*

We music teachers have a wonderful job! What other profession allows you to use your creativity, enjoy wonderful music, and change lives? It's thrilling to watch students learn focus and self-confidence while developing their potential and their love of music. Few things are more rewarding than taking students who are "blank slates" and turning them into dazzling musicians. I'm thankful every day to have found this means of feeding my family *and* my soul. But teaching *does* have its challenges—getting kids to practice, charging for make-up lessons, dealing with interfering or reluctant parents, and inspiring students to become successful performers. In this book I'll share with you my personal journey of teaching music and developing the creative solutions that make our jobs more effective and rewarding.

I've been a private flute teacher for more than thirty years. During that time, I've learned a lot, much of it by trial and error. Did my music and teaching degrees help? Yes, but I wish they had included more practical techniques. Through the years I've honed my skills to create a studio of students who are motivated to learn and work hard. I'm fortunate that my students have a track record of winning competitions at the local, state, and national level. Don't get me wrong—teaching students who win awards and scholarships to top colleges and conservatories is great, but awards and recognition are not my greatest reward. They're not even the best evidence of my teaching skills. My greatest pride comes from knowing my students enjoy playing and love their lessons with me. My greatest satisfaction is in seeing how my teaching inspires them and enriches their lives, long after our lessons together have ended.

In this introductory chapter, I will summarize a method that has helped me meet the many challenges we all face. It's a simple but life-changing method that will improve the quality and enjoyment of your teaching and make a more lasting impact on your students' lives. In short, the *Music for Life* viewpoint will transform your teaching style.

THE *MUSIC FOR LIFE* APPROACH

I decided to write the *Music for Life* series in response to requests I've received from all types of music teachers, from private studio teachers to those teaching at the college level. To follow in the series are books for students and parents, and instrument-specific teaching techniques books. You'll find these books to be not at all theoretical, but filled with helpful strategies and practical hints you can immediately apply in your studio. In this volume, *Making Music and Enriching Lives,* written for music teachers, I've included practical strategies and techniques to help increase both your results and your enjoyment of teaching. Best of all, you'll inspire students to develop a lifelong love of music: *Music for Life.*

With each chapter I'll challenge you to implement as many new ideas as possible into your next day of teaching. My goal is for you to build a studio of students who love playing their instruments and look forward to their lessons. I want you to be the teacher every student is clamoring for! First, let's start with an overview of the principles we will discuss in part 1 that form the foundation of the *Music for Life* approach.

Focus on Relationships First

For years, students, parents, and teachers have asked me, "How is it that your students always perform so well and love what they're doing?" It's true that my unique teaching techniques help, but I believe the biggest difference stems from my philosophy of teaching. That philosophy is deceptively simple: To be successful, you must base your teaching on relationships. Once you've established these mutually trusting relationships, you'll not only be a better teacher, you'll enjoy the process more, and your students will be happier and more successful.

My guiding principle is "Love your students and they'll love their lessons and their music." When you enjoy your students and form a bond with them, they will be open to the right balance of pressure and support. No matter how well you know your instrument or what great literature you can play, if you haven't formed a solid base of trusting relationships with your students and parents, the whole pyramid may tumble.

Why are strong relationships the key to getting results? The first reason is the difference these relationships will make in your own attitude. I truly love my students; most are like family to me. When I brag to people about my "kids" I often have to distinguish between my "personal" children and my students. If I didn't, people might wonder how many times I had given birth! Forming personal connections with your students inspires you to work harder to give them the tools they need to achieve their goals. Anticipate each student's arrival as you would a friend coming to visit—never as a paycheck walking through the door.

Secondly, knowing students as individuals makes you a better teacher. Students can't learn to play well from only a book or a CD; it takes personal interaction. The better you know your students, the better you know how they learn best, what inspires them, and what upsets them. Knowing I understand and support them, my students are more open to trying hard music and to my criticism. At times, my coaching suggestions can be blunt, but my students accept my approach and even thrive on it, knowing the criticism comes from someone who cares about them unconditionally.

A third reason to spend time building relationships is the meaning it adds to your students' lives, and to your own. Years ago my student Laura wrote in a Mother's Day card I received at our annual Mother's Day recital, "You may not be my biological mother, but you are a second mother to me. You have encouraged me, comforted me, and listened to me through our many years together." How important it is for kids to be able to confide in a trusted adult outside of the family, someone they can learn from and depend on.

To create mutual trust, you must let your students get to know you, too. One day when I was in seventh grade, I was shopping at the local Safeway with my mom. As we turned the corner toward the meat department, I spotted my math teacher putting a package of chicken into her cart. I was shocked! I had never imagined my teacher doing such a normal everyday thing as shopping for groceries. Students need to know their teachers are real people, too!

Transfer students have come to my studio who couldn't even remember their former teacher's name! (Perhaps that's why they are their *former* teachers?) When you laugh at your own mistakes, relate anecdotes about your life, and tell students about your successes and failures, they see you as more than just a teacher. They grow to trust you as a mentor and a friend whom they will work hard to please.

Form strong ties with parents, too. Parents can give you insights into their children, and involving them in students' music training almost always boosts student achievement. Invite parents to lessons and recitals. Chat with them at contests and competitions. Communicate regularly through a monthly letter or e-mails. Give them ideas on how to help their children practice and how to reward them for their progress. You're missing a valuable resource if you don't use parents as part of your team.

Instill Pride and Respect in Your Students

Treat being a member of your studio as a privilege. People often remark about how my students love me and their lessons. "Of course they do," I reply, "That's the first thing I teach them!" At the first lesson I tell students the same password, or secret phrase, they must use to belong to my studio: "I love my flute teacher and my flute lessons very much!" Requiring this password for entry begins to establish our "mutual admiration society."

I talk about my studio as an elite club in which students are lucky to be members. What is the price of admission? Practice and participation! I use phrases such as "All my students have good tone and you will, too" and "All of my students practice an hour a day." This generalization lets them know what is expected to stay in this special club. Typecast them individually too, and in a positive way. Make observations such as "Katie, I can always count on you for beautiful phrasing." Even if your positive spin is only "Here you are again, right on time!" give them a reputation to live up to.

Welcome students into your studio and foster the feeling that the next hour will be a special event. Relay that feeling of their importance by having a vibrant, attractive studio, by dressing in a professional manner, and treating students as important and fun people. Greet them with a warm hello and a smile and expect the same from them. If students come into my studio without a happy greeting to me, I have them march right back outside and come in again. "Hi Bonnie!" they'll say, laughing. "It's great to see you!" We joke around even during the most serious lessons and I try to make each lesson a fun time.

Deepen your student-teacher partnership by making students feel important and appreciated. Take time during every lesson to compliment. Even if it is about the cool book bag or the cute hair clip, one compliment can go a long way. Be interested in their achievements in and out of music. Get excited about their winning soccer game and their hard-earned A in math. Make it your goal to never let a student leave a lesson without hearing at least one bit of flattery. When students do something especially well, drop everything, and give them a huge compliment. Occasionally stop them in the middle of the piece and say, "That was beautiful. Could you play it one more time for me to enjoy?"

Write little notes in students' manuscript books for them to later discover at home. Imagine the mileage you will get by sending an e-mail compliment such as "Wow! I could tell you practiced this week!" They'll read that sentence and run right to their instrument. If you really want to make an impression, compliment them in front of other people, or let them overhear your praise. Run out to the car after a lesson to tell parents, "He deserves an ice cream cone on the way home!"

Build Team Spirit

Encouraging friendships within your studio helps students feel they are playing on the same team. My students start getting to know each other through pictures on a bulletin board in my studio. At the first lesson I "introduce" students by referring to their school photos and those of studio events we have enjoyed. New students see pictures of retirement home concerts, contest winners laden with flowers, reward parties in our hot tub and at restaurants, students posing with famous flutists, and lots of smiling faces at our epic Mother's Day recitals.

As I describe these events to new students, I talk about how they, too, will be inducted into this "Hall of Fame" by participating in these events. I brag about my other students and predict how much they'll enjoy meeting them. Another fun way my students get to know each other is through ensemble playing. Thirteen-year-old Lucy is not the most faithful when it comes to practicing. When asked why she keeps taking lessons she frankly admitted, "For the ensembles and the parties!" Later in this chapter and in chapter 13, we'll talk in more detail about hosting fun musical events.

Group events build team spirit and provide opportunities for more experienced students to serve as role models. Fostering teamwork is also crucial in a studio of high achievers to prevent jealousy and rivalries. In chapter 3, "Instill Pride and Respect," I'll show you creative ways to generate a feeling of belonging and pride among the students of your studio. You'll also learn how to set studio values for students to uphold and how to maintain their respect for you and your status as a teacher.

Expect More from Yourself

Being a music teacher isn't a profession, it's a passion. (You know we're not in it for the money!) Teaching is not something you do; it's who you are. Carefully examine your motivation for teaching. Some people pursue a career in education because it's what they've wanted to do all along; others teach because they never realized their own musical ambitions. Don't view teaching as second best to performing or something to occupy yourself until you "make it big." Make teaching a choice, not a consolation prize. The best motive for teaching music is not because you love music; it is the desire to enrich lives. Without this motivation, even the most talented instrumentalists will be unsuccessful. Look forward to every day and have fun with your students. Show your students your zeal and dedication and rejoice in the progress each student makes. Appreciate your good fortune in having music in your life and being able to change the world through your students.

As President John Kennedy advised, "Ask not what your country can do for you—ask what you can do for your country." Well, I'm no John Kennedy, but I can tell you the harder you work for your students, the harder they'll work for you. Expect more from yourself than you do from your students. Instead of looking at the clock and inwardly groaning that you still have fifteen minutes to endure in the lesson, worry about how you will be able to fit everything you've planned into that last fifteen minutes. Don't just be a teacher, be committed to being a *great* teacher.

Let me tell you about a private music teacher I met whom I'll call Marie. Marie has taught for forty years and maintains a teaching load of fifty students. She dreads her daily teaching routine. Who wouldn't? She doesn't enjoy her students or their lessons and is frequently disappointed by their results. "My students don't practice and they sound horrible," Marie moans. "I don't know if it's the books I use, parents who aren't supportive, or that my students are plain dumb or lazy." "How come *I* never get the good students?" Looking perplexed, she adds, "I need some of your magic. How do you do it?"

Well, I can tell you I have no "magic," although sometimes my studio feels like the Magic Kingdom—a fun place where dreams do come true. Marie puts in many long, hard hours with her students, yet she only works with them on band music and teaches them nothing about music theory or history. They never enter contests, she doesn't hold recitals, and she has never attended a professional music conference or read any educational literature. Most telling of all, Marie uses the same teaching techniques *she* was taught forty years ago. Who wouldn't feel bored and frustrated?

Marie's full teaching schedule is only partly to blame. The sheer number of students is not as critical to teacher burnout as is attitude. Don't be content with the "status quo"; commit yourself to working harder. You may be doing more, but it won't seem like more work because you'll have control over your environment, you will feel more fulfilled, and your students will be more successful. The results will energize you!

Of course we all have students whose playing we'd rather no one else ever heard, but if your students are consistently not making the grade, ask yourself what more *you* could do. Chapter 4, "Show Students Your Commitment to Excellence" shows you how to have the same high standards for yourself that you expect from your students.

Teach Students to Be Their Own Teachers

One of the best ways to create lifelong musicians is to teach students to become independent. Start by teaching the whole musician, not just the instrumentalist. Teach students the basic building blocks of music theory, history, rhythm, and musicality, and they will be able to solve their own problems. Teach them so well that they become their own teachers.

Not all teachers use this approach. One transfer student came to me after taking two years of lessons. When we reviewed what she had learned, she told me she could play all her scales. "Great!" I said, "Can you tell me the key signature for E major?" "Oh," she said. "I don't know my key signatures!" When I asked another transfer student how she decided where to breathe, she said, "Wherever my teacher tells me to." My own first piano teacher used to write in the names of all the notes, circle the sharps and flats in red, and then play the piece for me so I could hear the rhythm! If she had trained me in basic skills, my own flute students wouldn't laugh at my piano playing now!

If you teach your students to play scales, then teach them how scales are built. If they play Mozart, then tell them about Mozart's life. If they play Bach, tell them about the performance practices in the Baroque period. If you want them to learn how to sight read, teach them how to count. This may sound obvious, but you'd be surprised at how many students only know a couple of pieces which they learned by rote. If you only concentrate on the music and not the *building blocks* of music, you are cheating your students. They may sound good on those two pieces you've worked on together but they are nothing more than trained seals. When students know the basics, they can master music on their own.

Train your students to become independent musicians and creative thinkers. Instead of always telling them your way, ask, "What do *you think*?" When they face a technical problem at lessons, teach them how to figure it out on their own; don't solve it for them! If they don't know how to count a rhythm, don't play it for them. Have them go through the steps of marking the beats and counting out loud. If the runs are a big jumble, show them how to iron them out by taking out the slurs, slowing their playing, and using different rhythms. If they don't know how to phrase, teach them about sequences and appoggiaturas. If they make a mistake, ask, "What was wrong with your pitch?" or say, "Your rhythm wasn't right in that measure. What did *you* play and how *should* it be played?" Chapter 5, "Promote a Love of Learning and Independence," will help you guide students to solve their own problems at lessons and at home.

Create an Atmosphere of Achievement

Setting high standards and getting results go hand in hand. Many consider me a tough teacher because I expect my students to practice an hour a day, attend flute events, and participate in studio recitals and contests. None of these requirements is a surprise to my students because I tell them my standards and requirements when I first speak to them.

Once you've communicated your standards, how do you get students to reach for them? Just ask them! Students are like husbands and housework; they will only do as much as you ask them to do. (Male readers, forgive my stereotype.) Are you hesitant to ask students to practice because they're too busy or they might think it's too hard? Are you afraid of seeming pushy, or are you scared they'll quit? Maintaining these high expectations may not always make us popular, but requiring students to sustain high standards means you *care*. I guarantee you will be shocked at what they will accomplish when you ask them to do more.

Each of us as teachers must decide the level of performance and commitment we expect. I know a piano teacher whose only requirement is that her students show up for lessons *breathing*. Another teacher only accepts new violin students if they promise to practice three hours a day, have two lessons a week, and declare they are conservatory bound by eighth grade. For most of us, our personal goals and standards are somewhere in between those extremes.

Hold students to high standards from the first lesson. Perhaps you will lose a few prospective students, and you may even have to "fire" one or two who choose not to fulfill your expectations, but tough love gets results. Ultimately students will appreciate you and love their music even more.

Why is it worth the trouble of imposing high standards on your students? It's worth it because life will be much easier in the long run. Setting high standards can be tough at first, but it's no different than the standards parents must set. It may be easier to let our children skip school, eat only junk food, watch TV, and play video games all day, but in the long run we'd end up with children who are unprepared to lead productive lives.

The same philosophy holds for your students. Sometimes it's easier to let things slide, or to pass students on when the piece is "good enough," but a determination for excellence pays off in the *long* run. When you have clear, consistent expectations for your students you'll hear better music, you won't have to be a policeman, and you won't burn out: you'll be having too much fun. Your students won't want to quit, either, because once they've been through "boot camp" they will be too excited about getting good to stop.

My student Anna said, "Some of my friends talk about how nice their teacher is, but my friends play so bad, I think that not being really nice all the time makes you a better teacher." When you impose high standards, students will improve so quickly that their enthusiasm will make teaching so much fun; they will love their lessons and you will love your job. The word will get around that you have high teaching standards and good students. Isn't this the clientele we all want to attract? Create an atmosphere of learning and achievement and you'll be surprised what your students can do. In chapter 6, I'll show you, step by step, how to achieve these results.

Expect More, Get More

How do you get a studio of talented students? *Expect them to be talented!* "But my students can't play hard music/memorize/play musically/perform under pressure," you think. I counter your doubts by asking, "Have you ever *expected* them to?" You've probably heard of the science experiment that began at the start of a new school year. The teacher was told that half of her students were bright and the other half about average. At the end of the year the academic records of the two groups held true to what she had expected. But here's the twist. Those bright and average students were put into groups at random! The only difference was in the mind of the teacher. Their academic performance had nothing to do with their innate ability but everything to do with the teacher's bias. Research has since proven many times this "expectation" or "Pygmalion" effect.

Treat your students as if they will become accomplished musicians and they'll begin to believe they can be. From the beginning talk about how good they are going to be. Pick a strength to compliment in beginners, even if it is only their ability to sit up straight and hold the instrument. Build on that strength. Act as if it is unusual for someone to learn as quickly as they do and they will learn more quickly. You will be shocked at what they *can* and *will* do if you only ask. What you expect, you're likely to get!

Encourage students to work for their *personal* best. If students play a piece well one time, expect them to play it that well every time. Although she wasn't a teacher, my mother knew instinctively to do this. I'll never forget the day I made my bed by myself for the first time. Excited with my big-girl achievement, I pointed with pride to my slightly rumpled bed and waited for my mother to praise me for being such a clever girl. Instead, my mother simply replied, "That's wonderful, dear. Now you can make your own bed every day." "Oh, no!" I thought. Making it once had been a fun new experience, but to make it *every* day? Use my mother's standards for your students. Ask, "Was that your best? Are you satisfied?" When students master a technique once, expect them to master it every time.

When students play below their abilities say, "That was not up to your level." If they ask, "Should I try that again?" Always say, "Yes!" Never let sloppy playing pass, even if it is a beginner or the last student of the day. Teach your students pride in their playing by shipping a piece back home until it is played right. When they have finally conquered it, say, "Now you can be proud of what you did!"

Attitude Is Everything

Strengthen students' self-esteem by showing you believe in them and care about them as individuals. Visualize a positive future by saying things such as "If you keep practicing this way, I'm sure you'll be able to play the Beethoven next year." Positive reinforcement is like money in the bank that can be drawn out when the student faces a problem or criticism. When students know you appreciate and believe in them they will develop resilience to see them through the toughest times of becoming a musician.

Have confidence in your ability as a teacher, too. Tell your students, "We can do anything. We are a great team!" Attitude is more important than aptitude, and if you think you can, you can. And that applies to both teacher and student. Chapter 7 will show you how to commit yourself and challenge every student to be a star by having high performance standards.

Make Practicing a Priority

"Doug" drags into his lesson every week and gives the same answer, "Umm . . . not so good," when you ask, "How did practicing go this week?" Each week you review the same piece that never improves with so little playing in between lessons. What can you do with problem practicers? Tackle the problem even before they begin taking lessons. Set general time guidelines for each new student, varying them according to ability, age, and the student's goals. During your initial phone interview, tell parents and students your standards and practice requirements. Help them understand the importance of practicing and that you expect a consistent commitment to practice if students are to remain in your studio.

It's hard for many students to fit practice time into their busy schedules but if they're committed to improve, they might need to cut back on the time they spend with other activities such as TV, video games, phone calls, and socializing. Some students may have to choose between playing a sport and becoming a top-notch musician. For others, music is one of their many hobbies and their practice time reflects that. Chapter 8 will help students prioritize their interests and plan their practice time accordingly.

What do you do for students who put in the required amount of practice time but don't accomplish much? For more targeted practice sessions, teach students what and how to practice. Encourage them to set daily practice goals instead of watching the clock. Sample goals might include: play page eight with no mistakes or one section five times in a row with no mistakes; memorize from letters G to L, or learn the notes from letters A to C. Determine time and quality practice goals and coach procrastinators.

If a student is still not succeeding, find out why. Does the problem stem from lack of motivation or your teaching techniques? Give the student a chance to succeed by varying your teaching style and going back to the basics. In chapter 14, "Use Practice Tricks for Fast Results," I'll show you how to help your students get the most from their practice sessions in the least amount of time.

Help Students Retain Their Knowledge

You may be asking, "But how can you find time during lessons to chat; teach music theory, history, musicality, and sight reading; give them time to fix their own mistakes; and still get through new music?" I have devised a system that has saved me loads of time over the years. It lets students know the important things they need to remember from each lesson and helps them retain them. I save time (and patience!) at the lessons because I don't have to repeat myself. I call this method my *Music for Life* two-note-book system.

My students bring two notebooks to each lesson. One is a manuscript book in which I write down not only their assignments, but almost everything else I say, including theory homework, music history, musical terms, and clear suggestions for improvement. I put a bullet circle in front of every fact or suggestion that I want them to remember. They are then responsible every week for copying these bulleted items into a second book, a three ring binder I call the *Music for Life* book. This binder contains ten tabs with headings such as theory, history, musicality, tone, posture, intonation, musical terms, and position. Their *Music for Life* book becomes their own personal catalog of everything they have learned and an easy reference for me. I'll go over this notebook system in more detail in chapter 9, "Increase Success with the *Music for Life* Notebook System."

Set Goals to Fulfill Student Needs

We've all heard the adage "If you don't know where you are going, you won't know how to get there!" Goals give students an end point to aim for, but make sure each goal has value and meaning for the individual student. Set long-term goals that fulfill students' individual potential, wishes, and needs.

Set clear short-term goals for each technique or lesson. Praise students for every new accomplishment, but let them know that next week it will take even more to win your praise or a fun sticker. Each pass under the "limbo bar" takes more effort. Say, "This week you got a sticker because you played the D minor scale without mistakes, but next week to earn a sticker you must not only play without mistakes but play with beautiful tone, and the week after that you must have the scale memorized."

For older kids, use a harder piece of music as a carrot to get them to practice more. Say, "This piece is so great, but it's difficult and will take a lot of practice. Are you *really* sure you want to play it?" Laugh as you watch them jump up and down and beg to practice more! To a seventh grader, say, "You don't want to sound like a seventh grader, do you? I think you can play like a ninth grader!" If students sit fifth chair in the band, set their sights on third chair and then first. Always kick it up a notch. If you have built a solid relationship with them, they will be able to take the pressure and accept the challenge.

In chapter 10, I'll give you more ideas on how to set meaningful and realistic long- and short-term goals for your students. You'll learn how to set attainable technical, musical, and performance goals, and I will arm you with ideas for using goals to boost effort and achievement.

Use performances as motivators too. Students will always practice more before the "big test." Every year I invite at least two master teachers from colleges and conservatories to give master classes in my studio. We also have in-studio concerts and retirement home concerts for "dress rehearsals" before contests and competitions.

All of my students who have taken lessons for more than one year participate in contests. Some of you may shy away from contests because you don't want to pit your students against each other. Some worry that underperformers will feel bad. Others are reluctant to create more work for themselves. When you read chapter 22, "Prepare Students for Performance," and see how much they gain from participating, you may change your mind.

Offer Constructive Feedback

We've all heard the adage "Practice makes perfect," yet "Practice, *the results of which are known,* makes perfect" is a more accurate statement. If you don't know your goals, hours of practice won't help. Receiving honest feedback on performance is an essential part of skills development, regardless of the subject. I used to play a little tennis, but never having lessons made improving difficult. I *tried* to concentrate, but my practice rarely made me better because I had no feedback on what or how to improve.

I kept thinking, "Keep your eye on the ball," but I needed a teacher and honest advice.

Besides being their cheerleader, give your students constructive feedback on their playing using tangible, specific examples. Don't just tell them to play it better next time. How you give feedback, how specific it is, how high your standards are, and how much you involve the student make all the difference.

Recognize Results *and* Effort

Human nature motivates students to work harder when their work earns praise and tangible rewards. Nothing is more crucial to the success of your studio than recognizing and rewarding your students' hard work. Recognize students for their results *and* their effort. Anyone who practices to the best of their ability deserves recognition regardless of how much they have improved.

Psychologists tell us that children of all ages would rather be praised than punished—but they would rather be punished than ignored. "Ignoring" your students by accepting any level of achievement never works; they need your continual, honest response to their efforts.

Sometimes in our zeal to teach, we forget to praise. Catch your students doing something and exclaim over their accomplishment. Almost every student does something right. Remember to point it out. Be creative with your praise. Rather than saying "Good job!" say, "You didn't hesitate once during that tricky run!" Or "Did you hear your big, juicy tone?" When you point out shortfalls, try to blend in a little humor. Reward effort with your attention, stickers, notes, and prizes.

Help parents set up a system to reward accomplishments. Start by determining desired behaviors like memorizing a piece or the always-hoped-for practicing without complaining. Determine meaningful rewards like going out for ice cream or earning more computer time. In chapter 11, I'll give you ideas on setting up a recognition and reward system.

Foster Happy, Confident Students

How do you have happy students? Start by adding variety and fun to your lessons. Learning an instrument involves lots of practice and repetition, but the efforts you and your students make are not worth it if it's all drudgery. Amuse yourselves with a weekly cartoon on the music stand or by asking students to bring jokes to liven the start of the lessons. My black lab, Angie, always gets a laugh from students when after a few sour notes, she rolls over and plays dead. Try the unexpected to spice up your lessons. Do something different and vary your routine. Music can be serious, but learning music is supposed to be fun! In part 3, I've dedicated chapter 21 to turning around complaints and doing something different.

Inspire your students with the power and joy of music. Choose music that motivates them to practice. Share your joy of music and your music values, and by all means, play what you love.

Compliment your students and show them you genuinely enjoy being their teacher. Every one of my students has heard me say many times, "I am so lucky to have you for a student!" and "What could be more fun than teaching a student like you?" Sometimes I'll say to a student, "Can you believe how much fun we're having and I get paid, too?" Show you sincerely enjoy your students and watch them beam.

Regardless of their level of playing, revel in their progress. Avoid the mistake of demanding perfection, being too blunt, or hurting their feelings. If you do, admit the teacher is not always right.

I confess that not every student is a joy to teach. If you're not excited about a student, then fake it! If you appear bored during lessons and uninterested in your students, they'll feel bored, too. If you want your students to be thrilled about taking lessons, then show them your own pleasure and enthusiasm. Excitement is more contagious than the flu! Remind yourself of the good things about teaching, act enthusiastic, and then tell your students. Chapter 12 will help you make music lessons a fun experience for the teacher and the student.

Host Special Music Events

Recitals, concerts, and other musical events are too expensive, too much work, too long, and too boring, right? Besides, every student fears and dreads them anyway. Wrong! When recitals are done in a spirit of fun instead of competition, they can be great motivators. Among other things, they're an excellent way to reward big accomplishments, entertain students and parents, and create camaraderie among the families in your studio.

Holding in-studio contests encourages students by putting peer pressure to work. I've hosted swimming pool parties for students who learned all their trills, hosted hot tub parties for those who practiced double over the summer, and taken ensembles to lunch when the judge praised their dynamics. Students will work extra hard to be included in the winning group with their music friends. In chapter 13, I'll offer creative ideas for hosting recitals and other music events your students and their families will enjoy.

Expect Exceptions

Even teachers who follow these principles to the letter will not solve every problem every time. While every child has the potential to be a musician, not every child *wants* to be one, or is willing to do the work required. We can say and do all the right things but sometimes it's not meant to be. Personalities can be mismatched, some students make other priorities, and others are not interested in learning. No matter how heroic our efforts, we cannot reach *every* student.

Students who don't progress can be draining to a teacher's mental and physical health. When this happens, determine whether you've given your all. If the answer is "yes," have the courage to help these students make a change. They might choose to stop taking lessons, go to a teacher with different standards, or stay with you and commit themselves to a serious practice plan. Chapter 25, "When It's Time to Say Goodbye," will help you make and follow through on this difficult decision.

But the good news is that by following the principles I've discussed, most of your students *will* be success stories. Will every *day* be a success story? You know the answer to that question. We've all had days when we felt overworked, underpaid, and defeated. Our best intentions have been misunderstood or our love and caring seems unappreciated. I have days when between hosting musical events, communicating with students' parents, preparing for competitions, ordering music, scheduling rehearsals, doing bookkeeping, teaching lessons, and my own practicing, I feel as if I'm juggling fifty plates that may crash down on me at any moment. My head is so "full of people" and jobs to accomplish that I can't turn my attention to other priorities when my teaching day is over. On days like these I may wonder if all the effort is worth it.

I then imagine the money music teachers could make if they applied their level of intelligence, training, creativity, and work ethic to a "regular" job. I picture receiving that steady paycheck and the luxuries it could bring me. Then, a moment later, I remember what that paycheck would "cost": working in a big downtown office with days filled with mandatory meetings, bosses to please, and a shrinking bottom line. I'd have to substitute a rush-hour commute to a stark office building for a quick walk downstairs to my warm and inviting studio. No thanks! No corporate perk could compare to the opportunity to play beautiful music and enrich lives. Comparing the two life choices, I'm thankful I chose to be a music teacher.

LOOKING AHEAD

In this introductory chapter I've shared with you ingredients of the *Music for Life* relationship-based teaching approach. In the remaining chapters of part 1, "Enriching Lives," we'll look more closely at these principles and other ways to motivate your students.

In part 2, "Making Music," you'll learn about the technical aspects of teaching music. I've included tips, tricks, imagery, and exercises to help your students practice more effectively, become confident sight readers, and memorize pieces more easily. I'll show you easy ways to teach students how to practice, play musically, and learn other skills essential to well-rounded musicians.

In part 3, "Tackling Your Toughest Teaching Challenges," you'll find answers to the knotty problems we teachers face, such as conquering stage fright, starting beginners, the differences between teaching girls and boys, teaching adults, and knowing when to say goodbye.

In part 4, "Running Your Private Music Studio," both beginning and experienced teachers will find tools to develop a business plan, set up a studio, write a studio policy, and handle other issues small business owners face. You'll save time with practical tips that will make your music room and schedule more efficient.

Teaching may have its challenges, but when you put your heart into it, you will reap the rewards. Helping people use their talents and grow as musicians and people can be the greatest job on earth. I'll provide you with the proper tools to make it easier. Let's start with chapter 2, where I'll talk more about how to build solid, productive, and trusting relationships.

TWO

Focus on Relationships First

MAKE RELATIONSHIP-BUILDING A PRIORITY

John flies into the music room bursting with excitement over his winning three-point basket at the championship game. Later, Kris shows you her college essay, about how she tamed her stage fright, that earned an A. Next Paul, a plastic surgeon, keeps you in stitches as he describes his frantic morning at the hospital. And finally, Tom arrives with a batch of his mom's famous oatmeal cookies—perhaps she hoped you couldn't scold her son with your mouth full?

One of the biggest rewards of teaching music is the opportunity to know a wide variety of people. These student-teacher-parent relationships *are* my teaching. I believe in the saying, "No one cares how much you *know* until they know how much you *care*."

A trusting relationship between student and teacher creates a beautiful duet. In this chapter I'll talk about how to strengthen the important bonds you form with students and their parents. College professors who teach advanced students may feel less of a need to establish close ties with their students, but even they will benefit from this relationship-based model. No one approach to teaching can guarantee 100 percent success, but applied consistently, these ideas and techniques will transform your teaching style. First let's talk about the benefits you'll reap when you base your teaching on relationships.

You'll Be a Better Teacher

When you know your students, you'll see them not as "violin students," contest scores, or paychecks, but as unique individuals with interesting personalities and important lives away from your studio. The better you know them, the better you will be able to teach them. When you know your students' individual needs, you can adjust your approach to their learning styles, emotional make-up, challenge levels, and technical strengths and weaknesses.

You'll Be Inspired

Many musicians decide to become music teachers because they love *music*. A better reason would be because they love *helping people*. I gain inspiration and energy from my students when I know and care about them as individuals. I'm motivated to work harder when I see their dedication to their instruments and their love of music grow-ing. When you are passionate about the music and genuinely enjoy your students, your enthusiasm spills over to them. It's a win-win situation.

Your Students Will Work Harder to Please You

When students trust and respect you, they'll be open to your instruction, criticism, and expectations. When they see you as an important person in their lives, they'll be reluc-tant to let you down. When students want your admiration they will put in their best effort and continue to do so through good times and bad.

You'll Have a Lasting Effect on Their Lives

Conversations you have with your students may affect them longer than the music you teach them. My students visit me years after they have stopped taking lessons and love reminiscing about the fun times they had and my (sometimes unsolicited) advice. Ana, now an adult, said, "When I first came for lessons, I thought I was only going to learn about music. But I got a big lesson in life, too."

My own two children, Scott and Kyle, love their piano and strings teachers and have established strong bonds with them. Even if my boys didn't practice, I'd be willing to pay for them to spend that hour a week with these fine role models who have taught them so many of life's lessons. Likewise, your guidance, wisdom, and friendship are in-valuable to your students as they seek to become not only successful musicians, but well-rounded people, successful in life. *Never underestimate the influence you may have on your students' lives.*

KNOW YOUR STUDENTS

How do you create strong relationships with your students? The answer may seem ob-vious: spend time interacting with them. Take time from every lesson to show your in-terest by talking and asking questions. You might consider this a waste of valuable lesson time, but believe me: it pays off.

Talk to Your Students

Greet each student with a welcoming smile even if the previous student made you wish for a new profession. Start each lesson with a little conversation to set the mood. Some-times students (especially adults!) need to talk or vent a little when they arrive directly from school or work; then they can settle down to the business of the lesson. Ask about their hobbies, family, weekend plans, or about what happened at school that week. After hearing students' litany of stories about friends and activities, I say, "Didn't you forget to tell me about one VERY important thing you did?" They always smile and say, "Oh, yeah, and I *practiced,* too!" "Good answer!"

When students seem distracted, impatient, sad, or upset, be willing to drop every-thing to find out more. Encourage them to speak up when they have concerns—even if they are about you! The more students talk, the better you'll understand their personalities and how to reach them (although beware of the student who wants to talk the lesson away to avoid playing scales). Our job is not to be a psychiatrist, but to pay attention to what is happening in our students' lives. Everything, from illness or a basketball tournament to finals or a fight with a parent, can bear on their attitude and performance.

Foster a Positive Attitude toward Life

Show students you understand their problems and then help them put their woes in perspective. "I know you had the worst day of your life because of the hard math test and the rotten peanut butter sandwich for lunch, but let's talk about how important that will seem tomorrow." Step back to lighten things up with conversation and a smile when students get upset, disappointed, nervous, or frustrated during lessons. Be positive and show them how music lessons can make the world a brighter place. I always kid my students and tell them that their lesson is the best hour of their week. At the end of a lesson that began with the weight of the world on their shoulders, I say, "See, aren't you happier now after you've had your lesson?"

Practice the Fine Art of Listening

Be genuinely interested in what your students are doing and happy for their accomplishments in and outside of music, even if it's that dreaded soccer schedule that eats up their practice time! Show them your interest by giving them your full attention. Undistracted listening demonstrates to students that nothing else is more important than your time with them. Research shows that we learn most of what we know through listening, yet most of us absorb only a small portion of what we hear. Active listening helps to retain more of what you hear and will make your students feel they are the most important people in the world when they are in your studio.

To be a good listener, listen more and talk less. Be open-minded and give genuine importance to their opinions; you might learn something! Demonstrate your full attention by leaning forward slightly and focusing on your student's face. Let students struggling with words finish what they want to say without interrupting. Show your interest with responses like "Is that right?" or "I didn't know that," "That's interesting" or "I'm glad you told me that." Make mental notes and watch your students' surprise a month later when you remember their best friend's name or what they received for Christmas. Listen to your students with the same interest and intensity with which you listen to your favorite concerto.

Consider a Student or Parent Survey

You may find it enlightening to ask new students and parents to complete a survey that asks about their motivations and interests. Talking about the results might break the ice and help you more quickly get to know about their life in and outside of music. Writing about interests provides an opportunity for less verbal or outgoing students to express themselves. The survey might ask, "Why did you choose your instrument? What is your favorite subject in school? Do you play in any music group?

What are your goals for taking lessons?" and even "What do you think makes a good teacher?"

A parent survey might ask: "What are your expectations or goals for your child in music lessons? Whose idea was it for your child to take lessons? How many hours does your child spend in after-school activities each week, e.g., soccer or ballet? How much daily practice time can your child commit to? Can you help your child practice? Do you plan on attending your child's lessons? Does your family have music in the home? Do you attend any musical events as a family? Does either parent have previous musical education or background? Would you be interested in helping to plan or assist with our fun in-studio musical events as your time permits?" The more you know your "clientele," the better you can serve them.

Share Student Information

A bulletin board in my music room displays all my students' pictures. To know students even better, post their pictures along with personal information (with their permission) for all to see. Students enjoy learning about each other. You might include information about students' families, pets, sports, musical accomplishments, and other interests.

PARENTAL INVOLVEMENT—IT WORKS!

Form Strong Ties with Parents

Why are close relationships with parents important to your program? Parents are experts on their children, and their support is crucial to their children's success. Parents who see themselves as partners in their children's music education rather than "customers"—as in "the customer is always right"—are more likely to support you and your requirements. They'll be more supportive of your teaching methods and more apt to encourage their children to fulfill practice requirements at home. When they have successfully "bought into" your program they'll more willingly help with recitals or parties, buy music, spring for new instruments, and pay to support their children in outside musical events. Parents are a valuable resource and usually fun, interesting people who can enhance *your* life too. Get to know them better and help them become involved.

Educate Parents on Their Important Role

Parents play a pivotal role in their children's music education, yet many have no idea of the extent to which they can positively or negatively influence their children's love of and pursuit of music. Some have the attitude that participating in lessons and practice is not their responsibility; all they need to do is deliver their children to lessons and pay the bill. These parents miss out on a great opportunity to bond with their children, as well as a chance to learn about and appreciate music.

I have my sad stories about parents, as do most teachers. The mother of one of my flute students refused ever to come to our annual Mother's Day recital; she said she would much rather be at the dog show than listening to her daughter play classical music. Another student told me her father had ordered her to be finished with practicing by the time he got home from work because he "needed his peace and quiet" while he watched TV and drank his cocktails. Another mother asked me if her daughter could have lessons only every other week, not because she couldn't afford it, but because what was *she* supposed to do during lessons? Another parent refused to even transport the child to the lesson because "Music is *her* thing." One father did not think that the money for lessons was worth it and the daughter had to beg every week to continue lessons (and I had to fight to get the check!). Life is made of choices, and because these parents placed lower priority on music education, their families missed out on many of the joys of having a child who plays a musical instrument.

Most parents want to help their children do well, but they don't know how or where to start. If parents don't know what is expected of them, it is our job as teachers to educate and guide them. Most importantly, we need to communicate to them how important they are to their children's success. We can make the parents' job easier and more fun by giving them concrete ways to be involved. Assisting with daily practice, attending lessons, setting high but realistic expectations, and encouraging music playing are only a few of the things parents can do to help their children succeed. Most importantly, they can be the cheerleaders every child needs, especially when taking on the challenge of learning an instrument. Book 2 in the *Music for Life* series will give parents and children loads of ideas on how to make learning music a fun and successful experience.

Keep Parents in the Communication Loop

Keep in touch with parents through regular e-mails or newsletters. Parents appreciate being kept up to date on studio events and their children's progress. The more informed parents are, the more they feel part of the process and invested in their children's musical education. E-mail is the easiest way to stay in touch with individual parents and students. Try to stay off the phone as much as possible because five phone calls can last five hours as you chat with each parent, but five e-mail messages can take less than five minutes. Welcome parents' e-mails and phone calls and respond quickly.

As I mentioned in chapter 1, sending e-mails to ask how the week's practice is going, to congratulate a student on having a good lesson, or to keep parents informed about their children's progress is thirty seconds well spent. If I feel something is troubling the student or their dedication is waning I call the parent, but I also contact them when the student has had a particularly wonderful lesson.

I send out a regular group e-mail, the *Flute Flash*. It contains reminders, with dates and directions, of upcoming events, news about students' triumphs, thank-you notes, and general notes of encouragement. (The *Flute Flash* can be printed out and posted on the refrigerator.) Sometimes I forward cute animal pictures or cartoons. Anything to keep in touch.

To use e-mail efficiently, make contact group lists with all parents' and all students' e-mail addresses. When you send the e-mails, address the e-mail to yourself, then blind carbon copy (BCC) the student group list. This way everyone gets the e-mails but everyone's e-mail address is kept private. Remind families to regularly check their e-mails.

Schedule a Yearly Check-Up

My friend Laura, who teaches violin, told me about her annual meeting with the student and the parent. She does it during the Christmas season when kids are not practicing that much anyway, and schedules the meeting during the child's lesson or reschedules to make sure the parent can attend. Laura tells her students and parents that this meeting halfway through the year is a chance for everyone to sit down together and say how they think they are doing and to give helpful suggestions to the others in the parent-student-teacher team. Laura, the child, and the parent sit in a triangle away from the music stand and face each other. She starts first to set the tone and requests that everything said be honest, but polite. During the meeting she takes notes to help her remember the conversation during upcoming lessons and also to let all participants know she values their input. Laura may start by saying, "I've noticed. . . . How can I help?" The child's turn is next. When the child has a tough time speaking up or when the parent tries to interfere, she hands the child a stone with the word "harmony" painted on it. She uses this stone like an Indian talking stick: whoever holds the stone has the right to speak. Laura tells the students that listening to each other is an important part of making music and that she and the parents (with an eye to the parents) respect what the students say.

Laura finds that this meeting keeps everyone on track and prioritizes what is important, namely the welfare of the child. She feels it reduces tension and even raises her student retention rate. Parents can never say they weren't "warned" about a problem, and not one has ever complained about paying for a lesson spent in this way. Scheduling a time brings all the interested parties together to brainstorm and prevents the teacher from being blindsided when the parents race into the studio with some sort of rant. Once again, communication is the key.

Ask for Parents' Help

Parents can also be a big help to the teacher. I have strong relationships with my students' parents and many of them help me with secretarial and computer work, make phone calls, transport students, bring food to musical events, and help me remember all the things on my studio "to do" list. Some parents answer my phone during lessons or make copies for me. I depend on them to help me have a successful studio. I appreciate parents' help and always go out of my way to thank them. Working together brings us closer and also gives them insight into the many jobs and responsibilities of a music teacher.

Involve Parents in Lessons

We have already briefly discussed the controversial topic of parents coming to lessons. There are two sides to this issue. One of my colleagues has made a firm rule that no one is to come into the house except the student. She has her reasons. One father was such a strict parent that whenever his children played, they would look first to him for approval and ignore the teacher. Another parent made so much noise clicking her knitting needles and talking on her cell phone that neither the student nor teacher could stay focused. Another mother interrupted with suggestions and told her two daughters that they didn't have to play the four songs assigned, only two, and since she didn't like the Christmas book, they didn't have to play their assignments in it either. My colleague has even had knick-knacks stolen and had her toilet overflow! No wonder she doesn't welcome parents into her house.

Luckily I have had the opposite experience. I love to see parents at lessons tapping along with the music, clapping after pieces, praising their children, asking for clarification of new information, and, of course, laughing at my jokes. I insist that parents of beginners attend lessons. These parents become part of the learning triangle and are a great help to their child and to me. I sometimes give the parents assignments for the week: sit with a timer and time the long tone exercises, record how many times each scale was played, work with the child on a new rhythm, make flash cards for key signatures, or have the child give a concert at home. I have had such wonderful working relationships with some flute moms and dads that they have become good friends and supporters. We work together as a team. I appreciate a second pair of ears to record what I have said, and I invite their comments when they can give me insight into their child. The parents who attend lessons fairly frequently are the same parents who attend recitals, offer their homes for ensemble rehearsals or parties, bring me treats, take an active role in their children's practice sessions, and ensure that music is an important part of their family life. An added bonus to having parents at lessons is that they get to know you and your program and develop an allegiance to it. When they see what a great teacher you are, they won't want their children ever to quit!

If you're uncomfortable with parents attending every week, ask them to stop in once a month at the end of the lesson for ten minutes. If they don't attend, make contact every so often by following your student out to the car, or sending home notes. Facilitate this communication by hosting parties and recitals with receptions that allow time for casual conversation.

Handle Disruptive Parents

What do you do with parents who interfere? Well, as you have probably guessed, I have a fairly strong personality, so I work to make sure I have control of the lesson. If a parent keeps talking, I say, "Boy, we have so much to get accomplished at this lesson, we better not take any more breaks." If the parent still talks, I turn away and address the child only. Later in the lesson I call on the parent to congratulate or applaud their child, so they know I appreciate their presence but that their involvement needs to be that of a parent and not that of a teacher or judge.

Many musician parents have a hard time being quiet during the lesson. When I attended my son's viola lessons, I couldn't help letting out an *involuntary* moan as he played out of tune or missed the same rhythm repeatedly, so I was asked to stay away. He needed to focus on his teacher and not my responses. Many older students do fine without parents at the lesson, but care must be taken to still keep the parents informed and involved.

How do you ask a parent to stay away? As uncomfortable as it may be, it is sometimes necessary to say out loud: "I need Tyler to trust me as a teacher, and if you second guess my decisions or interrupt, I cannot gain that trust. Tyler and I need to build our relationship and it would be easier if we had some time alone together." Perhaps the parent would hear it better if the request to stay away from lessons came from the child.

LET STUDENTS KNOW YOU

Teachers are real people, too! In chapter 1, I recalled my surprise at seeing my seventh grade math teacher shopping at the grocery store. Only then did I realize that besides being a teacher, she was also a normal person with everyday needs. Too often, teachers intentionally take on the role and image of "teacher" and only become "themselves" again when they leave the classroom or studio. Let your students see you as a complete person with feelings, opinions, and interests outside of the music studio. One of the pluses of teaching at home is that students see you in your "natural habitat" and more easily see you as a real person. Sharing parts of yourself makes you more approachable.

Balance your conversations with information about yourself. (My students always know whom I'm voting for!) With your shared love of music, you and your students can relate on so many levels. Allow students into your life by showing them you too have feelings, interests, and challenges. Alisa recalled, "I had a piano teacher who was not a friend, and I never practiced. It was like she was a robot that taught piano. She never talked to me or admitted her mistakes and she made it seem like *she* was perfect and I wasn't, so I quit."

Students enjoy hearing about your hobbies, your family, and your interests. Look for incidents in your own life students can relate to. If they're nervous about taking private lessons, tell a story about how you felt when you started, or even relate the story of another student who learned to become comfortable with you. Laugh at your own mistakes with students. Be human and caring.

BASE YOUR RELATIONSHIPS ON TRUST

When you've built your relationships with students upon earned trust, students know you care about them, even when you're being firm with them. With trust, your students are more willing to take chances, make mistakes, and ask when they need help. They try things out of their comfort zone because they believe in you. Without trust, your relationship can go no further. The following student/teacher relationships may be doomed:

"You should have heard Maureen play yesterday," the guitar teacher whispers to her star student, a high school classmate of Maureen's. "She's so slow, I don't know if she'll ever get out of book one! She'll be more prepared next week after the scolding I gave her."

"I know Tom asked me to write his recommendation for college, but I am so busy right now, I can't get to it," the cello teacher confides to the mother of another student.

"Patty isn't really ready for the contest next week," a teacher thinks, "but I'm going to have her compete anyway. Maybe she'll learn a lesson about preparing earlier next time."

"Matthew, I don't know why you are so nervous about this recital," chides Matthew's trumpet teacher. "Don't be such a baby about it. No one else is scared like you are!"

Getting to know your students is the first step to building relationships with them. The second step is preserving and strengthening those relationships. Building new relationships takes time, but rebuilding relationships in which trust has been damaged can take far longer. Students must know you will always put their best interests first. As a trusted friend, rather than a paid acquaintance, students need to know you will always be there for them, even when things may not be going well. Janna, who is now in college, concurs:

> The friendship I have with my flute teacher is so important to me. It makes lessons more enjoyable because after these eight years we are more like equals. Because I trust her, there is an open atmosphere of give and take, not take, take, take from the student's point of view. I used to be too shy to say anything, but now I'm not afraid to say my ideas on the music and we work together.

Show Students and Parents They Can Count on You

Demonstrate personal integrity and a commitment to following through on promises made. Strive to be the kind of person you would want *them* to become. Treat your students (even the underperforming ones) with the same respect and friendship your other friends enjoy. Don't talk behind students' backs, especially to other students. If you must use students as negative examples, give them fictitious names. Let students know that their feelings, secrets, and even tears are safe with you. We'll talk more about putting the student first in many of the following chapters.

LETTING GO: THE DOWNSIDE OF RELATIONSHIP BUILDING

I've talked about the many benefits of basing your teaching on relationships and you may be wondering, "Does it always work out?" Let me answer by sharing some personal stories. I had a student whose family I greatly admired. They showered me with gifts and attention and they felt like personal friends but they would not even return phone calls once their daughter graduated. I realized the parents had been nice to me so I would continue to teach their daughter, not because they cared about me.

When another student's mom was in the hospital, I devoted a lot of time listening and supporting her and even sent food to the family. At a lesson a few months later, I told her I was concerned about the number of lessons she had skipped lately (her reason was that she was "too busy"). Later that night, her mother called, fuming, upset that I had talked to her daughter, and she cancelled the lessons.

Another successful student whom I had taught for six years and for whom I had done countless extra lessons and added gestures of support e-mailed me the day of her lesson and said she felt like trying out another teacher. I never heard from the family again.

I once gave a high school girl free flute lessons for six months because her parents said they couldn't afford to pay me. Imagine my surprise when I heard she had transferred to another flute teacher and then left to attend a top California college that cost as much as my house.

I had a lazy student for about six months. This girl probably practiced about six minutes. When we decided it was not working out, her mother told everyone I was not supportive and her daughter was blameless.

We all have our poignant stories. The downside of building a relationship is becoming vulnerable. You may feel the amount of caring is a one-way street when some parents and students are willing to take, but not to appreciate. Is all the effort worth it? Wouldn't an eight-to-five job be easier and less stressful?

True, throwing ourselves into our teaching leaves us more vulnerable to being hurt, but this same commitment makes us better teachers. The more we care, the more our students thrive and the more personal satisfaction we gain. It's been said that "Virtue is its own reward." When you do things for your students, do them because you want to help them, not because you want to get something back. If you give extra lessons, offer make-up lessons, arrange performances, open yourself up to your students, and put in extra effort, don't wait to be thanked by all. It won't happen. The only expectation you can have is knowing you're doing your best. Sometimes it doesn't seem worth it, but then you realize that to be a good teacher, you must take a chance. You've heard the saying, "It is better to have loved and lost than never to have loved at all." Committing yourself to your students won't always turn out the way you had hoped, but it's what good teachers do, and when it works, it's magic.

LOOKING AHEAD

This chapter emphasized the importance of building solid relationships and offered ways for you to strengthen your bonds with your students and their parents. The time you spend implementing these ideas will reap huge rewards as students become more committed to you, their lessons, and their music. Next, in "Instill Pride and Respect," we'll talk about how to increase students' self-pride, and create team spirit and a sense of belonging in your studio.

THREE

Instill Pride and Respect

Terri left her violin lesson in tears. "I'll never be any good," she cried. "I practiced every day this week and my teacher still told me everything I did was wrong. I can't learn the spiccato bowing, my elbow is never at the right height, and my vibrato is too shaky. I don't even hold the cello right! My teacher will never be proud of me. Why do I even try?"

Every student has had a frustrating week of practice, a tough lesson, or a disappointing performance. Being corrected at lessons and being judged in performance can make us feel like human punching bags. Students who lack self-esteem are less able to weather the inevitable frustrations and disappointments and more likely to avoid trying new tasks.

Teachers who instill pride and self-confidence in their students allow them to reach higher and succeed. What is pride? Most dictionaries define it as a feeling of self-respect and personal worth. Some use it interchangeably with self-esteem. Why is self-esteem so important? Students with healthy self-esteem have a more optimistic outlook because they feel capable. They are more open to criticism, and they accept compliments graciously. Students with strong feelings of self-worth realize their value as a person is not dependent on their skill as a musician or any other one facet of their lives. Let's look at how to help students develop that underlying sense of self-confidence, control, and optimism that is so valuable in music and in life.

SHOW YOUR PRIDE AT LESSONS

Let students know you admire them. Seeing your pride in their accomplishments in and out of music strengthens their pride in themselves and bolsters their courage to try new things. Give them the idea that they're funny, smart, and fun to be with. Laugh at their jokes and "ooh" and "aah" over their accomplishments. Compliment their good attitude and their ability to practice consistently, complete their homework, and work hard. "I know you can do it!" goes a long way.

But tailor your compliment to the student. After I heard 15-year-old Alisa's stunning solo performance I exclaimed, "Your playing was impeccable!" She looked bewildered. "Is that a *good* thing?"

Make your goal be to give students at least one well-founded compliment per lesson (but make sure they understand you!). Say, "Am I ever lucky to have a student like you!" "I think you're phenomenal." "Let's work on this piece to show off your beautiful tone and phrasing." "I have never heard that phrase played better. You are so musical." "This piece is a winner and so are you." "I'm amazed at your progress. Who would have dreamed two years ago that you would sound like this?" Literally pat them on the back or shake their hand after a big accomplishment. "This is a big step up and you did it! I would never have given you this piece unless I had complete faith in you."

Write extra notes in their manuscript book. "Fabulous job on scales today; Congratulations on seventy long tones; Beautiful tone today; Keep up the good work! You are doing great!" If students feel comfortable with the gesture, put your arm around their shoulders and say, "We're a great team." Look in their eyes and honestly say, "I am so proud of you." Watch them float out on a cloud. Students blossom in an environment where they feel capable and valued.

Linda took lessons as a teen and as an adult. She recalls that feeling of pride in a job well done. "As a person that would, um, periodically be ill-prepared for my lesson, I can imagine how hard it would be for a teacher to feel proud of students that slack off. But when I actually was prepared, Bonnie was nothing short of thrilled. She influenced my life and my skill in a positive way which in turn encouraged me to practice a bit more the next week too." Encouraging students to respect themselves enough to succeed and move forward in music encourages them to move forward in other areas of their life too.

SHOW YOUR PRIDE IN PUBLIC

Share your pride in your students' performances by asking them to play for friends, relatives, and other students and parents. Ask students with back-to-back lessons to perform for each other, no matter what their level. "Listen to Zach play *Yankee Doodle*. Can you believe he has only had eight lessons?" Point out their accomplishments in front of their parents and others. Attend their solo performances and be the proud teacher (armed with flowers). I often brag about my students; I can't help myself. I hope I'm not perceived as acting superior; I'm just bursting with pride and giving them the credit.

ENCOURAGE STUDENTS' SELF-PRIDE

When students perform well, remind them of how far they've come. "Wow! Did you ever dream you could play this well?" "How do you feel after such a great performance?" "That was a huge accomplishment!" Self-pride is so important that some teachers avoid telling students they are proud of them, but instead say, "Aren't you proud of yourself?" When students' feelings of self-worth come from within, they don't grow dependent on outside sources for approval.

TREAT EACH STUDENT AS SPECIAL AND UNIQUE

Everyone wants to feel they are unique. Single students out so they feel they have a special place in your studio. My sister Cindy's son, Stephen, plays trombone. When he plays exceptionally well, his teacher compliments Stephen using his Greek name. "Beautiful tone, Stavros!" Hearing his special name, Stephen beams.

Lauren plays so musically that when I want her to interpret a passage I only have to say, "Just do your 'Lauren thing' here." When Lauren hears this she knows that her performance is her responsibility and that I trust and admire her. To make students feel special give them a pet name or typecast them in a positive way. Say things like, "You are such a good memorizer, this won't be a problem for you to learn," or "You're known for your wonderful tone; where was it?" "Your spiccato bowing really needs work but you're such a quick learner, I know you'll have it by next week." "Now it is time to put your own personal stamp on that sonata." "You are so good at learning the cello; I can't imagine you'll have any trouble tomorrow on the math test at school."

Students will also feel special when you note important events such as earning a driver's license or remember their birthdays with a candy bar or pencil. Celebrate the anniversary of their first lesson by laughing at how far they have come since their humble beginnings. Many times my students show up for their anniversary lesson with cake or presents. Honor your students and make them feel they are one of a kind.

INSTILL PRIDE IN BELONGING TO YOUR STUDIO

Everyone, young people especially, has a strong need to belong, to be identified as a member of a select group. One of the best things you can do to motivate students is to set up an environment where they feel they're part of a special and successful group. Pride develops not only through satisfaction in your own achievements, but through those you associate with. That's why people identify so strongly with sports teams. "We won!" they exclaim from their place on the couch. Ultimately, we want our students to experience both individual pride and the pride of being part of a group of students they respect.

Induct Students into Your Elite Club

Promote an elite group identity. Create the feeling that being part of your studio is an honor with the price of admission being more than handing you a check. Show them they're special, not because they are better than everyone else, but because they work hard to belong to a special group.

When students in your studio hear each other, they know the studio standards to live up to. If everyone sounds wonderful, they will get the picture early on that they need to fit into this class of achievers. Anticipate success by saying, "All my students have good tone, so you will too." "You know what it takes to be part of my studio." Early on, say, "All of my students are good. You're one of my students, so you'll be good, too."

As I said in chapter 1, at the first lesson I teach my new students the password to enter my studio: "I love my flute teacher and my flute lessons very much." Most of the students have fallen in love with my dog, Angie, who attends every lesson. Now many students have amended the password to "I love my flute teacher, my flute lessons, and my flute *dog* very much." Almost every card or thank you I receive from students ends with this saying. It may sound silly, but this tradition sets the mood for a mutual admiration society and creates greater loyalty to my studio. Rituals provide symbolic communication and the comfort of knowing you belong to something bigger than yourself.

Promote a Family Atmosphere

My students tell me that taking lessons from me is not just about taking lessons, but adoption of a certain "lifestyle" that's required to be part of my studio. My studio is not just a room but a "club." I welcome new students and their parents into our "flute family." Immediately they feel part of something special and can identify with the larger group. They quickly learn the "flute culture" of my studio through seeing pictures on two bulletin boards in my music room and by hearing stories of past recitals, concerts, parties, and contests. They know that they, too, will be part of these exciting events soon. The younger students look up to the older ones (their big flute sisters and brothers) and try to follow in their footsteps. The older ones offer advice and support and cheer on the younger ones.

Introduce students and their parents with back-to-back lessons to widen their circle of friends within your studio. Have them play for and applaud each other. Encourage carpooling and ask students to attend each other's performances to solidify friendships.

In chapter 16, "Multiply the Fun in Chamber Music," and chapter 13, "Host Fun Musical Events," I offer loads of ways to have fun and create studio unity.

Encourage Pride of Association

Help students feel part of a team by celebrating each other's successes. Our studio motto is "All for one and one for all."

To promote pride by association, encourage students to come to each other's concerts and root for their friends at contests. In the studio, post concert programs, recital pictures, and awards won. Send e-mails telling of students' achievements. Say things such as "Aren't you proud of Perrin for getting into the youth symphony?" My former students still come to concerts, call, and e-mail to ask how younger students are doing and remain part of the extended flute family.

Form Friendships through Ensembles

Music friendships can last a lifetime. I was well aware of that a few years ago when I watched three of my former students participate in a life-changing event. From my perch up in the choir loft, tears formed in my eyes as my past students, Laura and Erin, walked down the aisle as bridesmaids. Ana, the beautiful 28-year-old bride, completed the trio. I pictured the three girls as fifth graders, performing in the trio they named "Future Famous Flutists." Peals of laughter were common as their trio rehearsed. Now, I marveled at these three beautiful, mature young women. Though none of them plays the flute much now, their fun times in music have bonded their friendship for-ever.

Establishing ongoing ensembles is one of the best ways to strengthen friendships. Ensemble rehearsals are an enjoyable break from regular lessons and standard literature, and they make music fun.

Avoid In-Studio Rivalries

A few years ago I judged solo performances at a district flute contest. The player I se-lected would win the coveted prize of being sent on to the state contest. My judging went smoothly all morning. After lunch, as I seated myself at the judge's table, I no-ticed an unusual number of students streaming into the contest room. Before long, only standing room remained. The audience talked excitedly as if anticipating a spec-tacle. The door was flung open and heads turned as two smartly dressed girls marched in, each clutching flute and music in gloved hands.

After being seated, the obvious rivals glared at each other, then quickly turned their attention to stare at me, the judge. It was clear to me and the audience that this would not be a friendly competition. This was going to be a prize fight! The girls each took off their gloves and the competition began.

While each girl played, audience members turned around to glance at me, trying to read my expression. A few bold students craned their necks to read over my shoulder, hoping to catch a glimpse of my comments and the rating.

Both girls played well, yet without passion. Afterwards, warring factions clapped loudly for their favorite hoping to convince me of their choice. Who was I going to send to the state contest? For a moment, I wished I could have been beamed out of that room and not been in the middle of this apparently famous rivalry.

Unbelievably, I later learned that both girls studied with the same teacher! How sad. Both girls would have performed better and had more fun if their teacher had fos-tered teamwork and mutual support within her studio. The world of music can be cut-throat, but teachers must do everything possible to discourage these nasty attitudes in and out of their studio. This teacher had obviously done nothing (or not enough!) to discourage jealousy and resentment and had used competition between the two as a motivator. What could she have done differently? Many things.

One of the biggest bonuses to having a musical family, especially in a studio of high-performing achievers who often compete, is the feeling of support students have for *all* students in the studio. Discourage jealousy and make them feel that a success for one of them is a success for all. Let students know what excellent company they are in, but don't pit one student against the other. It might be tempting to use such compar-isons as motivators, but that tactic backfires in the end.

Avoid saying things such as "Sue played this in sixth grade and you're in eighth grade; you should be playing better than this," or "Tom's tone is so beautiful—why don't you sound like him?" Avoid assigning duplicate music for recitals or contests which would allow for direct comparisons. Don't rave about other kids' accomplishments to a student who competed against them. Above all, remind students that their biggest competitor should be *themselves,* not another student. They should always work toward a "personal best."

Lastly, don't act jealous of other teachers or their students. (I know, this can be a hard one.) Tell students you're happy for them and appreciate other students' and teachers' hard work and accomplishments.

INSTILL PRIDE WITH ACCOMPLISHMENT

True self-esteem, or *earned* self-esteem, comes from accomplishments. Nothing is more motivating than pride in a job well done and being recognized for the effort it took to get there. Performance, success, and pride are interrelated. Create a positive cycle: the better your students perform, the more pride they feel; the more pride they feel, the higher their performance. Nothing gives students more confidence than being totally prepared. As teachers, we must make sure they have a good shot at success and have done something to be proud of.

Recall Successes before Performances

Remember that just *recalling* past "wins" increases students' pride and self-respect. Before a performance, revisit those wins. Bolster confidence by reminding students of their hard work, accomplishments, and strengths.

"Do you remember how well you played in the recital six months ago? I know you'll play just as well this time." "I can't wait to see the judge's face when you play that Presto." "You have worked so hard. Today will be the fun part." "I am so proud of the way you played at the recital; I am really looking forward to hearing you at the contest."

After Successful Performances, Let Students Bask in Their Glory

"How do you feel after such a moving performance?" "You played that piece so beautifully at the contest; you must be so proud of yourself." "You should give yourself a pat on the back." "You did so well in the recital. I'll bet you can't wait to start a new piece." "Don't you feel great about overcoming your problem with stage fright?" "The audience was spellbound by your playing." "A year ago you could barely play a scale; today you played a concerto!"

After Disappointing Performances, Help Students Look to the Future

One of the greatest gifts we can give our students is self-satisfaction and the ability to look beyond problems of the day. Students who have developed a healthy sense of pride are much less apt to be crushed by a single performance. They are better able to see the big picture and to realize that one bad week, lesson, or contest does not define their abilities or worth as a person. Being a musician takes a healthy ego and resilience after "defeat." Improving students' ability to bounce back after disappointment is so vital I will continue to talk about it throughout the book.

Self-respect and self-confidence grow when you remind students of their strengths and successes. Some students habitually brush off compliments and launch into a list of things they could have done better, especially right after a performance. Remind them that after a performance, no matter how they felt they did, they must bow, smile, and graciously accept compliments. Encourage students to appreciate, and not discount, their accomplishments, even when the performance hasn't matched their definition of "perfect."

Don't listen to moaning about the three missed notes in measure thirty that ruined the whole performance. "Let's look at the whole performance in perspective. Sure, you messed up section G, but think back at how you might have played this piece six months ago. Though this particular day did not turn out the way you hoped, be proud of your improvement." When teachers emphasize *mastery* over winning and losing, students see themselves as more successful. They know they're improving, no matter the outcome of their performance.

RESPECT YOUR STUDENTS

Respect is not the same as obedience, nor is it fear. Fear destroys self-confidence; respect builds it. Fear is learned. Respect is earned. Think of respect like a boomerang: you must send it out before it comes back to you. The best way to teach students how to show respect is to be respectful toward them.

Model Respect with Your Words

Speak respectfully. Be mindful of how you phrase corrections, even when your patience is bankrupt. Sprinkle your teaching with phrases that show you value your students, like "I'll be there for you." Acknowledge their efforts by saying "Thank you." Or even shaking their hand. When they're confused or stumped, ask, "How can I help?" Even when you're frustrated or disappointed, use helpful, not hurtful, language. Instead of saying: "I'm disappointed in you," say, "Do you think you gave this your best effort?" Instead of "That was bizarre!" say, "Let me show you how I might have played it." Instead of "What were you *thinking*?" say, "Next time (or from now on) I want you to . . ."

I know my own students will be reading this chapter and laughing. OK, I don't always use those sweet, kind words, but even when I give you a bad time, you know it is done out of love! If students know you love and respect them, they will even love your kidding and dramatic language.

Model Respect with Your Actions

Model a respectful student/teacher relationship. It's simple: treat students the way you like to be treated. If you make teaching a priority and take lessons seriously, your students see the value you put on learning. Be dependable. Show up for lessons on time and don't cancel at the last minute unless you have an emergency. Do what you say you're going to do when you say you are going to do it. Return calls. Maintain a clean, organized, and stimulating studio. Dress in a professional manner. Be organized in the lessons by using the time efficiently and be organized for competitions and concerts by choosing the piece early, calling the accompanist well in advance, and sending in the forms early. Above all, take your job seriously and be courteous and dependable, even when they're driving you crazy!

MAINTAIN RESPECT WITH STUDIO STANDARDS

One of the things I love about teaching privately is that I get to set the rules! Let students know they must meet certain obligations to retain a spot in your studio. These obligations include taking responsibility for their learning, using common courtesies, and maintaining practice standards. The "rules" in my studio also include participation in concerts and contests. Each teacher must decide on the rules necessary to make the studio run smoothly and then be upfront about relaying those requirements to new students. I strongly suggest using a studio policy as a way to identify and communicate your standards.

Establish Standards of Student Responsibility

Students need to value your time and only cancel a lesson if there is illness or a real emergency. They must arrive at every lesson on time with all necessary books (and the check!), have their lesson homework completed, and be ready to learn. Students must understand it is their responsibility to order music, arrange ensembles, or trade lessons when they have a conflict. If students do not live up to your standards, don't be afraid to call them on it. They will never know unless you say something.

Two former students remembered how this sense of responsibility remained with them into adulthood. "Bonnie's lesson mandated undivided attention from everyone in the room. Closed doors and no distractions. The biggest rule of conduct: come prepared or be prepared to suffer the consequences. That was a wake-up call for my own actions, especially at a young age" (Mike, adult).

"You only have to show up late a couple of times to know that your lesson doesn't get to flow into the next person's time just because you got stuck in the wine section at the grocery store on your way to the lesson" (Linda, adult).

Establish Standards of Student Conduct

I am appalled and saddened when in the "real" world and exposed to trashy TV, movies, and ads. I hate hearing people casually using swear words and treating each other rudely. I wouldn't let anyone put a bag of trash in my living room and I don't want my house polluted by trash on TV or trash from anyone's mouth. I once saw a T-shirt that read, "A PBS mind in an MTV world!" That describes many of us.

In my studio I expect and maintain standards to make it a sanctuary for beautiful music and beautiful people with a core value of mutual respect and admiration. Teach students to shake hands firmly, look people in the eye, and speak up when asked a question.

I once had a student who frequently said, "That's annoying!" or complained, "Do I *have* to?" When I asked her to replay a phrase, she rolled her eyes. Every five minutes she looked at the clock and heaved another sigh. She consistently missed lessons and was openly elated when I told her I'd be away on vacation. When she handed me the check I felt like a servant. After repeated talks about attitude and manners, I terminated her as a student, giving her a final lesson about treating her *next* teacher nicer. Though you are a friend to your students, make it clear you are still the teacher and must be treated with respect. Students work harder for a teacher they admire. Older students who have been respectful can undergo a gradual metamorphosis as they grow "too comfortable" in the studio. Those who have studied with you a long time and have become very successful may become a little flip or sarcastic because they think of you as just another friend. Saying only once, "I love you, but remember, *I* am the teacher, and *you* are the student. OK?" usually cures the problem.

If a student talks back, remember that your response is going to determine what happens next. Don't respond with sarcasm or by raising your voice. You can't control your students, only yourself. Say, "I would never speak to you in that tone of voice and I expect you to speak to me with respect." When you model control, you show them how to control themselves.

Expect your students to be courteous and polite even though you are close friends. I recently talked to another flute teacher who told me she didn't like teaching because "I don't like having to be the boss." Well, you must be the boss or your students will not respect you or value what you teach them. Stress to students the importance of treating others the same way they like to be treated. Help them understand the harm they can cause by thoughtless, unkind words and actions.

To maintain student standards of conduct, *never* allow students to

- Walk in and ignore you. Expect them to smile and say "Hello." If they don't, have them go outside and try it again.
- Leave the lesson without saying "Goodbye" or "Thank you for the lesson."
- Dress inappropriately.
- Ignore your questions.
- Overlook their mistakes or disregard your suggestions for improvement.
- Treat you or other students in a discourteous or impolite manner. Expect them to say "please" and "thank you."
- Talk back to you.
- Use slang that should be reserved for school friends. Point out their misuse of cer tain words. "Like" is a popular one as I write this, as in "I like went to school and then she was like . . ."
- Demonstrate a negative attitude during lessons, coming alive only when it is time to leave. Asking, "Am I boring you?" usually perks them up. (Or you could threaten to put an ice cube down their back.)
- Argue when you try to teach them something new or repeatedly question your advice.

Manners, pride, and respect are inseparable. Enhance students' feelings of competence and self-pride by providing them with a balanced mixture of acceptance, limits, and expectations. Earn their respect and they will show you theirs.

LOOKING AHEAD

The first three chapters of *Making Music and Enriching Lives* have concentrated on building and strengthening relationships. In the next chapter, "Show Students Your Commitment to Excellence," we'll talk about how to earn the respect of your students and their families by expecting more of yourself as a teacher, musician, and community participant.

FOUR

Show Students Your Commitment to Excellence

Violin teacher Lisa begins each lesson full of energy for her students. She gives them her full attention every moment they are together. When beginning students play, she reacts as if she has just heard the New York Philharmonic. Lisa locates special music for students, prepares handouts, and shares new information she reads. She organizes ensembles, enters her students in contests, and holds fun recitals every year. When students have trouble playing, she works and works to find the solution. She keeps her own instrument skills sharp and continues to learn and grow as a teacher. The result? From the youngest student to the oldest, the most talented to the least, her students play to the best of their abilities. Even more importantly, her students are dedicated to their music and love what they do.

EXPECT MORE FROM YOURSELF THAN YOU DO FROM YOUR STUDENTS

Commit to setting high standards for yourself. You'll see positive results when you become *proactive* and give the same commitment to your job you ask your students to give to their lessons. When students see you taking this job of music seriously and working hard to make them play better, they will reciprocate. Like Lisa, work to be the best teacher you can be. Only then will you have the right to expect the same from your students and be able to say, "I'm working hard and I expect you to do the same."

Have a Plan

Following the Boy Scout motto, be prepared. Do you have a plan for every lesson and a long-term plan for each student? Or do you teach whatever happens to come to mind that day? Teachers need plans as much as pilots need flight plans, coaches need game plans, and business owners need business plans. Ineffective teachers come to lessons unprepared, wondering what to teach their students day by day or meandering through the books with no thought to the individual. At the beginning of each lesson, outline what you want to accomplish. Make sure lessons have a balance of scales, technique, music theory and history, and repertoire.

Keep track of what you've taught each student, where you've left off, and where you're headed. I'll give you the perfect system for organizing yourself and your students in chapter 9, "Increase Success with the *Music for Life* Notebook System." Save time by maintaining an organized music and CD library that allows you to easily find the piece you're looking for and use printed handouts for students in order to save lesson time.

Evaluate the Lesson Content

Ask yourself, am I *really* teaching students during lessons? Our job is to provide new information in *every single lesson,* not just a road map determined by assigning new pieces and encouraging our students to keep playing through the book. When each student leaves, ask yourself: Did he learn any new techniques today? Did we focus on making music and not just playing the notes? Did his playing improve at the lesson? Did he get information on music theory or history? Did we concentrate on tone and intonation? Did he learn new musical terms? Did he leave with a desire to learn more?

Demonstrate Your High Standards by Teaching the Best Lessons You Can

Give each student your full attention at every lesson, even if you're hungry or tired or sick of hearing book 1. Teach beginners with the same passion and dedication as you have for advanced students. "Twinkle" can turn into Tchaikovsky if you give students your all. Through your actions, show the importance of the lesson. The more excited *you* are about the world of music and how it relates to their instrument, the more excited *they* will be about practicing.

Don't confine your teaching to the books. Use demonstrations, handouts, and gimmicks to catch their attention. I use a new idea, gimmick, cartoon, or handout almost every week to enrich the lessons. These extras might include composer action figures, composer bios, a new song I learned, or a funny way to teach breathing. This month my students got treats for updating their notebooks. They also got a picture of Beethoven, Easter candy, an exercise ball to teach posture, a flute painted with fish and crabs, and a joke list of things to do to bug your band conductor. I'll offer more ideas for enrichment in chapter 21, "Troubleshoot Problems and Turn around Complaints."

If you only see your students at lessons, you're not giving them a well-rounded education. Give them plenty of performance opportunities. Prepare presentations for parents during lessons, and hold informal studio concerts and more formal recitals. Plan extra events and throw parties.

As we saw in chapter 1, when you expect more from yourself, your students will follow in your footsteps. In the rest of this chapter, we'll review your responsibilities to your students, from striving for excellence in your instrument to being a positive role model. All of these duties affect the quality and success of your teaching. First, let's examine your personal teaching standards and the type of students these standards attract.

DEFINE THE VALUES AND STANDARDS
OF YOUR STUDIO

Remember Lisa's accomplished violin students? Wayne is the opposite. His students play so badly that even doting parents are eager for the sour notes to end. Yet Wayne seems content with his students' poor performance and gives them undeserved accolades. Apparently, "good enough" is certainly "good enough" for Wayne. Why would these potentially talented kids strive to get better when Wayne is satisfied with mediocrity? Does Wayne believe his students aren't capable of playing better, or does he lack confidence in his ability to bring them to a higher level? Maybe he doesn't care to bother.

Determine What Kind of Student *You* Want to Teach
and What You're Willing to Give

I admit I'm a hard-charging "Type A" teacher. Other teachers prefer to be less goal-oriented and to cater to "recreational" musicians. It's OK to be a "Type B" or even a "Type Z." Students need all kinds of teachers. What counts is that no matter how you do it, you give each student *your best and the opportunity to reach his or her own potential.* Techniques that work for me may not be right for teachers having different expectations or personalities. By writing this book, I hope to inspire you to create the studio and attract the students that are right for *you.*

Before you ask yourself what you're willing to sacrifice to make your students successful, you must decide for yourself what success is. What level of achievement is the goal for *your* studio? Do you prefer to work with college-bound music majors? Young beginners exploring music? Adults playing for fun and relaxation? Is your "mission" to push students to do their best or to bring music into your students' lives no matter their commitment? If you dream of teaching enthusiastic, high-performing students, then commit yourself to making it happen. Or do you prefer a more relaxed studio of average students and the lifestyle it brings? The choice is yours. As the saying goes, "What you expect, you generally get." Do some soul-searching to decide what kind of students you want and the level of commitment you're willing to make.

Music Is for Everyone

As much as this book is about setting high standards and attaining goals, there is a flip side. We never want our students to think that music is only for the elite. If we make them feel that music is only for the top performers, then we are turning away a lot of kids. Given the reality of making a living as professional musicians, we must realize that we are mainly training future audience members, not professional performers. We want them to attend concerts, give their own kids music lessons, and make music a lifelong friend. They won't do that if they've been turned off by feeling inferior. So many kids quit because they feel they were no good at music when in reality it was the teaching that was no good. Music is not only for the most talented and hard-working students. Students have different aptitudes and goals, but no matter what these may be, we want our students to realize they must work hard to realize those goals. If you never expect the best from your students or let them see the possibilities, then you are robbing them of their potential. Even kids who don't seem to have innate talent can go farther than you expect with a positive push.

Develop Expectations and Standards for Each Student

Preset standards provide a tool for guiding and measuring progress. Ask yourself, "What skills and concepts do I want this student to know by the end of the school year? How can I measure progress to know if *we* are succeeding?" List what you hope each student will achieve by the end of the year.

Standards measure not only how well students are doing but how effectively you're teaching. For example, your standard might be that after two years of lessons, Sandra should have learned eight scales, finished book 2, memorized three pieces, and played three medium-level sonatas with few mistakes. If she hasn't met those standards, figure out what went wrong.

HOLD YOURSELF ACCOUNTABLE
FOR STUDENTS' RESULTS

Unlike Lisa, who produces fabulous students and loves her job, and Wayne, who has terrible students but is satisfied with mediocrity, we have Michael. He hates teaching saxophone. One student after another arrives at his studio having devoted little or no time to practice since the week before. Squeak, splat, screech. How can he stand it? During lessons he looks at the clock, watching the minutes crawl by. His mind is half on what the student is playing and half on what he will eat for dinner that night. The only part of the lesson he looks forward to is being handed his check. His happiest days are when he has to cancel lessons to play a gig. He marches his students dutifully through the same books, at the same pace, regardless of how quickly they progress. He looks upon them as saxophone players on a conveyor belt moving through his studio and out the door, not as people to whom he is committed.

Michael sees no need to involve parents; to him they're only signatures on checks. He doesn't sign up his students for contests because he knows they aren't good enough. Nor does he attend their concerts because he would be embarrassed. He's too busy to hold recitals. Michael can't understand why none of his students are ever high performers. And he's so tired at the end of each teaching day. "It's my rotten luck," he claims. "Other teachers get the good students and I get the lazy ones with no talent!" Before placing blame on his students or materials, Michael needs to first look at himself. Instead of whining about terrible students and bad luck, he needs to take responsibility for making them better.

When Students Fall Short, Look to Yourself First

A student at one of the top conservatories told me of a teacher who, at the *last* lesson of the year, told his student, "You haven't had one good lesson all year!" How devastating! This girl was obviously talented and committed enough to have gained acceptance into this conservatory. I contend that the blame for "no good lessons" must also lie with the teacher. When students fail to meet your expectations, don't just blame them for being unmotivated; first analyze your own role in their success or failure.

As you read this chapter, take time to be introspective and ask yourself some tough questions. Find out the answer to *Are my students as good as they could be?* Listen to other teachers' students at competitions or in recitals; how do your students measure up? Can you spot any trends in your students' problems? Do they all play out of tune? Are they rhythmically challenged? Are they boring to listen to?

If your students don't perform well, take a hard look at your effectiveness and hold yourself accountable. Private music teachers don't get annual job performance reviews so we must analyze our effectiveness ourselves. Assess your results each year and determine how you can help your students achieve more.

When Your Students Don't Measure Up

Ask yourself: Are my expectations clear and concise? Did I teach them how to practice effectively? Are students still struggling with the basics of note reading and counting? Do they have long-term goals to aim for and timetables for completion? Do my students complain about the music being boring, or about spending too long on one piece? Have I created performance opportunities to motivate them to work toward a goal? Do I provide them a well-balanced "meal" of technique, theory, and literature? Do they leave each lesson having learned something or improved their technique? Do I give them confidence with my words and actions? Have I invested myself in turning struggling students around? Are my students losing interest? Am I? I'll offer you lots of suggestions throughout this book to inspire you and your students and make you a more effective teacher.

BE AN EDUCATED AND SKILLED TEACHER *AND* PERFORMER

Kerri was a good middle school flutist. She took lessons from me from sixth grade through ninth grade. Then she quit, saying she didn't have time to practice and keep up her grades. After graduation she attended a university in a different field from music and never resumed her private lessons. I lost track of her until one day I happened upon her website—advertising herself as a flute teacher! Kerri claimed that although she had little training, her love of music was enough to qualify her as a music teacher.

Joan had played a little flute in high school band and after college decided it would be fun to pick it up again. After two years of studying with me she was still a mediocre student, and she quit because her lessons were too demanding. A few years later Joan realized her art degree wasn't landing her any jobs and she was thrashing around for a career. Then she had an idea: "Why not teach private music lessons? Anyone who can play a little can do that."

Joan and Kerri were partly right. It's true that anyone who can play an instrument can teach music lessons, but not everyone can do it *well*. Joan and Kerri are fictitious names but their stories are not. They both set up teaching studios with little training and their students suffer because of it. To respect their teacher, students need to feel confident in the teacher's mastery of the instrument, its literature, and music basics. Mediocre teachers doom their students to match their own low level of achievement. Even beginners deserve teachers who know their stuff.

Strive for Excellence on Your Instrument

Conscientious teachers learn everything possible about the instrument and literature, not just the fingering chart and beginning tunes. They bring their performing experience to the lessons. If you teach more than one instrument, make sure you know them well. Just because you play the saxophone does not mean you are a clarinet teacher.

I cringe when I hear of mediocre 16-year-olds with plenty of students who have chosen teaching over babysitting. Can teenagers be good teachers? Perhaps some can, if they are advanced performers and under the tutelage of an experienced teacher. Unfortunately, usually the "good deal" teachers turn out to be not such a good deal for parents when in the end their children have missed the opportunity to learn from a skilled and experienced teacher.

Students will be excited to study with you if they feel you are an expert and committed to teaching them. Do you have to be a virtuoso? No. You don't need to be the best performer, just the best teacher. If you are not the most advanced player, find a teaching mentor to help. Also know when it is time to pass a student on to a more advanced teacher.

Stay fluent on your instrument. Know the major etudes, solos, concerti, ensembles, and orchestra literature. Be well versed in its idiosyncrasies of tone and pitch, and know the standard and trick fingerings for difficult passages.

Seek New Challenges on Your Instrument

One of the most wonderful aspects of music is the steady stream of new things to learn. In fact, studies have shown that playing music is one of the few things that can help stave off Alzheimer's. I hope this proves to be true, as I imagine 100-year-old musicians living at the musicians' retirement home, the "Fermata Inn"! Stretch yourself on your instrument. Play in a musical group that challenges your skills and expands your repertoire. I recently left my comfort zone by recording a jazz CD with my flute/violin/guitar trio, and recording a CD of Jewish wedding music with my string quartet. It's fun to try new things.

Perform in public. Play gigs or plan a solo or ensemble recital. Perhaps you might perform in your students' recital. They will appreciate knowing you can relate to their struggles with learning new music and performing. You might even be more sympathetic when they complain about performance deadlines and stage fright!

Summertime, when your workload may be reduced, is a great time to recharge your batteries. If you have time, brush up on your skills with your own lessons. Attend a music summer camp or seek out other instrumentalists for a concert or just for fun.

Have you considered learning a new instrument? I'm a poor guitarist, violinist, and violist, and I'm a fair pianist. But learning these instruments broadened my understanding of music far beyond my experiences as a flutist and vocalist. By learning a new instrument you'll learn ideas and techniques that will relate to your own teaching and you'll benefit from experiencing the new student's perspective. You may not be so hard on your piano students when you hear how bad you are on the banjo!

For those of you who are tops on your instrument, remember that playing well is a completely different set of skills from bringing out the best in people. Don't assume because you can play Mozart that you can motivate others to do so. Even a virtuoso performer may need to work to become a virtuoso teacher.

Always Play Musically

"If I have to play 'The Indian Song' one more time, I'm going to scream!" you think as you dutifully plunk it out for your student. Play for and with your students, but make sure you always play your best, even if it is that old "Indian Song." Let them hear your beautiful tone and phrasing. When students can play just three notes, show them how beautifully those three notes can be played. Students will pick up your sound just as babies imitate their parents' accents. Play duets and solos for them to imitate. Demonstrate musical phrases so students can pick up on the subtle nuances. Approach all music with a commitment to beauty. Always play your best and you'll inspire them to do the same.

CONTINUE TO LEARN AND GROW
AS A TEACHER

How many times have you told Sue to correct her position and improve her tone? It's been frustrating to repeat yourself lesson after lesson. No matter how many times you say the same thing or how loudly you say it, she still doesn't get it. Now her mother is on the phone, stumbling over telling you something. Finally she blurts out. "We have decided to have Sue study with another teacher. We're happy with what you've done for her, but we all feel it is time for a change. After three years we think it would be beneficial for her to get some other viewpoints, so we won't be seeing you tomorrow." What could you have done to make a difference in Sue's playing *and* her parents' decision to change teachers? New ideas! Are you sounding like a broken record? It's time to get out of your time warp!

Seek New Information

Look for new information and inspiration to capture your students' attention. Stay current on teaching techniques. Instead of repeating your explanation, learn an alternative. If you've been teaching the same music the very same way for years, then you *and* your students must be bored. When even your long-term students are eager to see what you have in your bag of tricks, they won't have to look elsewhere. Try the ideas listed below to stay sharp and creative. And, of course, *finish reading this book*!

- Subscribe to trade magazines such as *Clavier, Keyboard Companion, String Teacher, American Music Teacher, Flute Talk,* and *Flutist's Quarterly.*
- Attend national music conventions for your instrument or the Music Teachers National Association (MTNA) convention.
- Complete the MTNA teacher certification.
- Read books about your instrument, biographies of composers, and books on general music, teaching, and philosophy.
- Listen to singers and artists of other instruments.
- Join your local instrument club.
- Listen to the radio when you're doing other tasks to familiarize yourself with a wide variety of pieces. Listen to CDs of master artists.
- Always seek new literature. Ask other musicians, listen to the radio, go to concerts, buy CDs, try out pieces at music stores, order catalogs, and ask publishers for recommendations. So much music, so little time! (Especially if you teach violin or piano.)
- Read books about general teaching techniques and even business motivation books.

Reenergize with Other Teachers

What do two teachers who run into each other at the grocery store talk about? Not the price of rutabagas. Their students, of course! "My student learned this piece . . . can you believe it?" "Mine is struggling with learning . . ." Do you and other teachers share problems and techniques? "Have you ever experienced this? What in the heck am I supposed to do?" or "I learned this new teaching trick; you've gotta try it!"

Gather knowledge and *courage* from other music teachers. Join a professional music society such as the National Music Teachers Association, or local and national groups featuring your instrument, such as the National Flute Association or the National Association of Teachers of Singing. There's no one right way to teach. Get to know other public and private teachers of all instruments and compare notes; they may have creative solutions for handling difficult situations. Everyone appreciates receiving support and encouragement. You're not alone!

If you're an experienced teacher, offer to mentor someone who is learning the ropes. You'll find great satisfaction in sharing your knowledge and experience with someone who is starting out professionally. Your involvement is especially valuable to private studio teachers who can feel isolated. One once told me "Sometimes I feel like I'm the only piano teacher in the world!" It's wonderful for teachers to network and share ideas.

- When your students participate in contests or master classes, don't leave after they finish playing. Sit through other contestants with a pen and notebook in hand.
- Join an online chat room or mailing list (such as the Flute List) devoted to your instrument.

• Invite a guest teacher when you go on vacation and ask them for suggestions.
• If you have children, attend their lessons.
• Find a buddy with whom you can vent your feelings and laugh. Other teachers help us keep our perspective; their students may be worse than yours!

Look to the Experts

Jamie has a big orchestra audition coming up and brings you the music. You've never played in an orchestra and aren't sure how to coach her. Sam is playing trumpet in the band and wants your help learning how to improvise on his solo. You've always needed music for every note or you're lost. Kim is performing a concerto with her youth orchestra. You've never played it, but recall that a violinist in the professional orchestra in town performed the same concerto a month ago. How can you solve these dilemmas? Ask for help!

No teacher knows everything; you can always learn from others. If you think you already know all the answers, you either are not being truthful or are naïve. Don't feel threatened by other teachers of your instrument. There are plenty of students to share and the knowledge gained from other teachers can be added to your own bag of tricks. Some students may feel they should change teachers after a certain number of years but if their lessons include input from outside teachers, they won't have to. They'll have the best of both worlds: a caring teacher with a long-term plan and fresh ideas from other experts.

Schedule visiting artists to hold master classes for your students. When world-class flutists come to Seattle for other events, I invite them to give a master class at my home. If you don't live in a major metropolitan area, contact the state college or even invite a teacher of another instrument to visit your studio. Students will work extra hard for this great opportunity to meet and learn from talented teachers! College master classes give prospective students and teachers a chance to meet and learn about each other.

LIVE BY A CODE OF ETHICS

We want to be skilled on our instruments and committed to teaching, and we also owe it to our students and to our profession to be honest people with high moral values. After all, imparting life lessons is part of what we do for our young students. That's what *Music for Life* is all about. Model to them your personal integrity. Act in a professional manner toward your colleagues and students. Take time to reflect on the far-reaching repercussions of your actions. Let's talk about "tricky" ethical situations and see where some teachers have gone wrong.

Keep Your Students' Best Interests in Mind

This is the theme from so many chapters. Be loyal to your students. Put their needs above your own. If they have outgrown you, let them go. And please, be truthful about their talent and their chances of making it in the music world.

Gabrielle was proud when her student declared music as his major. Then she made the mistake of promising him that if he worked hard, he'd be accepted into an elite school, and even get a scholarship. Her promises never came true. Declaring a major is only the first step in the long road to becoming a professional. Encourage your students to achieve *realistic* musical goals, and never make promises you cannot guarantee. Sadly, most students will not make it in the professional world. Our ultimate goal should be to give them a lifelong love of music and never promise they can make their livelihoods in it.

Treat Fellow Musicians Fairly

Mary Ann felt sorry for her students. "Everything is so expensive these days," she told them. "You can copy my music so you don't have to buy your own."

Mary Ann's students may be saving a few dollars, but if many people copied music rather than bought originals, composers, publishers, and music stores would soon be out of business. We owe it to these artists to support their business, which in turn helps our own.

Gail was the violin judge at the district competition. After hearing one of the contestants, she walked out in the hall to talk to her. "You played fairly well," she told the young girl. "But you have some areas that need fixing that your teacher has obviously missed." She handed her a business card. "Why don't you give me a call and let me help you?"

Whether you know the other teacher or not, stealing a student is unethical! When judges and master class teachers are coaching a student, they must be particularly careful not to criticize the teacher. The decision to change teachers should come from the student, and preferably with the former teacher's recommendation and approval.

Be Clear in Your Expectations

Richard walked out of his fourth lesson in disbelief. "She never told me when I signed up for lessons that I would have to play in five recitals every year! I had no idea I had to memorize so many songs, hire an accompanist, pay my teacher extra for the recital time, help rent a facility, and bring refreshments. I want out!"

Students and families have the right to know what is required of them up front so they can make informed choices. Teachers must be forthright about their studio expectations from the initial phone interview so students can begin lessons with their eyes wide open.

Place Honesty before Profits

"Learn to be an accomplished pianist in just three months!" the advertisement proclaims. "Try our secret method and amaze yourself and your friends by playing all the great composers with only minutes of practice a day!" This advertisement is as believable as the one that claims, "Take our magic pill and lose ten pounds a week while watching TV and eating chocolate." How I wish they *both* were true! Don't promise results that can't happen.

Thomas told all his piano students that as a service to them, he would purchase their music and they could pay him directly. He failed to mention that he was marking up the music store's price to make a substantial profit. Music teachers provide a service, not a product. We may purchase music for our students as a convenience, but not to compete with real businesses. If you purchase music, charge the student the same amount you yourself paid.

Shirley told her students they could save money and time by having her accompany them at contests instead of hiring a professional. The problem was that her mediocre piano playing sabotaged her students. Don't put earning money above your students' performance.

Life is full of choices and tricky problems like these. I've done things I considered to be honest and blameless that other teachers might question. If you are not sure whether you're doing the right thing, ask a trusted friend: Is this the best way to handle this? Is there anyone I need to inform first? Will my actions hurt anyone? Might they be misunderstood? Have I told the truth without omitting any facts? Life is full of challenges. Good luck!

Make Your Music Room a "Center of Civilization"

A great teacher is a link to the intellectual development, refinement, and educational contributions of centuries. We are carriers of tradition. We teach our students more than music; we pass on to them culture, history, and beauty.

Carry on the tradition of excellent performance from former generations. "This is the way Van Cliburn plays the Tchaikovsky concerto." Credit former teachers and players with your teaching tricks. "I learned this trick at a master class by Isaac Stern." Talk about period history and art in the world when the piece was written. "Debussy's music is so like this Monet painting." Explain the etymology of foreign musical terms and broaden your students' vocabularies. "The Italian word *segue* means something follows. This is a word we use in English too." By sharing the beauty of music you are contributing to your students' futures and possibly even their children and grandchildren's futures.

Share Your Music with the Community

As the last note resonated, our audience burst into applause. Well, except for the man in the third row who had fallen sound asleep. And the white-haired woman who left in the middle of the fifth piece because it was past her bedtime. The rest of the retirement home audience, many wearing hearing aids, felt the music move straight to their hearts. They loved seeing the "youngsters" in their Sunday best. "Thank you so much," I heard over and over. And "When are you coming back?" One lady grasped my hand and nearly swooned. "What a night!" she exclaimed. Even the gentleman who told my student before she started playing, "Keep it short!" was clapping enthusiastically. How easily we pleased them.

Sharing your musical gifts with your community adds purpose and meaning to your teaching. Offer your services to community organizations such as schools, churches, and retirement homes. Offer to help the band or orchestra teacher. Help with the school musical, concert, or fundraiser. Don't confine your students' music life to the room in which you teach. Bring them to malls, churches, schools, hospitals, fund raisers, and local events. Do your part to promote the value of music in your community and beyond.

DOES SHOWING YOUR COMMITMENT TO EXCELLENCE TAKE TOO MUCH WORK?

Do you feel exhausted after reading this chapter? Is being a great music teacher too overwhelming? A "Far Side" cartoon shows a mosquito with a gigantic, bloated stomach biting a man's arm. If he remains there taking in more blood he may explode! The caption reads, "Pull out! Pull out!" Like the mosquito, we need to set limits for ourselves. And like the bitten man, sometimes we fear our students will "bleed us dry." Even the best and happiest teachers have days when they question the profession they've chosen.

I believe the best way to feel reenergized is to remember why you choose to teach. Recall that gratifying feeling you have when, after explaining the rhythm in a fifth different way, your student's face lights up. "*Now* I get it!" Remember the kids who walked into your studio as shy wallflowers and now exude confidence playing in front of any audience. Think of the miraculous gift of music you have given to your students *and* to all who hear them. Remind yourself of the wonderful contributions your teaching has made in your students' lives and the friendships you have gained. Above all, believe in what you're doing. You're not teaching notes, you're touching lives.

LOOKING AHEAD

Now that you've committed yourself to excellence, let's see how you can make yourself obsolete!

FIVE

Promote a Love of Learning and Independence

Zoe beams as she walks into my studio. "This week I practiced five etudes instead of only the two you assigned," she says. "And I played the *whole* duet, not just the first movement. Actually I played the next duet, too." Her eyes sparkle with pride as her words tumble out. "This weekend I got a *lot* done. I ordered the music and set up a rehearsal time for my ensemble. Oh, and then I updated my *Music for Life* book and I filled out the entry form for the contest. Last night I finished reading the music theory book. And then I had some more time so I memorized the concerto." Then she looked a little apologetic. "I tried to get in three hours of practice a day last week, but it was finals week. Next week, I promise I'll do more."

I am not making this up! My student Zoe is enthusiastic and independent. And she is not my only wonderful, over-achieving student. I feel I should be paying some of these students for the privilege of being their teacher! Some of us may be lucky enough to have one or two of those dream students, but most students need our help to get that way. Sustaining a studio full of hard-working, enthusiastic students isn't luck; it's the result of finding the right techniques to motivate each of your students. I say "each" student because there's no single magical formula for motivating every student. They all have different wants and needs.

In this chapter I'll help you create opportunities and experiences that motivate students to love learning and achieving. But don't let the word "motivate" mislead you. In the following pages you'll find no special "motivational" techniques. Why? Research repeatedly shows that good everyday teaching techniques motivate students more than any special efforts to target their motivation directly, and good everyday teaching techniques are what this book is about. In fact every technique I recommend in this chapter, I've touched on earlier or will in future chapters. Good teaching practices bear repeating now as we consider how to foster an atmosphere in your studio that helps students become capable, self-motivated, and life-long learners, not by chance, but by your design.

DEVELOP AND NOURISH STUDENTS' LOVE OF LEARNING

Students who have developed the character strength "love of learning" value learning for its own sake. Students with a love of learning are more likely to have confidence in their ability, enjoy challenge, discover new things or tackle problems on their own, and even think more positively about the future. To spark a love of learning in your students, create opportunities that encourage their natural curiosity and desire to learn, and that build self-reliance, self-confidence, and self-esteem.

Help Students Find Value and Meaning in Their Studies

Studies have shown that the two things necessary for learning are understanding the subject and finding meaning in it. Of the two, finding meaning is surprisingly more important. I, for example, might understand the subject of car engines, but because I'm not interested in them, I'll probably soon forget every detail about crankshafts and pistons. I find this same phenomenon with my students when I teach them music theory. Only when I point out in the music how theory will help their playing do they seem to take an interest and remember the facts. Students always want to know, "What's in it for me?" Help them see the value of each new step. "I know learning third position is tough now, but then you'll get to play so many more great pieces that go higher." We'll talk more about adding meaning by meeting needs in chapter 10, "Energize Students with Goals."

Share Your Enthusiasm

Just as students won't work hard if you don't, they won't be enthusiastic about learning when you act bored or indifferent. As I've mentioned before, your most important motivational tool may be your enthusiasm. Studies have shown that students who are engaged by a teacher's enthusiastic delivery of *in*accurate material learn more than those listening to a dull, boring teacher who delivers accurate information.

Sometimes it's less *what* you say than *how* you say it. What atmosphere do you create in the lessons? Are you happy to see each student? Even the last student of a long day? Do you glance at your watch frequently or do you act as if each lesson is too short? Are you thrilled with your students' smallest accomplishment?

Share your love of music by raving about your favorite pieces, composers, and performers. Be excited about the music and genuinely pleased when they play. At least *pretend* to love "Twinkle" and demonstrate it with the care you would a demanding piece. Pique students' interest in a new piece by assigning it a couple of weeks before you bring it out in the lesson. Say, "This is one of my favorites. I can't wait to hear what you think of it." Rave about what they have learned and tell them how eager you are to take them to the next level. "You are going to get so much use out of this trick I am about to teach you." Or, "Wait until you learn this next step; it's going to make such a difference in your playing." "If you think book two was great, wait until you play book three!" Listen to CDs and rhapsodize. Even if your personality is more laid back, crawl out of your shell for lessons and get excited! Students may think you're crazy at times but they'll pay attention.

HELP EVERY STUDENT FEEL SUCCESSFUL
Create Early Successes

To develop the drive to achieve, students need to experience success. Get beginners up and running soon. Ensure their success by assigning pieces that are challenging yet doable. Give them opportunities to feel competent as soon as possible. Cindy's son Mark recently began taking violin lessons. His teacher started him in a booklet of familiar, easy-to-play songs he had created with notes represented as letters. Even his youngest players gain an immediate sense of mastery. Please, please be careful about choosing literature that is too technically or musically difficult and don't rush too quickly through the book. (I never want to hear Bach and Mozart slaughtered again!) Be sure the child is proud of the performance of a piece before moving on. And never let any good playing go unnoticed.

Encourage Struggling Students

Commiserate with students when they have trouble with a new technique or concept and keep encouraging them that it will all be worth it. "It's hard learning something new and feeling inept, but that's what lessons are all about. Stumbling over a new technique means you have climbed up one more rung on the ladder of success." Relate your own problems learning something to struggling students to let them know it is normal, not stupid, to make mistakes.

Learning takes time and repetition. If students struggle with new techniques or concepts, return to a level they did understand and introduce the new concepts even more slowly this time. Offer frequent, early, and positive feedback to buoy their belief that they can succeed. Avoid an impatient tone if they don't remember something you've already told them five times. (OK, I do get a little irritated on the tenth repetition!)

Gradually Increase the Difficulty of Assignments

Once students have experienced success, gradually increase the difficulty level. Pick pieces that are incrementally challenging and build on skills students have already mastered. When students move up to a new level, reassure them they can handle it. "I know you are a little afraid to move to hour lessons after half hour lessons but you are so much more advanced now. I need an hour to teach you all the things you can learn." Say, "If you can play Clementi, you'll be able to tackle the Mozart next." "Once you can play 'The Spinning Song' up to tempo, you can move on to the Bach Invention." Remind students of their progress over time so they will be excited for the next step even if it is not the final step.

CREATE INDEPENDENCE BY TEACHING
THE WHOLE MUSICIAN

Susan was blown away when her new student, Jenny, came for her first lesson and played the Mendelssohn Violin Concerto. "Oh my!" Susan said. "That was fantastic. What else have you been working on?" "Nothing else, just the Mendelssohn." "Have you played any other compositions from that musical period?" Jenny looked puzzled. "Musical period? What do you mean?" Questioning some more, Susan asked, "Do you practice scales?" "Sure, all the time," responded Jenny. "Great. Can you tell me the key signature for A major?" "Oh. I know how to play my scales but I don't know about the key signatures." Susan moved on by suggesting they sight read a new piece. "It might be something you'll enjoy working on," she added. "Start here at the beginning." "Could you play it for me first?" Jenny pleaded. "I'm not that good at counting."

Without theory and history background, Jenny was missing out on an important part of her music education. I feel strongly about the importance of teaching the *whole musician*, whether that musician plays flute, piano, or the *kazoo*. As music teachers we have an opportunity to give the gift of music, not just the gift of becoming fluent on a particular instrument. With competitions, recitals, and tryouts, it is tempting to teach to the test and concentrate on those few pieces each year that will make students (and you) shine in public. But if students only learn a few pieces by rote, they are left with nothing after these pieces are forgotten.

Drill the Basics

Don't just teach students music: teach them *about* music. Include the basics of counting, music theory, sight reading, ear training, intonation, music history, musical terms, and musicality in every lesson to give students understanding and skills that go beyond performing. "But my students know all that stuff," you may be thinking. Is that true?

Quiz your students. Have them say note names or chords fast as a speeding bullet. Ask them to mark the beats or teach you a rhythm. Ask them in which period composers lived. See if they can play all the scales and arpeggios with no mistakes. Ask the definitions of musical terms in their music. Get away from real music and drill the fundamentals. You'll be surprised.

What's in it for students? Concentrating on the basics makes sight reading, learning, and memorizing more accurate and efficient. When students know *why* things work, they will be able to analyze music and figure out solutions on their own. The skills they learn now will last a lifetime and enable them to explore music on their own after they have left your studio. They can transfer this knowledge and approach to the learning of a new piece or a new instrument and, indeed, to other aspects of their life.

What's in it for you, the teacher? Your job becomes easier as students take over the learning process for themselves. We've all heard the saying, "Give a man a fish and he eats for a day, but teach him how to fish and he eats for a lifetime." Our main objective as teachers is to encourage students to develop their own musical thinking and creative problem-solving processes, thus making us obsolete. I tell my students they have two choices: one, they learn the basics to become independent thinkers; or two, I come live with them. I'll be there to help whenever they need it. (They all choose number one.) Trust me: the time you spend on the fundamentals now will pay off tenfold in the future.

Include the Building Blocks of Music in Every Lesson

How can you cram all this information into a short lesson? You can use books specifically designed to teach note names, counting, chords, and theory, but more importantly, you can sneak it into every lesson. When students reach the first piece that's not in C major, teach them about key signatures. When they reach a piece based on arpeggios, teach them how to build them. Ask: What scale did you just play in that duet? What key did this piece modulate to? Is this section in major or minor? What does this musical term mean? How many ledger lines does high B have? If we are in 6/8, what kind of note gets three beats? What period is this piece from and what does that tell you about the trills? What happens to the pitch when you play softly? What is the road map for a minuet and trio?

Make music history a part of each lesson. Talk about composers as if they were your friends. Sprinkle your conversation with "gossip" about composers' lives and the times in which they lived. Require students to write a short biography about the composers of the pieces they play. My students have a weekly assignment to bring me the name of a classical music piece and composer they heard during the week. They read to me out of a music history book while I take notes, I talk to them off the top of my head about the composer, or I give them a handout. They then copy this information under the appropriate musical period in the history section of their *Music for Life* notebook (which you will read about in a coming chapter). This music history takes only five minutes of the lesson but enables students to see composers as real people, understand the performance practices of each period, learn to play musically as they heard on the CD, recognize composers and periods, and grow to love their favorite pieces.

Sneak music skills into conversation. Use the real musical terms. Instead of "slow down," say "ritard." Say "crescendo" instead of "get louder" and "accelerando" instead of "get faster." "Let's play the B major arpeggio forte" or "Go back to the beginning of the sequence." "Where does the theme modulate?" or "What form of the minor scale was in that phrase?" The possibilities are endless.

To help organize teaching the basics, dedicate certain weeks or months to drilling specific skills with students of all levels. Though I try to include the basics in every single lesson, August and September in my studio are National Sight Reading Months, October and November are dedicated to music history, the summer months are for scales, and January and February are theory and ear training. After the spring contest season we concentrate on tone, intonation, and breathing exercises and etudes. I set aside a portion of each lesson to go through sight reading books or exercises I have created.

Create handouts so you don't waste lesson time writing. Handouts I use include Name the Chord, Figure out the Mystery Word (made up of notes on the staff), Learn to Build Scales, How to Play Appoggiaturas, the Anatomy of Breathing, Tone Tips, and Pitch Tendencies. I catalogue my handouts in file cabinets for easy retrieval.

Avoid Becoming Indispensable

"No! Me do it!" the toddler cries as she grabs the pitcher away from her mother. Drinking the juice was secondary to being able to pour it for herself. From an early age children yearn to be autonomous. The need to feel independent is inborn and motivating. The child who can pour her own juice feels she has some control over the world and beams in pride. She begins to believe in her abilities and is eager to do more things for herself.

Put this human need for independence to work for you in the studio. Teach students to be autonomous and to think for themselves. Once they know the basics, give them the tools they need to solve their own problems. Respect and trust your students' ability to make decisions; doing so builds self-esteem and self-confidence. From playing scales to managing stage fright, each skill students master is another step toward making the teacher obsolete. Just knowing they have the skills to analyze and solve their own problems boosts confidence.

HELP STUDENTS BECOME ACTIVE LEARNERS

The brain that works is the brain that learns. If you teach "at" students they will retain a portion of what they hear and then forget most of it the next day. When they learn actively, they retain much more. Students learn by doing, by creating, and by solving problems. They'll be more motivated when you give them more responsibility and control over their own learning.

Independent learning is effective learning, and it will not happen if you become a crutch for your students. Imagine a child whose parents do everything for him. While he watches TV, they clean his room and pick up the trail of candy bar wrappers he left behind. When he's out playing, they check his homework and correct his answers. Next they clean the mess he left from eating his snack. What are his chores? He doesn't have any and wouldn't have a clue how to do them. What happens when this child enters the real world with no life skills? He falls flat on his face without his parents holding his hand.

Don't train your students to use you as a crutch. When they blindly do what you say, or worse, just imitate your playing, they will never learn to think for themselves and will always need you to hold their hands. Once students know the basics, be a *facilitator* who encourages, provides feedback, and supports their efforts—not someone who provides all the answers. When you supply struggling students with every solution, you rob them of the chance to figure it out. Students must learn to figure out *for themselves* what went wrong. If you tell them the "answer" to every mistake, they will learn how to play only *that piece* but not *how to play.* Avoid playing every new piece for them or they will only learn how to imitate you and will not learn how to sight read on their own. I tell my students, "The 'nice' teacher would just play this for you and solve this problem, but the good teacher helps you figure it our on your own."

When students make a "dumb" mistake, say, "What did you do wrong?" *Take your time and let them answer.* When they realize the mistake, be sure *they* mark the music, and not you. Assure students, "I'm not asking you to tell me what mistake you made to embarrass you or to make you feel guilty. I am asking you to figure out mistakes on your own so you will always be aware of them and can fix them when you're not at the lesson."

If students can't remember a previous technique, ask them to look it up in their student notebooks. You'll learn how to create these unique notebooks in chapter 9, "Increase Success with the *Music for Life* Notebook System." Teaching students to be responsible for their learning is an ongoing process that takes your time, patience, and support. Help your students to gain independence by learning to solve their own problems.

Keep Students Actively Involved in Their Learning

Emphasize the *method* of problem solving. Model problem-solving skills by analyzing a piece with students and thinking aloud as you go so they can hear your thought process. "First look at the time signature and figure out what kind of note will get the beat and how fast you want to play. Mark the beats in the first four measures. Say the rhythm out loud by counting apple, apple, huckleberry, huckleberry while tapping. Next say the names of the notes out loud in rhythm. Then finger the notes while you say them in rhythm. Now you are ready to play!" After you help students break down a difficult spot, make a point of saying to them, "This is how you can figure it out on your own." Review your problem-solving methods with students, asking them, "Do you remember how we got here?" When students have trouble with a new concept, such as a tricky rhythm, say, "I don't understand this concept. Can you teach me?" ("But don't expect me to pay you!") They will understand once they've had to explain it.

Respond to problems with questions: "How could you make the tone on that note better?" or "Should this be an up-bow or a down-bow?" "How did *you* play and how is it *supposed* to be played?" If students make a rhythm mistake, ask, "Can you check that rhythm?" or "Do you know what you did wrong rhythmically there?" Make them tune on their own and when hearing pitch problems, ask them if the note was flat or sharp instead of correcting the pitch yourself. Almost always reflect the problem back to students and then guide them to find the answer.

Teach students general rules, such as "Use terraced dynamics in a sequence" or "Always breathe before a pick-up," and then recall the rule when you review new pieces.

Help them generalize within the piece. "Where did the first phrase start?" "With a pick-up on beat three." "Where did the second phrase start?" "On beat three." "Then where do you think the third phrase starts?" Resist answering the question "Is this right?" Suggest ways for students to decide for themselves.

Fourteen-year-old Simon loved the thrill of discovery. "I found this really cool Scherzo but it looked way too hard. Then I decided to use the ways you taught me to figure out a piece, like marking the beats, using the metronome, and analyzing the chords. It's fun knowing how to figure out music on your own. It's like having my teacher there without her yelling at me!" (Thanks, Simon!)

Teach Students to Be Creative and Critical Thinkers

Critical and creative thinking are complementary aspects of thinking. Creative thinking involves generating ideas, solutions, and different ways of doing things. Critical thinking involves evaluating, analyzing arguments or suggestions, and making decisions. We use these skills to solve real life problems, moving back and forth between creating solutions and then deciding if they'll work. Students need both thinking skills to move their learning beyond memorization or parroting you.

Invite students to ask questions and empower them by valuing their opinions even if they differ from yours. My son Kyle loves to play Bach unaccompanied suites on his cello. His teacher's and my concern is that he likes to play them in a Romantic style—not exactly as Bach intended. While teaching him about the Baroque style, his teacher allows him to put his personal stamp on the music. Sometimes learning to be innovative is more important than being right. Of course, if Kyle later decides to audition for a job or a contest, his teacher and I will advise him to audition in the style appropriate to the music, to show he knows the correct Baroque practice.

To help students begin to form their own opinions and style, ask, "What do *you* think?" Give them time and bolster their courage to think on their own. When starting a new piece, ask students for their ideas on dynamics and phrasing. Encourage them to experiment using the general rules you have taught them to figure out phrasing on their own.

Help Students Become *Creative* Thinkers

- Allow them time to think of one or more answers. Show them it's all right not to have an instant answer.
- Ask students to play simple songs with different emotions. Experiment making the same tune sound mournful, cheerful, angry, or wistful.
- Ask students to help you analyze a piece. Ask: "Would you rather accelerando or ritard here? Should this section be a gradual crescendo or forte-piano-forte?"
- Listen to recordings and ask them to form opinions on different styles, tone, and interpretations. It's fine to allow students to listen to the CD recording first, but then put it away to help them develop their own style.
- Give them a little leeway in interpretation. In the long run it may be much more important for them to put their own feelings into a piece than to play it totally in the correct style.
- If students play fingerings differently than printed, ask them to back up their choices with good reasons.
- When they have applied a novel solution, say, "That isn't the way *I* might play it, but you did it so convincingly your way that it works."

Help Students Become *Critical* Thinkers

- Ask questions that seek clarification: "Can you give me an example of another place in this piece that has the same phrasing?"
- Probe assumptions: "The rule says we should breathe after a long note rather than a short note. Do you think that would work here?"
- Contrast viewpoints or perspectives: "How would Mozart want this to be played? Why might Brahms disagree with him?"
- Ask about consequences or results: "How would the mood change if you played the largo section the same as the presto?"
- Ask students to draw conclusions: "What can you conclude from looking at the dynamics or the tempo of this piece?"

In this chapter we talked about the importance of teachers not only disseminating information, but inspiring students and equipping them with the skills and knowledge they need to continue learning long after their lessons with us have ended. Beyond teaching your students music skills, help them develop a love of learning and the tools and motivation to become their own teachers, skills that will carry them throughout their lives.

LOOKING AHEAD

In our next chapter, we'll talk about more skills and attitudes that will serve students throughout their lives. We'll talk about how to help them persevere when they get discouraged, how to demonstrate the value of hard work, and how to teach delayed gratification. Let's turn to our next chapter, "Create an Atmosphere of Achievement."

SIX

Create an Atmosphere of Achievement

We all wish for those ideal students—the ones who play perfectly and love their teacher, their lessons, and even long hours of practice. Disciplined and committed students set the bar high and work continually to reach it. Your students can develop these qualities when you create in your studio an atmosphere of achievement.

SET HIGH STANDARDS

When my students' friends hear I'm their teacher, they often say, "She's really hard, isn't she?" or "If she's your teacher, you must be super good!" Setting high standards and achieving good results go hand in hand. I didn't always have that reputation. When I first started teaching, I thought my students were doing pretty well until I went to a contest and was surprised by other students' high levels of performance. "How did those kids get that good?" I wondered. And then, "If they can do it, my students can too. It's time for us both to work even harder." *Ask and ye shall receive* became my new motto. Every year I expect a little more from my students and believe they can do it.

You've heard of high school seniors who graduate without ever learning simple math and knowing how to read. You do your own students a similar disservice when you pass them from one piece to the next before they have played them to your standard. Let students know that studying music is serious as well as fun and requires hard work.

If you're not sure what standards you should set, attend contests with your students and work to have them perform as well as the winners. Many students are the kings and queens of their school music programs, but hearing other students lets you both know what's possible at their own age level.

It may seem harder at the beginning to correct every mistake and demand "perfection," but the payoff will be worth it. The basic good habits you demand prepare students for whatever path they choose. Have a long-range plan in mind even with beginning students. When you hear young Matt's terrible playing habits, ask yourself, "Will Matt's tone/vibrato/position enable him to play a major work when he is 17?" If not, work on fixing the problem now. Letting things slide now can cripple him later, and you never know who will turn out to be a superstar!

When you maintain high standards you may also notice lower student attrition. Why would students quit less often when you're tough? Parents appreciate your work ethic and that you're passing it along to their child. Some students may initially chafe at your expectations, but soon most of them will be grateful for your commitment to making them their best. When they discover both pride in their accomplishments and the joy of making music, they will be ready for even more.

Communicate Your Standards Early On

The following "horror story" is not fiction. It happened last month and is burned into my memory.

The phone rings. "Hello."

"Hi, this is New Girl's mom. We were wondering if you had room in your schedule for a new student. My daughter, New Girl, is in tenth grade and has been playing flute for six years. She's very bright, is a great student, and practices without being told." "That's my type of student!" I said. "What are you looking for in a new teacher?" "She wants someone who will push her and we heard you would be that person. I think you will enjoy working with her." We set up a trial lesson.

A week later, "New Girl" arrives for her trial lesson. "Let's get started. Play me something. How about a scale?" "I hate scales." "OK, then play whatever you would like." New Girl picks up her flute to play from memory. Slouching in the chair and with fingers flying (way off the keys) she plays something resembling music but with no beat and no discernible tune. Her tone resembles a sick and dying foghorn. She turns to me, waiting for my compliment.

My heart sinks in disappointment. "Even though we'd be starting from square one," I think, "Miracles do happen." I tell her that, as with all my transfer students, we will go back to the beginning to fill any "holes" in her education. This also provides an opportunity for me to let her know how I like things to be played. "Do you understand?" Silence. "I guess," she finally answers.

We move to playing a beginning book of duets. Between songs I ask her questions to determine what she has already learned. To my straightforward theory questions such as "What is the key signature for B major?" she replies, "I know the answer; I just can't put it into words." "What does *allegro* mean?" "I know that. I just can't think of it right now." I tell her I assign weekly theory homework and she reacts as if I had asked her to compose a symphony. "I have enough homework at school!" she protests. "My school is *so* hard. Today I had a *really* hard day. My teachers made me . . . blah, blah, blah."

We turn to working on her embouchure. At this point it resembles a frog sucking in bugs. I ask her to make her lips pout and to practice by blowing a kiss to her mom. She looks at me with disdain. "I don't *want* to kiss my mother." Her mother wilts. New Girl says she is unwilling to try more embouchure exercises at home.

Next we tackle her breathing problems with a long tone contest. Hers are fifteen seconds; mine are forty. "You'll need to play twenty long tones every day." "Twenty? *Every day?* I don't have time for that." "No? Let's see. Twenty times fifteen is three hundred seconds, which equals five minutes. You don't have five minutes a day to improve your breathing?"

"No. I can't practice every day. I'm way too busy for that." Mom interjects. "New Girl, you told me you would practice for an hour five days a week." "I *never* said that! Mondays, Wednesdays, and Fridays I have soccer, Tuesdays is math team, and I haven't even started gymnastics. That's five days a week. And I have so much homework. How can I do twenty long tones every day?"

"Wow," I say. "It sounds like you don't have enough time to commit to flute—at least not in the way I will require. I only accept students who will practice every day, are excited about learning, and want to work with me to get better." The lesson ends. We exchange pleasantries. I say goodbye to "New Girl." *Forever.*

During the initial phone call or trial lesson I tell prospective students and their parents about my program and my requirements. They sign up with their eyes open. Being up-front about studio expectations avoids problems down the road. I also ask new students how well they do in school. This is a *generally* good predictor of how committed they will be to lessons.

After hearing about my program, most students (and parents!) are excited to start. The majority of students stay, and once they are through "boot camp," thrive on the challenge and feelings of accomplishment. Others decide I'm not what they are looking for and I refer them to a teacher with fewer requirements. A few students start lessons with good intentions, but after a few months realize they're not up to the challenge. That doesn't mean that I am too tough or they are too lazy. It means our goals are not a good match.

Create an Atmosphere of Achievement

A great teacher is tough, and in being so, helps create an atmosphere of achievement. I could easily forget a student's flat D-sharp, ugly tone, or cloddy phrasing, but I'd be lowering my standards. When students make mistakes or don't play musically, hammer away to correct them before moving on. Say, "That may have been good enough for many teachers, but you're stuck with me!" Don't let sloppy playing slide by because you don't think they can do better or you don't care enough to make them better.

Expect a lot even from beginners. Assign only pieces that they can master. Imagine you heard the student's performance on a CD. Would it be acceptable if you didn't know the age of the student? Tell them, "No matter what level you are, play your music beautifully. If you can only play 'Row, Row, Row Your Boat,' then it should sound just as good as mine." Or "If you are playing the Bach Violin Concerto then you had better play it like Bach!"

Be clear in your assignments. How will they know how well to play if they don't know what you expect? You'll learn more about giving assignments in chapter 9, "Increase Success with the *Music for Life* Notebook System."

Teach students how to practice for "perfection." Work with them so they aren't careless in practice at home. Suggest they ask themselves, "What would my teacher say?" (I have offered to make a life-sized cutout of me with my finger pointing to make my presence felt at their homes, but all have declined.) And remember that while you're being a demanding teacher, you should be a fun and loving one too.

Tell the Truth

Be nice. Be kind. Be fun. Be *truthful.* If students play well, let them know. If they play poorly, be frank. They won't know what your standards are unless you are blunt. Students want to know the rules. Sugarcoating makes for a lovely teatime but a lousy lesson. I'll talk in more detail about giving honest and constructive feedback in chapter 11, "Recognize and Reward Results and Effort."

TAILOR EXPECTATIONS TO THE INDIVIDUAL

Will setting high standards help you make a superstar out of *every* student? Sorry, no. Students have different mental and musical capabilities, learning styles, levels of interest, instruments, time commitments, and parental support. Adhere to a certain standard, but tailor your requirements to individual needs and capabilities.

All my students must maintain a certain standard, yet the expectations differ for each student. You may give a half page of an etude to one student and two pages to another. An A lesson for one student may only be a D's worth of effort for another. Regardless of their level, I expect every student to play musically and with few mistakes. Even if they are playing "The Happy Farmer," that farmer should sound ecstatic. When you demand a lot, students realize you're serious about making them better, and take their own commitment more seriously too. When they work harder their fast progress will shock them, and they'll be hooked on music for life.

Ask for Your Students' Best

My student Ana is on her school track team. Every week she can't wait to tell me about her performance. Does she tell me how many runners she beat? Ana's more excited to tell me whether she beat her Personal Record (PR) than to tell me her overall ranking. Ana's main competitor is herself. When she shaves five seconds from her total time she is ecstatic and then commits to doing even better the next week. What a great attitude!

Encourage students to compete against themselves to improve their personal best. Say, "I've heard you play more musically than that. Do *your* very best." "Play that phrase until you are proud of it." Teach your students to be as particular as you are; ask them, "Was that B the most beautiful you've ever played?" "How would you rate how you played that sonata?" "Are you satisfied with that grade?" "You have beautiful tone; why aren't you using it all the time?" "Most seventh graders would be thrilled to play like that, but you are not the average seventh grader, so don't be satisfied with that performance." Though not all students are created equal, they can all be winners when they compete against themselves to better their PR. If they can play it once, insist on the same level every time.

When students are not happy with their performance at a lesson, usually agree with them and ask what could be improved next time. When a student turns to you and says, "Do you think I should play that again right now to get it better?" *always* say, "Yes." When their performance of a piece at the lesson has been below par, ask them if they want to play it again now or take it home to perfect it. Most of the time they'll opt to try it again, and this time they will concentrate. If they want to take it home agree with them that it does need another week of better practice to reach their personal best.

Are Your Expectations Too High or Too Low?

Are the expectations you've set for a student too high? Expectations that are too high make students feel as if they're constantly failing. Students may give up, or put too much pressure on themselves to meet them. If you have any doubts, review the assignments at the end of the lesson with the student. Ask if it is the right amount for the week and also inquire if they feel the overall work load is too much and adjust the assignments when necessary. When students agree that the work load is right, they are then also committing to practice the required amount, and they will feel like partners in their learning.

If the student has been assigned the same material week after week and is still struggling, work on practice methods at the lesson. Get part of the assignment good and leave the rest for the student to work out at home. If their progress is still slow, rethink the assignment to something that uses the same skills but is a little easier, or backtrack to an etude to build up the particular technique needed. Many times I have students go back and repeat a technique book but with higher standards the second time. Usually they don't think of this as a sign of failure but as a way to really master the material and be ready for the next step.

When students persist in saying their workload is excessive or "This piece is too hard!" they may be right, at least this time. Ask yourself if you're moving too quickly and whether it is time to change gears. Remember that learning a particular piece is not as important as learning technique and enjoying music, so if the student has just learned the piece wrong or has a bad attitude about it, it may be wise just to drop it and move on. In chapter 21, "Troubleshoot Problems and Turn around Complaints," I'll give you ideas and strategies to keep students working and interested.

On the other hand, are your expectations so low that students feel you have no faith in them to do better? Do they think the best thing about your teaching is that you are so nice and so easy? If you are casual about their commitment and accepting of any level of progress, they will be too.

Stretch Students to Higher Levels

Gradually ease beginners and transfer students into the rigors of exacting lessons. Praise them for small accomplishments and then remind them that with each lesson you'll raise the standard. New students may need time to adjust to shifting standards, but don't give up. Some lucky teachers have the opposite problem with students who already play beyond their years or playing experience. Don't get caught up in the numbers; these kids need challenges too. No one is ever the best; keep stretching.

To gradually increase your standards tell students, "You got a sticker for playing the scale in whole notes, but next week it must be memorized. And the following week you will need to play it in quarter notes to get the sticker." "You played that pretty well, but we're going for perfect here." Or "You got all the notes and rhythm right, but that's not enough. Now go back and make it music." Say, "I know you are in ninth grade, but you don't want to sound like a ninth grader, do you? I think you can sound like a tenth grader." If you give stickers or other rewards for great lessons, hand them out liberally at first and then make them harder to attain.

Mikaela, a student who has since graduated from high school, remembers the "shock" of her first lessons at age fifteen:

> I was scared. I'm an overachiever, but the standards were so much higher I felt I couldn't exceed them. When I performed for Bonnie there was no "shock and awe" like I'm used to in the rest of my life. I had to get used to my standards always rising because no matter what I did, I could always do more. I knew I could not always be the best, but I always *tried* my best.

IMPROVE STUDENTS' WORK ETHIC

Learning to play an instrument may be the most difficult undertaking in our young students' lives. In this culture, movies, TV, and video games lure kids, making it hard to get them off the couch and into the practice room. How can teachers encourage the self-discipline needed to learn an instrument?

First, emphasize consistency in practice and attendance. Through regularity we acquire the habit called self-discipline. Praise students who practice consistently instead of in spurts. Remind them that it is not always the most talented players who get better but the ones who work every day. Emphasize the point with practice charts or rewards for the most days practiced in a row, or weeks with six days of practice. Say, "Remember the fable of the tortoise and the hare? The hare was more talented but the slow and steady tortoise won the race. *Hard work wins over talent when talent doesn't work hard.*"

Teach self-discipline in attendance. Make it uncomfortable when students try to cancel. Ask them to reschedule instead of missing the week. Give your schedule to students and ask them to trade with one another when they have a conflict and call you with the change. Students will cancel less if you charge by the month no matter how many lessons are taken. Money talks!

Teachers should also cancel as few lessons as possible. If you are always canceling lessons for performances without offering make-ups, your students will quickly assess where your priorities lie.

Teach Time Management

Aren't we all tired of the students who come in to each and every lesson whining, "I had the worst day/week/month at school? I had so much homework I couldn't practice. I was going to do the theory assignment right before I came to the lesson but we had to leave early. I would have practiced more but we had company. I was up until midnight every night doing two big projects I was assigned a month ago. I was going to practice three times a day on the weekend because I didn't practice during the week, but then we went away on a trip. I'll start the new piece after this one is perfect. I know the competition is next weekend but I *promise* my pieces will be memorized by Thursday. *Really!*"

Projects, homework, tests, sports, and *practice* always compete for students' time. Teach them time management skills so that every week and every lesson is not full of stress. Help them schedule their school *and* instrument projects early and check along the way to be sure they're right on track. Remind students that preparation put off until the last minute can't always become an emergency where the music has to suffer. If students consistently cancel lessons to finish homework or come unprepared to lessons because of a last minute paper, test, or project, work with them on time management. Offer ideas such as playing twenty minutes after an hour of study, practicing right after school before they start homework, playing at the same time every day, or playing two sessions on Saturday. If students have trouble spreading their music workload equally over the week, help them to set daily goals such as learning just two lines of a song, or working on two pieces one day and the other two pieces the next. Enlist parents' help to check on their child's progress during the week and help them stay on target. Chart long-term practice goals on a calendar and pretend the deadline is early. I'll offer more ideas on time management in chapter 14, "Use Practice Tricks for Fast Results." Students will appreciate these time management skills later in life, whether or not they become music majors.

Teach Delayed Gratification

Students see star athletes and famous performers but don't always realize the years of practice that made them so good. They can't see how playing boring scales and annoying etudes is worthwhile. It's hard to imagine being able to play "cool" pieces soon when all you can play now are "stupid, easy" pieces. Delayed gratification is a tough lesson. Learning to start with nothing and chip away at a task with consistency is one of life's biggest lessons *and* assets. There is no way out of hard practice for a future goal.

Help students persevere. If the piece is long, or the technique challenging, remind them of the end result and cheer them on along the way. Say, "The fun piece is full of arpeggios. When you learn these, playing this piece will be easy." "Learn how to double-tongue better and then we will tackle the big piece." "Remember last year when you were only in book one? This year you're in book two and next year the fun really starts with book three. You'll get there if you keep practicing!" "When your etudes are done, *then* you can play solos." "Wait for this big concerto. In two more years you will have improved enough to do it justice." "Remember that anything worth doing is worth doing well, and that will take time."

IS MAINTAINING HIGH STANDARDS WORTH THE INVESTMENT?

I believe it is. Just as the work spent teaching the basics will make your job easier in the long run, so will the blood, sweat, and tears you invest in setting high standards for students from the start. Our goal as teachers is not only to disseminate information but to encourage our students to reach their highest potential. Equip them to do so. Go beyond teaching instrument skills. Teach them to always strive for greatness. Give them a solid foundation and the desire to always do their best, and the rest will be almost easy.

LOOKING AHEAD

In the next chapter, "Attitude Is Everything," we'll talk more about expectations, but with a twist. We'll move from having *high* expectations, to having *positive* expectations. We'll talk about the power of self-fulfilling prophecy, and how you can encourage students to use positive self-talk and visualizations. You'll see how dramatically taking a positive view of your students' abilities can affect their views of themselves and their chances of success.

SEVEN

Attitude Is Everything

SHOW STUDENTS YOU BELIEVE IN THEM

That's a beautiful sound. Aren't you excited?" It was Abigail's third lesson. On her fifth try she had gotten a tone on the flute headjoint. "Wow!" her mom and I exclaimed. Abigail smiled. "Now see if you can tongue to start the note." With lots of encouragement, she tongued about every fifth note. "You're a natural! Do you think you could play two notes without breathing between them?" Another demonstration and Abigail succeeded. Mom and I were as impressed as if we had heard James Galway playing the Paganini *Moto Perpetuo* in one breath. "You're picking this up fast. Think how much you've improved in one lesson!" Abigail beamed. "Imagine how good you'll be by Christmas! You were born to be a flute player!" Abigail left believing she had special talent. I envisioned her first recital and vowed to make her a top-notch student. Success begins in our minds.

Help Beginners See Themselves as Musicians

Your outlook can determine whether your students succeed or fail. Think of each new student as a treasure box to be opened. *Assume* they will be great and most will meet your expectations. Talk to new students as if they will be wonderful musicians and believe they can be. Pick a strength in beginners and build on it, even if it is just holding the instrument or counting four quarter notes in a row. Act as if it is unusual for someone to pick up a skill so fast. Acknowledge their challenges and let them know they have what it takes to succeed: "You're smart, you're talented, and I will show you how to work, so of course you are going to be a wonderful violinist." Watch them sit up straighter knowing they can achieve anything as long as they work hard. Be excited for their future, and they will be too.

Maintain Positive Expectations

Maintain your optimism in the studio. When students arrive, ask, "Are you ready for another great lesson?" Frame challenges positively: "This piece is tough but I have faith in you." When students learn a new skill or have a better-than-average lesson, be enthusiastic. "I *knew* you could do it!" Show them you believe in their abilities. "There probably isn't a seventh grader on the planet who could play this piece musically, but I bet you can if you really practice." Act as though the sky is the limit. "You're working your way up to being a superstar!" Predict a rosy future. "This is going to be a standout year for you!" From the minute they walk into the studio, encourage their "can do" attitude. Keep smiling. It's the easiest way to buoy their spirits.

Picture Your Way to Success

Imagine the possibilities! From the first lesson, relate today's skills to their future. "You'll want to keep your fingers close because it will help when you start to play fast pieces." Describe contests they might enter, advanced and beautiful pieces they should aim for, and ensembles they can join when they reach a certain level. Give them concrete events to look forward to and strive for.

Keep a record of tasks they've mastered, such as scales or long tones. Use these records to set measurable goals to achieve and then beat. Share your visions of success. Favorably "compare" students to those more advanced. "Kasumi's first piece was *Hungarian Serenade* and yours is, too! You are going to be just like her!" Or "I remember when Janna couldn't get a good sound and she wanted to quit, but now listen to her. I am confident your tone will be as good as hers." We move toward what we imagine. Help students celebrate past triumphs and visualize future success, whether it is making it to the next skill, book, or recital. Encourage them to think like winners. Plan big. Aim high.

HAVE FAITH IN YOUR ABILITY AS A TEACHER

Just as you must believe that your students can be successful if they really try, you must keep the same belief in your teaching skills. If you learned how to become a good musician yourself, nothing is stopping you from bestowing that ability upon your students. Maintain your own positive attitude by associating with positive people, setting challenging personal goals, and looking for creative solutions.

Confer faith in your abilities by saying, "Put your trust in me and I promise you will get good if you practice." Let them know about your past successes as a teacher: "Lauren started with me in fourth grade and look at her now. You can do the same thing!" or "We can do anything; we're a good team!"

BUILD SELF-CONFIDENCE WITH POSITIVE SELF-TALK

Parker paced up and down the hallway waiting for his turn to play at the contest. "I was stupid to enter this contest! I'm not half as good as the girl in there playing now. People will laugh when they hear *me*! I'm so nervous I just know I'm going to mess up! I don't have what it takes. I'll never be any good!"

We become our own worst enemies when we engage in such destructive self-talk. Tell your students like Parker, "When you talk to yourself before a performance or even in everyday life, be kind. Imagine you're talking to your best friend. Now *be* your own best friend and talk to yourself with care and respect. Why? *What you say to yourself matters.* It affects how you feel and how you perform."

Negative self-talk destroys students' overall faith in their abilities. Attitude drives behavior; it can determine your future success or failure. If you think and talk to yourself like a winner, you will develop the self-confidence of a winner. We all have huge potential and must strengthen our belief in ourselves.

Whether You Think You Can or Think You Can't, You Are Probably Right

Help students become aware of self-defeating thought patterns and put a positive spin on them. If we tell ourselves we can't, then we probably won't. "I can't" gives you almost no chance of success. When most people say "I can't," they are really saying, "I won't . . . put in the time or effort, or discipline myself." When students say "I can't," respond with, "Yes you can, and I will help you!" Change "I have to be perfect" to "No one expects perfection." Don't berate yourself for the past with questions such as "Why didn't I choose a different piece?" "Why didn't I practice that hard measure more?" "Why did I play such a long program?" Replace "I should have" with "next time."

Strike these anxiety-producing phrases: "I know I'll mess up." "I'll get nervous and it will fall apart." "I'm stressed." "It's impossible." These words are not just a by-product of stage fright; they *cause* stage fright. During the important minutes before a performance encourage students to say "I'm *excited* about playing" or "I'm fine" rather than "I'm *nervous*!" Have them say "This will be fun" instead of "Help! I want out of here!" What we say can change how we perform. People who concentrate on what they *can* do are better and more confident musicians, and happier in general.

HELP STUDENTS TAKE RESPONSIBILITY FOR THEIR RESULTS

"Sam won the competition and I didn't even place?" moaned Jen. "It's not fair. He played last in the day I and played in the middle so the judge couldn't even remember me. Sam has a more expensive cello than I do. I forgot my rosin. His teacher is better and makes him practice more too. He's been taking lessons longer. I had such a hard week at school I couldn't practice. My piece was way too hard. The judge likes romantic pieces and I played Bach. I couldn't sleep last night because I was so nervous. I think I'm coming down with a cold."

I guess some people, like Sam, have all the luck. Or do people like Jen have all the excuses? Help students see the results of the choices they have made. Instead of listening to them blame someone or something, help them analyze how different choices might have produced a different outcome. Could they have memorized the piece a month earlier? Would performing more often have helped tame their stage fright? Was the program they chose too ambitious? Might they have been more successful if they had played with music instead of from memory? Was there a problem with technique the student didn't address? *Should they have practiced more?* No pity parties!

WHAT IF I FAIL? HELP STUDENTS
OVERCOME THE FEAR OF FAILURE

The personal nature of music exposes musicians to criticism and failure. Playing in front of an audience can be as painful as trying on bathing suits in front of them! Give students the courage to try by telling them to worry less about what other people will say or think or how they'll compare with other performers. There will *always* be performers who are better and worse. (And always people who are richer, smarter, and cuter, too!)

Don't fuel their fears by expecting perfection. Tell them, "When you make the first mistake be glad it's over and go on." After a tough performance or a competition loss, remind students that successful people look at their "losses" not as permanent and personal, but as feedback. Failure is about an outcome; it is *not* a personality characteristic. You may have failed to win, but *you* are not a failure. We all learn from trial and error. Help students "get back on the horse" by beginning right away to talk about "next time." Their future outlook can be the difference between a mediocre performance and a magnificent one. Read more about putting contests and concerts in perspective in chapter 22, "Prepare Students for Performance."

EXPECT EXCEPTIONS

The sad truth: It won't always work.

I recently made the tough choice to "fire" a student. Tiffany came to me from another teacher and I never would have guessed she'd had one year of lessons. My first inclination was to blame her teacher for not having set high enough standards. My instinct was partially right in that Tiffany had not been pushed to work hard, but after I got to know her, I realized that pushing her to work would be a next-to-impossible task. Each time I taught her a new fact she whined, "Do I have to memorize that?" or said, "That's way too hard!" Although she had arrived with a poor technique and an attitude that was even worse, I was *determined* to turn her around.

"You've written a book about motivation," I told myself. "You should be able to 'hook' this girl. Let's see how good you are." Full of enthusiasm and hope, I pulled out all the stops and used every trick in the book (literally!) to turn her around. I explained that her attitude was a choice that would determine her success or failure. I emphasized the importance of thinking positively, focusing on solutions and not problems. I helped her imagine how far she could reach with steady practice. I talked excitedly about new techniques, praised her for every small success (and trust me, they were small!), and tried to be the best teacher I could be.

Yet Tiffany did not want to change. When I taught her a new trick fingering on the flute, she fought back, saying, "I don't want to do that—my way is easier." I coaxed and cajoled her into playing with good tone on the D major scale but when she went on to play the F major scale she played with a tone that sounded as though she had never had a lesson. "Why would you choose *not* to play with the beautiful tone you have?" I asked. "Because it's easier," she said unabashedly. Dismayed, I gasped. "Well, you *asked*," she retorted.

Her mother aided and abetted her. Poor overworked Tiffany needed her mother to carry in her heavy book bag and flute. When she complained she was too tired to sit straight, Mommy cooed, "Sweetheart, would it help if I put a pillow behind your back?" Her mother asked me to be more "understanding" because "Tiffany had so much homework this week" (she was in the sixth grade) and "She had a cold . . . she didn't understand the assignment . . . she forgot her books . . . she's tired from playing soccer . . . she needs to rest on the weekends after a hard week at school . . . she was up late at a friend's slumber party . . . she's sensitive and doesn't perform well under pressure. . . ." Poor Tiffany!

We reviewed the same material week after week and her lessons took on a dull regularity. In six months she could not learn six key signatures. "You give me too much to memorize!" she whined. Even her mother had learned that D major has two sharps. Tiffany wanted to play better but wasn't willing to devote *any* effort to getting there. My positive attitude could not overcome her negative one. No matter how well you teach, most students will rise to the challenge, but sadly, not all. Believe in your students and help them see their potential. When your efforts have become a one-way street, give yourself and the student a break. Bail out! You'll learn when and how to make this decision in chapter 25, "When It's Time to Say Goodbye."

LOOKING AHEAD

In our next chapter, "Make Practice a Priority," I'll show you how to help students make practice a priority, tell you how to turn clock-watchers into goal-watchers, and offer help for dealing with procrastinators.

EIGHT

Make Practice a Priority

M usic teachers often ask me for advice. What do you think is their number one concern? Is it "How can my students win more contests?" or "How can I find more students?" or even "How can I be a better teacher?" If you noticed the title of this chapter, you've probably figured it out by now. Their number one concern is "How do I get my students to *practice*?"

Practice issues are on every teacher's list because the one hour per week students spend with us is not where fine musicians are made. Their success depends on consistent, effective practice when we're nowhere in sight. There's no way around it. Until the magic "music improvement pill" is invented (quickly followed, I hope, by magic weight loss and anti-aging pills), there's no way to improve on an instrument other than to faithfully practice. In this chapter I'll present techniques to help you reduce students' resistance to practice and to make practice time more productive. First let's talk about setting your practice requirements.

SET AND COMMUNICATE
YOUR PRACTICE REQUIREMENTS

Students need practice standards to help them fulfill their potential. You might assign fifteen minutes of practice, five days a week to a young beginner and require two hours, six days a week of a competitive advanced student. Decide what you will demand and what you will accept. Most students will rise to the level you require.

Again, during the initial phone interview you must let parents and children know you expect consistent practice. You don't have to make it sound like they are joining the army if they study with you, but when the parent of a teenager asks if ten minutes a day will be enough, you can clear up any misunderstanding right then. At the first lesson, review this commitment with students through your written studio policy. Ask if they can handle the required amount of practice. Request that parents commit to supporting this expectation.

HELP STUDENTS MAKE PRACTICING A PRIORITY
Give Beginners a Great Start

Emphasize the progress students will make with concentrated practice. I tell my beginning students that one *month* of lessons with a half hour of practice a day equals one *year's* worth of band with no practice, and one hour of daily practice will get them two years ahead. Wow.

Ease into the practice schedule with beginners to gradually accustom them to practice deadlines and the concentration they need during lessons. During the first few weeks ask them to keep their instrument available in a common room and play for a few minutes at a time several times a day without keeping track of the minutes they've played. When students put in their first good solid week of practice, emote over how much they improved in just one week. Remind them of the feeling of accomplishment they earned, and another reward: all the applause!

Gradually Increase Practice Requirements

Raise your expectations with your students' abilities. After the first few months I expect an average of twenty minutes of practicing per day. After six months, that time is to have increased to thirty minutes per day. By the one-year mark, unless the student is younger than twelve, I generally require an hour of practice per day. A rule of thumb for many teachers is a minute of practice a day for each minute of a lesson: students with forty-five minute lessons should practice forty-five minutes per day. Students who want to advance may lengthen their practice time by dividing their practice into two sessions per day.

Some students may even consider taking two lessons a week in the summer. This is a perfect opportunity to accelerate progress for late beginners and for those who are motivated to learn more. It's also an easy way to make up for lessons missed due to vacations.

Underscore the Importance of Regular Practice

Matt was in fifth grade when he started taking trumpet lessons. Full of enthusiasm, he pictured himself playing in band in a year. But his dream never happened. Every week he arrived at his lesson groaning about how tired he was from playing sports and how he didn't like to stay inside to practice. His parents thought he needed "down time" on the weekends. They took four weeks of vacation during the school year and the whole summer off from lessons. Matt spent so much time reviewing old material he never got off square one. Without consistent lessons and practice he was doomed to stay a beginner all of his life. Frustrated with his lack of progress and convinced he wasn't musical, he gave up playing.

Alexa came from a musical family. A naturally gifted player, she had a beautiful tone and a mature sense of musicality. She also had the mistaken belief that she could skate by on her inherited talent. Without consistent practice, she soon saw her harder-working friends pass her by.

I stressed in chapter 6, "Create an Atmosphere of Achievement," the importance of encouraging students to make practice a daily routine like brushing their teeth. Tell them they only need to practice on days that end in *y* or on days they eat! Advise them to schedule the daily practice as they would a dentist appointment. If they skip the appointment, they must make it up on another day. Encourage students to keep their instruments out. The hardest part about practicing is remembering to do it and then getting started. Make a fuss over them when their practice pays off. "I can tell you practiced every day. Don't you love it when you work hard and it shows?" or "Remember, there are *seven* days in a week. Force yourself to sit down every day, put Velcro on the chair, and the rest won't be so bad." Or "This piece was almost there. Too bad you only needed two more days of practice to have really wowed me."

First Things First

It's hard for everyone to fit more into their busy schedules, and some students may have little experience setting priorities and following through. Ask them to list their activities and the amount of time spent on them each week. Assign a priority number to each one. Ask, "Are you spending most of your time on these most important items? How much time do you spend on 'optional' activities such as chatting with friends and watching TV?" Review their lists and help them carve out time for practice. When students protest about being too busy, ask, "If someone offered to pay you $10.00 for every minute of practice, do you think you could find time for an hour and collect $600 every day? I predict you'd find the time to practice if you really wanted to!"

Students aspiring to continue their music education in college must put practice ahead of activities that don't contribute to their goal. If students want to win competitions and auditions, remind them, "If you're not practicing, the next person is." If they dream of becoming competitive musicians, remind them to start building their dream today. Students with hobbies other than music will need to choose how much time to devote to each. Remind yourself that, unlike for you, music is not the most important thing in every student's life. Imagine if you were to take pottery or photography lessons. You might enjoy these pursuits but only as a casual hobby. Some students view their music lessons in the same way, yet they still want to learn. The world has room for all sorts of musicians, but you don't need to teach those who don't commit to regular practice.

Make a Practice Agreement

When students consistently have trouble finding practice time, make a practice agreement with them at the end of each lesson. Say, "I've asked you to (assignment). Can you prepare all of that during the week?" If they think it is too much, decide together what to drop. Then say, "I trust you to return to the next lesson prepared. Can I count on you for this?" If they do return unprepared, they've broken their agreement with you. When students continually break practice agreements, realize it's not that they couldn't fulfill the terms, but that they've chosen not to.

Jump-Start Procrastinators

The most important time to practice is right after the lesson. Students retain more when they revisit a new concept within twenty-four hours. If they wait a couple of days after the lesson, they will have forgotten much of what they learned. Of course most students think they have already done their duty by coming to the lesson and they don't need to practice again that day. Try to convince them to at least try any difficult new technique the day of or at least the day after their lesson. "I know playing the dotted quarter and eighth rhythm is tricky. Be sure to practice at home today so you remember how it goes." Try these other ideas:

- Ask parents of beginners to sit with them on the first practice day to help them get organized and to review what happened in the lesson.

- Watch for students who don't do their work at home and then come to the lesson asking you to fix their problems. Encourage students to contact you during the week if they are confused. Guide them to use the techniques they have learned to solve problems on their own instead of waiting for help.

- If students consistently don't complete their practice assignment or written and technical homework, make them do it at the lesson while you sit there looking bored. A few times of catching up on homework while the teacher reads a book and eats chocolate can stop this bad habit!

- Students will work harder with a looming deadline. It's amazing how much they'll practice right before a contest or a private concert for parents.

- Students may procrastinate because they feel overwhelmed and don't know where to start. Break down the assignment into daily assignments and goals to help jumpstart their practice.

- Be wise to those students who "forget" to bring certain books (that they hate playing) to their lessons. Solve the problem by having copies of the book at the lesson and not accepting the excuse.

- Be hesitant to accept students who come every other week for lessons. Thinking they have longer to prepare, they usually only practice the few days right before the lesson.

- Purchase a remote control for the students' TVs that voices this message: "We interrupt this programming to tell you to practice *now*!" I'm kidding. Until this teaching aid is invented, how about a friendly e-mail reminder during the week?

If the Student Has Not Practiced

When students come to lessons unprepared, let them know you can tell they haven't practiced. (You usually can tell by the way they walk in the door!) If the student comes with an ill-prepared lesson, either refuse to hear it or make them do the practice during the lesson (while you eat chocolates again to keep in a good mood). Say, "You are wasting my time and your lesson time by asking me to listen to all these mistakes. My job is to teach you new material, not to listen to you practice. I will not listen to music that is this bad." Be very honest and firm with your disapproval. Practicing to make the teacher happy is not the best motive, but it's a start!

When students regularly come unprepared, try creating a practice chart to keep them on track. The chart need only include the total amount of time spent each day, a tally of minutes spent per assignment, or a list of what was to be accomplished.

Hold students responsible for their practice choices and results. Say, "When you make your goals, also make a plan to achieve them." Or "You can't compare yourself to Katy, who wins all the competitions, because you are not putting in the hours a day of practice that Katy does. When you practice faithfully as she does, you'll be successful like her."

TEACH STUDENTS WHAT AND HOW TO PRACTICE

Even the most motivated of students may not progress if they don't know *how* to practice. Our job as teachers is to simplify the process for them. We can't throw them out the door and then expect a finished product to return the next week. Ensure students know precisely what they must learn by the next lesson and how to go about it. You'll learn how to help them in chapter 14, "Use Practice Tricks for Fast Results," and in our next chapter, "Increase Success with the *Music for Life* Notebook System."

Emphasize Practice Quality over Quantity

The mother of my former student, Joan, ruled her daughter's practice sessions with an iron hand. She *insisted* Joan practice for one hour per day. If she missed a day of practice, her mother required her to practice for two hours the next day. If she missed three days, her mother called to cancel her lesson. The lesson would be a waste of time, she thought, without the obligatory seven hours of practice. Joan resented her strict practice demands and her playing skills remained poor. I finally convinced her mother to abolish the practice chart. The change was miraculous. Joan arrived at her lessons happier and well prepared. Now she focused on what she needed to improve, not how many minutes had ticked by.

When the only thing that matters is time spent, practice becomes a game of "beat the clock." We've all heard of (or been?) the kid who practiced piano with one hand and held a comic book in the other to get through the jail sentence of practice.

Teachers and parents can get hooked on the notion of a direct correlation between amount of practice time and improvement. Many conservatory students also feel they must lock themselves in a practice room tallying the hours and sacrificing their lives for their art. But amount of practice is not always the best indicator of progress. We all know *there's no getting around putting in a certain amount of practice time, but quality of practice is more important than quantity.* Hours of practice per day done incorrectly or without focus may be useless.

Measure Improvement, Not Time Spent

Emphasizing *quality* over *quantity* of practice time can convert students from clock watchers to music watchers. I rarely demand practice charts. I prefer to let students decide the amount of practice time they need to complete the assignment to my standards. If a student is doing poorly, or the parent tells me there has been little practice, we have a talk about commitment. Like dieters keeping a food diary and then weighing themselves every week, a few students need to keep a timed practice chart of how much (or how little) time they've put in during the week to realize the effect it has on performance. Most students will work harder when they know I plan to supervise their practice time.

Help students to form a daily practice *plan.* The plan could include the time of day they will practice and what they want to accomplish. To get students to focus on improvement instead of time you may need to abolish timed practice charts and remove the clock from their practice area.

Set Goals for More Targeted Practice Sessions

Students progress faster when they work toward specific practice goals. They enjoy bettering their latest accomplishment. Why is goal-setting so effective?

PRACTICE GOALS

- Force students and teachers to set standards.
- Help students feel they have accomplished something, especially on long-term projects.
- Help students manage their time better.
- Allow you to raise the standard of performance each week for each section. Week one the student's goal could be to play all notes correctly, week two, to add dynamics, and week three, to play up to tempo.
- Force students to concentrate on improving the hard parts.
- Make practice time shorter if you allow students to quit once they meet their practice goals.
- Encourage students who have put in less practice time to do better. When you comment on the poor quality of their home practice preparation and they say they are too busy to put in more time, tell them, "I'm not asking for more hours; I'm asking for better performance."
- Help students get better faster. Students without specific goals may not improve if they only watch the clock.

Set Specific Practice Time and Quality Goals

Help students set daily goals and make a pact that their practice is over when they have met their goals. My sons like this kind of practice because it's their only way to get out of practicing for the fully allotted time. Helping students identify and focus on goals buys them free time. Using this system, my boys tell me at the beginning of their practice what they want to accomplish and then call me in to "test" them when they think they are ready. Many times their "early release" program is wishful thinking on their part, but they learn that a standard must be met to achieve the goal. This way they battle against their own mistakes, not the clock, or *me.* Soon they will be able to make their own daily goals, be responsible for attaining them, and be honest in their assessment. This works out well because as they get older, they want me less involved with their practice (and their lives!). I have to try to trust their goals and judgment, a hard thing for teachers and parents to do!

Parents with no musical background may find it more difficult to perform these daily checks and may need students to check themselves. It doesn't matter how much time they spent to get the piece good, only that it *is* good. Give these students extra help in learning to be responsible for their self-checks and their improvement. During lessons you will be able to assess whether they achieved their daily goals.

Help Students to Develop and Record Their Own Technique and Practice Goals

Set weekly goals for beginners and then gradually transfer that responsibility to them. Students who have ownership of their goals are more eager to achieve them. Some students may need nothing more to keep them on track. Make sure students clearly record their goals in their notebooks; unwritten goals can mysteriously lower over a week's time.

The practice session goals you might assign are endless. For example, students will: Play from an assigned list of music and cross off the pieces they've finished. Mark wrong notes, circle key signatures and accidentals, and mark dynamics and breaths. Mark in the breaths and only breathe where they have been marked. Mark all fingerings or bowings and stick to them. Play the first two lines of the etude with no mistakes. Play all the notes correctly in several runs with smooth, easy connections. Increase the tempo to a determined mark. Memorize the third page. Play a section with the tuner until the intonation is correct. Play a difficult measure two times right for every time wrong. Improve the tone on the double-tonguing or double-stop section. Write in the breaths and dynamics in the *adagio.* Play the cadenza a new way every day. Practice the piano piece on the first day with only the right hand and on the second day with only the left until both hands play correctly together. Play runs two, three, four, and eight notes to a bow. Vary vibrato throughout the piece according to the mood. Write in beat marks and learn the rhythm on page twelve. Locate all appoggiaturas and mark in and play the dynamics for the phrases.

Evaluate

Are your students improving between lessons? If not, and they protest they *are* practicing, determine what is blocking their progress. Practicing techniques? At the lesson, give them a new piece and ask them to demonstrate to you their practice tactics. If they struggle even under your direction, look to yourself. Perhaps you need to readjust their assignments or your teaching methods.

LOOKING AHEAD

In this chapter we talked about ways to keep your students on the practice track between lessons. My suggestions included showing them the connection between practice and results, helping them make practice a priority, and holding them responsible for their practice choices and results. Our goal is to convert students from clock-watchers to music-watchers who can set their own practice and performance goals. Next, we'll look at a system that helps students retain the techniques and information you've given them and saves you from repeating yourself.

NINE

Increase Success with the Music for Life *Notebook System*

Kevin looks at you with a blank stare. You asked him to recall something you've told him three weeks in a row. You repeat yourself again. "The relative major is a minor third *above* the minor." How many times have you told students, "*Meno* means less but *poco* means a little?" Like me, have you come to the sad realization that what you teach your students and what they *retain* are two different things? Would you be interested if I told you I have a system that helps students understand their practice goals, remember key aspects of their playing, and retain information you've given to them? For the last twenty years I've used a notebook system to save time and frustration, motivate my students, and provide them with a valuable resource.

I came by the notebook idea out of necessity. One year I asked my three graduating seniors to bring in their old manuscript books in which I had written over the years. I wanted to review with them what they had learned before they left for college. While reviewing their books I had a revelation. Time after time I had rewritten the same music theory, definitions, and helpful hints. I lost track of the number of times I had repeated myself and obviously, so had my students. How could I preserve my sanity and not keep rewriting information? I also needed a way for students to quickly reference what they had learned. I solved the problem by developing the two-notebook system all my students use and enjoy.

How Does the *Music for Life* Two-Notebook System Work?

Students bring two notebooks to each lesson. The first is a large spiral-bound manuscript notebook of musical paper. In this manuscript book, I write almost everything I say during the lesson except "Hi, how are you today?" I draw a circle bullet in front of key information I want students to remember, such as suggestions for phrasing, dynamics, breathing, intonation, tone, articulation, fingering, and history and theory facts. On this book I have bestowed the imaginative title "Your Manuscript Book." Most teachers use manuscript books to record assignments, but the *Music for Life* manuscript book does so much more.

The second book is a three-ring binder with ten tabs, which I call their "*Music for Life* notebook." I ask students to rewrite the bulleted information from their manuscript book into their *Music for Life* notebook under tabbed headings such as tone, musicality, or music history. Let's look closer at how to use the two books and what they can do for you and your students.

BOOK 1, THE MANUSCRIPT BOOK

How Does the Manuscript Book Help Track Students' Progress?

Besides writing the weekly assignments in the manuscript book, I also note students' progress on individual pieces and their overall progress using the variations below:

Bullets

I draw a circle/bullet in front of information I want students to *always remember* so they can easily spot this information on the page.

Color

Each week we begin a new page in the manuscript book. I make it easy to find the current weekly lesson and assignments in the books by marking them with colorful, stiff adhesive notes. I'm amazed at how much time flipping through books these little tabs save. I use a different color marker pen every week to write specific homework assignments *and* to circle assignments in books. This colored marker system makes the notebook look colorful and fun and helps students know what to practice at a glance. This week's assignments are written in blue in the manuscript book and circled in blue in their music books.

Stars

I draw a star in front of each homework assignment so students can easily pick out what they are to do for the week. The assignment gets two drawn-in stars if they need to repeat it. Unlike a good movie, a five-star assignment denotes a problem, not a masterpiece. This system helps me track students' progress on individual pieces.

Stickers

Students who have a spectacular lesson get a sticker which I affix in their manuscript book by the date. I have a fun sticker box under the student chair and they carefully deliberate as they choose just the right one. I am more liberal with stickers for younger students, but as they progress, stickers celebrate only the best lessons.

Stickers may seem like a childish motivation, but even older students (including my 70-year-old male student) will work for them. Sometimes I'll jokingly say, "I know you had to practice two hours a day to get your piece this good, but wasn't it all worth it just for this sticker?" Students may laugh but still beam, knowing I've recognized their hard work. As another motivator, I sometimes hold contests with a reward party for students who get ten sticker lessons in a row. Watch them practice harder than ever to be included in that winners' circle.

I can also keep track of students' overall progress with the sticker system. When I flip through the manuscript book and see that one out of three lessons has a sticker, I know the student is on the right track. When two months have gone by with no stickers, it's time for the dreaded "talk."

What Should I Write in Book 1,
the Student's Manuscript Book?

1. Precise homework assignments

To help students get better results from their practicing, write down every assignment for them and denote it with a star. If you leave it up to students to remember what material they are to practice, they may always forget the scales and etudes. "Oh. I thought you told me to only work on solos and duets this week." Designate which pieces are to be learned over a long period of time and which need to be ready for the next lesson. Write instructions in easy to understand "kid" language and be sure they can read your sloppy writing (note to self). Draw pictures, circle important points, or write in huge letters to get their attention. At the end of the lesson, reiterate what was learned and what you expect them to accomplish during the following week. Before the student leaves, ask if they or their parent have any questions.

2. Detailed suggestions for improvement on practice goals

We talked about setting practice goals in our last chapter, and I cautioned against making the amount of practice time our main concern. Instead, be specific about what they need to improve and write it down so students can set daily practice goals. Avoid misunderstandings by including specific instructions on all aspects of technique and musicality. Before students leave ask, "Do you understand what you need to focus on next week?" Or say, "Achieving this goal can earn you a sticker next week!"

When students work on big pieces for several months, I label a page or two in their book with the name of their piece. Every week I write musical ideas for that piece in the manuscript book. Give students the responsibility of transferring these ideas into their music—don't do it for them! Write musicality hints such as "connect the phrases through the breaths," and include practice goals for the piece, such as learning the correct fingering, playing up to tempo, or memorizing a section, on this page. Make students beg to play the next section and only reward them when they've achieved their goals in the first section. These goals become a handy reference for long-term improvement without having to leaf through the lesson book.

Writing explicit comments in their manuscript books helps students *and* you, the teacher. The more notes you have from the previous lesson, the easier it is for you to reconstruct that lesson, know where you left off, and quickly focus on what the student was to have accomplished over the previous week. When you read "seamless connections between notes," you will know to pay special attention to that. When you have been giving the student lots of suggestions on a piece, sometimes wait to write them down and instead, ask the student to summarize the main points of the lesson and to dictate to you what should be written.

3. Colorful and graphic suggestions

Music is not a science. Music is not black and white. Music is about emotion, so be emotional! Use colorful metaphors and analogies to describe music's beauty and complexity. Graphic explanations create powerful images. Rather than say, "Crescendo at letter D," say, "Pretend you are screaming as you jump off a cliff!" Take time to write what they should play and suggestions on *how* to play it. Clear, detailed explanations avoid confusion at home. Try to give instructions that say what the student should do, not what they *shouldn't* do. It's like telling someone not to think about a pink elephant. If you say, "Don't play staccato," the word *staccato* may be all they hear. Better to say, "Play legato," and frame it in the positive. These explanations also show parents what their children learned at lessons the parents didn't attend and reinforce what they heard at those they did. Picturesque written analogies such as those listed below help students understand and remember how to practice at home.

Tone: "This note should sound like thick fog at the beach. Spray paint the room with your sound. No more tight lips as if you are sucking lemons. In this section, the tone should sound like a French woman saying she loves you. Keep an open throat: breathe with a yawn, fog up the mirror, and look like a wide-mouthed frog. Make the low notes sound like a bag of killer bees."

Vibrato: "This vibrato should sound like a mystery. Use vibrato like an opera singer just before she dies. Try dead battery vibrato. Accent the appoggiatura with a stinger of vibrato."

Musicality: "This phrase keeps moving to end in an explosion. That phrase sounds like a hovercraft, never touching down until the appoggiatura ending. String the notes along like pearls on a necklace. When you reach the climax of this section, plant the flag on Mount Everest! This piece should sound like drinking wine in a sidewalk café in Paris. This section is a conversation with a man screaming and a woman pleading. Play the notes of the phrase like skipping rocks over the water."

Breathing: "Breathe in through your toes. Suck in all the oxygen from this room so the rest of us are dying every time you breathe. Breathe like you are about to swim the length of the pool underwater. Expand when you breathe like an accordion. Fill up a balloon in your abdomen when you breathe."

Music Theory: Include tips here on how to build scales and chords, figure out minor scales, and play cadences. Music theory isn't so colorful, but it is important!

Intonation: "I'll pay you $1.00 if you can play this note flat in the contest! That note was flatter than a pancake. This note was so sharp I thought you were playing Concerto in D-sharp Major. Blow down to your toes on the C-sharp."

Fingering and Bowing: "Use the fingering written in the book unless you can prove the editor was wrong. Don't use creative faking. Break the bow on the double stop like swatting a fly. Drag the bow through peanut butter."

Posture and Position: "Velcro fingers. Watch out for Unidentified Flying Fingers. Don't conduct yourself when you breathe. When you're out of breath, don't bend back as if you're setting up for a back flip. Put a pencil in the end of the flute to remind you to keep it up."

Dynamics: "This note should crescendo like a flower blossoming. This phrase should sound like someone yelling 'Fire!' Hold the phrase forte until you run into the wall. Make a gradual crescendo and then flare out at the end like the bell of a trumpet."

Articulation: "You owe me one cookie for every wrong articulation. Don't sound like a woodpecker attacking when you play staccato notes!"

Colorful instructions and illustrations hold students' attention and make them easier to understand, increasing the chance they will put them into practice at home.

4. Inspirational messages, quotes, or "friendly warnings"

Write something for students to discover at home. Move or inspire them, or remind them to get with the program! "Great job on your scales today! Wonderful lesson! You can do it!" Or "Better scales next week or else! You owe me seven days of practice!"

5. Celebrations

Parents keep track of the date of their baby's first tooth or first steps. Why not celebrate a student's "firsts"? Use a yellow marker pen to highlight firsts in weekly lessons or make a special "first" page. Celebrate first memorized song, first duet, first recital, or first two-page song. My students and I always celebrate their first anniversary of living through lessons with me!

6. Notes to parents

When parents of young children can't (or shouldn't!) attend lessons, write a note to them at the end of each lesson. You could write about the practice focus for the week or summarize the student's progress in the lesson.

BOOK 2, THE *MUSIC FOR LIFE* NOTEBOOK

The second book in my system is a three-ring binder I call the *Music for Life* notebook. It includes pockets for storing handouts and ten tabbed sections arranged by category. You could call it the *Music for Life* notebook, or if you think this name is corny, create your own name or just call it the "music notebook." The ten tabs I use in my flute students' notebooks are listed below. Teachers of other instruments may think of other useful tabs.

Students fill sections such as music theory, ear training, and trill and trick fingerings with loose-leaf manuscript paper. Others, including music history and music terms, contain notebook paper.

What Are the Ten Sections in the Students' *Music for Life* Notebooks?

The broad range of topics I include represents my belief in the importance of teaching the *whole* musician.

1. Music Theory/Ear Training: This section's subheadings, such as scales, chords, rhythm, and ear training, help students easily locate the information they have written.

2. Music History: Music history is divided into sections according to musical period: Renaissance, Baroque, Classical, Romantic, and Contemporary. Each musical period section contains a brief definition of its characteristics and a list of its major composers. Students write performance practices and biographies of composers under the appropriate period. This music history section makes it easy for students to recall the musical period of each composer and see which composers lived at the same time.

3. Musicality Suggestions: This tabbed section contains help on everything that transforms playing an instrument from mere "typing" into living, breathing music. I include hints such as "crescendo to the appoggiatura and lift up on the resolution," "crescendo on a series of the same note," "the pick-up is softer than the note it leads into," and "music is tension and release."

4. Musical Terms: The musical terms section includes pages for each letter of the alphabet. This personal music dictionary makes it easy for students to find words they've already learned. Examples of musical terms under *A*: allegro = quick and lively; andante = walking speed.

5. Tone Hints: Ideas on tone production, timbre, and vibrato are included here. Examples of technique tips are "Blow up for high notes and across for low notes," "Support from your abdomen," or "Eliminate throat sounds by yawning." More general reminders include "Vibrato is a measure of emotion."

6. How to Practice: Suggestions on "chunking," changing rhythms, and much more.

7. Intonation Exercises: Here I list intonation exercises as well as pitch tendencies for the instrument.

8. Posture and Position Suggestions: Notes here, such as "Don't stick out your head like a turtle" or "Keep fingers centered in the middle of the keys," help students hold the body and the instrument to their best advantage.

9. Trill and Trick Fingerings: I list trill fingerings and other trick fingerings that aid in speed and pitch in this section. I provide examples of each on manuscript paper.

10. Breathing Exercises: These include exercises that expand lung capacity and use air efficiently, such as playing timed long tones, as well as hints on how to breathe for musical phrases—for example, "Breathe before a pick-up."

How Do Students Use These Two Notebooks?

Part of every student's weekly assignment is to review the manuscript book and write the bulleted information under the correct tab in their *Music for Life* notebook. For example, if I remind them to hold their flute up or keep their fingers close they would rewrite that suggestion from the manuscript book into the Posture and Position tab in the *Music for Life* notebook. If I teach them how to build a major scale, I ask students to recopy the information from the manuscript book to the *Music for Life* notebook under the Theory tab.

When students begin taking lessons, I help them decide under which category they should catalogue each tip or piece of information. Soon they understand the system and do it independently. It's not so important *where* they write the information as long as they write it, remember it, and know how to retrieve it. I keep a close eye on beginners' books, checking them at the beginning of each lesson while they play scales. With more advanced students, I periodically check their *Music for Life* notebook to ensure they are up to date and to review material they should know. This year I gave everyone one month to organize their *Music for Life* notebooks. Those with completed and legible books went "trick or treating" in my studio for Halloween gifts and candy. I pull the same trick on Valentine's Day week, Easter, and the Fourth of July.

Why Is It Important for Students to Rewrite the Information?

Writing switches on a part of the brain called the reticular activating system, or RAS, that keeps important information in our minds, ready to use when needed. Writing reinforces memory. When I taught myself Japanese, I filled many notebooks and file cards with Japanese words and phrases. The act of writing and then seeing the words helped me remember them. Even if students are not thinking about tone variables, they'll be more likely to use them after having written the facts and suggestions.

What If the Student Doesn't Take the Time to Read the Notebook and Transfer the Information?

At the beginning of each lesson, glance quickly at students' *Music for Life* notebooks to see if they have updated the material. If they haven't, tell them: "We need to stop here so you can finish your homework. Darn, I wish we could be playing duets now, but updating your book comes first." Young students may need a parent's help.

If you suspect a student doesn't even bother to read the manuscript book, try this sneaky trick: write a joke or personal note to the student in the midst of all the assignments and refer to it at the next lesson. I write notes between the lines like "Duets, Page 4, and #5. Hillary, did you read this book?" or "If you tell me you read this sentence before I bring it up at the lesson, you get a candy bar, Etude #6." Gotcha! If they forget to bring the *Music for Life* notebook to their lesson they are automatically disqualified from getting a sticker.

How Does the *Music for Life* Two-Notebook System Benefit Students?

The ten-tabbed *Music for Life* notebook gives students a record of what they have learned in a handy reference that's easy to check when they forget a suggestion. Reading the bulleted information helps students know what is important and helps them remember what and how to practice. The notebooks serve as their personal music journal and encyclopedia and handy, easy-to-use references if they forget a fact or suggestion. These notebooks also serve as a convenient storage place for handouts, concert programs, pictures, student e-mails, parent letters, or contest forms.

Students value their *Music for Life* notebooks and take pride in the knowledge they contain. Most decorate the front covers with drawings, a cartoon, or artwork. Many take time in the summer to enter the information into their computer and print neat copies for their notebook. In time, these notebooks become not just sources of information, but treasured keepsakes that chronicle their years of music study. We love looking back to see the childish writing and simple assignments that chart their improvement through the years. "Look at this!" a student will exclaim. "Did I really have that much trouble learning how to play a triplet?" When students graduate, their *Music for Life* notebook guides their continued improvement on their own or serves as a handy resource for their next teacher. They might even use it when they become teachers themselves.

How Does This System Benefit Teachers?

Having students rewrite important information in their notebooks saves you time and energy because you don't have to repeat yourself. The *Music for Life* system also helps you quickly review what you taught at each lesson and assess whether there are any gaps in the student's knowledge. This is especially helpful for transfer students who may not have learned according to your normal progression. When you glance under the theory section and see that you have taught major and minor chords, but not augmented or diminished chords, you can plan what to teach next. If writing this much seems daunting, consider asking students to tape or videotape their lesson to review at home. Not comfortable having your every word recorded? Parents of younger students might relieve you by taking detailed notes of their own at lessons.

Is Writing Worth the Trouble?

The time I spend writing in their manuscript book ranges from two to five minutes. I intersperse writing throughout the lesson, usually while the student is playing. Rather than eating up valuable lesson time, in the long run writing reduces wasted lesson time. While I listen to students play their scales and etudes, I cheat and get a jump on writing in their composer biography or their theory homework section. While I write a suggestion I read it out loud and have the student practice it. I've also substituted handouts for many concepts I teach to save me time and writer's cramp.

When students *do* forget something you have already taught them, refer to the tab under which it is already written and you'll get the last laugh. "How do you find the relative major of E minor?" I might ask. "I don't know," a student might say. "You never taught me that." "Look it up under the theory section in your *Music for Life* notebook. See that information written under the heading minor scales? That looks like *your* handwriting to me!" The *Music for Life* notebook system becomes an invaluable tool for achieving our ultimate goal of making students their own teachers.

In this chapter I let you know about my "secret weapon," a two-notebook system that tracks students' progress, saves time for teacher and students, keeps parents informed, and helps students retain more of what they have learned. I predict that after using this system for a few weeks, you'll wonder how you ever taught without it. My tabbed notebook system just might change your life!

In our next chapter, "Energize Students with Goals," we'll discuss how to determine what motivates each student, and devise a process for setting outcome, short-term, and long-term goals.

TEN

Energize Students with Goals

Goals guide our lives and give us focus. Elite athletes, top-performing executives, and achievers in all fields use the power of goal-setting. You and your students can, too. Goal-setting is a common thread weaving throughout this book. Whether the topic is creating an atmosphere of achievement, getting kids to practice, or conquering stage fright, goal-setting gets results. Musicians who set goals effectively are more self-confident, concentrate better, and feel happier and more fulfilled after their performances. Learning to set and achieve clearly defined goals is another valuable skill students can apply to all areas of their lives.

GUIDE STUDENTS' EFFORTS WITH GOALS

Remember that saying, "Hard work beats talent when talent doesn't work hard?" Regardless of talent level, the harder you work, the better a musician you will be. But working hard is not enough. My friend Charlie told me about his coworker, Tom, who worked extra hours each week, starting early and staying long after everyone else had left. "A dedicated and industrious employee," you might think. Maybe not. Those extra hours Tom put in did nothing to increase his productivity because he went from one project to the next, never setting priorities or deadlines. Without concentrating his efforts on the important tasks, he often never completed them. He was busy doing too many things and in the wrong order. Charlie left the office each night, thinking, "There's Tom, working *long* and *long* instead of long and *hard*." Goals direct your hard work.

SET GOALS TO ADD VALUE AND MEANING

To awaken an inner desire in students, look at things from *their* point of view. Using the "What's in it for me?" technique, find out what is important to them. How do they enjoy spending their time? What situations do they wish to avoid? Set goals that fulfill their needs and they'll be motivated to excel. Students might be willing to work hard to do well in a concert, learn a favorite piece, get a good grade, play with friends and family, keep up with their peers, use music as a diversion from stress and academic subjects, gain admission into a music camp or playing group, win an award, or get attention. Other reasons might be to appease parents who are forcing them to take lessons (not a good reason) or to avoid being yelled at in the lesson (oops—even worse!).

HELP STUDENTS TO SET ACHIEVABLE OUTCOME GOALS

Remind students, "*No one plans to fail, but many fail to plan.*" Specific goals produce better results than trying to "do your best." (Achieving small short-term musical goals that led to long-term ones has given me the skills and confidence to do more challenging things in life, such as writing this book!)

Once students have set their goals, work with them on a step-by-step plan to attain them. To illustrate the goal-setting process, let's follow the true story of my student Alisa from her beginning goal of playing hymns to her end goal of earning a spot in the Seattle Junior Symphony. Alisa has performed in the two lower youth symphony groups. Next are Junior Symphony and Classical Symphony and the top Seattle Youth Symphony. She has dreamed of being in Junior Symphony for more than a year now and has focused on her *outcome* goal of winning a spot at the fall auditions.

Outcome goals are the hardest to plan and achieve. Not that we all don't occasionally fantasize about winning the contest or the lottery. The trouble with outcome goals is that we risk failing because of conditions beyond our control. We can control our *own* behavior but not that of the judges or competing musicians. It's dispiriting to work hard to achieve an outcome goal, only to fail because of poor judging, an illness, an injury, or plain bad luck. Only so many spots are available in Junior Symphony, and many young flutists vie for them. While Alisa practices to earn a seat, competing students may be practicing even harder. Because Alisa has no control over her competition, her best playing might only earn her a disappointment.

I use long-term outcome goals to motivate my students and encourage them to participate in youth symphony programs, to challenge the flutists who sit above them in band or orchestra, and to enter contests. I always caution that the outcome is just *a by-product* of playing better and having fun with music. Long-term outcome goals are fine to use but students must keep them in perspective.

Enjoy the Journey toward Outcome Goals

When a student's outcome goal is their whole reason for taking lessons, teachers can be tempted to "teach to the test." They might concentrate on the contest pieces and not give students the depth and breadth of music and technique they need to be well rounded. Passing the test becomes the goal instead of learning to love playing. I once had a student whose sole goal was to compete in the state contest. Once she achieved that goal she quit taking lessons. Another student became so focused on earning first chair that when she didn't, she wanted to quit playing altogether. Outcome goals can be dangerous!

Respect Students' Ambitions

Teachers need to respect the goals students have selected. I have taught students I believed could win national competitions, but who didn't want to enter them. Other students could have moved up to advanced band but chose to hang out with friends in intermediate band. It has been hard for me to resist pushing students to commit to more.

On the other hand, many students come with the idea of learning a little flute, but with a little (or a big) push from me, they raise their aspirations. Regardless of their long-term goals, I always have a carrot (or chocolate bar?) in front of students. As for the goal of becoming a music major and deciding where to go to school, I leave that big decision *entirely* up to my students. I warn them about the dangers and delights of being a professional musician and paint a realistic picture. They know my goal is for them to be the best musicians they can be.

HELP STUDENTS TO SET SHORT-TERM GOALS

Once students have determined their long-term goals, ask them to write them in their student notebooks. Writing down the big new goal is not enough. Next they must develop an action plan that includes technical, musical, and performance goals.

Develop an Action Plan

Help students break larger goals into smaller goals with target dates for achieving them. Keeping goals small and incremental gives more opportunities for rewards students can appreciate right away. With each goal accomplished, students feel a sense of forward motion and pride.

Alisa wanted to learn *Carmen Fantasie* by Bizet/Bourne for her youth symphony audition. This was a perfect piece to help achieve her outcome goal, and even more importantly, she *loved* it! The first step in Alisa's plan was to set an overall schedule. Alisa got down on her hands and knees to beg me to assign *Carmen* to her but I would only agree if she promised to practice two hours a day! Looking toward the youth symphony auditions in September, she calculated the time she needed to be totally prepared and determined she needed to start working on the piece the previous May.

The next part of Alisa's plan was an agenda for learning the piece. She decided to tackle *Carmen* one page at a time, breaking down the long piece into short-term goals. Next she set deadlines for what she had to accomplish. She only needed to play a few pages for her audition, but her goal was to know the whole piece by that time. Her timetable included a schedule for learning the notes, gradually meeting the fast metronome markings, and memorizing sections of the piece.

Create a Series of Successes

Prioritize goals to avoid overwhelming a student and help them focus on the most important ones. "Your first goal is to learn this trick fingering. Then we'll start on the adagio movement. After it feels solid, you can start to memorize it. Then we'll talk about performing it in public." For beginners, break down each new challenge into the smallest possible steps, as in programmed learning. For example: Week one: Learn the notes. Play the runs tongued and leave out any grace notes. Week two: Add the right slurs and play slightly faster. Week three: Play slowly but with the metronome, and add the ornaments.

Make a big deal out of every small accomplishment. "Wow! You know five notes now!" or "You've learned the first page of the concerto. I bet you will learn the second page even faster!" Each small goal students achieve raises their energy and confidence as it points to forward progress.

Dr. Shelley Collins, professor at Delta State University, celebrates her young beginning students' small successes. Students earn a sticker on every page learned, throw the beginning book out a third-story window when they have completed it, have their picture taken in a graduation hat after the first full year of lessons or after graduating from the fife to the flute, and at the end-of-the-year party participate in the "flute toss" competition. (They have to promise that's the only flute they will ever throw!)

HELP STUDENTS TO SET MUSICAL GOALS

All three of the following goals are related to performance. Performance goals are easier for students to handle if you break them down even further into technical, musical, and final performance goals. Let's see how Alisa used performance goals to work toward her dream.

Technical Goals

To perform such a technically brilliant piece, Alisa had to concentrate not only on *Carmen* but on her basic skills. The first step she took was to double the number of technical etudes she played to build up her technique and stamina. She was willing to do anything to play her beloved *Carmen*.

Another challenge she faced was playing what seemed like hundreds of notes in one breath. Alisa still struggled with playing long tone breath-building exercises. Being able to hold a note for only twenty-five seconds hindered her ability to play long phrases. One day she asked me, "How long can *you* hold a note?" I told her my best was around forty-five seconds. Suddenly her eyes lit up. "*I'm* going to beat you!" With this challenge in mind, she began playing hundreds of long tones at home. Every lesson she had added one or two more seconds, and before she left repeated her vow, "I *am* going to beat you!" With her determination and hard work, in six months, she did!

Alisa brought this same determination to work on double-tonguing, on playing strong low notes, on even sixteenths, on smooth big skips, and on bringing out the melody surrounded by fast notes. As she worked on her technical goals in the piece, her overall playing kept improving, as did her commitment to her instrument.

Musical Goals

We know there is more to music than notes and rhythm. Alisa had to play each page of *Carmen* with beautiful tone and exciting musicality before she could turn to the next page. To achieve this goal, Alisa circled the dynamics and created her personal interpretation. She listened to recordings, watched a video of the opera, and had several piano rehearsals to help her really understand the music. She lived and breathed *Carmen*.

Final Performance Goals

A sign in my studio reads, "*But I could play it at home.*" Every musician knows what that sign means. Alisa's next challenge was to play her best *Carmen* not only at home and in my studio, but, most importantly, at her audition. Her goal was to play confidently enough to not let stage fright rob her of technique and musicality, and to enjoy playing and pleasing the audience. The performance goals she wrote in her book were to walk into the audition with a smile, announce her piece without stumbling, play her piece as technically well and as musically as she was capable of doing, bow and smile, *not faint*, and have a good time!

To achieve these goals, Alisa performed often to get used to playing in front of an audience. She played for the chair in her bedroom, then her stuffed animals, her little brother and sister, her parents, the neighbors in her condo (who were not always gracious), her friends, the students who had lessons before and after hers, the audience of a student recital, and just about anyone she could drag in off the street. By the time of the *real* audition Alisa was ready!

Her musical and performance goals helped her appreciate her successes along the way. Even if she didn't earn a seat, she would gain satisfaction and confidence from knowing how much she had improved. I am writing this chapter about Alisa's drama just three weeks before her audition for the Seattle Youth Symphony. If the judges knew I was writing her story for you, they might want to give this chapter a happy ending, but of course they will pick whom they deem to be the most qualified musician. I'll keep you posted!

To review goals with your students, ask them:

- Is your goal demanding, but reachable? Is it within your power to attain? Is your goal set so high you'll likely end up being disappointed?

- Did you set your goal high enough? "Shoot for the moon and if you miss, you'll still be in the stars."

- Is your goal written in the positive? Is it stated in specific, not vague words? "I'm going to try my hardest to play this piece fast" is not as helpful as saying, "I will play this piece ten metronome notches faster than I played it today, with no mistakes."

- Is the goal something *you* want and are willing to work toward? Playing principal in orchestra sounds impressive, but carries with it a huge responsibility. Be careful what you wish for!

- Is this *your* goal as opposed to your parents' or your teacher's goal? Other people can set unrealistic goals for you based on what they want. If your mother's goal is for you to win a conservatory scholarship and you've always dreamed of being a second-grade teacher, it's time to make some tough choices.

- Does your goal contradict any other goals? You may not be able to win first chair *and* be on the all-star baseball team. Don't sabotage one goal for another.

- Have you determined what you need to give up or reduce to achieve your goal? Will you have to say goodbye to long telephone chats, sleeping in, your favorite TV programs, or another hobby?

- Have you identified any obstacles to your goal, e.g., needing a new instrument or missing lessons during summer vacations?
- Did you write your goal in your student planner? Once students write down a goal, it begins to etch itself into their subconscious.

ADJUST GOALS AND EXPECTATIONS AS NECESSARY

My friend Mary Pat has a smart and capable 16-year-old grandson. He was not doing his best in school, much to his parents' dismay. One day he asked his mother if he could dye his light brown hair. "What color?" she asked. "Bright blue!" he said with enthusiasm. Sensing an opportunity here, Mom replied only with a number. "3.8." Shorthand for, "If you want blue hair you must earn a 3.8 grade point average in school. Otherwise I will say NO to this crazy color!" Mary Pat saw her grandson a few months later sporting bright yellow hair. "I thought you were going to dye your hair blue," she said quizzically. Greg's answer was short. "3.5."

When Greg and his mom realized a 3.8 grade point average wasn't going to happen they adjusted his goal to one more attainable, and everyone was happy. Goals motivate only when they are attainable. Sometimes they need to change to fit the individual and the circumstances. I hope my own sons stay with musical, not "hair" goals.

ENCOURAGE STUDENTS TO CONTINUE REACHING

A few years ago I taught a young boy, Carl. Each time I gave him a new etude or the next page to learn he started crying. "But I can't do that!" he'd say. "Learning new things is what music lessons are about," I told him. "As soon as you reach one goal, set your sights on the next one." Carl never wanted to reach out of his comfort level and resisted anything more demanding. But learning music means *always* stretching forward. As a teacher, be a little pushy, not complacent. Challenge students with harder or longer pieces you know they can play. If they don't rise to the challenge you can always change goals.

Entice Students with Suggestions of Future Goals

As we've talked about before, students need something to work toward and a picture in their mind of who they want to be. Have students fantasize where they would like to be in a year, two years, or after high school. Tell them, "*If you don't map out a route, you won't know where you're going or how to get there.*" Encourage students with what they might accomplish next. Say, "Good job on twenty-second long tones, *now* you can do thirty!" "This is a lot more difficult than anything you have ever done before, but if you work hard, I know you can do it." "Second chair is good, but how about going for first?" "One page a week in the etude is fine, but three is even better." "At next year's contest instead of playing a solo, let's go for the complete program division." "You can order that fun duet book when you can play a D scale through two octaves."

Make More Challenging Goals *Their* Idea

When students achieve a goal, ask them to renew their goal at a higher level. Hold back eager students a little and let them talk you into trying something harder. When Alisa was in fifth grade, every time I asked her what she wanted to play first, meaning a choice between an etude, scales, solos, or a duet, she always answered, "Carmen!" In sixth, seventh, and eighth grades when we chose contest pieces she continued to beg, "Carmen!" Finally I relented. She didn't view learning the piece as an assignment, but as a gift! Talk up a new piece and make your students beg to practice! Ha!

When you ask students to "stretch a little," ask for a commitment. "Your other pieces have only been one page and this piece is four pages; do you think you can do it?" "This piece goes super fast. Do you think you could get it up to tempo with some hard practice?" "This is a beautiful piece but it is very long. Are you sure you want to tackle this?" "I don't know; it's going to take a lot of work . . ." "If you worked hard, do you think you could memorize up to letter I? Wow, that would be something." "Can I count on you to learn this by March?" "How good the next three lessons are will help me decide which piece to choose for your audition."

BOOST EFFORT WITH COMPETITION GOALS

Preparations for auditions, seating tests, and concerts are great motivators because they encourage serious practice. Knowing a performance will be judged raises the value of practice to a whole new level. Who wants to look foolish in public? Motivation is the difference between auditing a class and working to get an A. A little stress does wonders for practice! During contests, students learn from judges, gain valuable experience dealing with stage fright, see how they compare to other students, and are energized when they or other students in the studio are winners.

Most students in my studio audition for Youth Symphony, participate in master classes, and enter three contests. Along the way there are recitals and seating tests in orchestra and band. Students always have a new goal and "emergency" to practice for. "Better get practicing; only three weeks until the recital!" "Dr. Ott will be here for the master class in only one month. You'd better work to get ready!" Sure, it is more work for me to arrange these events, but the payoff is in students who come to lessons prepared and eager to learn. These competitions are a big part of my program, not as end goals in themselves, but as opportunities to build students' motivation to improve.

Expect Participation in Concerts and Contests

Social reinforcement is a terrific motivator. Recitals, master classes, and ensembles create opportunities for students to hear each other and be motivated to keep up with their peers. When you tell students that playing in contests and concerts is part of your program, they will accept their involvement and want to do "what the other kids are doing."

Gradually ease more hesitant students into public performance. My beginning students memorize a piece every week and perform it as if they were in a recital. By the time they perform at their first public concert, performing is (almost) painless. Start with playing for their parents at the lesson, move up to playing in ensembles, and then finally launch them into a "solo career."

Recitals are a different story. I give students this opportunity no matter what their level. Students who can only play the notes B and A play the "A and B March." Playing before a friendly audience of parents and friends gives students a feeling of accomplishment and pride. Don't *we* love it when people compliment our performance?

Make Each Performance a Positive Experience

When you require participation, make sure students are fully prepared and leave happy. One year my student Linda had made slow progress on her contest solo piece, despite her weekly promises to practice more. The day before the big contest arrived and she was not prepared. "Sorry," I said. "If you play like this the judge will be irritated, you'll be embarrassed, and I will have to run and hide in the restroom. You suddenly have a bad case of the flute flu and will need to call in sick."

Why wouldn't I allow Linda to play in the competition? Wouldn't it do a student good to have her bluff called? Is it concern for the reputation of my studio that would cause me to force a cancellation? Of course I don't want a poor performer representing my studio, but that wasn't my main motivation for pulling her out. I do let students who aren't perfectly prepared perform because any public performance is "character building." But if the performance is a disaster, the student may walk away not with ideas of working harder next time, but with a determination to never *try* again. It's hard to give students who have embarrassed themselves the courage to get back on the horse again. It is the teacher's responsibility to prepare students well enough to keep their confidence intact.

Hold In-Studio Contests

Other kinds of competition work well in the studio. Kids try hard to be part of the winning group, especially if the reward involves candy or a party! Make competitions public by keeping a chart so the winners will be admired by all. A perfect time for an in-studio competition chart is right before music contests.

Try in-studio competitions for these feats: The student who: practices the most during a week or a month (charted half-hour increments), practices the most over vacation, on the weekend, or on Wednesdays, plays the longest long tone, improves the most in one month, earns the longest run of stickers, first makes it through the etude book, earns ten sticker lessons in a row or in three months, practices the longest number of days in a row, or learns all the scales. How about a competition for the student who brings the teacher the nicest gift? I'm kidding!

Place Friendly Bets

Have I turned my studio into a casino? No, but it has the fun and excitement of one (with none of the smoke) because I place "bets" with my students. My former student Joe recently visited me after having gone off to college ten years earlier. During the first five minutes of our conversation he made a confession: "I still owe you a batch of cookies because I played that measure out of tune and lost the bet!" When the stakes are high during a contest, we write the bet onto the student's music. Judges have quizzically asked, "What does a chocolate bar have to do with this phrase?"

Bets work for performance goals too. Simon was not excited about playing in the flute contest but in the end he felt it was worth it. He won one dozen homemade cookies for bowing, a dozen for smiling and working with the judge, and another dozen for sitting down and not beating himself up after his performance. (I think he was too busy thinking about the cookies to be worried about playing!)

Here are examples of other studio bets. "I will pay you $1.00 if you can play the last note of this piece (which is now unbearably sharp) *flat* at the next lesson and *in tune* at the recital." "If the judge compliments your quartet on your dynamics, I owe you a pizza party. If he complains about the dynamics, you owe me a batch of cookies (my choice). If he says nothing, we are even." "Here are ten M&M candies. I get to eat one every time you make a mistake on a scale." "You owe me a cookie for every key signature mistake." See how you can turn mistakes into sweet rewards for the teacher?

TEACHERS NEED GOALS TOO!

While we're on the subject of goals, I want to remind you, dear teacher, to set your own goals. Specific teaching goals produce greater success than aiming to "be a good teacher" or "have happy students." Do you want a certain number of students? Set a goal. Do you want your students to attain higher standards? Set a goal. Do you want students who are dedicated? Do you want to look forward to every day of teaching? Do you want to become rich and famous from teaching private lessons? Set a goal. Good luck!

POSTSCRIPT

And now back to Alisa. I am writing this postscript two weeks after her youth symphony audition. After a year of practicing with the mantra "Make It into Junior Symphony" going through her head, Alisa played *Carmen* quite well and made not a single mistake on the sight reading test. And yet, she *did not* get into Junior Symphony. She was admitted into *Classical* Symphony. Alisa presents an ideal example of why students are wise to focus on both performance and outcome goals. After her initial disappointment, Alisa reminds herself that Classical and Junior are on the same level; they just perform different repertoire. She is having a ball playing in her new orchestra, won second place in the state competition playing *Carmen*, and now has been reenergized with her new goal of moving up to the top Seattle Youth Symphony next year. And my goal? To find a piece as motivating as *Carmen*!

LOOKING AHEAD

Now that your students have set their goals, how will they know when they're achieving them? Our next chapter focuses on how to recognize and reward students for their results *and* their effort. We'll talk about ways to give students feedback about progress and performance, point out their shortfalls, and applaud their accomplishments. We'll finish with a discussion of how you can set up a motivating reward system with parents.

ELEVEN

Recognize and Reward
Results and Effort

Nothing is more critical to the success of your studio than your ability to recognize and reward your students' hard work. Providing honest feedback and constructive criticism are among the most important roles of all teachers. Psychologists tell us that children of all ages would rather be praised than punished—but they would rather be punished than ignored. "Ignoring" your students by not correcting their mistakes and saying they are always wonderful never works. Students need our continual and honest attention.

We've already discussed the importance of praise and rewards in previous chapters, and you might wonder why I'm revisiting the topic once more. My reasoning is simple: apart from sharing your musical expertise and forming solid relationships with your students, nothing else you can do as a teacher is as important as recognizing students for their efforts and their results. In this chapter I'll give you a plan to do so.

GIVE STUDENTS FEEDBACK ABOUT
PERFORMANCE AND PLAYING PROGRESS

Eric slouched as he played the violin etude. "Why would anyone write something with five sharps?" he thought. "Yikes! There goes another A-natural."

His mind was on the big baseball game tonight. Eric's coach had given him some batting drills and he couldn't wait to see if they improved his game. With his mind on hitting, he *missed* half the notes he played and forgot to look at the little numbers above them. "First and third positions are the easiest anyway," he thought. Finally he was through. "That was pretty good, Eric," said his teacher, Julie. "Let's go on to the next piece."

On to the dreaded shifting exercises. He felt like "shifting" right out of the room, but dutifully he went through the motions with the intonation only his mother could love. "You're getting better," Julie advised. "But next time try to play more in tune. Let's play your Beethoven."

Eric slaughtered the unsuspecting Beethoven and Julie suggested he listen to a recording. "See you at the next lesson! You're doing fine, but next week could you practice a little more?"

"Practice what?" he wondered. "I guess I didn't play as bad as I thought. When my batting is bad, my coach points it out right away and tells me how to fix it."

Why didn't Eric's teacher give him constructive and honest feedback? Didn't she know the standard for someone Eric's age? Didn't she know how to correct his mistakes? Maybe she thought he wasn't talented or smart enough to get better, or was afraid if she was honest he might quit? Didn't she care enough about his progress to make the effort to be involved in his lessons? Was she more interested in getting him through the books than in making him a musician? Was she too tired of her job to project enthusiasm and a desire to improve?

Students need constructive feedback, no matter what the subject. My son Kyle played on two basketball teams. One coach had them do drills and critiqued their technique, while the other coach just let them play practice games. Though Kyle groaned a lot about the first coach's constant feedback, guess which team won every game and which team won none?

At the risk of sounding like a broken record, I want to reemphasize that students deserve a teacher who is dedicated to helping them improve. If we don't really care how our students play, we're in the wrong business. Passing students on through the books without constant feedback will only allow them to play more, not better. The key is to provide specific feedback and deliver it in a way that enables students to listen without being defensive. This happens naturally when your relationship is based on open, two-way communication. Now let's talk about *what* to say and *how* to say it.

Give Constructive Feedback

After you've heard a student play a passage, give a general positive comment like "Good" or "OK!" Then be more specific with praise or corrections. Your goal is to encourage them to do better and not discourage them from wanting to try again.

Routinely invite the student to speak first. In chapter 5, "Promote a Love of Learning and Independence," I stressed the importance of letting students discover their own mistakes. Being independent fosters their skills of self-criticism. Ask, "What did you do right in this section and what did you do wrong?" "What did you think of your intonation/phrasing/bowing/position/pedaling/fingering/tone?" Let students be part of the discussion. Many times when students make a mistake, it takes only a look from the teacher for them to figure out where they went wrong.

Tangible, specific examples are helpful corrections. Telling students their playing is "sloppy" is less useful than, "You rushed the eighths in the presto section, you were flat on the top note of every big skip, the eighth note pick-ups were quarter notes, and the dotted eighths and sixteenths turned into triplets."

Point out the technical details *and* musicality. "The way you play that melancholy part tugs at my heartstrings." "The section at letter B reminded me of sharks." "You really made a difference between the agitato and the tranquillo sections."

Be Realistic

Some things take time, and it is better to ship the piece back home than to list a litany of mistakes. If students have been taught what and how to improve, it may be better to let them work on it by themselves instead of continuing to hammer away at the lessons. Say, "You know what needs fixing; bring it back when you've made some improvements." "We worked on the first page, now it is up to you to generalize what you learned to the rest." "Why don't we put this piece in the 'freezer' for a few months and revisit it later?"

Although it says in the Declaration of Independence that all men are created equal, sadly not all music students are. When students have done their best and still don't sound so great, your continued small fixes will have diminishing returns. Their best will never be "good enough." The next time you're tempted to correct a struggling student in minute detail, ask yourself: *Will this matter to her five years from now?* If not, let it go and rethink the assignment. Make a deal with the student: "You don't have to play 'French Folk Song' anymore if you play this etude with dotted quarters and eighths." The trusting relationship you have formed with the student is not worth risking over getting a particular piece perfect. Praise your students' *personal best.*

Tell the Truth

I sometimes shock students with my bluntness when they begin to study with me. Soon they learn to appreciate (and often laugh about) my honesty. My own "checkered past" of poor practicing led me to this method. I started taking piano lessons at age thirteen from a lackluster woman who had been teaching since the Stone Age. I was not an enthusiastic student and dreaded descending the stairs to her cheerless basement room with its curtains tightly drawn. I rarely practiced, yet my piano teacher always told me how *wonderful* I was. I wish that instead she had been honest with me and pushed me to excel. She praised my mediocre playing so highly I began to think I really was good and that only stupid people had to practice! She either didn't know better or didn't care enough to mold me into a better player. Maybe she was trying to be nice.

My teacher was very sweet but benevolence is not enough. People like to know where they stand, and the most meaningful praise comes from a teacher who tells it like it is. I've been told my middle name must be "Frank," but when I tell my students they've played great they are so proud (or they nearly faint). When I tell them they are *not* playing well, they know they had better run home and practice.

I know I have said this before, but please care enough to be honest with your students. When they play poorly, tell them, when they play well, praise them. This seems so obvious, but you would be surprised at how many teachers, wonderful players themselves, let bad playing slide. If they know how it should sound, why don't they demand it from their students?

Being honest and "strict" does not mean lessons should be a litany of corrections and hurtful comments; give your assessment in a compassionate way. Granted, telling the truth takes more energy and patience in the short run, but in the long run, it pays off in better performance and happier students. *Trust me.*

Have you always thought that corrections should be stated in the positive and not in a natural, straightforward way? "You played that wonderfully but it could even be better if you kept a steady tempo?" Studies have shown little evidence that negative feedback is detrimental to students' feeling about the lesson, the teacher, or their success if given in the spirit of helping, not hurting students.

Fifteen-year-old Annika, who transferred to my studio this year, says,

> When there is honesty at the lessons you can really get better. I like to be told precisely what was wrong and how to improve rather than be told, "Go practice," or "Make it better next week." When my lesson hasn't been good, I sometimes feel sad, but it makes me feel good that my teacher cares enough to make me better.

Point Out Shortfalls

If a lesson is not well prepared, make things a little uncomfortable. Refuse to hear sloppy playing. Say, "This piece is not ready—let's give it another week"; "You didn't give your time to this at home, so let's not waste our time on it at a lesson"; "My job is to teach you new techniques and musicality, not to point out sloppy mistakes"; or "Lessons are for learning new material, not practicing." If you don't listen to ill-prepared music, your blood pressure will stay down, and the lessons won't irritate you. Don't get angry, but don't be a pushover. Remind students they can do better: "I know it's hard to hear so many corrections. I'm not being picky because I think you are *bad*. I'm being picky because I think you can be really *good*." Sometimes all you need to say is "You can do better," or "I believe in you." Or just give them The Look. Remember to praise in public, correct in private.

Monitor Your Communication Style

Conduct yourself so students are not afraid. Well, maybe a *little* afraid. Be sure they work to hear your compliments, not just avoid your wrath. Don't become a human "Spell-check," where all you say are negative comments. Have times in the lesson where students do not feel they are being judged but when the two of you can just enjoy the music.

Make feedback a two-way process. Invite students to comment on how well *you're* teaching them. This invitation lets them know you take their opinions seriously and are willing to compromise on solutions. If they don't understand a concept or are having trouble with some technical difficulty, ask what *you* can do to help them improve. Sprinkle your teaching with "Do you understand?" and "How can I help you learn this technique better?" Sometimes a student's inability to learn is really the teacher's inability to teach.

Care as much about the integrity of the music and their education as about being "buddies." (They will end up liking you even more, and better yet, they will respect you.) Let your students know that you separate being irritated at them *musically* and *personally.* No matter how they perform, you are still on their side.

Use Humor in "Reprimanding" Students

A little bit of sarcasm said in a *non-threatening*, "loving" way gets their attention and adds humor to discussions with students who trust and respect you. Be playful and get your message across. If a student's lesson wasn't great, say: "This was not up to my standards or your standards. Let's pretend this lesson never happened." "Make sure I'm thrilled next week with your playing or you'll need to bring me cookies. Either way I'll be happy." "I'm not happy. And if I'm not happy, nobody's happy, so practice and I will be happy next week." "How inventive. Next week, let's try for what the composer wrote, OK?" "That was great typing, now let's hear some music!" "How about playing this in a key signature I've heard before?" Don't be afraid to be a little melodramatic: "My goodness! That was the most *horrible* tone I've heard in my *entire* life!" "That tone reminds me of a dentist's drill!" For the really horrible mistake I let out a squawk from the rubber chicken!

Applaud Accomplishments

Sometimes in our zeal to teach, we forget to praise. Even the best students need encouragement. If you are on a tight schedule in the lessons preceding an important event, say: "We're hurrying here. I appreciate how great you're playing and I don't have time to give you every compliment you deserve. Right now I only have time for corrections. Please assume everything is fabulous unless I tell you otherwise."

When students do something spectacular, stop in the middle of a piece and *rave* about what you heard. "Wow! Sorry to stop you but that was the best chromatic scale I have ever heard." "Play those last two phrases again; they gave me goose bumps." For even bigger smiles, praise them in front of someone else. Tell the next incoming student what a great lesson you just had. Say, "Are you lucky! Lydia put me in such a great mood."

REWARD EFFORT

We all want a pat on the back, not only when we have reached our goals, but for our efforts along the way. While I was writing this book (over a period of five years!), I would periodically send material or ideas to Cindy, who contributed so much to this book, and to Hal Ott, Professor of Flute at Central Washington University. I was thrilled every time they said, "Good job! Keep going!" Their praise spurred me on to continue writing.

Like me, students yearn for approval and acknowledgment for the work they are putting in. Reward students periodically while they are *learning*, rather than waiting for the final outcome, such as the concert or contest. "I know you still can't play the piece but your double stops are so much better!" Vocal and tangible rewards motivate students (and adults!) to keep trying.

Extrinsic Rewards as Motivation

Motivation is the reason people do what they do. Motivation can be *extrinsic*, as in the expectation of a reward such as candy, money, or a new CD, or *intrinsic*, as in the pride students feel when they've reached an important goal. Extrinsically motivated students play for tangible rewards from others; intrinsically motivated students play for their own reasons. As teachers, when we feel proud of a job well done, we boost our intrinsic motivation. Some of us would also appreciate more extrinsic motivation, too: money!

Many parents, myself included, have used extrinsic motivation when they've paid (or bribed?) their children to practice. I used to pay my sons twenty-five cents for every good practice *without complaining*. They earned enough to purchase the video game system I had refused to buy. I felt any means justified the end of establishing a consistent practice schedule that got them to the point where they felt good enough to be vested in the whole process. (Now as I still listen to the sound of video machine guns filling our family room I wonder whether this was a good decision!)

Is rewarding students for practice justified if it helps them lay a solid foundation of playing that, when they are good, becomes its own motivation? Or does this type of reward promote the mindset that practicing is a distasteful job that students must be compensated for? The jury is still out.

Some people feel that rewarding children to practice simulates real life. Practicing, especially for beginners, is a hard job, and people in real life get compensated for working. Others feel that music itself and pride in a job well done should be the only necessary motivation.

Studies have shown that extrinsic motivation can work well for the short term, but in the long term, students must be motivated from within. True motivation is internal, and the ability to motivate oneself to pursue important goals is one of life's most valuable skills. Teachers can't motivate students; we can only help them to motivate themselves. Let's talk about how to nudge our students in the direction of intrinsic motivation.

Recognize Effort and Results with Praise and Rewards

For rewards to be effective, use them only occasionally and when students don't anticipate them. Surprise students after a spectacular lesson or practice (I keep a stash of giant chocolate bars). Reward them when they need to get jump-started. Link the reward to improvement, not perfection. You might sometimes allow the student to select the reward most effective for them. (Sometimes the reward is the promise of no etudes or scales for a week!) Combine the reward with positive comments. The only incentive many students need is a smile and a "Great job!"

In chapter 9, "Increase Success with the *Music for Life* Notebook System," I mentioned a reward system of writing comments and using stickers and stars as feedback. These also help students, parents, and the teacher track general progress. Stickers are terrific motivators only if you award them for true excellence. Even advanced students and adults appreciate being commended for their hard work if the lesson is spectacular or they mastered a particular technique. Students comb through the box for the perfect sticker, which I affix by the date of the great lesson. Some ask to put the sticker on the front of their *Music for Life* notebook so they can keep an accurate count of their "badges of honor." When Mom arrives to pick them up, they call out, "I got a sticker today!" Mom is also thrilled (and sometimes relieved). Former student Mike remembers that in his younger days in lessons from grade school through high school, "Bonnie always enticed me with Muppet stickers for a job well done. I didn't even like stickers, but I sure as heck wanted those!" Teachers might also give small prizes such as candy and pencils, or post pictures of "victorious" students on the studio bulletin board.

Sometimes all it takes is a compliment. Surprise students by writing compliments about their lesson or technique in their assignment books. Write in big letters: "Wonderful Scale Playing" or "First Person to Sound So Good on Page 11" or "AMAZING!"

Help Parents Set Up a Reward System

Teachers can reward at lessons, but parents can reward all week long in the "trenches." A few carefully chosen bribes may spur students to reach higher. Parents might award points for: practicing every day, practicing *without complaining* (my favorite), practicing without being reminded, practicing more than required, keeping an accurate (and honest) practice chart, or accepting help from a parent during a practice session without a reenactment of World War II! Other causes for celebration might be memorizing a piece, having an extra-good lesson, playing in a concert or contest, or conquering another movement of the "impossible" piece.

Determine Meaningful Rewards

Anthony's grandmother came to his lesson two months ago armed with a big box of surprises for Anthony. She brought LEGOS, a water bottle, colored pens, a sketch book, playing cards, mechanical pencils, a pinwheel, a small first aid kit, and a candy bar. Perfect small prizes for a fifth-grade boy. Why? Anthony had been frustrated at several lessons when he couldn't easily learn a new technique or when his hard work at home didn't show in the lesson. Understanding Grandma worked out a structured set of rewards—not only for Anthony's *performance* but also for his *effort*.

Anthony's special reward system:

- If Anthony practiced every day, he got one prize from the box each week.
- If he paid attention and concentrated at the lesson, even if he didn't play well, he got a prize.
- If he practiced at least five days a week for a month he got a new video game.
- Unbelievably, the ultimate reward for a spectacular lesson was a *sticker*. He valued that sticker more than any of his toys.

Enlist parents' help to determine what means most to their child. When you or parents reward children for good behavior, use the opportunity to discuss the difference between internal and external rewards. Say, "The most important thing is that you worked hard to accomplish your goal. Don't you feel good about yourself? I want to reward you to show you how impressed I am."

These might be rewards worth working for: candy or an ice cream cone after a great lesson, a new dress for the competition, having friends over after practicing, a new toy, a CD player or CDs, a favorite dinner or going to a favorite restaurant to celebrate, more computer time (my boys love this one), a movie with friends, getting out of chores (my boys love practicing while I do the dishes), a day off from practice, or small monetary rewards, e.g., a quarter for every extra practice session. Do whatever it takes to acknowledge students' hard work and effort and to add a little extra fun into taking lessons. In the next chapter we'll discuss other ways to keep your students happy and looking forward to their lessons.

TWELVE

Foster Happy, Confident Students

Studying and teaching music isn't worth the effort if it's no fun. Make lessons something you both look forward to. Greet students with a smile, say goodbye with a smile, and have fun in between. Laugh at every lesson. Flashing a grin reassures your students and is the least expensive gift you can give to them. Smiles say, "You're doing fine and I'm enjoying you!" Along with the discipline, high standards, and serious work you expect, make teaching and learning music a joy!

DO SOMETHING DIFFERENT

Use Silly Learning Aids

I have several fun props in my studio, the most important being my dog Angie. We often laugh at her as she lies on the floor, feet upward, looking like the flute music has killed her. (She's really rolling over to get her stomach scratched.) I rotate jokes or cartoons on the music stand and give them out to be put in a special section of the *Music for Life* notebook. I use silly gags. A life-sized Winnie the Pooh gets dressed for the season and provides an instant audience. "Sammy the Sight Reader," a Martian-looking toy with three eyes, reminds them to look ahead when they sight read. A light-up ring adorns fingers that move too high or repeatedly use the wrong fingering. Scaly Sal, a scaly Stegosaurus, comes out to help them play scales. Keep the atmosphere light with jokes, tales of your experiences, poking fun at yourself, and doing silly things.

Give Students Choices

When my son Scott was fourteen, he wanted to play a Brahms Rhapsody. His piano teacher would never have chosen such an advanced piece for him, but once Scott heard it he fell in love. Although he worked on only a small section over a long period of time, the pride of playing something so big and real motivated him to practice more than any smaller piece could have. It also meant our family had to hear Brahms for a long time! Don't always dictate what students play; allow for individual input so the decision is partly theirs. When choosing contest pieces, ask students to listen to CDs and bring in their favorites. If students love a piece of music, they'll work harder on it, identify with it, and play it with more passion.

Add Variety

Variety can recapture your students' attention. Guest artists, recitals, parties, and other activities can break students out of the routine. Be open to new ideas and be willing to try new things. Use new music, handouts, and fun props. There are many ways to spice up your music room, music, and routines.

HELP STUDENTS EMBRACE YOUR PASSION FOR MUSIC

Demonstrate the Power of Music

Music can transport us to another place and time. It can define a generation. I'm a child of the '60s and still love John, George, Ringo, and especially Paul! Music reunites us with our past. When we hear a song we may think about our first concert or our first date. The opening line of "Hot Time, Summer in the City," flashes me back to summer strawberry-picking. Music makes our homes more relaxing and welcoming, and even brings us back to our childhood. Music can alter personalities. How many "shy caterpillars" have morphed into "butterflies" through the confidence mastering an instrument lends? Let your students know they are privileged to share this wonderful gift that touches our lives.

Link Music to Their Lives

Music is intrinsic to so many facets of our lives. Help students see what it means to you. Music has been my steadfast friend on my happiest days and on my saddest. It has enhanced my fondest moments and soothed my greatest heartaches. When my infant son died suddenly, I practiced for hours on end, trying to focus outside of my pain. I arrive for medical procedures armed with my CD player. Music in all its varieties adds beauty to my life.

Help students find value and meaning in their own music. Point out how they can share music by listening to or playing with others. Talk about its ability to aid healing, distract, and comfort during difficult times. Say, "The more you get into *music,* the more you'll get out of *life!*"

Share the Work and Lives of Great Artists

Introduce students to the "Greats." Talk about your favorite pieces and stellar performers. I rave about the Beethoven *Emperor* Concerto, the Brahms B Major Piano Trio, *The Planets* by Holst, *The Firebird* by Stravinsky, the Dvořák *New World* Symphony, and everything by Bach. I am a one-person fan club for Yo-Yo Ma, James Galway, Edgar Meyer, Murray Perahia, and Itzhak Perlman.

Talk about musical challenges these artists overcame. Get excited about every new piece you give your students. "Wait until you hear this piece; you're going to love it!" "This sonata has always been one of my favorites." "If you thought that book was good, this new book is great!"

Add music to your students' lives by bringing them to concerts and suggesting radio stations to listen to. Create a lending library of CDs. Give students a prepared list of your favorite composers, orchestras, artists, and pieces. Offer a general list of pieces they should know about. Ask them to tell you about their favorite music. Be open to a wide variety of music, from pop to blues. (Just hope it isn't rap!) Listen to your favorites together and let them experience the joy you feel when you hear wonderful compositions and artists. Your enthusiasm will be infectious.

Share Your Musical Journey

Talk to your students about your own journey falling in love with music. I regale my students with tales of the first time I ever sang in harmony ("Kum Ba Yah" at Girl Scout camp), my first concert (the Vienna Boys Choir in seventh grade), and the first time I heard a symphonic recording ("Scheherazade" in eighth grade, while babysitting). I tell them about the lasting friendships I formed during my university choir tour of Europe, the thrill of my first flute recital, and the beautiful choral and instrumental music performed by my friends at my wedding.

Inspire with Musical Events and Friendships

I've met most of my best friends through music. I find musicians to be bright, interesting, and creative people. (I'm sure every music teacher reading this will agree!) Encouraging friendships in your studio is a wonderful way of combining the social and the musical. In later chapters, I'll give you plenty of ideas for hosting fun musical events.

MOTIVATE WITH MUSIC

Choose Music That Entertains and Inspires

So much music, so little time. Don't waste your time playing or teaching music that neither of you enjoys just because it teaches certain techniques. Play what you love. Life is too short and there's so much music to choose from—especially if you are a pianist or violinist! There may be no getting around playing certain exercises (the shifting exercises I have played on violin and viola, and Hanon scales on piano come to mind), but mix obligatory pieces among pieces that are fun or uplifting.

Choose Music That Encourages Practice

It is a delicate balancing act to assign music that challenges students and yet doesn't discourage them. Make assignments challenging enough that they can understand why they need to practice. Get them excited about reaching a new technical level but don't make assignments so long or hard that students will feel defeated from the start. Avoid assigning music that is so childish it insults them or too mature for them to understand. Match the personality of the piece with the personality of the performer. Teens love drama in minor keys and younger students gravitate to fun, fast pieces.

Show You Appreciate Your Students' Playing

While we attended the University of Washington as college students, my sister Cindy and I shared a house. She often heard flute music wafting through the house when my students played from a beginning solo book. Last summer she visited during a lesson. When she heard a student playing from that same solo book, she asked, "Aren't you tired of hearing those same songs being played after *thirty years*?" "No," I told her. "I love to share these songs with new students. Time after time I'm thrilled to see their progress." It is hard for me to relate to disgruntled symphony musicians who tire of playing the great masterworks when I still get a kick when a well-prepared student plays "Long, Long Ago."

Enjoy your students' playing, no matter what the music or level of playing (if they play it well!). When one of your students says, "I love 'Hot Cross Buns,'" say, "Oh, that's one of my favorites too" (with a straight face!). Great teachers find beauty and emotion in all kinds of music. Delight in your student's triumphs no matter how small.

STAY IN TUNE WITH STUDENTS' EMOTIONS

Like the old advice for married couples, "Don't ever go to bed angry," don't knowingly let students leave the lesson angry or upset. Students' frustrations can stem from difficult music or technique, personal problems, fatigue, and yes, sometimes annoyance with their teacher. Regardless of what might be the cause, don't ignore their emotions. If you see tears starting to well up, stop everything and talk. Avoid overreacting and taking their frustration personally.

A certain amount of frustration is a normal part of learning any new skill. When they look dejected, give them a glass of water, a sympathetic ear, and a tissue. If they have misinterpreted you or don't understand the concept, strip it down to its barest essentials. If your instincts tell you something is bothering a student, don't be afraid to probe a little. Most students will say, "I'm fine," but even when they do, they almost always appreciate your caring. Follow through with a call to the parents if you are concerned.

If the student does something dumb, join in with a dumb story of your own. "Well, you think that's bad, wait till you hear the stupid thing I did." When you are not afraid to admit your own mistakes, students won't feel nervous or in jeopardy for making their own. When students make a careless mistake and shake their heads in disappointment, you don't need to point it out again. If things get tense, try to lighten up. Stop everything and chat. Do everything possible to let students know you are on their side.

Take Care When You Correct

While writing this chapter I received a call from the parent of my sixth-grade student Susan. Though she's not one of my more enthusiastic students, Susan has made slow but steady progress over her first year of lessons. Her lesson last week after a month's summer break was surprisingly poor. Her scales were atonal and her mistakes multiplied exponentially as she played. Her frustration level (and mine) grew as I made her keep repeating each scale until it was good. She left the lesson with neither of us feeling successful.

Susan's mom later called to tell me her daughter had not touched the flute during the past week and wanted to quit. She said Susan had sensed my impatience and frustration and she fell apart. Boy, did I feel bad. Her call was a harsh reminder of the power of my words and the importance of staying attuned to students' feelings. Susan's mom came to every lesson, but we had no time to talk privately. If I had known how my display of emotions had hurt Susan, I would have apologized and made a conscious effort to keep them in check. More importantly, I needed a reminder to put Susan before the music. I *feel* this way about every student, but sometimes my manner doesn't display it. I want so badly for them to improve that I may focus too much on improvement. Especially with beginners, I need to be more aware of their feelings and how my words and emotions could discourage them. I hope Susan gives me another chance.

A similar scenario played itself out earlier this year. Katherine put in her homework and practicing time and progressed but I needed to repeat my explanations so often that I felt I was teaching a patient with Alzheimer's. I dreaded Katherine's lessons but felt I had to keep her because she was faithfully practicing. One lesson my aggravation boiled over. I put my head in my hands and said, "I have said the same thing so many times, I don't know what to do!" Katherine looked crushed. I realized she could never keep up with the pace I desired and would feel better about herself with a slower-moving, more tolerant teacher. I should have come to terms with our mismatch much earlier. Now Katherine is happier with a new teacher and I am happier with the new student who replaced her. I hope Katherine forgives me.

Recognize the Teacher Is Not Always Right

"I was only wrong once, and that was when I *thought* I was wrong." Just kidding. Admit your mistakes. If you unjustly accused a student of not practicing, misheard a note or rhythm, or lashed out impatiently, apologize. More important, offer students unconditional support regardless of their performance.

Quickly apologize when you are wrong. If you point out a mistake and they say there was none, don't belabor the point to prove yourself right. If you were too harsh, apologize and take the blame. Say, "I got a little overzealous today trying to improve your tone. I apologize if I was over the top." Be careful of your tone of voice and avoid sarcasm with sensitive students who don't know you yet. They may misinterpret your humor. Say, "Maybe you're right." Even better: "Maybe I'm wrong." Follow up an emotional lesson by calling students at home or e-mailing them later that evening. This reassures that you don't forget them when they walk out your door. Say, "I noticed you were upset at the lesson. Was it something I said?" "Are you okay?"

I made mistakes with Katherine and Susan. From now on, if I feel like screaming when a student plays B-flat in the D major scale for the fifth time in a row, I am going to excuse myself to get a glass of water and calm down. Or silently count to ten. Or say nothing and smile until I can make sure what I say next will be helpful, not hurtful.

The message I am writing now is that no teacher is perfect; we all make mistakes. Learning to give appropriate feedback in a non-threatening way takes practice.

Postlude

Back to Susan. After my apology she did give me another chance. I tried something different at her next few lessons. Instead, of drilling her over and over on scales, I went three weeks without the mention of a scale. I replaced the scales with real songs with piano accompaniment. Then I let her bring in her own music and we ended up playing patriotic tunes and *Star Wars*. After one month, we decided to focus on only two scales per week and add more duets to her weekly assignment. I worked hard to maintain high standards while filling the lesson with encouragement and praise. Susan's mom made her a reward box with three levels of prizes, so now after every lesson Susan and I analyze how she did and give her the appropriate prize. Though Susan is still not crazy about practicing, she now skips into her lessons and last week brought me an award ribbon for "Best Teacher." I love happy endings.

ACT IN YOUR STUDENTS' BEST INTERESTS

Put Students before Their Performance

For a moment, think forward to the day you will retire from teaching. Looking back at those years of your career, what will matter most? Years after their lessons have stopped, what will your students remember? Playing the etude up to tempo, the scale without mistakes, the memorized piece? Yes, but more importantly will they treasure the foundation you gave them in becoming a caring individual, developing a life-long love of music, and learning about life? Students may practice more if they are afraid of your wrath, but you'll be left with students who can play the notes while hating their teacher and the music. Keeping the student's sense of self-worth intact is more important than any prize to be won.

Maintain Your Priorities with a Mission Statement

Successful organizations develop mission statements that outline their beliefs and priorities. Our mission statement as music teachers should read: "*The welfare of students comes first.*" Nothing you do or say should conflict with this paradigm. Did you push Stacey to perform before she was ready? Is Dan afraid you'll be upset since he didn't enter the competition? Is Sonia terrified she let you down because she didn't make the cut in the orchestra? Is Mary anxious about your response after her memory slipped in the recital? Are you disappointed with Nathan because he placed third and you expected first? Is Julie in tears because you ripped her playing apart? Are you so critical of Eileen's playing that she is losing her confidence? Are you pushing Tim to be a music major when deep down you know he'll never make it as a professional?

Do you accept the check from Rob's parents every month though he rarely practices and wants to play basketball instead of the trombone? Do you focus solely on

pieces that make students look good at recitals to the exclusion of skill-building repertoire and music basics? Do you continue to teach Sandra even though she has outgrown your expertise? Do you expect Sam to practice three hours a day, squelching his
love for his instrument?

Act in your students' best interest even when their goals are not what you had envisioned. If you focus on the product (prizes, recognition, scholarships, making a big
name for yourself) instead of the person, students will lose trust in you. They may also
lose their love of music. When you think of students as people first and students second, great music will easily follow. When your mission statement centers on *serving
others,* not yourself, you won't be disappointed.

LOOKING AHEAD

In this chapter I suggested ways to nurture a studio of happy, confident students. Sci-
entists tell us that people who laugh and enjoy life live longer. Using these suggestions
may not help you live to be one hundred, but at least you and your students will have
more fun along the way. Speaking of fun, in our next chapter we'll look at ways to host
a variety of music events that will provide goals for your students and opportunities for
their music friendships to flourish.

THIRTEEN

Host Fun Musical Events

WHY HOST MUSICAL EVENTS?

Recitals, concerts, and other musical events cost too much, are too much work, and are too long and boring, and students fear and dread them anyway. Right? Wrong. If recitals are done in a spirit of fun instead of competition, they can be great motivators and students will think of them as parties, not tests. Holding studio events also promotes friendships and creates studio unity. Learning music can sometimes feel like a solitary pursuit, but these events offer students a chance to be with "their own kind" and to gain inspiration from others. Parents also enjoy these special events and the chance to network with other parents. All the events at my house include fun, food, friends, and flutes. What a great combination! Here are some fun ideas for parties that will make you the most popular teacher on the block!

Parties

Bravo Parties

Use peer pressure to encourage students to work hard to be part of the winning team and gain public admiration. Pick a skill most students need and can achieve, make a contest of it, and then plan a bravo party for the winners. Accomplishments such as knowing all the high-note fingerings, trills, scales, or chords, or mastering a certain number of bowings or positions, work well. Reaching a certain page in the book, tackling a certain number of assignments, having the *Music for Life* notebook up to date, memorizing a certain number of pieces, practicing a certain amount over a time period, and practicing so many days in a row (with a parental affidavit) are also party-worthy goals. This year I had to pay up my ensembles with lunch and a hot tub party because the judge complimented their dynamics. If you think giving a prize such as a pizza party or a backyard potluck barbecue is a lot of work and money, think of how much more enjoyable lessons will be when every student attains the desired skill. A slice of pepperoni is sure worth not having to sit through hours of scales peppered with wrong notes.

Sight Reading Parties

Ensemble reading parties are practice for sight reading and a way for students to get to know one another. You can put all students in one big group coached by you, or provide music and a room for smaller ensembles. Even pianists can have sight reading parties: invite another instrument to join in, or play piano four hands music, play duets on two pianos, take turns reading measures, or (for weaker readers) just play one hand only in solo literature.

Improvisation Parties

Teach students jazz chords or twelve-bar blues and have them take turns improvising. On piano, one student can play the chords while the other improvises. For solo instruments, invite a jazz pianist or guitarist to come to accompany.

Concert Events

Arrange for students to travel together to see a famous musician perform, and host an after-concert party or go out for dessert. And of course celebrate a group recital with a fun party.

Beginning of the Season Parties

This is a good time for new and old students to get to know each other and an opportunity for the teacher to talk about goals and events in the coming year.

End of the Season Parties

Who needs an excuse? Host a party to celebrate making it through another year.

Skill Games Parties

Play music bingo and theory games. There are lots of resources for teachers to teach students skills through enjoyable games.

Reunion Parties

Miss all your former students? Invite them for a party over the winter break or during the summer. This Christmas I had fifteen students and their moms for a sit-down dinner. Six of my present students gave a very short recital and then we ended with sight reading ensembles. The alumni encouraged the younger kids while giving them role models.

Recitals

We all picture the big stage, the nervous child dressed in his or her best stumbling up to the piano, shakily starting the piece, getting hopelessly lost in the middle, bolting to the door, and vowing, "I will *never* play another recital as long as I live!"

It doesn't have to be that way! Recitals can be fun events and such valuable learning experiences for the students and their parents too. Why host recitals?

Recitals provide:

• An excellent way to reward and say, "Bravo!" for a big accomplishment.

• An easy way to train students (and parents) in concert etiquette.

• A fun way to entertain students and parents.

• A sneaky way to teach new skills.

• A solid way to build confidence and self-esteem.

• A wonderful venue to solidify student friendships.

- A tested way to calm nerves before an important audition, concert, or competition.
- A valuable preparation for being in the public eye, leading seminars, and giving speeches.
- An opportunity to show your appreciation to students and their parents.
- A venue for younger students to emulate more advanced students.
- An easy way for students to hear a menu of music they might some time want to play.
- A chance for you to bond with your students on a personal level and to get to know their parents better too.
- A public way to show off your students and market your studio.
- An opportunity to remind students of what a good thing they already have.

Recitals don't have to be scary. Your students will *look forward* to these fun recitals:

Mother's Day Recital

The most important event in my studio is our yearly Mother's Day recital, which I bill as *the* social occasion of the year. Every single one of my students describes the Mother's Day recital as "Lots of fun!" Because only ensembles play, there is no performance stress and the concert length is manageable. I have been fortunate over the years to have parents with spacious homes offer to host the recital. We wear party clothes, decorate the home, and bring fancy party food, so it feels like an elegant event.

Once each ensemble has assembled on the "stage," we begin with introductions. One member, using a microphone, starts off by introducing another one of the group, listing at least ten personal traits ranging from their musical accomplishments to their pet's name or their least favorite vegetable. The introduction *always* ends with, "And she loves her mother and her flute teacher very much." (See how I always work that in?) After the ensemble performs, each student's mom comes up front for a Polaroid picture with her daughter or son and is presented with a small gift I have bought, topped with a card signed by her child. This finale is a big hit! After the concert we share a delicious potluck dinner. The kids change clothes and play together for the afternoon and everyone has a good time and a lasting memory.

Every year this recital gets a little more dramatic, and the recital has evolved into "performance art." Each ensemble dresses up to reflect their piece. One year we had little red monkeys, girls in formals with tiaras, and a quartet featuring spring colors and flowers attached to their flutes. We've had ensembles dressed as pirates, and the unlikely combination of pajamas and crowns. Other years have seen a Yankee Doodle duet played by a boy in a full Revolutionary War costume and me looking ridiculous in Betsy Ross wig; a quartet with picnic supplies and flutes in baguette bags for "Flutes on Vacation"; and a trio wearing halos playing "When the Saints Go Marching In." One of my favorites was my second-grade boy student dressed up like my dog, Angie, as I led him into the recital room on a leash.

The acting has become wild, too, as each group performs a very short skit. Last year my two graduating seniors dressed in graduation gowns and marched down the aisle playing Pomp and Circumstance and introduced themselves as "Bonnie's graduating class." They thought it would be funny, but it brought the whole audience to tears as we thought of losing them from our flute family. One year my husband wore a Keystone Cops hat and gave a speeding ticket to a Telemann trio that was playing MM = 160 instead of the speed limit of 108! An adult duo danced the tango while a quartet played "La Milonga," and there was a mock "Funeral for a Marionette." Many times these skits include send-ups of the flute teacher and I have to take it in good humor. My all-time favorite was four girls who held a mock contest and imitated four judges they knew and "loved." "Welcome to the most important contest in your life, where if you make a mistake your whole career will be smashed to pieces!" What a cathartic event that was! Planning the skits and costumes for these recitals is half the fun. Let your students use their imagination and create an "event."

Anti-Contest

My friend Karen holds a yearly anti-contest in which my students have been involved. Her groups also dress up and perform skits. A big plus at the anti-contest is that you get to bribe the judges! Those lucky judges have been presented with cakes that say "Judges, we're the best!" They also have received blocks of cheese from a quartet of mice, fish from "The Trout Quintet," and even crowns. The music is serious but the staging is hilarious!

The Long *Recital*

One of the most daunting tasks of holding a full-scale recital is letting a large studio of students play full-length pieces without the audience falling asleep. Here's a solution that has been very successful. Announce that the recital is three hours long (gasp!) but that each student and family may come and go as they wish, as long as they stay for at least one hour. I have done this recital in private homes on the night before a big contest. Everyone brings buffet items that are set up in another room (I always have to have food!) and people drift in and out and can eat while they listen. (Don't you wish you could do that at symphony concerts?) The concert is almost nonstop, but everyone is happy (except perhaps the long-suffering accompanist!). The performers have a big enough audience to make them nervous, and the audience is well entertained and well fed.

New Kids Concert

One spring I held a concert featuring only my students who had taken less than one year of lessons with me. I called it "New Kids on the Block" or "New Kids in Shock." Students told the audience about their flute history and how long they had studied with me. It was a fun way for students and parents to meet each other and for new students to have a nonjudgmental audience.

Getting to Know You Concert

In the "getting to know you" concert, before they play, students give a small "presentation" that gives a little insight into their personalities and other talents. Audiences love learning more about the performers. Giving a presentation takes the focus off the playing and puts everyone more at ease.

One year two of my high school students made a collage of magazine cutouts titled, "Flute Lessons with Bonnie." A beginning student who had lived in Monaco sang her little piece in French before she played it; another gave a little speech comparing me to her old, *nice* teacher from another state. One wrote a poem, some drew pictures, and some brought old baby pictures.

In-Studio Master Classes

"Fun and helpful" is how my students describe our "You Be the Judge" master classes. I invite all of my students to pretend they are judges at a competition. I draw a chart of important categories such as phrasing, tone, and dynamics and ask all audience members to evaluate the performance. The students are very sensitive to their teammates' feelings (probably because they know they are next), and always begin with a compliment before the commentary. Even the very beginning students who aren't playing gain so much from having to analyze what they like and dislike. The younger students are in awe of the older ones, but still have great suggestions on stage presence. "You Be the Judge" helps students prepare for the real thing.

Try these in-studio master class variations:

- Each student must give one compliment and one criticism.
- Assign a different technical point to each audience member to evaluate. Technical points might include musicality, tone, dynamics, stage presence, bow technique, shifting, ensemble, pedaling, ornaments, breathing, announcing the piece, and especially the bow at the end.
- Give each audience member an anonymous judging sheet similar to those used in real contests they will encounter, to be turned in to the performer after the concert.
- Copy scores on which to write specific comments.
- Take turns having one student be the judge and coaching the performer (then they'll see how hard it is to be a judge!).

Guest Teacher Master Classes

Students gain so much from hearing a second opinion (and it's great when that second opinion agrees with yours!). A guest teacher master class gives students a nonthreatening goal and can spur more practice in the middle of the season. Students who have studied with you for years and might be thinking of changing teachers can learn from others and still stay in your studio. Inviting guest teachers is also a way to evaluate your own teaching. Is there something you have overlooked? Does this teacher know some new tricks? Does the teacher feel your students are well prepared? Networking with other teachers provides you with mentors and can also make future connections for students.

I try to hold a master class in November and one in January, and have had many fabulous teachers from colleges and conservatories around the country as they came through town for other events. If you don't live in a big city you can still contact teachers from the college or symphony in your state or even teachers of other instruments.

The cost for the master class is covered by the participating students. Auditing the class is free. Visiting teachers either coach a select five or six in front of an audience, or give longer private lessons which are open to the public. The master classes can run from two hours to two days and are always held in my studio. And of course, each master class involves food!

The Audition from Hell

Contrary to the name, this recital is the most fun! I try to recreate the most unnerving aspects of playing in an audition and coach students how to survive. I shake their stand, aim a fan on their music, talk and laugh, order pizza on the phone, and anything else I (with some help from the other players) can dream up. Read more about this crazy recital in chapter 23, "Conquer Stage Fright."

Group Performance Class

Many teachers give students a chance to play for each other once a month. Even if the pieces are not totally polished, these informal performances provide deadlines for the students, a chance for the teacher to review concepts, and a way for students to bond with each other.

Ensemble Recitals

Ensemble recitals like the one we host on Mother's Day really take the pressure off the performers. It's amazing how much easier it is to stand up in from of the audience when you have a friend beside you. Invite students' friends who play other instruments or team up with another teacher to join in the fun. Celebrate with a "Chamber Pot-luck" afterwards.

Solo Senior Recitals

Senior recitals acknowledge the hard work and accomplishments of the student's musical journey and are a great venue for celebration. For those who do not give senior recitals, the last lesson seems so anticlimactic. Seniors can perform their favorite music, learn new pieces, and invite friends in for ensembles. A few of my students have brought their music scrapbook/photo albums to share. One student invited her two former teachers and acknowledged the contribution we had all made to her training by giving us roses.

Students design professional-looking invitations and programs for their senior recitals. The programs should include a biography featuring musical accomplishments and a special dedication to the parents who made it all possible. (A thank you to the music teacher and accompanist is always appreciated too!)

The recital can be a grand concert in a performance hall or church, or a small affair in the studio or their home. One of my students, Katie, had a small family recital in my studio where she took her family down memory lane. Her printed program featured school pictures from fifth grade through her senior year in high school. Her mom nearly wept as Katie played her "big piece" from each year. What fun it was to see her grow up before our very eyes!

I am always proud but somewhat sad at these final recitals, as these kids have become special friends and accomplished musicians. The end of the senior recital is very emotional. We exchange bouquets of flowers, hugs, and a few tears. I send them on their way, knowing music has played such an important part in their lives, and I'm grateful for having worked with such special people.

Recital Alternative

Here's a fun and practical option. Instead of a recital, make a CD. The student needs to choose music, rehearse, decide on a program order, and design and print a program, insert, program notes, and CD label.

After the whole project is done the student can turn from artist to music critic and give a list of attributes and evaluate the CD. How is the ensemble? Tone? Musicality? Choice of music? Would you recommend this CD to friends?

More Fun Recitals

- Slide show recital. Slides represent the mood, country of origin, or something about the composer or the times in which he lived.
- "We are the composer" recital. Teach students composition or improvisation and have a recital of all original music.
- Around the world recital/dinner. Each section of this recital contains music written in the same country followed by food from that country. (Life's not too bad when you drink champagne, eat brie, and listen to Debussy.) This one is a favorite with adults.
- American music recital. Every performer wears red, white, and blue. How about hot dogs and apple pie for refreshments? (I get to revive my Betsy Ross wig.)
- Music history recital. Each solo or ensemble is previewed with a short history of the composer or details about what life was like in the time and place in which he or she lived.
- Composer of the month recital, featuring only one famous composer such as Bach, Mozart, or Beethoven. Students can really get the feel for the styles of the great composers.
- Meet the composer recital. This is similar to the composer of the month recital but carried a step further. Groups of three perform music of the same composer, followed by a group discussion of similarities in the pieces to detect a compositional style.
- "Mood music" recital. Each piece is accompanied by a poem, picture, program music story, or expression of how the piece affects the performer.
- Pops concert in the park. Children will love the casual feel, and the surprised people at the park will get a free recital—and maybe a chance to think about enlisting their own children in your program.
- Lecture-recital. The teacher can be the narrator in a recital that revolves around a certain theme, such as dance, music and art or literature, music from around the world, and program music. The preview lecture can include fun facts, pictures, or slides and should help the audience listen to certain things in the music when they appear.

• Program music recital. Students make up a story about their piece and share it before they play. It's amazing how knowing these stories first really makes the music come alive.

• Cooperative recital with another teacher. Why not have a recital that is half piano and half violin? How about a trumpet/percussion recital? The advantage to a teacher with just a few students is that planning and expenses can be shared, and the recital is more interesting.

• Family recital. Invite members of the families to perform with students. It's a great way to encourage family togetherness and for other family members to appreciate the student's yearlong effort.

• Holiday concerts. The music seems so much more fun when you are wearing angel halos, Santa hats, or reindeer antlers. Why not hold this recital in a retirement home and include a sing-along as the final number? Students enjoy wearing costumes for a Halloween concert and playing scary music. How about turning your home into a haunted mansion for a *truly* scary recital?

• Theme music recitals with movie or show tune music. To really get in the spirit, serve candy and popcorn during the performance.

• Animal theme concerts with subjects such as dogs, cats, or zoo animals. Refreshments can include animal crackers, Teddy grahams, goldfish, and gummy worms.

• Pajama party recital at a nursing home, with cookies and milk.

• Recitals at the shopping mall, bookstore, or even at McDonalds!

• Weather or season theme parties. Kids can dress outrageously in the season.

Recital Tips

• Holding only one recital per year really puts the pressure on students to make their only chance good. Performing in many events throughout the year gives them valuable experience and many chances to learn from their mistakes.

• If there is any interest, videotape or make a CD of the ensemble recital, and offer it to students for a small fee. Students will love seeing themselves, it makes a great present for doting grandparents, and it is a good advertisement for your program.

• Bring recitals to retirement homes. What a great way to bring the generations together! Students can also earn community service hours for bringing joy into the sometimes-dreary lives of retirement home residents. After the concert, performers can personally serve cookies and punch to each resident. The students will love all the compliments and the residents will enjoy sharing their own stories.

• To add excitement and ease nerves, decide concert order by "lottery." I buy big chocolate bars and put the kids' names on them. After each performer is finished, a chocolate bar is drawn out of the hat. The chocolate lottery adds a little excitement and provides each player with a treat.

• Keep recital length under control. No one wants to sit for three hours listening to even the best students play. Hold two recitals back to back. If you have many,

many students, hold several recitals and give parents the chance to choose the dates.

- Remember your audience when choosing music. A mix of musical styles and a few familiar pieces will be most appealing to a general audience.
- Adult students like recitals, too, as long as they don't feel like recitals. Hold playing parties in private homes and make the music just one part of the event. (A little wine makes everyone sound a lot better!)
- The first and last piece may be the most important. Start and end with a lively or memorable piece. How about a group piece for the finale?
- Intermixing solos and ensembles adds variety.
- Don't start recitals with the least advanced going up to the most advanced; this can cause rivalry. Intersperse ages, boys and girls, musical periods, moods, and advancement levels.
- Be explicit about concert attire. The rule in my studio: no jeans, no tennis shoes, and *no visible belly buttons*!

PLAN PARTIES AND RECITALS ON A BUDGET

You can host parties even if you don't have a big budget or a big house. Try these ideas: Invite a small group at a time to your house; make all parties potluck; take the kids out to McDonald's, for pizza, or to an inexpensive buffet restaurant; ask a parent to host a party; have a picnic at a park or in your backyard; use the facilities of a retirement home or church, and invite the members.

OTHER FUN MUSICAL EVENTS

Every musical event does not have to be a performance. Here are examples of music gatherings I have hosted at my house; I bet you can come up with some fun and interesting ones on your own.

- Alexander Technique workshop. This two-hour workshop from an accredited Alexander teacher was a great introduction into the method of moving the body. Each student got individual attention and we had fun hearing the before and after when students opened up their tone due to proper posture and movement.
- Piccolo demonstration. I play little piccolo so I invited Zart Dambourian-Eby, the piccolo player with the Seattle Symphony, to give a demonstration and hints for starting the piccolo and learning to play it well. One of my favorite (posed) pictures is of audience members with their fingers in their ears, a defense against listening to fifteen piccolos played at once.
- Extended techniques introduction. Here again, I am not an expert on all the funny things the flute can do, so Paul Taub, contemporary flute specialist, gave us a concert and taught us how to play the flute in ways we never dreamed possible.
- Smart Music demonstration. Smart Music is an ingenious computer program. It works for all instruments and is great for learning new pieces. At the beginning

level, small exercises appear on the screen. The amazing thing is that when you are wearing a microphone, it marks your mistakes! Who needs a teacher? (Just kidding.) It also allows you to choose different accompaniments for scale practice; if you want a swing trio or a gospel choir to play along with your G major scale, you've got it! At a more advanced level, it provides piano accompaniment to major works and even follows your tempo; when you ritard, so does Smart Music.

• College and conservatory speakers. Many of my former students are attending conservatories and colleges as music majors, so I invited them to speak to my current students who are thinking of following that path. We had an interesting presentation about how to decide on a college or conservatory, how to take auditions, what life was really like as a music major, and what preparation was needed. It was also a great way for the younger students to see their former role models and visualize themselves in the years to come.

• Music teacher surprise party. Some of my visiting college students were reminiscing about their former junior high band director, whom they had taken for granted but now in the wisdom of "old age" appreciated. I invited the band director to my house under false pretences and ten of his former students yelled "Surprise!" as he walked in the door. Each student had made him a card, the four older ones played a quartet, and we shared food and memories. He cried.

LOOKING AHEAD

I hope this chapter has given you some ideas to incorporate fun into your teaching. Hosting musical events can be both a reward and an inspiration for learning. And remember, it's not worth it if you're not having fun!

These first thirteen chapters have been about ways to motivate your students and enrich their lives. Now we look ahead to part 2 of *Making Music and Enriching Lives,* which addresses specific skills in making music.

Part 2

MAKING MUSIC

FOURTEEN

Use Practice Tricks for Fast Results

HOW (NOT) TO PRACTICE

Thursday's lesson wasn't that great, and Jim's teacher reminded him that he needed to practice on a daily basis. Jim vowed to *really* practice more for the next lesson. But on Friday the next lesson seemed so far away and hey, he needed a break. The weekend was crammed full of sports activities. He also had to work on the science project, his parents wanted him to help clean the house, and most importantly, he wanted to catch up on those computer games he had missed during the week.

Practice? He thought about it once, but couldn't find his manuscript book, and then it slipped his mind. Monday afternoon rolled around. "I've got to do homework and, oh yeah, I've got to *practice*!" But first, Jim had a snack and a little TV after school. Then soccer practice. Then dinner. Then homework. Then a friend called. *Then* practice. "I'm so tired, I think I'll just play the parts of the song we worked on last week and leave learning the new section until tomorrow. Yeah. This part sounds really cool when I play it fast. There were some weird notes somewhere on measures 20 to 26. I'll circle those measures . . . when I can find a pen. I'll play the whole thing now again, but faster this time so I can get done sooner. I guess I better try that stupid etude. How does this thing go anyway? I don't get measure five; I'll just wait to ask her at my lesson."

Tuesday is no better. "Where's my manuscript book? I guess I better learn those scales she told me to practice. Ugh. I'll play through the first three scales two times each and just tell her I didn't have time for the rest. How does she expect me to remember all those key signatures anyway? I'll try the etude again but skip those hard measures. Hmm. I wonder what's for dinner? I've got to ask Mom if Tom can come over on Friday. I wonder why the sky is blue? Where was I anyway?"

Wednesday. "Oh my gosh. My lesson is tomorrow. I can do the theory homework in the car on the way to the lesson. I'll practice for a whole hour today and play through everything. If I have another bad lesson she's going to kill me!"

Jim was doing everything right—if his goal was never to improve. Even though he was busy, he needed a plan.

You can get more done in less time, if you practice right. Teach your students these hints to make practice more efficient and effective. Give them the following guidelines and watch them zoom ahead.

Practice Hint One: Develop a Practice Routine

"Where do I start?"

Most successful musicians have a standard routine for practicing. Having a routine makes it easier to get started and to cover everything in a practice session. A good routine might include the following steps: a stretching exercise for your body; a warm-up exercise on the instrument to help your muscles and your mind get ready to play; scales, scales, scales to concentrate on all aspects of playing, such as tone, vibrato, bowing or breathing, and position. Next comes the assignment: etudes, working on pieces already in progress, learning a new piece or a new section, and finally, playing something just for fun.

Practice Hint Two: Establish a Timetable

"So much to do, so little time. How can I get it all done by the deadline?"

Long assignments can be overwhelming. Some students don't know where to start and where to end. Fear holds them back. Other students are allergic to scales and etudes, but love their duets and solos. Time flies for some students and the week seems like it has only three days. These kinds of students will all benefit from a daily practice chart with definable goals.

Try a daily practice chart

> Monday: Work on the first two lines of *Tune a Day* page 11, practice the D and G major scales, concentrate on the fingerings on page 3, and do ten long tones.
>
> Tuesday: E-flat and B-flat scales, first three lines of *Tune a Day,* the duet, and long tones.
>
> Wednesday: Do theory homework, scales, and long tones, *Tune a Day* page 12, and review duet.

This kind of time management helps students see one step at a time, keep track of their assignments, keep in control, and come prepared for the entire lesson seven days later. Students can write in the time spent on each assignment or just check it off. Read more about practice goals in chapter 8, "Make Practice a Priority."

Plan consistent practice

"My lesson isn't for six more days; I'll practice later."

Cramming doesn't work. Your brain needs time to digest what you have put in. Try to pick up the instrument every day even if you plan on only five minutes of practice (which will probably turn out to be much more once you get going). Practicing every day gets you in the habit, and you will ultimately end up with a greater number of hours practiced during the week than if it is all done in a couple days. Make practicing part of daily life like eating or brushing your teeth.

Keep track of long-term projects

"The contest is in three weeks? Help!"

Create a plan to be prepared by a deadline and get started now! Like building contractors who use flow charts, use a calendar for a countdown of days left before the performance. Make weekly practice goals to mete out equally what needs to be accomplished.

Practice Hint Three: Check Out a New Piece First before You Start to Learn It

"Can't I just play it through a couple of times first and worry about all that stuff later?"

If you stand at the top of the cliff and take the long dive into the river below without looking first, you may break your neck! Learning a new piece of music may not be quite so dangerous, but diving headlong into a new piece without looking first can be just as foolhardy. Discover as much about the piece as you can before you start so you don't waste your time on meaningless repetitions and learning mistakes. Amy Porter, flute professor from the University of Michigan, advises, "Take your music to bed with you and read it like a book. Pay attention to *everything* that's written."

Thought practice

"Practice without an instrument? Are you kidding?" My former student Sarah Bassingthwaighte, who now teaches flute at the University of Washington, uses this unique method for herself and her students. Thought practice takes place over the course of a week when the student is not allowed to play the piece but must discover everything possible about it to ensure a good start once the instrument is in hand. Thought practice helps you to recognize and correct mistakes before you actually make them, or more precisely, before you teach *your body* to make them. During thought practice, you can focus your practice and find the root of the difficulty by paring down the number of things you're doing. You don't need to worry about embouchure, tone, bowing, pedals, or fingers. Yes, you do need physical learning too; you can't just imagine you are a tennis champ and be one. But do the mind work first and all the way up to the performance, alongside your other practice techniques. The biggest benefit of this kind of practice is that you'll spend much less time doing things wrong and more time doing them right, and you'll become a better sight reader to boot. Also it helps develop the inner ear. You'd be amazed at how much time we typically spend undoing all the mistakes we made when we started the piece. The biggest obstacle is convincing the student it really works and keeping them from playing the piece for the first week. To some, it seems like you're not really practicing unless you're making noise (and the parents don't hear any sound, so they might be skeptical too).

Remember, it has to go through your brain before it reaches your fingers. Between the page and your instrument is your brain: the music goes through your eyes, through the brain, into the fingers and out the instrument. The things to concentrate on in thought practice overlap those in sight reading.

As with sight reading, analyze the form, key, meter, motives, and notes. Check out the rhythm, tempo, meter, and pulse, and clap the interesting measures. Work out the difficult passages by naming the notes out loud in tempo and in rhythm (say the sharps and flats). Pay attention to the key, accidentals, the form, patterns, and written instructions. Now look away from the page. How much can you remember? Imagine your fingers moving without actually moving them. Can you feel certain fingers moving sluggishly? Can you sense your finger mistakes? Sing the phrase. Be aware of any body tension.

Practice without the instrument for at least one week before actually playing the piece. You will be surprised at how much more closely you watch the score and how quickly you can learn something when you don't have to unlearn all the mistakes.

Practice Hint Four: The Right Notes and Rhythm Are Not Enough

"What do you mean, I have to 'feel the music'? This is just practice!"

Music isn't math or typing. Anyone can play the notes and rhythm, but there's so much more. Don't get so hung up on playing every measure technically right that you forget about the beauty and emotion of the piece as a whole. How can you convey this to the audience?

Practice Hint Five: Try to Enjoy Practicing

"This is supposed to be fun?"

Practicing your instrument shouldn't feel like completing a jail sentence in solitary confinement. Think of it as *playing* your instrument instead of *practicing*. Think of the other benefits of practicing in addition to learning the music and becoming a better musician. Learning a new piece can be as stimulating as doing a crossword puzzle. It can be a break from homework or housework and a chance to do something personally satisfying that's also good for you. If you are a child, it can make both you *and* your parents happy. Practicing may not feel like going to a party or riding a roller coaster, but it can be exciting and rewarding to learn new music. Remember that music is fun!

Practice Hint Six: Appreciate Your Progress

"Will I ever get good? Why is this taking so darned long?"

Learn to be patient with yourself. Rome wasn't built in a day and neither is the technique of a good musician (OK, except in the case of Mozart!). We've all felt like throwing our instruments out the window now and again but when we're impatient with ourselves, all of our energy goes into *frustration* instead of *learning*. Don't waste time beating yourself up or banging your head on the piano; just slowly and patiently concentrate on the job at hand.

Realize that everything is a process. Sometimes a new way to do something, such as double-tonguing or bowing differently, initially seems harder than the old way, but trust the teacher's path and goals. When I was young I decided that I could count on my fingers instead of learning the addition and subtraction tables because it was easier. Well, that only works up to the number 20 if you use your toes! I guess my first grade teacher really did have a better way. Learning an instrument *is* a lot like learning math: every grade has different material to learn and the material builds upon itself. You expect that it will take twelve years to learn math and you should expect that same step-by-step progress in learning music. There will always be the next level to attain no matter how good you are. That's what music and learning are all about.

"But it's such a waste of time to play the same piece over and over."

Practicing one piece makes all your technique better, so the work you do on learning a beginning piece today will pay off by giving you the technique to play a harder piece next month. Short-term successes have a long-term effect.

"But being good seems so far away."

To keep motivated during the "long haul," set small attainable goals and give yourself a reward: "When I get these eight measures right I'll take a break; when I finish my etude I get to play the duet; when I can get the tempo up to 120 I will go to another section; when I can make every breath on this page I'll eat a cookie (my favorite). Congratulate yourself for larger achievements such as finishing the etude book, playing in the recital, or just making it through another year of lessons. As in losing weight, think about the next five pounds, not the next fifty, and give yourself success along the way.

"But I practice and Nathan's *still* better than me."

Just as in any endeavor, science or soccer, people progress at different rates. You aren't going to quit the soccer team if you aren't the best player, nor will you drop out of the science class if the student across the aisle scores better on the first test. Try to accept your skill level no matter whether it is as good as the next guy's or where you really want to be. I've had students who started out great the first six months and then stagnated in their development, and others who seemed "hopeless" but turned out to be superstars. It is good for teachers to keep this in mind as we look at struggling beginners. You never know!

Practice Hint Seven: Practice with Focus and Concentration

"What was I supposed to be thinking about in this piece?"

"I can't remember because I have so many ideas in my mind at once. What are the sharps in B major? How do bees fly? How many beats in a dotted quarter note? How many quarters will it take to buy that baseball mitt? How many counts does this rest have? I deserve a rest from all this thinking."

There is no substitute for time and repetition, but you can cut down on both with concentration. (No, practicing in front of the TV during commercials won't cut it.) We've all read a page in a textbook five times with no retention because we were dreaming about something else. Keep your mind on the task at hand and make every minute count. I call this type of practice "microwave practice" because it is concentrated and goes three times as fast.

Sayoko, who first started playing flute as an adult, observes,

Learning to play an instrument is like learning to drive a car. There are so many things to think about at the same time! How am I going to shift gears? How can I look in the front mirror and the side mirror? Which lever is the turn signal and which one is the windshield wipers? How am I supposed to think about the notes, rhythm, dynamics, pitch, and vibrato all at the same time? I have to really keep my mind focused so I don't drive off a cliff!

Help concentration by practicing in a room with few distractions—and, conversely, sometimes practice where there are many distractions to learn how to ignore them. If your mind starts to wander, bring it back to the task on hand. Try to gradually increase the amount of time you can go without other thoughts sneaking in.

Timing is everything

"I can't concentrate that long."

Practice at the right time. Focus on your practice or wait until you are ready to concentrate. Don't practice if you're upset or worried or overly tired or hungry. (OK, OK, you're not *always* worried, tired, or hungry!) Break up your practice sessions. Even a few minutes' break can help clear out the cobwebs: walk around the house, step outside, pet the dog, feed the cat, grab a cup of tea, do some stretches, or play another song for a few minutes before returning to the task at hand.

Don't make the mistake the first time

"I keep making different mistakes."

A mistake isn't just an accident; it's a *possibility* you have given your brain. If you are learning the driving route to a new place and go a different way every time, your brain will understand each way as being a correct choice and will be paralyzed with indecision under pressure. "Do I turn left at the light, or right? Do I go past the school or turn before it?" Making mistakes in music leaves your brain similarly befuddled. "Which fingering should I use? Do I shift into fifth position here or stay in third? Where should I pedal? Where should I breathe? Should I be playing at the bow tip or at the frog? Was that an F-sharp or F-natural?" It is very hard to unlearn mistakes and bad habits, so try not to make them the *first* time.

Let the metronome and the tuner be your at-home teachers. Always keep them by your stand and rely on them for accuracy.

Teachers can help by not giving students pieces that are above their level. If students make so many mistakes and have to take time to unlearn them, they may eventually hate the piece or hate the instrument. (We hope they never learn to hate the teacher!)

Practice Hint Eight: Specifically Mark All Mistakes

"How can I remember not to play that wrong note again?"

Do everything possible so that mistakes are not repeated. Remember, *practice doesn't make perfect, practice makes permanent.* When you make a mistake, mark it! Never practice without a pencil. (Marking with a pen shows over-inflated self-confidence!) So many students say, "I always make that mistake!" "Well, if it was marked, I bet you wouldn't!" However, marking mistakes is not license to write in every accidental, key signature, enharmonic, or high note name.

To mark mistakes:

- For better retention, the *student,* not the teacher should mark the mistakes.

- Don't just circle the mistake but specifically mark what you did wrong. Write in the number of beats, add a sharp or flat before the note, circle the connection, put an arrow up or down for pitch, etc.

- The first time the mistake is made, circle it; the second time, circle it in red; the third time, draw a pair of glasses before the mistake; the fourth time, draw a skull and crossbones; the fifth time, go to jail!

- Try using different colors for each dynamic (yellow is piano, blue is mezzo forte, and red is double forte) or different colors or shapes for tempo changes such as *rallentendo, stringendo,* and *allargando.* Anything to easily draw attention to the markings.

- Don't circle *everything.* If you mark every D-sharp in E major, you will never learn the key signature. Use your brain!

- At the next practice session, first review the marked measures. Practice them first before putting them into context.

- If you don't want to mark up the music, use adhesive notes for trouble spots. When the spot is conquered, the note is ceremoniously crumpled.

- When it's close to performance time, make several copies of the music. Have the teacher mark in only *that week's* mistakes.

Speaking of marking mistakes: A friend of mine played violin in a community orchestra and shared a stand with a fourteen-year-old boy. The music had been used before and contained several markings from the previous performer. Eyeglasses were marked everywhere denoting places to really watch out for. The boy turned to my friend and innocently asked, "What are all those *bras* in the music for?"

Practice Hint Nine: Practice the Notes *before* the Mistake

"I stopped and fixed the wrong note. Why do I still miss it when I start from the beginning?"

You played the E-natural in the long run incorrectly. You noticed it, circled it, and then played the E-natural. You fixed the problem. Wrong. The problem is not the E-natural, but the notes leading up to it. Even if you mentally remember that the note is E-natural, your fingers won't remember. You must practice all the notes in the run before the missed notes to cement the run in your mind and in your fingers. Play the few notes before the E. Now go back farther and practice the two lines before the run and the two lines after. By George, you've got it!

Practice Hint Ten: Don't Practice Everything Every Day

"How am I ever going to get through all these pieces in one practice session?"

Warm-ups, scales, and exercises for basic technique such as bowing, shifting positions, tone, and breathing should be practiced daily, but students can be "spread too thin" by trying to work through every piece every day in a limited amount of time. Choose three pieces out of five, or two sections from each piece, on which to concentrate. Rotate pieces and start at different sections.

What do you do when company's coming for dinner and there's no time to clean the whole house? Just clean the living room, kitchen, and bathroom and don't allow the company in the rest of the house. Similar choices must be made when practice time is short. Come to the lesson with only two out of five assignments prepared well rather then having played through everything with little accomplished.

Practice Hint Eleven: Don't Skip the Hard Parts

"Why can't I just practice the parts I know and wait for my teacher to help me on the hard parts?"

Students are expert at diversionary tactics. They skip the hard spots or even switch pieces so they don't have to deal with them. They surf through the fun parts and put in their time. Stopping at every roadblock is easy and gratifying to the ego because everything sounds good and practice is no trouble at all. But nothing new gets learned. *Don't wait for your teacher; be your own teacher.*

Practice Hint Twelve: Don't Always Play Straight through the Piece

"What do you mean I didn't practice? I played it three times from the beginning to the end without stopping!"

There's a big difference between playing and practicing. Playing without stopping is play; practicing is problem solving. It's fun to hear the whole song, but this is practice, not a performance.

Practice the same way you would memorize a poem, stanza by stanza. Pick a section to work on and be sure it is better before you leave it. When you make a mistake, don't start back at the beginning of the piece or even the beginning of the section. Correct the measure of the mistake and only then go back.

Teachers can get students to focus on perfection instead of distance by covering the second page of a new piece with paper, or even not giving them the second page of the piece, until the first page is learned (or even memorized).

For long-term projects, start with the hard section first; it will take the most time to conquer. Sometimes if I'm not sure whether a piece is a good fit with a student, I will ask for the tricky parts to be learned first. If good progress is made, then I know the piece is doable.

Don't always start at the beginning of the piece at each practice session. Play only a few sections, work backwards from the end or play the hard parts first. Allow yourself a run-through as a reward.

Practice Hint Thirteen: Take Small Bites

"How am I ever supposed to learn the really hard parts?"

Divide the hard sections into tiny parts and take small bites. (We all need to learn this lesson with *food,* too!) Work to focus your eyes on signposts of only one note, measure, or beat at a time; looking at the whole run makes us feel like we are taking off on a roller coaster. Play a difficult run or measure one beat at a time with a break afterward. Play first with each note articulated, then faster, then with the correct articulation, then as fast as possible. Now go on to the next beat or measure. When this is mastered, play the notes in one-measure groups, then two-measure groups, etc. This is a practice trick called chunking. It allows the brain to concentrate on only one small piece of information first. When practicing in small chunks, be sure to put them all together afterward to get the transitions from section to section, and to understand the structure and emotions of the piece.

Chunking is a good technique for mastering long runs with many notes as well. Subdivide into groups of no more than five notes at a time and then chunk them. Subdivide a seven-note run into 3+4 or 4+3. A nine-note run becomes 3+3+3. Thirteen notes might be 3+3+3+4. (Another little trick: For five-note runs think Hip-po-pot-a-mus, or, for the high-browed, I-gor-Stra-vin-sky.) Even when the piece is learned, continue to subdivide for a clean performance.

Practice Hint Fourteen: Chew Slowly

"Why do I have to practice slowly? This is a Presto!"

Don't race through practice; it is not a contest. Practice slow, slower, then slower yet. Some younger students, especially boys, have a really hard time with this. They like to prove that they don't need to work slowly and that they can get good fast, without gradually working up the tempo. (They don't like to ask for directions, either!) Success comes much faster when we play slowly ten times correctly, rather than fifty times fast. Trust me! (And please convince my sons, who want to turn everything into the *Minute Waltz*!)

For faster results, teachers and parents can get this point across by making a deal to trade in one hour of fast practice for 30 minutes of slow practice. Teachers might also give students a speed limit: "You can't play this section faster than MM=92."

Asking for a piece to be played a certain number of times a day can encourage students to play too fast, just to be done.

If you play too fast, you either can't hear your mistakes or are so focused on the speed that you want nothing to interrupt it, and will ignore the mistakes. But while you can fool some people some of the time, you can't fool all people all of the time!

Practice Hint Fifteen: Gradually Build Up Speed

"It says *presto*! How can I ever get it that fast?"

It's a long way from andante to presto, but these pointers can speed the way. First, make sure the piece is airtight at a slow tempo before edging it faster. Any confusion about notes and rhythm will cause it to stay slow. As I said before, chunking is a good way to increase tempo.

Analyze technical problems that may be holding back the speed and devise ways to conquer them. If big octave leaps, flying fingers, major shifts, double-tonguing, or crossing over hands on piano is the problem, take a time out. Use other etudes and exercises to fix the technique, then revisit the piece.

Give students a metronome goal to work toward at home, or ask them to keep a running account of the speed they reached every week. After creeping incrementally up the metronome, they should give the piece an overnight rest to help it sink in, and return to a lower metronome marking.

The teacher can trick students into a faster tempo by holding the metronome so they can't see it. Move the metronome up as they repeat the section. If there are any mistakes, the metronome gets moved back a notch. Without knowing the notch they are on, students will have the confidence to go faster. Surprise them with their accomplishment.

Sometimes try the tempo at a breakneck speed, just to see if it's possible, but concentrate on relaxed hands and fingers (and neck, back, and shoulders). Tension slows down movement, so practice playing only as fast as you can without a clenched fist and a furrowed brow. Playing too fast is a good diagnostic tool, as unreliable parts will fall out under pressure. Take the piece down a few notches from its all-time high for the actual performance, and the original tempo marking will be easy.

Practice Hint Sixteen: Practice Enough
Perfect Repetitions to Ensure Success

"I played it right two times. Isn't that enough?"

A sign posted in my studio reads: "BUT I COULD PLAY IT AT HOME." I remember playing a piece "perfectly" at home then falling apart at my lesson. How could this happen? I theorize that after twenty tries I had finally gotten the hard parts right and considered them fixed, but the little bit of nervousness I had at the lesson made the mistakes come back.

Repetition is insurance, but playing something wrong ten times and right once is not good odds. Don't count the phrase as learned until it can be played ten times right and one time wrong. Practicing is only really over when there is no chance of a mistake.

Repeat:

• A certain number of times (twenty times on measure 40).

• A certain number of times played correctly (five times right, no matter how many tries).

• A certain number of times played correctly in a row (five times in a row with no mistakes).

• For a predetermined amount of time (five minutes on each section).

• The number on the die that was rolled.

• The number your teacher told you.

• Until you can't stand it anymore!!

Motivate students to repeat difficult passages

I can't think of any better way to learn tough sections than to repeat them (correctly). Some phrases may need to be repeated fifty times, but racing through them one after another, making the same mistakes each time, does more harm than good. Try these tricks for making careful repetitions more fun, and read Philip Johnston's book *The Practice Revolution* for more innovative ideas like these:

- Track repetitions on a chart (get your star stickers ready).
- Practice each repetition in a different chair in the house.
- Stand at twelve o'clock of an imaginary clock and play a repetition at each hour.
- Draw a "game board" on a piece of paper; the student gets to move a "game piece" towards the finish line with every correct repetition.
- With every correct repetition, the student colors in one section of a coloring book or uses one more LEGO brick to build a masterpiece.
- Put ten pennies on the stand. With every mistake, the teacher takes away one penny.
- The student stands at one end of the room and with every correct repetition gets to take one step closer to the door—until he escapes!
- Track how many good repetitions can be done in one minute. Each scale or measure played with a mistake must be repeated five times and does not count.
- Time how long it takes them to play all the scales perfectly and work for lower times each week.
- Assign several exercises and ask students to measure their pace using the metronome. Tell them to surprise you at the next lesson with how many notches they have moved.

Practice Hint Seventeen: Try Different Practice Methods

"I played that same measure over and over and it's still wrong. What else can I do?"

When concentrating on a problem spot, try to approach it from different angles. Attacking the problem many ways helps to solve it and keeps the player engaged, interested, and willing to practice longer. Try variations such as playing single notes on stringed instruments as chords to check intonation, playing chords on the piano as single notes, playing without any ornamentation, or writing out hard rhythms in half time (sixteenths become eighths) to make counting them easier.

Teachers: When helping students find a solution to a problem, make sure they understand the general application of the practice method so they can use it in the future. ("Step one: We played with no slurs or ornaments. Step two: We put the slurs back in. Step three: We added the ornaments. Now you know the steps to solving the next piece.")

Use the practice methods for difficult passages (see next page).

Be successful with "programmed learning"

In programmed learning, a simple fact is stated, then the student regurgitates that fact. ("The sky is blue. What color is the sky?") The next small step is added. ("The grass is green. What color is the grass?" Then, "What is green and what is blue?") This method can be applied to learning music. Start as easy as possible and use each step to build.

PRACTICE METHODS
FOR DIFFICULT PASSAGES

FOR EACH:

1. Change the tempo.
Alternate playing notes fast and slow. Quarter notes can be played out of tempo, but slurred notes should be played as fast as possible.

2. Use dotted rhythms.

3. Build the passage from both ends.
Play the first two notes as fast as possible, then the first three notes as fast as possible, then the first four notes as fast as possible, etc.
Then play the last two notes as fast as possible, then the last three, etc.

4. Play one time very very slowly with perfect connections, tone, and pitch. Then play three times very slowly, once more a little faster, once again too fast, then

LEAVE IT!

For beginners learning a new song:
(Work on only one or two measures at a time)

1. Say the note names.
2. Sing the rhythm using the Kodály method (*ta* = a quarter note, and *tee-tee* = two eighth notes; a rest is said "shh"). "Ta Ta Tee Tee Ta" while tapping.
3. Say the note names in rhythm.
4. Say the note names in rhythm while fingering the notes.

5. Play one or two measures three times in a row perfectly.

6. Use this method on the next one or two measures.

7. Now play the first four measures until they feel easy.

Practice Hint Eighteen: Listen to Yourself and to Others

"Are you sure it was out of tune? It sounded good to me!"

It is easier to hear when someone else is out of tune or has a scratchy sound than to hear it in yourself. The answer? Buy a cheap voice recorder. Record yourself at normal speed and then play back the recording at half speed to examine vibrato and connections "under the microscope." Review the recording with a teacher or parent, while watching the music and marking mistakes and places for improvement. Always include in the review the wonderful things about the performance too!

Listen to others

"How am I ever going to sound as good as the CD?"

When you learn a language, you learn by mimicking. Learning music is the same. Ask the teacher to demonstrate, and go to concerts. Listen to CDs, play along with them, or buy Music Minus One play-along CDs. Listening to professionals gives students valuable insights they might pick up on their own. You understand how to play better by surrounding yourself with good playing.

Practice Hint Nineteen: Never Put Mistakes to Bed

Short-term memory lasts about one hour, but long-term memory kicks in after about twenty-four hours and becomes permanent. Always leave the piece with all the right notes even. Make sure the last run-through is good so your brain will store the right information and not the mistakes. Better yet, practice in six-hour intervals—such as 9 a.m., 3 p.m., and 9 p.m.—to really cement learning.

Practice Hint Twenty: Just Do It!

Now that you have learned the (twenty!) basic practice hints, try these ideas for even more successful practice.

If something is hard, make it harder in practice

- To master a difficult high note in a phrase, replace it with a harder note and then come back to easily play the original. For example, if the last note is a high E, play a high B instead. Now come back to the original. Instead of reaching up and straining to get the high E, it will seem easy compared to the harder B.
- If it is hard to diminuendo to *mf,* practice the diminuendo to *pp.*
- Play the piece faster than necessary, and then relax at the required tempo.
- If it is hard to play many notes in a bow or a breath, add to that number.

Work from a point of strength

- When teaching beginners new notes or working on tone, play a note that is easy and gradually stretch outwards.

- Practice first without ornaments to get the rhythm stable, then put them in.
- Of course, play slowly and then build up.

Change the articulation

- Trade slurs for separate notes.
- Slur in twos, threes, fours.
- Play everything tongued or on separate bows, then everything slurred. (This will really help get the rhythm steady and the notes even.)
- If the pattern is four notes slurred, play the first note separately and slur the next three notes. (This helps with a feeling of forward motion.)

Change the rhythm

- Play sixteenth notes in patterns of dotted eighths and sixteenths, sixteenths and dotted eighths, triplets, and whatever you can think of. (This method of practicing puts the focus on different notes and different connections.)
- Put fermatas over difficult notes or notes that are missed in a run.
- Practice by putting one big pulse on every note of a run. Do it slowly then speed up. Gradually transition to accents on every beat, then on beats one and three, then just on one of each measure.

More Practice Tricks

- Practice from the score. Learn entrances, harmonic structure, and when there is freedom to use rubato.
- Practice with just fingers, not blowing or bowing.
- For a grupetto (three notes slurred followed by a staccato note), circle the melody note to let your eyes focus on it and to set it apart musically from the repeating pattern.
- Just because you fingered the note does not mean it sounded. Count on your ears and not just your fingers for accuracy control.

Teaching Tricks for Practicing

- Play the game "Who hears it first?" If students catch the mistake they repeat the measure twice; if the teacher catches it, the measure is repeated five times.
- Concentrate on one aspect of playing at a time. Pull practice jobs (tone, key signatures, articulation) out of a hat and make a game of focusing on one job.
- Line up ten candy hearts or M&Ms on the stand. Choose a focus such as dynamics or key signatures. Each mistake means the teacher gets to eat a candy.
- Ask, "What do you think I am going to say about that phrase?" Reading the teacher's mind can be a good thing *most* of the time!

FIFTEEN

Musicality Makes the Difference

WHAT IS MUSICALITY?

Musicality is the difference between typing and communicating. It combines the elements of phrasing, dynamics, rhythm, articulation, vibrato, tempo, texture, timbre, and tone. It blends individual interpretation, musical rules, and styles of musical periods and composers. Musicality requires yet another crucial ingredient: *emotion.* Emotion puts excitement and meaning into every note. When we play musically we succumb to the emotions of the music and share them with our audience. When we play musically, we show our audience we are in love with the music, and we persuade them to love it too!

My former student Brooke, who is now a music major, describes musicality from the heart. "For six years I played as all beginners are taught," she recalls:

> I read the music, fingered the notes, and produced a sound. Then I changed teachers. She changed my flute playing, and ultimately my life. She helped me see that I had completely missed the essence of music. My music was dead.
>
> To me, music had been black notes on white paper and my playing reflected that. I never realized I could play the music and simultaneously *feel* it! A whole new world opened up to me. I discovered phrasing, contrasting styles, and emotions. I discovered that music is not just sound; it is a *lifestyle* which completely envelops the listener and performer. People outside a musical lifestyle don't understand why we can be so involved. But we have been to the other world of music and back, and in doing so have tasted a little bit of heaven.

Can Musicality Be Taught?

Many teachers feel that musicality is the "frosting on the cake." "I'll wait to talk about musicality," they say, "as soon as the student can play this sonata . . . or is in book three . . . or has had lessons for four years . . . or is 13 years old . . . or *when hell freezes over.*"

Can we teach someone to play musically or is it an innate talent? "Yes," to both questions. Teaching the natural-born musician is like opening doors in the house where they live. You demonstrate, they walk in and say, "Aha!" Other students may take longer, but they too can be taught step by step. They will gradually learn to generalize rules they learn to all music, and begin to express themselves. So don't wait! Start right away to make musicality the foundation of *every* lesson.

As difficult as it may be to teach beginners to be musical, it is equally difficult to talk about musicality without demonstrating with live music, but I will give it a try. Consider the following information suggestions, not rules. Music isn't math, and performers should put their own distinct stamp on the music.

How Do You Teach Beginners to Be Musical?

Show the similarities between spoken speech and music

Our personalities come out through our speech and through our music. When students play with no expression, speak to them in a dull, monotone voice, placing equal emphasis on each note. (The student will look at you as if you have suddenly become a robot.) Now speak with natural inflection. Notice the natural rise and fall of speech. Hear how most sentences settle at the end and intonation on questions rises on the last word. Between sentences we take a breath. One sentence leads thematically to the next. We take a longer break between paragraphs. Apply all these things to music and you will understand why a phrase is called a "*musical sentence.*"

Create a musical attitude from the beginning

Once again, raise your expectations. Excuses such as, "She's only 8 years old" or "he's only been taking lessons for six months" cloud what students can achieve. Expect musicality on every piece from the beginning. Simple tunes played musically will be much more inspiring for beginning students. When beginners can play three notes, practice playing them smoothly. Sing while the student plays or sing the beginning songs together to teach phrasing, connections, and breathing.

When students wonder why they must also play purely technical pieces musically, remind them that scales and etudes practiced unmusically will result in literature being played unmusically too. Every note is a rehearsal for the real thing.

Listen to good music

Imagine you wanted to learn to speak Japanese. Where to learn it best? Why, in Japan, of course! Practicing one hour per week with a Japanese tutor would help but if you only heard Japanese in that one hour, progress would be slow. Similarly if the only Japanese you heard was in the fractured accents of fellow students, their bad habits and bad grammar would hold you back. The same reasoning applies to music. The best way to learn to play musically is to listen to people playing musically.

Encourage students to listen to classical radio and CDs and to attend concerts. Play lots of duets so students can blend into your sound and phrasing. Even if it is "Oats and Beans," make sure you play with the same tone, phrasing, and excitement you want your students to use. Encourage students to practice with a pianist (easy if the teacher plays piano), play along to accompaniment CDs, or use computer accompaniment programs. Playing in ensembles is also one of the best ways to teach students how to listen to and imitate others.

Provide other tools

Start with a solid technique. As I know from playing violin, even if you know how you want it to sound, if you don't have the technique, no one else will know! Always play scales, arpeggios, and etudes musically. Listen for tone, tone color, dynamics, connections, and articulation that will translate into real music. Don't ever fall into the speed trap, thinking playing fast and making no mistakes is making music. That's just moving fingers.

Discuss the music with your students. Tell them about the composer and the period, and give them an image to grasp. "Silent Night" and "Flight of the Bumble Bee" are obvious examples. Teach musical terms, which give insights into the composer's wishes. Words such as *amabile, cantabile, brilliante, giocoso, deciso,* and *maestoso* help set the mood.

Check posture and position. Musicality comes from the whole body, not just the fingers. If students stand stiff-legged, sit rigidly or slumped over, or have bad hand position they will find it harder to express themselves. Consider videotaping so they can see how they look and sound.

Musicality Is Many Notes on One Gesture

Listen to the beginner playing a scale. One note trudges after another, sometimes with a big break in between notes, an accent on each one and no feeling of motion or connection. The music sounds as if the time signature is 1/4!

Now listen to the professional. We hear many notes grouped together as in one thought, even on a scale. When we talk about phrasing, we are talking about grouping notes together in a musical sentence. Even staccato notes need to feel connected.

One way to feel notes as groups is to think in fewer beats per measure. The fewer pulses you feel the more flow the music will have. If the piece is in 4/4, play it in 2/2. Play 3/4 in one big beat per measure and 6/8 in two beats per measure. Of course slower pieces demand more subdivision, but never with accents on each beat.

Patricia George, professor of flute at Brigham Young University–Idaho, has devised this method for her renowned "Flute Spa" workshop. She uses it successfully for teaching beginners (or anyone, for that matter!) how to feel groups of notes together. Try it! You will be amazed at the results.

To understand and feel the larger musical beat:

1. Stand up and play a scale. Bounce up and down (from the knees) on each alternating note: G (down), A (up), B (down), C (up), etc.
2. Now play two notes on each bend: G, A (down), B, C (up), etc.
3. Now try four notes to a gesture up and down.
4. Next, instead of bouncing up and down, move back and forth with each group. (Even pianists can move.) Put one foot ahead of the other and lean forward for four notes and backward for the next four. This more closely parallels the movement of musicians mirroring the phrase with their body. Pianists can still move slightly back and forth with the phrase.
5. Now extend those four-note groups to eight. Eight beats forward and eight beats back.
6. Now do the same grouping but only move forward on each phrase. Eight beats forward, then move back quickly and play the next eight beats forward. These eight beats can then be extended to four measures or eight measures.

7. Try the same sequence on a song. Think and move in one-measure, two-measure, and finally four- or eight-measure phrases.

8. Another easy variation is to play just two notes on a gesture. Then play three, and build up.

Music Has a Feeling of Forward Motion

Music isn't static. Every phrase has to go somewhere and that somewhere is *forward*. Each note must connect to the next; phrases relate to each other and sections grow into each other. Music with forward motion is like a person who is relating an exciting story. "Wait until I tell you what happened next!"

For a feeling of forward motion:

- Read notes in groups, not one at a time. Just as beginning readers transition from reading C-A-T as separate letters and sounds to seeing words, transition from seeing one note at a time to thinking of chords, scales, and sequences as one unit.

- Think horizontally, not vertically. All music has an invisible arrow pointing forward. (You need special 3-D glasses to see it!) Mark an arrow above the phrase or between phrases to remind students of the forward motion of the music.

- Each phrase has a destination. Imagine playing on an escalator instead of marching in place, or picture a moving train. You may have to jump off to take the breaths or change bows, but you must keep running alongside the train to jump back on. The forward movement cannot be interrupted until the destination is reached.

- Ask students to circle the note that is the climax of the phrase. If they are indecisive, try different alternatives.

- Try to read the whole measure and keep your eyes scanning ahead to the next phrase, so you can anticipate what will happen next and be prepared.

- Lighten up! Phrasing should feel like driving a hovercraft, barely skimming the surface, and only landing at the climax. So many beginners play with a "down" feeling; ask them to pretend to stand on their toes when they play and to play with a light touch.

- The more technical the passage, the more the need for forward phrasing. Thinking forward will actually make it easier to play technical passages, especially those with lots of skips.

- After practicing measures or phrases for accuracy, put them together every day to understand how phrases and sections relate.

- Walk across the room while playing to get the feeling of moving forward toward a destination.

- When playing a section with four sixteenth notes to a beat, change the slurs for practice to get a feeling of forward motion. Group the *last* three notes of beat one with the *first* note of beat two, the last three notes of beat two with the first note of beat three.

- Better yet, play as if there are no bar lines.

Music Is Tension and Release

What if there were a book called *Nothing Happened*? The characters would be introduced, every character would be equal, and every day would be the same. No questions asked. No problems solved. The last chapter the same as the first. What a boring book!

Music is like a good story. In fact, it is a *great* story! Music has to have both *motion* and *emotion* to be music instead of just notes. Think of any good story. The characters and the setting are introduced in the first few chapters, but, as the drama unfolds, clouds appear on the horizon. Each successive chapter gets more intense until the tension builds to an exciting climax. The problem is resolved in the last chapter with the good guys living happily ever after. Each musical phrase, section, and piece must create this same tension and release of a good story line. The most exciting part is never at the beginning, and also not necessarily the highest note or the last note either. Build tension gradually to the most exciting part, explode, and then relax.

Body Language

I recently observed an outstanding young violinist perform a concerto. Even before she began to play she started swaying back and forth. By the end of her performance I felt as if I had witnessed a concert on the Titanic! The opposite held true at a concert by a professional violinist. This man held his body so straight during the entire concerto that he looked like a statue with a built-in tape recorder. I closed my eyes to tell whether he was playing without expression or whether his body language made me feel that way. Audiences like *listening* to a performer but also like *watching* their emotions too (that's why they don't just pop in a CD). But to communicate, body language should reflect phrasing and not be random movement.

How many younger players have you seen who tap their foot or show every beat with their bodies? Bobbing on each note will not only tell the audience that you are accenting every note but it will *force* you to accent each note! You cannot play a smooth line while moving your body to each beat.

Conversely, even if you don't *feel* the long phrase, moving your body to the music will cause you to play it as a phrase, not notes. It may feel silly, but to begin to understand phrasing, start moving your body and the phrasing will follow. In general, move forward when the phrase gets more intense and lift up at the resolution of the tension at the end. Watch a video of a famous artist on fast-forward, and you will see their descriptive body language.

To teach phrasing, help students mirror the music in their bodies

- For the very stiff student, begin by just swaying side to side with the music or walking around the room.
- Demonstrate a phrase for the student and use "body language" to show the expression of the phrase: as the music gets more intense and louder we move forward. Tell her to notice this same movement in chamber ensembles, pianists, conductors, and even in entire symphony orchestras. Next have the student model your motions. With a hand on the student's shoulder, physically move her slightly from back to front.

- (This trick is from Amy Porter, professor of flute at the University of Michigan.) Have the student start out with the body twisted to one side and looking backwards. Then while the student starts to play the phrase, put your hand on his shoulder and gradually turn so he is twisted to the reverse side. It is almost impossible to accent every beat when you are being moved in a sideways motion.
- Prepare the first phrase with the body. Pianists need to prepare with the fingers touching the keys first, followed by a relaxed and slow wrist drop. String players need to breathe and lift the bow. Wind players need to take a deep breath in tempo and mirror the emotion of the piece with body language.
- Practice good posture and movement. The mirror is an honest teacher. How about an Alexander Technique lesson?
- A firm core is necessary to support long phrases. Tighten up your gut but not your shoulders.
- Be careful of becoming too stiff and tight when playing loud, dramatic music. The feeling of the music needs to be mirrored in the body but tightness will not only ruin the music, it will ruin your body too.

Helpful Hints for Phrasing

- *Every note is important.* Sink into every note so that it means something and can be heard. Every note is like a word in a solemn vow, not like reading the lunch menu. Putting words to music helps students think about every note and emotion.
- Be sure to play the last note of the phrase to its full value, with beauty and vibrato. Don't chop it off because of a breath or bow change. Cut off on the downbeat of the rest. The phrase end is like the last bite of a delicious meal to be savored.
- Be aware of what's going on around you in the piano accompaniment or in the other instrumental parts. Be conversational.
- Work on technique so it doesn't hold you back musically.
- Sometimes we can make up for lack of breath or technique by our style and contrasts. We can play more slowly or take additional breaths or bows if we put in lots of accents, phrasing, and style. If your playing is exciting and involved, the tempo won't matter so much.
- Wide intervals are usually expressions of soaring emotions. Use lots of expression in big leaps and emphasize the bottom note before the high leap.
- When the phrase end is a descending pattern, make the ending feel ascending. Lift your instrument to lift the phrase. (Sorry, this doesn't work on the piano!)

MUSICALITY AND DYNAMICS

If you want to get someone's attention, *whisper.* Or SHOUT! Dynamic contrast is what counts and is one of the most important of the elements that make classical music interesting. When I am listening to classical music on the car radio with my husband (who likes everything soft), we are constantly adjusting the dial because of the rapid fluctuations in dynamics. He turns it down when it gets loud and I turn it up when it gets soft. Beethoven, with his rapid changes in mood and dynamics, keeps us busy.

How do you imagine Beethoven himself might have played? He was a wild and crazy guy, and we must be too! Classical music can give shy people the courage to come out of their shells. This is *not* the time to be subtle.

Helpful Hints for Musical Dynamics

Playing loudly
- A certain dynamic level is necessary for the audience to feel you are playing to them and to become involved. Play loudly enough in exciting music that the listener feels a part of the "surround sound." Ask students to play scales and other technical exercises at a full-bodied volume to get used to projection.
- Help shy students capture the feeling and physical demands of playing very loudly by having them pretend to yell to the next house or at their siblings! (Never at their teacher!)
- Let the orchestra play the full range of dynamics, but the soloist in a concerto (especially flutists and cellists) must usually be strong. The cadenza is the chance to play very softly to capture the audience's attention. There is a difference between tutti and solo dynamics.
- Play all the way through the last note of a big *forte* phrase as though you are running full tilt into a wall. Keep the support and intensity going to the very end. Sometimes thinking of putting a stinger on the end of the last note will help keep the intensity.
- Sometimes you must contain your power. No one pays attention to someone who yells all the time. Remember, music is about tension *and* release.
- Never play louder than you can play beautifully.

Playing softly
- Don't slow down on soft passages and speed up on fast ones.
- When the last note of the phrase end is descending, play it softer.
- A pick-up is softer than the note it leads into.
- To give a sense of forward motion to a very long note, start out very softly with no vibrato, add vibrato, and then add volume and widen vibrato. (Be careful not to overuse this trick.)
- Don't automatically put a diminuendo on every phrase end.

Crescendo and diminuendo
- Dynamics are an expression of emotion, not an end unto themselves. Playing loudly and softly means nothing without the feeling behind the dynamics. Don't just turn the radio dial up and down; turn the emotion knob up and down too.

- Generally, each note crescendos to the next in a phrase. Gradually crescendo to the climax of the phrase so the climax note doesn't stick out, but is the culmination of the previous notes.
- Crescendo on repeating notes or phrases like your mother calling, "Come here. Come Here! COME HERE!!"
- Put lots of excitement in ascending chromatic scales.
- Crescendo through the rest to connect phrases. Make sure the first note of the second phrase is louder than the previous note. If you come in softer than before the rest or a breath, it will feel like a new beginning.
- A crescendo or diminuendo refers to the next level down or up; it does not necessarily mean to play as loudly or softly as possible.
- When you see the word crescendo, immediately start softer, and then crescendo. This dynamic contrast will make the music more exciting .This trick can be used not only for one phrase but for a long section that gradually crescendos. Find places like the beginning of a run or after a rest to back off and build again.
- Crescendo like the bell of a trumpet. Play a gradual crescendo, then flare out at the end. On a wind instrument use most of your air on the last few notes, and on a stringed instrument, save your bow to the end and then move it quickly.
- Don't let changing dynamics change the pitch.
- To help students notice dynamics, mark them in different colors. *Forte* seems bright red and *piano* is light blue. Or mark all dynamics in one color and all tempo markings in another to make them stand out.
- Pretend there is a volume meter (or actually pick up one from Radio Shack). Play a *forte* passage. Now make the needle jump up to *ff* and *fff*.
- Assign a number to each dynamic. In a series of "hairpins" (soft/loud/soft) on a gradual crescendo or in a sequence, the numbers might go 1-3-1, then 2-4-2, and 3-5-3.
- Practice pieces at home with the correct dynamics. Never just run through the notes, waiting until the performance to play softly and loudly, or you won't feel the dynamics and may run out of steam in the performance.

Matching dynamics
- Don't play loudly on long notes and automatically play softly on short notes! This is such a common problem and it breaks up the phrase.
- Don't play louder on slurred notes than tongued or bowed notes.
- Trills must match the dynamics of the rest of the piece. In Baroque music, lean into the upper note of the trill first.
- Sometimes practice being only analytical. Play *exactly* what is on the written page. If it says *mezzo forte,* don't play *forte.* If it says crescendo on beat three, don't start the crescendo on beat two. Let the composer do the work for you.
- Counteract the natural volume tendency of your instrument. (Pianists are lucky here.) The flute is naturally louder at the top so sometimes we need to crescendo

as we go lower so the bottom doesn't drop out. The bow is naturally louder at the frog, so work harder at the tip to keep the volume even.

Accents

Phrases and sections need changing dynamics, but sometimes individual notes need an extra kick too. When I was young, my mother had a mixer with several speed settings and a button called "burst of power." You chose the appropriate setting but pressed the "burst of power" when you hit a lump. Many phrases need a "burst of power" on the climax of the phrase or on a special note that you love. Bring out individual notes with special accents.

Remember to play accents in context. An accent in a *forte* section can mean "Give it all you've got," but an accent in a soft, lyrical phrase can just be a warm bump. Using a tenuto mark instead of an accent can make the accent feel part of the phrase instead of a sudden shout. Remember, accent important notes, not the notes on the beat!

To accent a note, vary:

• Volume (softer or louder)

• Vibrato (faster or slower, wider or narrow)

• Articulation (a harder or softer attack)

• Length (makes it longer or shorter, or play a fermata)

• Tone color (clear, edgy, unfocused, using a harmonic, or playing on a different string)

MUSICALITY AND EMOTION

Twelve-year-old Anna has a new idol:

> I went to Sir James Galway's concert and it was totally amazing! I could tell what he was trying to say with his music. He didn't sound at all nervous and by the way he played you could tell if the song was sad or upbeat. He seemed so happy in his playing even when he played sad songs. He was totally present in the moment. It seemed like he was in the heart of the music. When he played, I could picture it. He almost made the music come to life like it was real.

Music is about feeling, not just moving fingers; if you are not emotionally involved, your instrument is just a machine. Say to your student, "You are not a dull, boring person, so don't play like one!" Be "in the box" technically, but "out of the box" emotionally, to connect with the music. In addition to the topics covered above in forward phrasing and changing dynamics, try these tricks to make the music more exciting.

To build excitement:

• Don't let up between phrases. Use a steady air stream or bow tension. As mundane as this sounds, this is *very* important.

• Change the vibrato speed. Use faster vibrato when it is exciting and slower vibrato for contrast in the surrounding parts.

• Play with your whole body. Support! Use more energy and get into it!

- Enunciate each note clearly. Use a harder attack with the tongue or more distinct finger articulation on non-woodwind instruments. Don't forget to rosin that bow!
- Play more accents and play louder. Use a faster air stream or bow and put "stingers" on accented notes.
- Don't play any dead notes! Tell students each note must pass the "heaven or hell test." If the note is vibrant, you go to heaven; if it does not pass the Excite-O-Meter, you know what happens!

Teach Students to Feel the Music

Even from the beginning, ask students to choose a feeling (excited, nervous, angry, urgent, wistful, innocent, melancholy, etc.) for a piece. A fun way to get started is to ask them to choose one of the Seven Dwarves for each piece or section. "Does this sound like Sleepy, Happy, Grumpy, Dopey, Bashful, or Sneezy? Or Doc?" (P.S. Don't have vibrato like Snow White's!) For the student who is not creative, collaborate with them to make up a list of mood adjectives.

To help students feel the emotion, ask them to pretend it is a scene from a movie. "What's happening on the screen here?" Or ask them to imagine scenarios involved with different emotion. Angry: Your brother just stole your diary and is reading it to all his friends. Melancholy: You remember all the good times you used to have with your best friend until he moved away. Ecstatic: Your parents decided that since you had such a great year of practicing they would take you and ten friends for a week at Disneyland!

Ask students to pretend to write a friend a long letter describing the action and the moods of each section of a new piece. Make up words to sing with solos so that every note has meaning like the words in a song or poem. I sing these lyrics to the first movement of the Schubert *Arpeggione* Sonata: "Oh, I love him. I love his face, his smile, his grin. I love his mother, and his baby brother. But most of all I love him . . . and his name is Jim." Your students will think you're crazy, but they will begin to play each note like the word in a song.

Even though it is only one student, conduct! They will follow your phrasing just as they would follow a regular conductor's. I find this helps them think of long phrases, movement, and dynamics.

Encourage Independent Thinking

As we have mentioned in previous chapters, teachers need to be careful to not always dictate. There are many ideas of how to make music come alive, as evidenced by all the CDs, performances, and editions of the same music. Teachers can help students be creative. Play a phrase or piece for the student in different ways. Ask, "What are the moods of these pieces? What is the same? What is different? Which one do you like best?" Demonstrate a phrase or piece. "Can you play it yet another way? Can you play it *two* different ways?" Use cadenzas to help free students from the bonds of strictly following the notes.

Turn the tables around. Demonstrate playing very badly. The student must now become *your* teacher. Be very literal about suggestions and do only as you are told. (Ha! Now they see how hard it is to teach musicality!)

If the score contains no markings, students should add them. Where do you think it should get louder or diminuendo? What note should you accent? Should it slow down here? Where should you breathe? Should you play staccato? If there are markings, always be willing to change what the editor (not the composer) has written. Advanced students can use urtext editions so they know exactly what the composer intended and can add their own ideas.

We can express our individuality and emotions with our phrasing. When possible, if a student makes different choices than you might, take a deep breath and acknowledge that they played with their own style. The only absolutely wrong way to phrase is to do nothing. Be brave. Try *something*.

Realize Composers Can't Prescribe Every Nuance

Ask students to imagine they "meet" someone only through that person's photograph. You may get an impression of that person through what you see, but you cannot grasp who that person is without actually hearing them. Composers pass down their written music, but without hearing them play it (darn, don't we wish that was reality?) we have to interpret their notes and put our own stamp on them.

How can the same written music be capable of different interpretations? Ask students to say a simple sentence such as "Yesterday he gave me the flowers and then ran away." Now tell them to emphasize a different word every time they repeat the sentence to see how it might change the meaning and importance of each word. "*Yesterday* he . . . yesterday *he* . . . yesterday he *gave* . . ." Our personal stamp gives the music meaning.

Communicate with the Audience

In high school I acted in a play. I quickly learned my lines, but in rehearsals felt too inhibited to let myself get into my part. (I've changed.) I thought that when the real performance rolled around, I would suddenly transform into an actress. It never happened. My performance mirrored the inhibitions of my rehearsals. Many students feel the same inhibition of expression. I can almost see the protective glass box some build around themselves during contests or concerts. The audience listens to their sound hit the glass wall and fall flat.

Now I realize that it's more embarrassing *not* to get into the role. Instead of ignoring the audience, the best performers invite them in to see the show. The best way to communicate with your audience is to absolutely love what you do. People can feel your joy; don't be afraid to share it.

To communicate with your audience
- Take an acting class or work in a restaurant to get used to interacting with the public.

- Play with confidence. My seventh grade physiology teacher was an older gentleman with a bow tie and a strict attitude. We stood up to answer his questions. One time I answered, saying, "The larynx?" He boomed back, "Is that a question or an answer?" "An answer?" I replied. Perform like an answer, not a question. Sell your piece.

- In rehearsal, learn to throw caution to the wind and play with wild abandon. Don't worry if all the notes of the run are there or if the pitch and tone are perfect. Be an actor! Give yourself to the music.

Teaching tricks for communication

- Stand or sit in front of students while they play. Look directly at them and say, "Play as if you're talking to me." I ask my students to aim their sound right at my forehead. When you're "in their face" like this they can't ignore their "audience."

- Instruct students to imagine the music flowing to the audience like sound waves rolling forward or like throwing a ball to a point ahead.

- Ask students to write a story that accompanies the music and to think of each section as an act in a play. Host a recital in which each student tells the story before playing and gets feedback on the audience's emotional response.

- Practice for someone, even if that someone is a chair. Pretend a judge is in that chair. Play for stuffed animals and posters on the bedroom wall.

Be an Actor

In her senior recital, Melissa planned to play two modern, "inaccessible" pieces. She worried that her musically "naïve" relatives would think it was crazy, modern stuff. "We should *always* play as if we're performing for an uneducated audience," I told her. "They might not understand the style, or the notes and harmonies, but no matter what the piece, they should understand our emotions." Contemporary music, in particular, sounds like a jumble of notes if the playing doesn't include contrasts and a feeling of commitment. Melissa was a big hit at her recital as she "bared her soul." Even her relatives who knew nothing about music were drawn in by her passion.

Good actors and actresses *become* their roles; we have no feeling that they are reading a script. Audiences are not impressed that actors have learned so many lines or can say them fast. Audiences get excited when they believe and feel what actors have to say. If the music is sad, *feel* sad. When it's exciting, *be* excited! Decide what character your piece is, and then play it in that character. Play with your spirit, not just your fingers.

Actors exaggerate their speech, their movements, and even their make-up. We must do the same (except maybe for the make-up part). Many times I will tell a student, "I know you are doing x, y, and z but I can't hear it!" Be obvious and do way more than you think may even be tasteful. Hit the audience over the head and don't be shy. Lose yourself in the music. If you think you are "over the top," you are probably "just right."

Music Is Theatre

Never lose an opportunity to move your audience.

- Play melodies from exciting arias. Pretend you are in full costume on stage.
- Pretend you are your favorite pop singer or your favorite actor. Do they act inhibited, or do you feel they are speaking right to you?
- Feel the emotion in your body. I once watched flutist Amy Porter give a recital. At one point she glared at her accompanist. I thought, "What did that poor man do?" until I realized she was so caught up in the music that her whole demeanor reflected the emotions she was feeling and communicating.
- Remember that in performance, you are on the stage from the minute you walk into the room. Wear distinctive clothing, walk in with dignity, and look like a star.

MUSICALITY AND RHYTHM AND TEMPO

Composers write certain rhythms for certain effects. If we play a triplet like three sixteenths and a sixteenth rest, it won't convey the same meaning. First practice without the instrument and count out loud (COL) to concentrate on accurate rhythm. At the same time, remember that rhythm can be subtly stretched to emphasize the notes you love.

Know the musical style for different rhythms.

- Dotted eighth notes are played shorter than written.
- The second note of a two-eighth-note slur should be lifted.
- Short notes lead to long notes.
- Repeated notes are separated.

Speed alone does not necessarily mean excitement; we aren't racing to the finish line. Know when rubato (robbing time from one note to give to the other) is appropriate and use it for expression.

- Know your tempo markings in order to be faithful to the composer's wishes.
- Keep the tempo steady and don't slow down on soft parts or when the going gets tough.
- Don't be afraid to play rubato in Romantic era pieces. Take time to enjoy each note. But when you play rubato, *bend* it, don't *break* it!
- Practice from the piano or orchestra score to see where solo instrument and accompaniment must totally line up, and to find more opportunities for rubato.
- Ritard before a fermata in the middle of a piece; don't do a crash landing.
- Hold the first note of a run, especially if it is a low note. This gives the note a chance to sound and gives the feeling of confidence. It also helps us to not rush. Try it; it makes a huge difference!
- Slow down on the last few notes of a run to counteract the natural tendency to rush and get it over with. If you feel like you are slowing down, you are probably just playing it in rhythm.

- The great majority of the time, ritard at the end of the piece. A ritard should be proportional to the speed of the piece (no giant ritards on prestos).
- Impose speed limits. Just because you can play it that fast does not mean it makes musical sense or that the audience can even *hear* it that fast.

MUSICALITY AND "BREATHING"

The word *cantabile* means "singingly." (Sometimes I mistakenly write down "*sin*ingly" in my students' notebooks, and the parents must wonder what I am teaching their children!). All instruments must phrase like singers. Play everything, no matter how simple or boring (yes, even scales!), like a song. In the following discussion, the word "breathing" can be interchanged with "beginning the phrase."

Pianists and string players, don't tune out this section! Even though you don't need to blow your instruments to make them sound, you still must make the phrases breathe. Wind players take a breath, string players decide on an up-bow or down-bow, and pianists let their wrists "take a breath."

I once judged a contest and asked the performer how she decided where to breathe. "At the end of each line on the page or every four measures," she said. Employing that same formula in writing would place a period after every four lines or at the end of the line on the paper. It doesn't make sense. Why is the placement of breaths so important? Where you breathe defines the phrases just as punctuation delineates phrases, sentences, and paragraphs.

There are no concrete rules for where to breathe, but here are some places that are a good bet.

General rules for musical breathing/phrasing
- In a rest
- At the phrase end
- Before a pick-up
- In between double notes (two Es in a row)
- When the phrase changes direction (the phrase goes from high to low, then starts going high again)
- After the tonic (the name of the key)
- After a long note rather than a short one (breathe after the eighth, not the sixteenth)
- After a low note rather than a high note (the breath won't be so obvious)
- Between members of a sequence
- After an appoggiatura
- When the piece starts over like the beginning (or when the theme returns)
- After the note that is the end of one phrase and the beginning of the next (some phrases have no distinct end and run right into the next. Breathe after the connecting note)
- After beat one

- Between repeated notes
- Where the composer tells you to!

Helpful hints for breathing musically
- There are two kinds of breaths: to live and to phrase. *Plan every breath* according to the phrasing of the music. The end of the phrase is not when you run out of breath!
- Don't abruptly cut off the note before the breath.
- Take time from the note before the breath to come in on time on the note after the breath.
- Take time to breathe. If you have two beats' rest, use them.
- Make the breath part of the piece. Breathe in the mood of the piece. Don't apologize for breathing.
- Take silent, motionless breaths. Don't gasp or bounce.
- Even pianists and string players should use their breath to prepare an important phrase and at the beginning of the piece.

MUSICALITY AND MUSIC THEORY

Music theory can give you clues to musicality. Truthfully, I was never a big music theory fan in school, but when students understand how learning music theory can help them phrase beautifully and intelligently, they will become more vested in learning it. Even if you don't naturally feel the phrases, there are certain "rules" that can be applied. If you begin to try to phrase "mathematically" using these rules, at least that will be a good start.

What clues does the structure of the piece provide?
- Do sections repeat? Is it sonata form? Is the form AB or ABA or AB-C-AD? Mark the same and different phrases in the piece. It's exciting to return to familiar themes. Make a distinction between sections with a slight separation and then more energy.
- Pick-ups: A pick-up is softer than the note it leads into. Every pick-up should have an "up" gesture.
- Sequences: A sequence is a pattern starting on different notes. CDEC, DEFD, EFGE, etc. (If you want to hear examples of sequences listen to almost anything by Vivaldi, who sometimes used the stencil as a compositional technique.) Every member of a sequence should be louder than the last. Use terraced dynamics (dynamics in steps as opposed to a gradual crescendo). On the first member of the sequence play *piano,* on the second member, *mezzo piano,* and on the third member, *mezzo forte.* Point out the terraced dynamics with a different number or dynamic level. Refer to each member of the sequence as a stair step. Stair step 1 = *p;* Stair step 2 = *mp;* Stair step 3 = *mf.*
- Music *usually* gets louder as it gets higher. When in doubt, crescendo according to the architecture of the phrase by playing louder as it gets higher. The soprano in

the opera never dies on a low note! *But* the highest note is not *necessarily* the most important or the loudest note.

- Crescendo on a note tied over the bar line and add vibrato. (Sorry on both counts, pianists.)
- Crescendo on a series of the same note as if you are repeating the words, and place a slight accent on the last note.
- In the Baroque period, play an echo on an exact repeat, then return to the original volume.
- Chromatic scales create excitement. Usually crescendo and accelerando on a chromatic scale when playing in a freestyle section like a cadenza.
- Pick out the main notes of a phrase and play them musically, then add the supporting (passing tone) notes.
- Accent an unexpected chord or harmony.
- Different chords serve different functions. For example, the tonic (I) chord has a feeling of rest, and subdominant (IV) and dominant (V) chords create the tension and release of a cadence (ending). Study chords in detail to understand their functions.

Accent Non-Chord Tones

Enjoy the tension of non-chord notes and lean into the dissonance. Crescendo on a suspension (a note held over from the first chord when the chord changes, creating a dissonance). Then relax into the resolution when the note changes to become a chord tone. Don't shy away from trills in the Baroque period that start from the above, nonchord tone. Most importantly, learn to spot and hear the ubiquitous appoggiatura.

Recognize Appoggiaturas

Appoggiaturas are upper or lower neighbor non-chord tones that delay the inevitable next note. Appoggiaturas are much like suspensions and usually happen at the end of the phrase, creating a dissonance before resolving into the final chord. Appoggiaturas are everywhere (listen to Mozart), and are almost always the climax of the phrase. Students learn to recognize them quickly by ear when you mark the dynamics and point out the appoggiatura and the resolution. Play the phrase first with the appoggiatura (sounds exciting), then without it (sounds boring). Then end the phrase with the appoggiatura (sounds unfinished).

Here's a fun trick to let students experience the emotional and physical feeling of an appoggiatura: Have them stand in a doorway with the outside of their wrists pressed *very* hard against the inside of the doorjamb. Have them press for about one minute, then walk away from the doorjamb. Their arms, still feeling the tension of pushing (the appoggiatura), miraculously float up when released in the resolution. Amaze all your friends at the next party.

To bring out the tension and release of an appoggiatura phrase, crescendo throughout the entire phrase. Build tension to the appoggiatura and then accent the tension of the appoggiatura with more volume and faster vibrato. The appoggiatura has the only "down" feeling of the phrase. Show the resolution of the following note with a softer dynamic, smoother vibrato, and a lifting feeling. To help the feeling of the release, wind players should blow up, string players should use an up-bow, and lifting the arm weight off the last note will help pianists.

MUSICALITY AND CONNECTIONS

What do smooth connections have to do with musicality? Everything! Stiff fingers and jumbled connections between notes make disjointed music. But gliding from one note to the next will connect the notes and give forward motion to each phrase.

Keep a Gentle Touch

Your instrument is your friend; don't slap it and don't fling your fingers off! Always keep fingers *curved and close*. Winds can practice by fingering without blowing to hear the impact of the finger on the instrument. Take the tension out and don't squeeze the instrument. Pianists should keep a free wrist and relaxed elbows to gently roll from one finger to the next and create a smooth line.

On the other hand, in your effort to have a gentle touch, be sure every note sounds! Be careful of *ghosting* the notes, where the note is fingered correctly but the key or finger does not depress all the way or there is not a strong enough bow or breath to make the note sound. Just because the note was fingered does not mean it was really played. Use your ears to hear every note clearly.

Move Fingers Together

Playing perfect connections makes the space between the notes sound tidy, but can also turn notes into phrases. Think of the notes flowing into each other with no "bumps." Ease one note right into the next and the notes will be felt in one gesture.

When you hear "jungle rot" (those messy fingering slips between notes), analyze what finger didn't move when it should have, and then do the opposite. Circle bad connections and treat them as mistakes.

Helpful Hints for a Steady Air Stream or Bow

Think of each note as being on an escalator, not the stairs. Even pianists can think, "Don't take your bow off the string." Keep the tone sounding no matter what the notes are. A big skip to a high note should not be jerky or separated. It should feel like an outgrowth of the low note, almost like over-blowing the low note or playing a harmonic.

Teaching tricks for a steady air stream

- Play the flute "with a little help from my friends." Student and teacher play the same flute *together*. The student keeps blowing a steady air stream while the teacher fingers the notes. (This is especially "fun" when there is a big height discrepancy!) Doing this team playing allows the student to focus only on the air stream and to realize it doesn't have to change because of short or long notes or different articulation.

• Tune flat and blow it in tune. To get the pitch up, focus on a strong, steady air stream.

• To ease into a smooth register change, add the notes between the skip to practice a steady flow between notes.

For stringed instruments

• Don't clutch.

• Lift the finger you are sliding when changing positions. If you can hear the intervening note, you are clutching too hard.

• Keep the bow speed even.

• Don't allow changing positions, changing strings, or different bowings to interfere with connecting notes.

• Don't let playing at the frog, tip, or middle change your phrasing without your permission.

• New students can finger the notes while the teacher moves the bow. Then the student puts his hand on top of the teacher's. Finally he moves the bow himself to feel a constant, straight bow.

MUSICALITY AND TONE AND VIBRATO

Tone Color

A mother croons a lullaby to her baby, a sergeant barks at the recruit, a young man declares to his fiancée his undying love, a woman wails when told her son has been killed. Strong emotions speak in different voices! Tone of voice, or timbre, also conveys emotional meaning in music. A full-bodied open sound declares, and a round hooty sound conveys mystery. Tone color is especially important on stringed instruments. Each string has its own sound, and the same note played in different positions or using harmonics conveys different meanings. Experiment not only with dynamics, but with tone color, and create a gray, yellow, blue, red, or purple sound!

Vibrato

Vibrato is a measure of emotion and should not remain constant. Vibrato can vary in speed (fast and slow) and in amplitude (change in pitch). Generally, a faster vibrato indicates intensity and a slower one, relaxation. A wider amplitude can be used for a calm part or an intense part. Be careful: a too-fast vibrato sounds like a billy goat, and one too slow sounds dull and lazy.

Teachers should introduce vibrato on long notes, then scales. Next move to a piece with an easy rhythm of whole, half, and quarter notes. Week one, play four vibrations on each quarter note; week two, play three or six; week three, play the piece faster; week four, play even faster and use vibrato only on half notes and longer. Practice different vibrato speeds by moving the metronome up notch by notch and also by playing varying numbers of vibrations per beat. Using scales, play up with three vibrations per beat and down with four, up with five and down with six.

Helpful hints for vibrato:

- Try these forms of vibrato: narrow and slow, wide and slow, narrow and fast, wide and fast. All portray different emotions.
- Use vibrato most of time (if it is appropriate for your instrument), unless trilling or playing fast passages.
- Don't "count out loud" with vibrato. In other words, the vibrato should not be precisely timed to, say, a sixteenth note in the music.
- String players start the vibrato before the note, and keep it going after the bow has stopped.
- Don't start out each note without vibrato and add it later. You can use this trick occasionally but be careful not to overdo it.

Use more vibrato on:

- Higher notes
- Solos, rather than chamber music
- Music from the Romantic era
- The first note of a slur
- Interesting accidentals
- The note before a skip of a fourth or more
- The highest or lowest note of the phrase
- An appoggiatura
- The climax of the phrase
- The note you *love*

Use less vibrato in:

- Music of the Renaissance, Baroque, and Classical periods
- An ensemble (to blend in)
- Fast passages
- Quiet, reflective moments

MUSICALITY AND ARTICULATION

Articulation is about the beginnings and the endings of notes. How hard is the attack and what is the length of the note? Articulation gives playing style. Ignoring slurs and staccato markings can completely change the meaning of the piece. Just as we enunciate words clearly to give them importance and meaning, we must do the same with notes. The attack and length of the note depends on the mood you want to convey.

Helpful hints for articulation:

- Use a strong attack (bow, tongue, and finger) to add clarity to runs.

- Use the lower part of the bow for the best attack. Remember to rosin!
- String players have a huge arsenal of bowings. Learn the best for each effect.
- The larger the ensemble, the shorter the articulation must be. Staccato that is appropriate in band will sound like a woodpecker in a solo.
- Separate a series of the same note with a sliver of silence so each note is clearly heard.
- Know the difference between -, >, ≥, and ^ accents.

Some of these hints for achieving greater musicality in your studio may sound mechanical. But as beginning actors use specific exercises to overcome inhibitions and become expressive thespians, so must beginning musicians learn to unlock their ability to communicate through expressive music.

Soldiers on the battlefield are told that bravery is nothing more than acting unafraid when they are fearful. The same could be said for playing musically. Students learn by "acting as if" they are musical. Before long they won't need to act. These techniques and exercises will allow them the freedom to express their musicality in any way they choose.

SIXTEEN

Multiply the Fun in Chamber Music

Whether you choose chamber music, a duet, or an orchestra, the rewards of playing in ensembles are endless. Ensembles are exciting, challenging, and fun.

You play second violin in the orchestra. The trumpets blare, the drums boom, the flutes trill, and you feel the special camaraderie of musicians united in their efforts to bring their audience great music. Together you bring Brahms alive. It's heaven.

You and your quartet get together to have dinner and then play chamber music. You have played with them so long you can read each other's minds. You're preparing for a concert, but rehearsing is so much fun.

You meet someone at the bus stop. She plays violin, you discover. "Oh, I play a little too," you tell her. "Want to get together and sight read some Mozart duets?" Two months later you feel like best friends with each other *and* with Mozart.

"I don't know any other kids who play instruments," a teen says, discouraged. "All my friends think I'm geeky for practicing so much. They can't understand why I wouldn't rather be watching TV." The teen's problem is solved when he joins the area youth symphony. A year later he and other wonderful, "geeky" kids are bonded by their love of music.

I love to play in ensembles! I am fortunate to play with wonderful musicians in Seattle, and I direct Silverwood Music Ensembles (silverwoodmusic.com). I am so lucky to perform in trios with violin and cello, cello and harp, violin and piano, and in a jazz trio with guitar and violin. I also get to pretend I am first violin in a string quartet. Which is my favorite? The one I'm playing in at the moment.

I've learned so much from playing ensembles and made so many good friends. Ensembles have also given me the ticket to play at interesting places and events. I have had fun performing at a christening party for an antique teddy bear, a cigar smokers' dinner, a party for the Goodwill Games hosted by Ted Turner and Jane Fonda (yes, they were together), a lunch for President Clinton, and a party for an African head of state. I've played with Silverwood Ensembles at business dinners for clients of Microsoft and Boeing, and on boats, in the mountains, and by the beach. And literally thousands of weddings and parties.

For me, playing in small ensembles is the best. I skip the pressure of solo performance and the stress of playing in an orchestra, and I can put my own special stamp on the music we play. If you've never played in an ensemble, you've missed out on a wonderful learning experience and a great time.

If you haven't included ensembles in your teaching curriculum, you're missing a golden teaching opportunity. Most of our students won't be become music majors or professionals. Sadly, many won't even play their instruments once they leave high school. Chamber music can change all that. Give students the skills to sight read and have them play in groups. They'll have more fun and be encouraged to work harder now, and if some day they choose to play in an ensemble, they'll have the skills they need to fit right in. What a wonderful gift you can give them now to encourage "music for life."

Why have your students play in ensembles?
- Ensemble music, especially for strings and piano, is some of the best music there is.
- Performing in an ensemble takes the pressure off each individual and is a great way to ease students into performance.
- Learning to interact with ensemble members is a valuable growing and maturing tool for teenagers. It forces them to "get out of themselves" and communicate with the members of the group, the first step to communicating with an audience.
- Ensemble playing is a great antidote for prima donnas. It forces players to think like a sports team and not like soloists.
- It teaches leadership.
- The skills students learn through ensembles make their solo performances better too.
- It is valuable ear training as each member tries to listen to all the parts at once.
- It's an easy way for students to make friends and for parents to get to know each other too.
- It beats the monotony and loneliness of playing by oneself all the time and adds to private lessons.
- It's a way to teach more than one child at once.
- It's tons of fun!

Perhaps most importantly, learning the skills to play in ensembles may be the one thing that keeps students performing past high school. Once students become good sight readers and know how to "play well with others," they will have the tools and desire to join musical groups and just get together with friends the rest of their lives.

HOW TO BEGIN

If you've never had your students perform in ensembles, the task of starting a chamber music program may seem daunting. Your mind may swirl with questions: How do I know which music to choose? How do I find other instruments to play with? How do

I schedule? How do I convince parents it is a good idea? My first piece of advice for teachers is, relax! Start small; don't feel you have to start a huge program.

Find Ensemble Members

Even young and inexperienced students love ensembles. To start beginners, play duets at the lesson; it's an easy way for students to learn by modeling the teacher's behavior. If students are too shy to play at recitals, play a duet with them to get their feet wet. Even simpler than playing with the teacher is having beginners work with a metronome, anything to get them to think of another part while they are playing. Once you move past playing with the teacher, how about starting only one or two kids? Give the advanced students more enrichment or use chamber music to turn around students who have considered quitting.

Where do you find other students for yours to play with? Call the local youth symphony and ask for teachers' names. Call the school that has the best music program. Contact a teacher of another instrument and describe the student you need a match for and ask if that teacher has a "corresponding" student. Attend a contest and approach students who might be a good match. Collaborate with a teacher of another instrument and share the coaching responsibilities. Even family members can be ensemble partners.

Chamber Music Is Different from Private Lessons

Chamber music means music among friends with no designated leader. As the teacher, try to leave the teaching model behind and work to become more of a *coach*. Having fun at the rehearsals and giving students the skills to become independent leaders is as much the goal as polishing the piece.

There's a lot to think about when playing in a group, so choose easier music than what each member can play individually. Chamber music rehearsals provide a chance to lighten up, so let groups play more "popular" music or music the students choose. Create rehearsals that are relaxed and full of laughter.

Choosing Compatible Ensemble Members

To form a cohesive group, match students by level and within a three-year age range. A precocious 6-year-old may be able to handle the music, but will not fit in socially with more sophisticated high school kids. If possible, match students to those within a twenty minute drive to facilitate home rehearsals. Gender is also important to consider. Grade school girls and boys and some in middle school still think the opposite sex is "yucky." They'll be happier in same-sex groups, while high school ensemble members may appreciate another chance to flirt with the opposite sex.

Let members of a group of about equal strength choose their part at random. Hold the sheet music parts upside down and backwards and let each student blindly choose the part they will play. If a group of like-age students want to play together but differ in ability, look for music with hard upper parts and less challenging lower parts. Don't be afraid to have students switch parts for a hard measure or two if one member is holding back the tempo.

Hold Effective Rehearsals

Tune up. You know the joke: How do you get two viola players to play in tune? Shoot one! Okay, don't go that far. Take ample time to tune at the beginning and retune during the rehearsal when everyone has warmed up. Let one person play the tuning "A" (cello in a string quartet, first clarinet in the clarinet ensemble, always the piano if it is part of the ensemble) and the others take their A from him. Younger players may need to tune one at a time, and then try it all together. It's much easier to hear pitch when someone else plays, so encourage students to help each other. "Was she sharp or flat?" Even though it's faster, don't always use the electronic tuner in rehearsals. If you only rely on the tuner you will learn how to look, not how to listen.

Organize the sheet music. If you're using copies, paste them on cardboard so they can be written on and won't fly off the stand. I always purchase the original but students use copies to mark up. Be sure all parts are from the same edition. Number the measures in the margins. And always come armed with a pencil.

To make rehearsals more efficient, when you go back to rehearse a section, begin by counting off your place out loud: "Before letter B. One, two, three, four, five, six measures." That way the whole ensemble is right there with you at the same time. When counting after letter B, count letter B as measure zero. Say, "After letter B. One, two, three, four," and you are all ready to play. For young groups, decide together who has the important part in each section and write in that person's name. This helps them easily remember who is the leader and when they should play out or be in the background. Point out when two parts have matching entrances or rhythms so they can get cues from each other and be aware of matching articulation and rhythm.

Practice students' parts first individually at their lessons so they come prepared. If possible, listen to recordings so they know how all the parts fit together. Keep the pace fast and don't spend much time rehearsing individual parts. If necessary, help the group at first by counting out loud, next using the metronome, later conducting, and then phasing out so they become their own leaders. If ensemble members need more work on their own parts or time to learn how their parts interweave, arrange for extra rehearsals on their own without the teacher.

Make It Lots of Fun

Arrange for social time. A group feels and plays much more like a group if the members feel they are friends. You'll be surprised how by knowing each other's favorite ice cream, cat's name, and most hated vegetable they begin to think, feel, and play as more of a group. Ensemble rehearsals may be half music and half laughing among friends, and that's the point.

Use humor, especially when correcting individual members. Everyone wants to be an equal part of the group. Kid students by saying, "There goes Alec, he just had to be the center of attention so he played during the rest!" or "Sarah just loves her tone on that D; that's why she held it for three extra beats!" The first few times things fall apart, just laugh. (It might not be quite so funny later on!) Avoid personalizing mistakes. It's easier to hear "Flute 2, you missed your entrance," than "Rick, you missed your entrance!"

Place groups bets: If Sean comes to the rehearsal late, he brings the cookies next time. If Mary Beth plays G-natural in A major, she brings cookies. If Holly doesn't look at the leader at least at the beginning and the end, again her fine is to bring cookies. Anything for cookies and to make the point. I also use bets for performances and have students write on the top of their music: "If the judge says our dynamics are good, Bonnie takes us out to lunch or hosts a hot tub party!"

GIVE STUDENTS OPTIONS

Back off and encourage students to learn leadership through ensembles. Which piece do you want to play? Who really, really wants to play first? Which tempo do you think is best? How short should the pick-up note be? How loud is the part at letter D? Should we take the repeat? When students are given power to help run the ensemble, they develop the skills to continue playing ensembles in the future.

Make the group as independent as possible. Delegate ensemble responsibilities to the members. Let them figure out attire, transportation, copying music, and rehearsal scheduling. Leave the secretarial jobs to them and the teaching to the teacher.

There are many ways you can promote a group identity: Give them permission to help decide on new members and which pieces they play. Let them get creative with an ensemble name: Flirty Flutes, Beethoven's Boys, and Tom's Tubas give the group character. Encourage every member to contribute ideas and to verbalize them. Arrange for them to sometimes rehearse on their own. Create performance opportunities that give them not only goals but happy memories together.

If the group wants to continue over a long period, decide on goals. Do they want to sight read new material every week, keep a notebook of music always ready to perform, look for performance opportunities, or prepare for a contest or concert? How often do they need to meet to obtain these goals? Keeping ensembles together over the years creates group unity and many times lasting friendships.

Avoid Scheduling Nightmares

How do you schedule rehearsals? The easiest solution is to ask one student to stay fifteen minutes after the lesson and the next to come fifteen minutes early, and you can have an instant duo or trio if you include the teacher. If possible, pair students who attend the same school so they can hold extra practice sessions before, during, or after school and might even be featured in a school concert. Students can also trade, giving up their lesson for ensemble practice so there is no extra time or money spent. If you must schedule extra rehearsals for a large group, I have found that Sunday is the best day.

If you're already too committed during the school year, try chamber music in the summer. You could make it a weekly event or designate an entire week for a chamber music summer camp. Summer is also a great time for sight reading parties. The parties can be supervised by the teacher if all the players are in one group. Alternatively, you can hand out music to several groups and position students in different rooms, and listen to the laughter reverberating around the house. Reading parties are an efficient way to choose performance pieces for next year and to get music reviews. Keep a list of students' reactions ("movement 1: fun; movement 2: boring"). You'll know which music to keep and which music to use for wallpaper or for wrapping fish.

Make scheduling easier
- Never let the group leave until they have planned the next rehearsal. When trying to decide on a schedule, ask students to say when they are free instead of getting into a litany of all their other activities. ("I am free Monday, Wednesday, and Friday from 4 to 6, and Tuesday after 7 p.m.")
- If the rehearsals are to be with you, give them a copy of your schedule so they can work around you.
- Set up a phone tree so each person takes responsibility for notifying someone else and it doesn't become your job.
- If one person has to miss a rehearsal or wants it scheduled for another time, that person is responsible for calling everyone. Students may suddenly become free if they have to make all those tedious phone calls.
- Enlist parents' help. Ask them to monitor the rehearsal schedule, make phone calls, provide transportation, and offer their home and help for rehearsals.
- Try trading off lesson times for ensemble rehearsals to avoid extra time for you and extra charges for the students. Week one, the trio meets at Nancy's lesson time, week two is at Jason's, and week three at Maren's. If rehearsals are with students of two adjoining lessons, carve the rehearsal out of the middle.
- Ensembles are an addition to the normal lessons, so don't be discouraged when students devote less time to rehearsals than you would like.

Paying for Ensembles

If ensembles are not during lesson times, decide your payment policy. A few years ago one of my students had three free ensemble rehearsals with me in one week but had to miss her regular lesson because she had a conflict. (She had to stay home to study!) Her father deducted the lesson fee from my check because he said the other times she was there were only rehearsals. (They felt like lessons to me!) Now I charge a per-person fee (no matter the size of the group, so that duets are not financially penalized). A more lucrative method is to divide up the regular lesson fee per person, but that requires more math.

TEACHING STUDENTS TO BE TEAM PLAYERS

The Blue Angels precision flying team epitomizes teamwork. When flying in formation eighteen inches apart, solid teamwork is critical. When the Blue Angels take off in unison, their flight leader sets the pace. Each pilot doesn't measure how fast to go or when to turn; they follow their leader. Even their narrator on the ground follows, matching the rhythm and timing of the leader's choreographed moves. A seamless performance.

Playing chamber music has similar qualities. We follow the leader and collaborate to play as a team. Ensemble playing is great conversation among friends, all of equal status. Someone once said, "It's amazing how much you can accomplish when it doesn't matter who gets the credit." In ensembles, playing the fastest, the loudest, or with unique tone and vibrato won't win you any points. Good ensemble players keep their noses and ears out of the music on the stands and tune in to each other. They learn to think and sound as if one player. This ability to listen makes you—and your students—better musicians. Enjoy a musical laugh. Learn to hear and think as a cohesive group, and blend. Enjoy the high energy of ensemble playing!

Look

Watch one another to begin and end sections together. Look at the other players when you pass off a melody to another instrument and when you play a melody with another player—and when something special occurs, so you can all enjoy the moment. In a large ensemble, if you are looking at a conductor, position the stand so you can see him or her over the top.

Recording with a video camera is an invaluable tool to let members hear their performance and to show whether they really are leading and watching. It even points out those members who are being a little too theatrical. The camera never lies.

Listen

Match tone and tone color: If Sue has a wispy sound and Clare, the leader, a solid tone, then Sue must try to match Clare by playing firmer and louder. Match amplitude and vibrato speed: If the leader has a wide vibrato, then the other players must blend or keep out of the way; avoid the attack of the killer vibrato bees.

Match articulation for attack and length: whoever plays the theme first sets the stage. If the leader first plays the eighth notes short, then all the eight notes are short. If the first player with the theme uses a sharp attack, then the others must follow suit. If the violins play pizzicato, the woodwinds need to play really short to match. Give careful attention to first notes and cut-offs; don't come in early or stick out at the end. The bottom line is: did you start and stop together?

Match the pitch. The only thing worse than one person playing out of tune is *four* people playing out of tune! Mark places in the music where there are unisons or octaves to tune up. The more players on one pitch, the softer they should each play for blend and pitch.

Match emotional playing styles. The violin player in my quartet plays with wild personality and passion. I have to really listen hard to match her rubato and glissandos when we play tangos. To really match each other's style and articulation, practice playing the same theme together.

Match dynamics. If the leader plays the opening *forte,* everyone else should too. Be careful about taking dynamics too literally, though. Sometimes inner parts or lower parts must play louder than their dynamic marking to be heard or softer than marked to allow the melody to stand out. To do this you must understand the limitations of each instrument in mixed ensembles. A trumpet playing with a flute should adjust all dynamics down one notch at least. And remember, the most impressive effect can be when the ensemble plays extremely softly.

Watch the balance. Give as much care and attention to supporting parts as you would to playing a solo; every part and every note is important. Even if you have whole notes, follow the melody-player's lead in phrasing and dynamics and always play musically.

Always know who has the melody or most important material. One tip for students is to mark names in the music, so they remember who the star is at that point, or to color-code when they have the melody or a supporting part. The balance can be affected by placement of players, so experiment with seating for better projection and blend, and make sure the player on the first part is positioned so his sound projects to the audience. Have someone go to the back and middle of the concert hall to judge balance and volume.

Become a team. To sharpen listening skills, practice one rehearsal facing away from each other so each player must depend entirely on his ears and not his eyes.

ENSEMBLE BASICS 101

How to Start and Stop

One year I judged a motley trio of junior high clarinetists. They burst into the room in time to play. Sweaty and dressed in torn jeans and T-shirts, they jostled to see who would stand where. When they were finally ready to start, the leader shouted, "One, two, three, four, ready, set, go!" I don't know if I heard the rest of the piece because I was (inwardly!) laughing so hard. Here's a more subtle approach.

How to Teach a Student to Lead

1. Let your ensemble know what kind of note gets the beat. If you are in 4/4, does the quarter note get one beat, one half beat, or two beats? Before starting, make sure everyone is watching you with instruments in the ready position.

2. Instruct the student who is leading to start with the instrument in "home" position. I tell my flute students to imagine the flute resting on a "shelf."

3. Think of at least one full measure before beginning.

4. All instrumentalists use their breath to begin the piece (even pianists and string players). Breathe on the beat before the entrance and make the breath the length of a beat and in the mood of the piece. Breathe audibly so the rest of the ensemble is assured that this is the time to start. For example, in 4/4 time, with the music starting on the downbeat, you would silently count one, two, three; breathe on beat four; play on beat one. While breathing, lift the instrument a few inches above the "shelf." The cue for the rest of the ensemble to start is when

the leader's instrument returns back to the shelf/home position. You are giving a visible downbeat, just as a conductor does.

5. To cut off at the end, do the opposite. Start out with the instrument on the shelf, bring the instrument below the shelf, and when it is returned to the shelf, stop playing. Make both of these motions fairly small and up and down, not in big circles as though you are twirling a baton. This method is a little hard for pianists (those pianos are so darned heavy!), so the pianist must give these cues with a lot of eye contact and some head motion.

Follow the Leader

When we speak about an ensemble leader, we may be talking about the person in charge who takes responsibility for the group in setting up the gigs, hiring the players, selecting the music, and handling the money. Another definition of the leader of an ensemble is the person who is the artistic director and chooses concert programs and players. Still another definition of the leader is the person who is playing the first part. In the following discussion, we will use the word *leader* to refer to the person in charge *at the moment* in the music and who sets the tempo and style. Even though there may be a designated leader such as the first violin, the clarinet with the highest part, or the piano in the piano trio, these roles change throughout the music as the important line shifts from person to person (even the violas get their turn!).

What is the leader's job?

Listen! Listen! Listen! The leader must be aware of everything that is happening in the ensemble. Communicate this by making eye contact, and expect it in return. Make the beats very clear, especially if you hear something amiss or feel a ragged tempo. When things get unsteady, it is the leader's job to look at the ensemble and nod until everyone is playing together again.

The leader must make musical decisions too. What is the tempo? What is the articulation? Where do we start and stop? As much as he must be strong he must also be open to suggestions and bend over backwards to not behave in a dictatorial manner. Ensembles with all members contributing ideas and interpretation make for good company.

What is the "follower's" job?

Look! Look! Look! Watch for tempi, dynamics, and other cues, and try to be the leader's "clone." Look to the leader for clean beginnings and endings. Match the leader in style and articulation. For clean starts and stops, quickly memorize the first and last measures to give the leader your undivided attention. If you are not the leader at the moment, don't try to set the tempo, tap, or beat time with your instrument.

What if the leader is not doing his job? Diplomatically use "I" terminology when asking for something. Instead of "You are not giving a clear beat on measure 12 and there's no way I can follow you," it would be better to try, "I'm not clear on my entrance at measure 12." Or "Could you give us two preparatory beats instead of one?"

To avoid getting lost

Everyone gets lost sometimes, but you can do several things as "insurance" against falling apart. The first is to know exactly *where* you are supposed to play. Check over the music before you start. Work out the road map. Where are the repeats? Is there a da capo? Where is the coda? If the sheet music is your own, it is a great idea to draw lines and arrows to help remember your way, or at least to circle the coda and signs.

Number the measures in every margin or every five measures. It makes rehearsals go faster and can be a great safety net. ("Measure 39," whispered when you are floundering, makes you glad you could easily find it.) Plan "getting together" spots where you can all meet if you get lost (for example, meet at letter B, where we all have the same rhythm).

At rehearsal, look at each other's parts during a tricky passage or get a copy of the score to see how your part fits in. Request that someone in the group give you a cue on a tricky entrance. A "Look at Ellen" written in your comrade's score can give you added insurance for an unsure entrance.

Now that your eyes are trained, you must train your ears. Always know where beat one of each bar is. No matter what happens during a complex bar or an inconvenient page turn, get back on beat one. Practice feeling beat one when listening to music on the radio. Listen to how your parts fit in. If something sounds wrong, even if you felt you counted correctly, be willing to adjust.

Always pay attention to the other players' parts to get your cues. If you are lost, you can think, "I know what the clarinetist has at letter H; at least I can join back in there." Be extra cautious during long rests, which are dangerous traps. Keep counting during the rests. Use your fingers if you need to (held down low, of course). To keep track of beats and of measure numbers, count "**one**-two-three-four, **two**-two-three-four, **three**-two-three-four." The first number denotes the measure of rest, and the others denote the beat.

Help! I'm lost!

It happens to everyone. How do you recover? Keep going! If you make some mistakes, probably no one will even notice. But if you stop you may cause the group to stop and they won't be happy. Keep beat one in your head at all times and try to stick it out through the rough patches.

How do you get through the hard parts? Listen to the other players. If you can't figure out that tricky rhythm, there is a good chance it appears in someone else's part and you can copy their counting. When a flurry of notes is too hard, play what you can catch. Play note one of each group of four sixteenths and come back in on beat one. (This was my saving trick when I played viola in a community orchestra. Yes, they were desperate for violas.)

Ask for help. If you are playing in the wrong place for more than two measures, look to someone else for help and a whispered measure number. But above all, never let them see you sweat. If you do get lost, never signal this fact to the audience with your demeanor. Keep your facial expression calm and your body serene; you will soon find your place again, and 99 percent of the audience will never know you had any mishap.

Ensemble Etiquette

Ron Patterson, professor of violin at the University of Washington, once played in an orchestra where the violinist sitting next to him kept *almost* hitting him with the tip of his bow. His wife, Roxanna, also a gifted professional, remembers a violist one chair below her who would "accidentally" tip over her music stand. Another friend recalls sitting first flute and hearing the second flute snidely say, "How did you get this job? Do you know the conductor?" One of my students had to deal with the jealousy of other girls when she played solos in her band. To unnerve her while she played, the two girls who sat below her glared and made faces. These players needed to learn some manners! Even if you are not friends, be musical friends when you play together.

Support your team members

- Whether you play chamber music or perform in an orchestra, you're in this together. Everyone shares the result, good or bad. If this is an ongoing ensemble, the number one rule is to come with music prepared. Mark any mistakes you make and fix them!

- Help each other out. If you and another player have the same difficult entrances after long rests, look at each other or silently name the measure number for reinforcement. If someone is lost, point to the place in the music or whisper the measure number.

- Make page turns easy. The inside player turns the pages. Turn soon enough not to miss any notes on the next page. Turn quietly and wait to turn until after someone has an important solo.

- Know orchestra etiquette: In an orchestra, if you have a question, the first person you ask is the section leader. Usually it is best not to ask a question directly to the conductor unless it is an emergency. It's better to wait until after rehearsal.

- Don't practice the first chair player's or the visiting soloist's solos within earshot before the concert. Avoid doing anything that would indicate disrespect, even if you don't admire their musicianship.

- Quit whining about your boring part. Work hard to become a better player, and you'll get better parts.

- If you must carry your cell phone make *sure* it's turned off before the performance. (I'll never forget the look of embarrassment of the face of the cello soloist when his cell phone rang in the middle of the concerto with the Seattle Symphony!)

- Never turn around and look at the person who made the mistake in the ensemble. Don't wince when things go wrong or give any other negative visual cues to your listeners.

- If you play a different part than your neighbor, don't read over his shoulder.

- Don't eat, chew gum, read a book, talk, or do anything that distracts you, your colleagues, the conductor, or the audience. Whether you are sight reading with friends, performing in a student ensemble, or playing in the New York Philharmonic, be professional.

Make friends

- Getting along socially makes a huge difference in getting along musically. Plan some social occasions to get to know each other and solidify the team.

- If there is a personality problem with a member of the group, try to work it out *away* from the rehearsal. Start the conversation out with pointing out all the things that are right, before discussing the things that are wrong. Most "personality conflicts" boil down to different interpretations of members' goals, roles, and procedures.

- Look upon your fellow members as colleagues, not competition. Don't be afraid to ask for help and pay compliments.

- If you'll be even five minutes late, call to let them know you are coming.

- Try to schedule rehearsals with more than twenty-four hours' notice.

- In small ensembles, learn to discuss musical phrases, dynamics, and articulation. Try things different ways and agree as a group on your interpretation. Even if there is a leader in a small group, democracy can work.

- Be diplomatic about offering suggestions. Instead of saying "you," try to substitute "we": "We always seem to slow down at letter D." "We're out of tune in the soft section." "It's hard to hear the melody in measure 12."

- Every moment you are on stage, you are on display. No frowning, no flirting, no fighting. Use your best posture and smile to look like you're having the time of your life.

- Don't talk incessantly about all your other "more important" ensembles or gigs and how wonderful you are in them.

- Have fun!

For the professional: Etiquette tips for success in the job market

- Return calls promptly.

- If you have to cancel, find a replacement immediately.

- Try to always answer "yes." If you are unavailable most of the time, they will probably give up on you.

- Take turns playing the top part.

- When you have to drive to a gig, know where you are going. Get clear directions. Learn to use the www.mapquest.com website. If necessary, make a trial run the day before so you won't be lost or late. Allow extra time for those traffic jams.

- "Early is on time, on time is late, and late is unacceptable." Don't make the people in charge worry about you. It's better to arrive early for the gig and read a book or magazine for fifteen minutes than to be fifteen minutes late. I *used* to hire a violinist who arrived at the last second. As we were tuning I was madly calling him on my cell, and moments later he would saunter in! He was a wonderful player, but I couldn't afford more heart attacks.

- Bring everything you need. Don't expect someone else to bring your stand or your stand light, your music, water, snack, or pencil. String players need extra strings and mute, and cellists a "doughnut" endpin holder. Unless your mother is on the job with you, be self-sufficient.

- Dress professionally. (No ring around the collar or unwashed hair.)
- Pay attention. Keep your eyes on the conductor or ensemble leader and not on the audience. (I admit the beautiful dresses in the audience sometimes distract me.)
- If the "performance" is only playing background music in a noisy, crowded room, play your best even though it seems no one is paying attention. That party might be the occasion when the Nordstrom executive hears you play and signs you for the company's private parties.
- Offer to help put the chairs, stands, and music back. Do everything possible to make the life of all the members fun and easy.
- Say "thank you" to your contact person before you leave the job. Express your pleasure in playing, not just in the check.
- Even when you get paid, ensemble playing is still about having fun!

Nothing is more fun than making music together. Through chamber music, your students become better musicians, gain new friendships, and grow to love music even more. That all adds up to a greater commitment to their instruments and their lessons. And don't forget to include the joy of playing chamber music in your own life. Go ahead and take the plunge!

SEVENTEEN

Take the Fear Out of Memorization

Opening night is finally here. You step out onto the large dark stage packed with waiting orchestra members. You face the audience, take your bow, and sit at the piano ready for your part to begin. As the orchestra soars through the magnificent introduction, you lift your hands to play the first note. Then suddenly your mind is a blank. "What note?" you inwardly scream. The audience gasps and stares. Your hands hover above the keyboard as the orchestra races on without you. Sweat forms on your brow. The audience titters. The director puts down his baton and the music stops. Everyone glares at you. You dash off the stage without looking back—never to play the piano again!

Shaking violently, you wake up in a cold sweat from this horribly vivid dream the night before the performance. A nightmare! And anyway, you don't even play the piano. You're a clarinetist, for heaven's sake! Immediately you panic about forgetting the clarinet concerto you've memorized.

Is memorizing a nightmare or a necessity? Does it help with performance or add to effort and stress? Yes. Memorization impacts a performance. Many people feel that they perform much better when the "music is in their head instead of their head in the music." Playing from sheet music is like reading from a storybook. The story is there, but something is in the way: the mechanics of reading. A performance played by memory feels to the audience as though the performer is telling his personal story, without the distraction of the middleman.

On the other hand, I sometimes think too much emphasis has been placed on memorizing. Even superstars performing concerti with orchestras sometimes play with the score in front of them. If students playing by memory feel nervous or can never quite get it together, allowing music makes perfect sense. Weeks and weeks of lessons spent on drilling memory seem like a huge waste of time. Some contests require memorization (almost all for concerti), but for nearly all judges, while memorization is a plus, playing with the music doesn't lower their rating. My choice is to teach all students *how* to memorize, but not necessarily require they all perform from memory.

ARE MEMORIZATION SKILLS INBORN OR ACQUIRED?

Some lucky students naturally memorize with the repetition of normal practice. Others must painstakingly learn a piece note by note, and this ability is not necessarily in proportion to the student's level of overall talent. Though it comes easier to some than others, we all have the capacity to memorize.

Make memorization part of your expectations for students from the beginning, and most will accept the challenge. I ask beginners to memorize a short piece every week. At the lesson the student stands up in front of me and the parent, announces his name and the piece, performs, bows, and then is rewarded with tumultuous applause.

Four main ways to memorize:

- Memorize the intervals or how the piece sounds.
- Memorize how the music looks, like taking a photograph.
- Digitally. Let your fingers do the walking. (This is the scariest, because if something breaks the sequence of fingers then you are sunk.)
- Theoretically. Analyze patterns such as the scales, sequences, and arpeggios.

HOW DO I MEMORIZE?

Start Small

As with other programmed learning techniques, start easy and build. Memorize an easy, structured piece before a more adventurous one. Look for a piece with lots of scales and arpeggios and repeating patterns.

Memorize music the way you memorize a poem. Learn the first two lines, then the next two lines, and then put all four lines together. Memorize one section the first day, the next section the second day, and then review.

As with all practice, slow and steady wins the race. Make sure fingering and notes are excellent so nothing needs to be "un-memorized." Make careful note of pedaling, bowing, shifts, hand placement, phrasing, articulation, and dynamics to establish correct memory patterns.

Use Your Pencil to Remember the Structure of the Piece

Write the analysis of the music in the part. Name the scales, arpeggios, intervals, cadences, key changes, chord progressions, sequences, repeats, and form. This is theory in action. Write down as much as possible about the piece without playing it. Pretend you are talking on the phone or writing a letter about this cool new piece and want to relate every juicy detail. "Letter B is in G major and starts on a D. It has a repeating pattern of three notes up then skip a third down. The fourth phrase starts on an E, the next phrase on a G, and the next on an A." Use this as a general framework for memorizing.

Label phrases that are *almost* alike. Even silly names like Oscar (starts on a G and ends on a D), Big Bird (starts on a G but ends on a C), and Cookie Monster (starts on a B and ends on a D) can help differentiate similar parts. Analyze every memory mistake. Did you mix up the sections? Does this phrase go up and the next down? Did you miss only two notes in the run or the whole run? Clearly mark every mistake.

Use Good Time Management Skills

Start memorizing from the moment you start learning the piece. It is foolhardy to practice the whole piece and then count on memorizing it three weeks before the performance. I often won't let students proceed to the next page until they've memorized the current page, to keep their memory work on target. Divide the piece into small sections to tackle, and set daily goals that are marked on the calendar for a countdown of weekly practice goals before the big performance.

Don't expect memory work one day to be perfect the next day. But be consoled that even if you have to start again from scratch, your learning curve will be faster the second time. Always review before adding on new material, and practice transitions between sections so you not only know what to play but in what order it appears. To solidify a memorized piece, put it in the "freezer" for a few months and then thaw it out for the final touches.

Approach Memorizing from Different Angles with These Tricks

- Cut the piece of sheet music into sections and put them in a bag. Pull out a section from the bag and start to play there. This gives practice in starting anywhere, so if there is a memory slip, students won't need to retrace to the beginning.
- Memorize the letter or numbering system of the music for fast reference if you get lost. When the pianist whispers, "letter F," you know right where to start.
- Practice singing the piece. It's essential that your brain and ear, not just your fingers, know the song.
- Rehearse the music without your instrument. Memorize every note, marking, and fingering. Learn to hear the music in your head as vividly as you would in your ear. Reassure yourself that you are not going crazy when you can't ever get the piece out of your head!
- Practice with the full score and look for cues that help entrances and other tricky parts.
- Listen to the CD repeatedly. Listen in bed, in the car, while brushing your teeth, walking, eating dinner, and anytime possible.
- Play along with the CD or work with the computer accompaniment programs.
- Be prepared to play the piece at different tempi. If you can't play it slowly, you don't really know it.
- Most memory lapses occur during a difficult technical part. Be aware and be prepared.
- See chapter 22, "Prepare Students for Performance." The more relaxed and focused the performer, the lower the chance of memory breakdown.

Test Yourself

- While memorizing a piece, keep referring to the music. Play three times with the music and one time without to make sure your memorization is accurate. Without referring to the music, our own mistakes become our reality. Remember the game called "gossip" or "telephone"? One person whispers a sentence in the next person's ear, and so on around the circle. Inevitably the sentence turns out to be a garbled version of the original. Keep checking the music to make sure all the notes, fingering, bowing, articulation, dynamics, etc. are exact, and not your own rendition.

- Tape-record your playing to pinpoint memory failures.
- Test yourself without your instrument. Write out the music to a difficult section on manuscript paper.
- If you are not a pianist, play a difficult passage on the piano to make sure your memory isn't just finger memory. This helps you see the note names and intervals in black and white.
- If you are a pianist, can you play the piece on a table or on a keyboard with the sound turned off? Can you play each hand separately? Practice with the teacher playing one hand or trade off playing every two measures. Hint: Most mistakes occur in the left hand.
- Make a separate copy or use different-colored markers to circle that week's mistakes at home or at the lesson.
- Practice playing the memorized piece at the beginning of the practice or spaced out several times during the day to simulate only getting one chance during a real performance.
- Play many practice runs before the real concert. It is amazing how distracting an audience can be. If your memory is going to slip, have it be at church or the retirement home, not at the contest. Never play by memory for the first time in public!

Trick Yourself

- Play with the music to see how far you can read ahead, and then turn your head away.
- Move the music farther and farther away on the stand so you can barely read it and are guided by the architecture of the phrase.
- Start with memorizing the last section to make sure it gets as much attention and remains fresh. Remember, those are the last notes the audience or judge will hear. Then add on sections going backwards. As you keep playing, you will always be more comfortable as you move into more familiar music.
- Photocopy the piece in a reduced size and tape it together. Keep it on the stand as a safety net. Glance at the "topography" of the piece to recall sections you already memorized.
- Be patient.

IF I'M NOT LOOKING AT THE MUSIC, WHERE DO I LOOK?

Reading the music not only gives us a safety net for playing the right notes; it also provides a buffer zone between the performer and audience. But what are you supposed to do without that music stand to protect you? Where are you supposed to look?

Closing your eyes during reflective or emotional parts of the piece can be a natural response. It also increases the emotional impact on the audience. Playing with closed eyes throughout the performance, though, has the opposite effect. It makes the performer seem to be in a trance and hiding from the audience.

Looking at the instrument is a safe bet and makes the player seem to be enveloped in the performance. This technique is especially effective for pianists and string players. But flutists who try to look at their instruments will become stiff-necked and cross-eyed!

Looking at judges during a contest is a bad idea. When judges look puzzled or perplexed, or start to write, some performers may become overly nervous or distracted as they try to read the judges' minds or react to the feeling of being criticized. Judges will give you an adjudication after the performance, so don't try to second-guess their opinions while you play.

It's not a good idea for students to watch the teacher, either. During contests, I sit in the back of the room, sometimes with my head down and my eyes closed during my students' performances. They always try to read my expression, and if I burp, sigh, or sneeze they fall apart! Some of my students look at their parents and say this helps them remain calm. For others, this is distracting too.

Looking up toward the ceiling breaks concentration and makes the performer appear to be asking for divine guidance. Looking at the floor makes performers seem embarrassed or afraid. Well then, where *should* you look? Look wherever you feel most comfortable. Change where your eyes rest. If you continually fix your eyes on a particular spot, you begin to look like a robot. Look at the accompanist during crucial moments to keep the ensemble together. During other times, a safe bet is to make the audience *think* you are looking at them, but in reality look over their heads and stay in the music.

Memorizing need not provoke fear and a desire to bolt from the room. The goal of memorizing is not to play it perfectly, but to have the means to find your way back after the inevitable mistake. Even if you are not a "natural" at memorizing, these tricks make it easier and add to your understanding and communication of the music. Give it a try.

EIGHTEEN

Help Students Become Confident Sight Readers

The orchestra was assembled for the first rehearsal of the season. Scores were handed out and the rehearsal began. The music was difficult, yet everyone was sight reading it well. Everyone but the new concertmaster! He looked confused and kept asking for measure numbers and looking at the fellow sitting next to him for cues. The conductor and other orchestra members were mystified because the concertmaster had a fine reputation as a performer. What was going on?

Then, at the next rehearsal, a miracle occurred. The concertmaster played every note without even glancing at his music! What happened? Five days earlier he could barely sight read the notes. How had he learned the music so quickly? The answer: he had learned the music by ear while listening to a recording. This is a true story!

Sight reading is one of the most important skills well-versed musicians can have. When I play gigs, I often work with musicians whom I've never met. We introduce ourselves, hand out the music, take a brief second to look it over, note any repeats, set the tempo, and then we're off! Many times people compliment us, saying, "You play so well; how long has your group been together?" We laugh, look at our watches, and then fib, "Oh, for *years*!"

Sight reading, or sight playing as it is sometimes called, is more than reading music; it's being able to read music *fast* for the *first time*. Good sight readers are invaluable in musical situations such as playing in "pick-up" groups. They also play more musically while reading music for the first time because they can pay attention to phrases and musical nuances instead of just the notes and rhythm. Good sight readers learn music quickly, too, because they recognize repeating patterns instead of seeing everything as new material.

And don't forget, sight reading can be tons of fun! I have many fond memories of sight reading parties when I was in college. Two other flute players and I often made a delicious meal, had a glass of wine, and then played for hours in the kitchen. (The wine and the kitchen acoustics made us think we were really good!) Get together with friends to play new music and you'll build your sight reading skills and friendships.

OVERCOME YOUR FEARS

My friend Judy, a prominent choral conductor in the Seattle area, was asked to give a sight reading seminar to a group of high school choir students. She started out her presentation by asking the group, "What is the *best* thing about sight reading?" The quick reply from the bass in the last row was, "When it's over!" Nonplussed, Judy continued, "What's the *worst* thing about sight reading?" A tenor retorted, "When it starts!" Judy had some attitude- and confidence-building to accomplish that day.

The biggest roadblock to sight reading is attitude. Students look at a piece and think, "I can't play this! I don't know how it goes because I've never heard it, and it's too hard to figure out by myself!" But when children are old enough to read a book, they are old enough to read music and to learn new pieces on their own. The teacher's job is to give them the skills and courage to do so. With the right guidance and practice almost anyone can become a confident sight reader.

In the first part of this chapter, I'll offer tricks for teaching sight reading. The next section helps teachers guide beginning through advanced students step by step through the learning process. I know you have much to cover during lessons, but if you give your students the skills to sight read, they instantly become better musicians. So let's get reading!

HELP STUDENTS BECOME
BETTER SIGHT READERS

We've stressed the importance of teaching the basics, but in sight reading it is *essential* for students to have the information at their fingertips. (Get it?)

Teach Beginners to Read Notes Quickly

Some teachers of beginners only teach students to learn songs by ear, and others just associate a note on the page with a fingering. As soon as students can read words, I think they can read music. When I was in junior high my first piano teacher wrote in the names of every note (and circled the sharps and flats in red) for the first two years of my lessons. I couldn't have been that dumb!

It's easy to teach someone to read the note names. Start with G on the treble clef or F on the bass clef. "See how the clef tells us the name of the note?" Review the alphabet, saying it forwards and backwards. Then expand out from the original G or F. "The treble clef tells us this is G; what is the note right below it?" Write a bunch of Fs and Gs, then keep expanding to E and A and beyond. The student will pick it up in no time.

When students learn a new clef such as alto or tenor clef, don't keep referring to the treble or bass clefs for comparison. "Let's see, the tenor clef is five notes above the bass clef, but yikes, now I'm in treble clef." (I still get confused playing the viola!) Teach them to recognize the notes on their own clef without translation. The same advice goes for enharmonic notes.

Young beginners may need to use flash cards or computer theory programs but most can learn on the spot. Drill students on note recognition by having them say the note names in rhythm before they play a piece, and other times having them say note names out loud or write them in the music as fast as possible. Work especially hard on notes with ledger lines. Always hold students responsible for knowing the note name. When beginning students make a mistake, ask, "What is the name of the note you missed?"

Drill letter names with "mystery words" written with notes on the staff, or have students make up their own "mystery words" for you to guess. Try these mystery words: add, cab, dab, egg, cage, bead, café, babe, fed, beg, ace, bed, feed, beef, fee, bad, ebb, face, fade, deaf, gag, fad, gage, bee, age, deed, dead, edge, added, ebbed, caged, badge, faded, faced, dabbed, bagged, beaded, cabbage. Write sentences on the staff and replace the letters A through G with notes.

Teach Beginners to Recognize Rhythms Quickly

Give a feeling of the beat: Start beginners by swaying side to side and saying "One-two" or "tick-tock." Progress to marching to songs and then saying the number of the beats out loud, "One-two-three." If students have a hard time feeling beat one, play short songs for them or have them listen to pieces to figure out the time signature and clap on beat one.

Use a pencil: Get students in the habit of physically marking the beats, and then transition to mentally marking the beats. Instead of using numbers, draw a straight line precisely where the beat is and where you will tap. To help beginners keep a steady beat, ask them to tap and point to each beat with a pencil to help their eyes track forward as they count out loud.

Practice rhythmic dictation and encourage students to compose their own songs. Hearing a rhythm and writing it down develops the ear and the ability to analyze whether what is written is what was played. It also develops a complete understanding of note values and an awareness of how music is notated.

To increase this understanding, when students make a mistake, always ask what rhythm they played and what it should have been. "I played a quarter note and it should have been a dotted quarter." Or play a measure with a wrong rhythm and have them correct you. Beginners should tap so they feel the beat with their body. As soon as they can consistently tap steadily, gradually phase out tapping (except during very difficult rhythmic measures). Students can clap along as the teacher plays, they can sing the note names and clap, or they can count the beats out loud ("one and two and . . .").

Tricks to fix the rhythm problems:

When students stumble on a rhythm, insist they mark the beats and say the rhythm out loud before you come to their rescue. Please, don't play it for them! Give them the tools to figure it out on their own. Try these tricks: Use words such as "pizza" for dotted rhythms, "ice cream cone" for triplets, and "huckleberry" for four sixteenth notes so they can quickly recognize and hear rhythms. Check out *String Rhythms* by Sally O'Reilly for more food rhythms. If a piece has difficult rhythm, count more beats per measure while sight reading: Play 4/4 measures in 8/8 or even 16/16. For hard-to-understand rhythms, take away the scare factor by writing the notes out in half time with sixteenths transformed into eighths, and quarters into half notes. Get away from the music, and write out and play the rhythm to a tricky measure on one note.

Use Music Theory to Help with Sight Reading

Sight reading is really applied theory. Learning the rules and patterns of music theory is not just an intellectual exercise; it is basic to playing, understanding, and sight reading. Consciously search for recurring melodic or rhythmic patterns. The more second-nature these patterns become, the more easily you will play them in new situations.

From the very beginning, help students understand how music is built and how theory can help in sight reading. Insist they memorize their scales and arpeggios! They should know them backwards, forwards, and upside down and be able to play them from memory and spot them at a glance. Knowing scales and arpeggios helps them read faster and "guess" more accurately. Have them analyze out loud or write the chords and scales above the measures.

Insert theory questions throughout the lesson and especially while sight reading: "What will the next chord be?" "If we are in F major, what is the last chord of the piece?" "The first three notes were G, B, D. What should the fourth note be? (Yes, G!)" "You played C, D, E, F, G, B, and C. What scale is this, and what note did you miss?" "What form of the minor did this phrase use?"

Always look for patterns: Try color-coding to help students see patterns. Make G major arpeggios blue and D arpeggios pink on every dotted eighth and sixteenth, and green on every dotted quarter and eighth, or purple every time the clef changes. If the music is a sequence (or other pattern), ask students to define the pattern and then play the second and third members without looking. "The sequence started on C, went up two notes, skipped a third then came back to C. What would the second member of the sequence be?" (Play Vivaldi to teach sequences!) Be aware of phrases that are "almost" patterns. Pick out non-chord or non-scale tones to see the scale, which is the foundation. "This is a D major chord with an added G; this is a D harmonic minor scale without a G."

Lots of scales help pianists and string players to understand the concept of patterns with fingering and anticipate what fingering will most likely happen next. Help students experiment with fingering and positions to develop the skill to anticipate and use the easiest fingering.

Use Your Ears as Well as Your Eyes

Sing solfège (do-re-mi) to help students hear in their head if a note they played is right or wrong, and to learn arpeggios more quickly. I use moveable *do* because I feel that helps students understand the function of every note in the scale (G is *sol* in C major but *fa* in D major). Show students familiar tunes without the title and ask them to name the tune. Practice playing by ear to increase interval recognition. When asking a student to start at a particular spot in the music, don't name the measure number; *play* the measure so they must associate the look of the music to the *sound*. Trick them by playing a passage and then deliberately making a mistake. Ask them to tell you what went wrong so they learn to compare the *sight* of the music with the *sound*. But beware of students who only depend on their ears. It goes without saying: don't play every new piece for your students or they will never learn how to sight read.

Practice Sight Reading at Lessons

Be sure to include sight reading at the lesson. Start students sight reading using very simple music with plenty of repeats and patterns. Make sure the sight reading music is below their technical ability, so their first attempts are successful. When students are reading a piece for the first time, sometimes have them stop to correct mistakes so you know they are aware of them. Other times have them keep going no matter what. Students soon think sight reading is a great game, but be warned: they may become so skilled that they may fool you at the lesson when they haven't practiced!

To incorporate sight reading into the lesson you can use special books designed for sight reading or read through pieces. For fun, cut a piece of music into small sections, mix up the order, and quickly read the new phrases. Students like the surprise and will understand how patterns make good music. For other rhythm drills, use a white board, flash cards, or computer programs.

Include sight reading in the normal lesson material. Have students sight read a couple of measures from their new assignment. Work through a solo or duet book fast, by sight reading the easy songs at the lesson and assigning the hard pieces for home practice. Use jazz tunes to stretch advanced students' rhythm reading and ear training.

Make Sight Reading Fun

If a student isn't prepared for a lesson, use the time to sight read duets and solos. Make it fun and laugh at mistakes. Give students plenty of new repertoire to learn. If they only work on two or three pieces a year, their sight reading will never improve. Host different kinds of sight reading parties. Create a lending library of fun songs, pop music, or movie scores, and encourage students to play "just for fun" and think about an incentive program for students who participate. Sight read duets and solos that are new to you at the lessons. Share your enthusiasm for sight reading and learning new things.

SIGHT READING CHECKLIST FOR NEW PIECES

Once you know the basics of music and have a new piece to sight read, where do you start? Most importantly, *preview your music first.* If you are sight reading in an audition, don't feel rushed. Always take your time to look for these important elements:

The key signature: Say the name of the key and the sharps or flats to yourself (e.g., key of A major; F-sharp, C-sharp, G-sharp).

Key changes: Be especially careful when adding or subtracting just one flat or sharp or when playing in those pesky keys with six or seven sharps or flats.

Accidentals: Accidentals can be accidents waiting to happen! Remember an accidental holds for the full measure. People often play the accidental correctly where it's marked but miss it later in the measure. Don't translate; think of E-sharp as E-sharp and not F, or the F-sharps will become F-naturals.

Tempo: Memorize the meaning of common tempo markings. Know the difference between *allegro* and *allegretto, andante* and *andantino.* Scan the piece to look for the blackest (fastest) notes, for they will determine your speed. Watch out for words that mean tempo changes, such as *accelerando, stringendo,* and *allargando.*

Time signature: Figure out what kind of note gets the beat in the marked tempo. A quarter note may get two beats in an *adagio,* one beat in *allegro,* and one-half beat in a *presto* tempo. Before you begin to play, mentally mark the beats in the first two measures and in any tricky parts. Count out two measures to yourself before you begin. If the first few measures have divisions of eighth notes, say, "One and two and." If there are patterns divisible by sixteenths, such as dotted eighths and sixteenths, say, "One-e-and-a, two-e-and-a" or "huckleberry" while you are thinking the exact rhythmic patterns of the first two measures.

Tricky rhythms and other difficult parts: Here again, mentally mark the beats and say those tricky rhythms to yourself. Pay special attention to all the measures with accidentals, hard high or low notes, and notes on many ledger lines.

Patterns: Watch out for rhythmic patterns such as syncopation, for scale and chord patterns, and for repeat patterns such as sequences.

Fingering: Note unusual fingerings, including crossing over hands in piano or harmonics on stringed instruments.

Clefs: Beware of changing clefs in instruments such as cello, which uses three clefs, or piano, which can have two treble or two bass clefs.

Repeats: Know the road map before you start. Where are the repeats? Is there a da capo? Where are the sign and the coda? Make a mental note of the repeats as you play. It never hurts to circle them if you have a chance.

LEARN TO SCAN YOUR SCORE QUICKLY

One of the reasons good sight readers can play music fluently is that they look ahead to "speed read." Good drivers and good sight readers have much in common; they include more in their field of vision so they can respond quickly to what's ahead. When you sight read, can you see two lines at once, or the top line and the title? How far ahead in the piece can you see? When you play, do you look ahead for brake lights in a tempo change, or a traffic jam of thirty-second notes? Your *eyes* must move ahead of your *hands*.

• Read bars, not beats. Continuously move your eyes from left to right and down the page. Practice duets and look at both parts at once.

• Build your speed. Use a flash card, or put an index card on the music, revealing only two measures. Look quickly, and then look away again while you play.

• Practice playing while someone provides a distraction. Quickly scan the score, look at the person, and quickly look back. When playing with a group, look quickly at the music and then directly at the conductor or ensemble members for good communication.

• Make a game of seeing how far you can play ahead when the music has been taken away. Teachers can close the book before the last two measures to test if the student knows what's ahead.

• Do visual exercises: look at the beginnings and ends of lines, quickly back to the key signature, from one rehearsal letter to the next, and back to the repeat sign while playing. See how quickly you can jump without getting lost.

• Practice reading piano chords from the bottom up, since the bass clef is the one that usually gives the most trouble.

Keep these good habits while playing:

- Sit straight in front of the music so your eyes can easily track.
- Wear glasses that allow you to see.
- "Check your rear and side view mirrors." Don't bury your head in the music or forget to look up at the conductor or other ensemble members.
- Maintain a steady beat. Tempo is most important. It's better to make a mistake in notes or rhythm than to play the notes perfectly but out of time. Set the metronome and keep up.
- Count up to the number of beats in each measure in your head. Never count how many Gs there are in a phrase, but know what beat every G is on.
- Be aware of beat one so that if you mess up a measure, you can jump back in on one.
- Play musically. Even though you are sight reading, don't forget that this is music.
- If you are playing the piano, a stringed instrument, or guitar, don't look at your hands. Glancing back and forth from the hand to the music slows you down. Keyboard players need to be sure they sit in the middle to get a feel for the keyboard. Memorize by touch where the two and three black key patterns are, much as in reading Braille. Practice scales in the dark or put a newspaper, book, or scarf over hands to get out of the habit of looking.
- Relax and have fun. Give yourself permission to make mistakes. It's only sight reading!

IMPROVE YOUR PLAYING AT HOME

Find some fun pieces to play by yourself at home. This improves your sight reading and is a wonderful way to get into the habit of playing for fun, not just practice. Purchase the *CD Sheet Music* CD-ROM, which has over 500 "free" pieces to print out on your computer, or play along with the songs on computer programs such as Smart Music. Better yet, invite friends over to sight read chamber music.

FAKE IT WHEN NECESSARY

All orchestra members know that some music is downright *impossible* to play. We all have music that is way over our heads, but we still want to sight read it. How? Fake it! On the piano, when I accompany my students on major concerti, I am sometimes reduced to playing only one hand and sometimes only one note. In the devilishly hard sections I play my own chords and make sure I have the correct rhythm. When I played viola in a community orchestra I was sometimes reduced to playing just the first note of every group of four sixteenths in order to keep up. I am not a master of these instruments, but I am a "master" at faking! The more practice you get, the less faking you will need, but in real life situations it can come in handy.

If you are unsure, leave out the extras:

- If you must choose between playing correct notes and correct rhythm, choose rhythm.

- Play the outside notes of the chord.
- Play the chord instead of a florid arpeggio pattern.
- Play the chord in a different inversion or in a different octave, whichever will cause the fewest mistakes.
- Leave out trills and grace notes.
- Re-tongue ties or slurs to help with the rhythm.
- Play just the first note of a group of sixteenths or a triplet.
- "Sit out" an impossible measure and come back on beat one of the next.
- If you become totally lost, move your hands or pretend that your part has rests!

Students can learn sight reading skills with a thorough knowledge of the basics and lots of practice. Show them how this fun "game" can open up new worlds of music.

Part 3

TACKLING
YOUR TOUGHEST
TEACHING CHALLENGES

NINETEEN

In the Beginning

Children begin music lessons from birth. They hear the radio playing, mom singing lullabies, cartoon music, and the music of family members at home. Later, if encouraged to sing, dance, and share the joy music brings to their parents, they will seek music on their own. Children who are hushed while singing, told not to bang on the piano keys, or stopped from playing their pots-and-pans instruments will not feel that music is part of their lives.

When should formal musical education begin? Children as young as two enjoy programs that introduce them to the world of music and awaken their own talents. Very young children learn best in a group lesson setting. These fun and informal classes include lots of singing and movement. Children will be encouraged to explore rhythm, form, and melody. They may learn to recognize the instruments of the orchestra, walk and jump to rhythms, and play recorders or percussion instruments. These preschool music programs should emphasize fun and group play, not performance. Parents who participate with their children in these early music exploration classes gain insights into when their children might be ready for private lessons. If parents ask you to teach a child who is not quite ready for private lessons, refer them to programs such as these:

American Orff-Schulwerk Association (www.aosa.org)
Dalcroze Society of America (www.dalcrozeusa.org)
Excel-ability Learning (www.excel-ability.com)
Kindermusik (www.kindermusik.com)
Music for Young Children (www.myc.com)
Suzuki Association of the Americas (www.suzukiassociation.org)

WHAT IS THE BEST AGE TO START PRIVATE LESSONS?

There is no unbendable rule that dictates the optimum age for every child. Much depends on the maturity and eagerness of the student and the teacher's style and teaching methods. Piano and stringed instruments tend to start earlier; woodwinds, brass, and percussion start later.

I prefer to start children when they are in the third through fifth grades. At that age they have the necessary focus, work ethic, and breath control, *and* they can understand my jokes. I'm not patient enough for tiny baby steps, so accepting students in this age range is optimal for me (although my 6-year-old student Abigail may change my mind!). In my experience, I can see no great advantage in starting preschool children on the flute because the "older" beginner usually catches up quickly. The advanced teenage player will be the one who practiced the most, not the one who started the earliest.

Many teachers have a differing opinion, having been successful teaching preschool students. The Suzuki program, a forerunner in early education, advocates starting children as young as 3 or 4 years old. This method has produced excellent results with some young children. Suzuki provides a wonderful community of music for children through parental involvement and group lessons and offers innovative ideas for teaching the very young child. I don't intend to debate here the pros and cons of the Suzuki method or to provide a dictum as to the appropriate age to start beginners. Teachers, parents, and students must analyze what will work best for them. Here are some variables to consider.

Some Advantages of Starting Early

YOUNGER CHILDREN

- May learn best before age ten, according to some studies.
- Integrate music into their lives before extracurricular activities crowd it out.
- Think of themselves from the beginning as musicians.
- Learn by rote and quickly develop their listening and memorizing skills.
- Enjoy the sense of belonging and the role models group lessons provide.
- Gain confidence when initially playing ahead of their peers.
- Need more parental involvement, which brings the family together in music.
- Develop more fluid and natural technique through years of lessons.

Some Advantages of Starting Later

OLDER CHILDREN

- Are better able to sit still and concentrate.
- Have developed the needed fine motor skills.
- Have the necessary breath capacity.
- Base their learning on reading music instead of imitating, learning closer to "real life" music situations.
- Better understand music theory as it presents itself through the music.
- May choose to play their instrument, instead of it only being the parents' idea.
- Are less likely to "burn out" by adolescence.
- Progress faster and in more exciting ways, requiring less patience from the child, parent, and teacher.
- May, after a few years, catch up with their peers (especially in woodwinds), saving years of time and money investments.

Is Your New Student Ready to Start Lessons?

Last year a parent begged me to take her second grade daughter as a student. When I hesitated, her mother confided, "Annie has been asking for flute lessons all year. I think she's ready." Annie arrived and spent the first lesson tearing up my music room. This little girl needed parental discipline, more years to mature, and/or hyperactivity drugs. When we finally got the flute to her lips she acted uninterested in trying to get a sound. I knew flute lessons for her were over when soon she declared, "I think I want to play the saxophone instead!"

To determine a child's readiness, ask:

• Can the child sit still for twenty minutes?
• Can she perform small motor tasks with both hands?
• Are her hands big enough to hold the instrument? Does she have the necessary breath control for a wind or brass instrument?
• Is she fairly organized? Does she take care of her belongings?
• Does the child show an interest in music? Does she ask for favorite songs? Does she sing?
• Does she feel comfortable talking with adults? Will she take direction?
• Is she mature for her age?

When Is It Too Late to Start?

It's never too late! My gentleman student started to play flute when he was seventy and has continued lessons through age eighty-three. I started flute lessons when I was a freshman in college and have made music my profession and passion. We all can learn and improve at any age.

Former student Mikaela talks about her "better late than never" attitude to starting lessons as a teenager:

> Playing an instrument is not a project to be completed, but something you keep improving on for your entire life. During my first few months I alternated between loving the flute and my progress, and feeling discouraged by how far behind I was. Now I can see the advantages of beginning later. All my motivation came from myself. My parents never reminded me to practice. I did it because I wanted to. It doesn't matter at what level I'm playing now, as long as I like what I'm doing and continue to improve.

WHAT STYLE OF TEACHING DO BEGINNERS NEED?

Most children need to gradually adjust to the demands of paying attention during lessons and devoting free time to practice. Rigid teachers may drive them away from the instrument altogether. At the same time, a warm and fuzzy teacher who provides little structure may progress too slowly and drive them away too. Young beginners need a teacher who is sweet and relaxed and then gets progressively tougher. Some children may need two teachers or a teacher who can adjust expectations as the child matures. I try to be a tolerant cheerleader for my beginners and then gradually turn up the heat while I dole out lots of praise and stickers.

Tailor Lessons to the Beginner

- Set appropriate expectations for each age. *Generally* expect second graders to progress half as fast as fourth graders.
- Stay attuned to the child's personality. Shy children need more time and a gentle voice. Rambunctious children need more spice and fun.
- Group lessons allow children to be with their friends and feel less individual pressure.
- Give students choices: "Do you want to play half the page or the whole page?" "Do you want to review this page or move on?" "Now that you've learned the new notes, do you think you're ready for the new scale?" "Do you want to play with the music first before you play it from memory?" "Do you want to play the duet part alone before I join you?"
- Make the lessons fun! Joke around. Exclaim about every new skill learned.
- Applaud with the parents after a particularly well-played piece.
- Never base assumptions purely on age. The first grader may have more talent, intellect, and desire than the sixth grader. You never know.

Help Students Focus

- Two short lessons a week may be more manageable than one long one.
- Avoid spending too long on position and posture in one sitting or you will lose your audience. (Most young boys show little interest in their thumb position!) Instead, intersperse suggestions throughout the lesson.
- Set small short-term goals. Reward new skills with stickers, pencils, and candy.
- Too much talking can be dull. Try "hands on" demonstrations such as keeping a piece of paper on the wall by blowing, bouncing a ball to show rhythms, or blowing bubbles to demonstrate embouchure. Put practice jobs in a bag and draw them out.
- Take time to talk and laugh and get to know each other. Music lessons should be loads of fun.

Starting beginners may be one of the toughest times in the "life cycle" of growing musicians. Enjoy the chance to build correct technique from the ground floor up and awaken a love of music.

GENDER DIFFERENCES IN TEACHING

Teachers fine-tune their teaching styles to accommodate each student's unique personality and ability. We must also adjust to our students' gender. Boys and girls are equal, but their brains are different. While some accepted male/female differences stem from society's stereotypes, many are hard-wired. Most parents and teachers have instinctively felt the differences between boys and girls in their behavior, interests, and learning styles. A friend who is a PE teacher told me that boys are dogs and girls are cats! With many exceptions to the "rule," decades of research has proven that boys and girls have cognitive, neurological, and hormonal differences. We'll discuss these differences along with practical advice on how to help both sexes flourish in your studio.

Boy Brains

1. Boy brains love competition. Set up a challenge for them and make the end results measurable and public. Post a scale chart on the wall, check off practice assignments, set metronome marking goals. Say, "I'll bet you can learn this page in twenty minutes!" or "Let's see who can learn four new scales the fastest."

2. Boys learn at an early age to suppress their emotions. From the beginning we categorize boys as "strong" and girls as "cute." Don't expect young boys to play gentle or sad music; they love big, fast, crashing chords. Create science fiction or action stories to help boys express themselves through music. "This phrase is where the terminator rules the universe."

3. Boy brains are optimized for spatial tasks. Teach them how music theory works and give them a chance to compose.

4. Boys are more impatient; they want it done now and fast. Slow pieces bore them and staying on the same piece for a long time brings them to tears. They would rather play the same piece fast fifty times until they get it right than achieve the same result by playing it five times slowly. They love to prove they don't have to go slowly. "You can get out of ten minutes of practice if you promise not to play this piece over MM = 100."

5. When boys say they can't hear you when they're watching TV, they may be telling the truth. Boys have laser focus and they hear less well than girls. Offer a handful of suggestions instead of overwhelming them with a steady stream. Allow time between activities for them to regroup and shift focus. "Let's work on the tone and intonation today. Next week we'll focus on phrasing and articulation." Or "Tell me about your baseball game before we move on to the duets."

6. Boys don't make social connections as easily as girls. Don't expect them to practice just to please the teacher or because they are afraid of getting into trouble. State a reason and a goal for practice. "You have to play sixteen notes on a bow before you can play this piece. This exercise will help." Or "The recital is only three weeks away and you don't want to feel embarrassed."

7. Boys exhibit more learning and behavioral problems. Eighty percent of students who drop out are boys, and girls outnumber boys at almost every college. More boys are diagnosed with dyslexia and Attention Deficit Disorder (ADD) than girls. Tailor your teaching, assignments, and timetable to their abilities. Repetition may be the key here.

8. Boys want excitement and the fast-paced action of video games and sports. They want the teacher to entertain them too. They love to laugh and goof around. Maintain a high energy level, tell them jokes, give them pet names, and laugh!

9. Boys want to feel instantly successful and respected. Start small and go in incremental steps with liberal praise. Let them be involved in decisions and give them leadership roles when possible. "I admire the way you worked so hard at the counting. How do you think we should tackle the intonation problems in this new section?"

10. Boys develop finger dexterity later. Though they still want to play the fast stuff, don't expect a fluidity until much later.

11. Boys are less verbal. This is a problem because most teachers are women and teach the way they were taught—with lots of words! Keep explanations short or you will lose boys. Be more hands-on. Research has shown that they don't see or hear as well as girls. Make the music room bright and speak loudly!

12. Boys may be less organized. Help them set up practice schedules and a system to remember to bring all their books to the lesson!

13. Boys love talking about things, not feelings. Let them regale you with stories of their hobbies and sports and integrate that information into the lesson. "You look like you are reeling in a fish when you bend over backwards when you are out of breath." Or "I want you to slam that note like you were making a slam dunk in basketball."

14. Boys are more upfront. They let you know what they like and hate; respond to them with candor and honesty. If they play well, say so. If not, be straight with them. "That tone stinks more than a skunk!"

15. Boys like to associate with power and influence and bask in reflected glory when their sports team wins. They want to be associated with a winning music teacher too. "Mr. Morrissey is my teacher and he's the best!"

16. Boys are less introspective. They may not understand why they do things or connect their actions with an outcome. Many times they don't even hear their mistakes: Don't let them become overly dependent on the teacher or parent for corrections. Play games like "Who hears the mistake first?" and ask "What do you think?" or even just "What mistake did you make?" to make them hear themselves.

17. Is it any surprise that boys fidget more? They have less serotonin in their brains, so they may need to wiggle and walk.

18. Boys can be loads of fun. Take that energy and channel it to music.

Girl Brains

1. Girls sometimes shy away from competition. They don't like to stand out or risk hurting their friends. Remind them that they are competing with themselves and that the results of any contest are secondary to learning.

2. Girls mature faster emotionally and are not afraid to talk about their feelings or to express them in music. Take advantage of that desire and encourage them to express themselves in their music.

3. Girls are more interested in the product than the process. They might view learning music theory the same way I'd view learning how a car engine runs. They don't care about pistons, either; they just want to drive.

4. Girls have more patience and understand that the steps they take now will lead up to success later. Recognize their efforts.

5. Girls can better multi-task. They can keep tone, technique, intonation, and breathing in mind at the same time. They have no problem jumping from one activity to the next.

6. Girls are people-pleasers. They have more of a hormone called oxytocin, which is linked to bonding. They will practice to earn the admiration of the teacher or to just stay in her good graces. Playing ensembles is a big motivator for them.

7. Girls do better in school and have a more linear learning curve.

8. Girls have a higher tolerance for "boredom." They will repeat the same measure over and over because you told them to.

9. Girls envision long-term goals and are willing to work to achieve them. On the other hand, they may have a lower sense of self-esteem when they have reached those goals. Revisit their accomplishments. Encourage them to take musical "risks" and reach higher.

10. Girls outpace boys in fine motor coordination.

11. Girls' "language centers" in the brain mature earlier than boys'. Girls learn best through words. They have larger vocabularies and follow long explanations.

12. Girls tend to be more organized and love making things pretty. This trait helps them organize their materials and their practice time. They especially appreciate decorating changes in the music room.

Beginners of both sexes and all ages need your patience, attention, and love. With these ingredients you'll give them the best chance to succeed.

TWENTY

Make Learning Fun (and Less Painful) for Adults

WHY TEACH ADULTS?

Imagine inviting a good friend into your house once a week to make music and get-ting *paid* for it. What a great deal. Teaching adults can be as rewarding to the teacher as to the student. Adults who decide to take music lessons are almost always inquisitive, interesting people, and you can learn as much from them as they do from you. I've had adult students from all walks of life, and at every lesson I've gotten to learn about their life's work and to become better acquainted with these fascinating people.

In a purely practical vein, teaching adults can be lucrative. As people continue to live longer and enjoy fuller retirements, retired adults are a new market for teachers. They usually have the disposable income to spend on lessons and have more flexible schedules to allow them to come in "off" times. Teaching adults can be both profitable *and* rewarding.

The benefits to students of a "certain age" of learning music:

- Bringing out a creative side that many times has been subverted in this automated world. How wonderful to talk about the phrasing or emotions of a piece when the rest of the day is filled with facts, figures, stress, and deadlines.

- Having something to share with others when performing. No matter how basic, music coming from the heart is always a gift.

- Connecting with a teacher. Private music teachers usually become cheerleaders, confidantes, and coaches.

- Meeting new people through group playing and concerts. What a way to build a so-cial life; it sure beats hanging out in bars! (Musicians hang out in measures. Get it?)

- Reducing stress. Adults learn to channel emotions through the music. Some of my adults have told me that practicing the flute at night is better than drinking a mar-tini, and having a flute lesson is better (and cheaper!) than going to a "shrink."

- Distracting from bodily pain. Adults experiencing the pains of older age will find music gives them something to concentrate on instead of their worries or their aching bodies. Instead of complaining about this and that body part causing trouble, how about the *musical* kind of organ recital?

- Fulfilling childhood dreams. So many adults think, "How I wish I had never quit music lessons." Or more specifically, "How I wish my mother had never let me quit." (It's never the father's fault!) Taking lessons now is in some way paying tribute to their parents, who had wanted them to learn music. Adults who never had the opportunity to learn music can now realize their dreams, and those who thought they were just no good at it, but probably just had terrible teachers, get a second chance.

- Being a student again, which can make you a better parent. Experiencing the joys and frustrations of learning increases empathy and awareness for the learning process. It's not so easy to say to a child, "Why didn't you get an A on that test?" when you are upset that you can't play the runs in the upcoming recital piece.

- Keeping mentally active. Your brain: Use it or lose it! Recent studies have shown that the three things that help keep the brain nimble and ward off Alzheimer's disease are playing board games, reading, and *playing a musical instrument.* Music can bring a significant improvement to long-term mental functioning. The wonderful thing about learning an instrument is that there is always so much more to discover. Learning keeps you young!

- Maintaining finger dexterity. I've had students who use the flute to battle against arthritis and even one surgeon who used it as physical therapy after his hand was severely cut.

- Carving out personal time. Many adults, especially parents of school-age children or those now caring for their own parents, feel their lives revolve around pleasing others and performing jobs. How gratifying it is to escape the daily routine and do something that provides self-actualization and growth.

- Gaining a sense of accomplishment. Learning an instrument builds self esteem. It also gives you something to talk about at cocktail parties. How fun at an older age to be learning something brand new!

- Scheduling a focus to the day. Jack, who is in his eighties, says, "For my wife and me, the almost daily practice sessions are never a chore, but a real joy—a joy of entering into and beginning to understand the world of music and musicians, of meeting the challenges each piece presents and of sharing a special time with each other. It's a lot better than watching TV!"

- Learning about music in general to become better listeners. Concerts are much more fun when you have an educated ear and know about the structure and history of music. My husband, Don, knows as much about classical music as I do about rugby. When we both attend a concert or a rugby game we are seeing the event from two very different perspectives! Adult beginners probably will not become professional musicians, but they will love becoming active, informed listeners.

- Gaining a sense of tranquility with the solitary practice and the soothing sounds of music. How many adults wish they could be "sent to their room" as they instruct their children to do when they misbehave. Practicing is a time of calm (except during those frustrating moments!) and a private time we all yearn for.

HOW IS TEACHING ADULTS DIFFERENT
FROM TEACHING YOUNGER PEOPLE?

When I first started learning violin at age 22, I could hardly stand to hear myself. I had assumed that since I sang and already played flute and piano, the violin would be fairly easy to pick up. But my expectations were so much greater than my reality. It was so frustrating knowing how I wanted to sound, but not being able to do it.

On the other hand, when I took my first tennis lessons around that same time, I didn't expect to be instantly lobbing the ball over the net and winning matches. Why was I so disgusted with the horrible squeaks and squawks on the violin, and so accepting of the tennis balls lost in the bushes? Music meant so much to me, I wanted to be good right away.

Adults can set unrealistically high standards for themselves. Many adult music students are highly skilled in their own fields and expect to get good at music fast too. It can be a very humbling experience for these high-powered professionals to learn a brand new skill and feel like children again. Being a novice musician requires building character and learning *patience* as well as learning scales. Adult flutist Sayoko has some sage advice.

> Most adults who start lessons have been very successful in their other life and now have decided that making money isn't the meaning of life and want to turn to art or music. The problem is that they feel they should be instantly as successful in music because they are used to being smart, quick, and competent. We adults need to realize that the journey is half the fun. My advice is: *Don't rob yourself of the joy of learning.* By being so tough on yourself you can get crushed under your own weight. Just sticking to it is an accomplishment in itself. I have sole discretion on whether I quit or not; no one is forcing me to take lessons or practice. I am just proud of myself for committing to the long term of learning music and look forward to the fun along the way.

Though they have many time limitations, adults are sometimes still filled with regret and feel a pressure to move ahead fast. "Why didn't I learn to play an instrument at a 'normal' age? How can I be a senior citizen and still sound like a pre-schooler?" They hear professionals play and think, "That's how I want to sound," and then set unrealistic standards for themselves: "At this rate I'll have to live until I'm 130 years old before I sound good!"

Creating realistic goals is sometimes a challenge. Practicing, like homework, is one of a kid's jobs. They have goals like getting to sit principal chair, winning the contest, or even just pleasing their parents. But to adults, music lessons are just a hobby. Taking the pressure off performance can be liberating for adults, but it also may be hard to keep them practicing when there are no tangible goals.

Adults' schedules also tend to get in the way of regular lessons and practice. Practice must take second or third place after all of the other responsibilities of work and family. You may have to be flexible about your attendance and make-up lesson policy. Lessons every other week may be the solution for adults to fit music into their hectic lives.

Adults and children have different physical abilities too. Adults do not have the quick-firing nerves that younger people do; they can understand concepts faster than they can physically produce them. On the plus side, adults have bigger hands. They can more quickly adjust to holding the instrument or reaching farther and can progress faster than young children to music with big chords, large leaps, or higher positions. On the other hand, an adult's hands may not be as flexible as a child's.

Children have another advantage too: their parents. Mom and Dad drive them to lessons, help them practice, and root for them along the way. There's no one at home to help adult students with hard measures and disappointing performance. Spouses and children of adult beginners may not be so supportive, or may even be jealous of the time spent on music. Adults are indulging their personal interest and sometimes even feel guilty for being "narcissistic."

The adult learner does have some advantages over the child, though. Adults appreciate the opportunity to learn. Kids have all their classes at school and extracurricular activities, whereas adults are grateful for the opportunity to do something for their sanity. Adults bring a lifetime of learning to this new endeavor and have an ability to figure out problems on their own. Adults know how they learn best and are more able to communicate their needs on the instrument.

Adults like the academic side of music. They are interested in theory and history, and they love learning about all forms of music, not just the particular piece they are playing. Their learning is far-reaching. They love their instrument, but they also utilize what they have learned for more educated and enjoyable listening to CDs and concerts.

And finally, adults are usually very appreciative of the teacher, as they understand the challenges we face in putting up with them!

Support Adults' Goals

Adults' reasons for taking lessons are usually vastly different from those of the rest of your studio. You must accept their goals and make them yours too. Most of my adults are not looking to set the world on fire, but are just happy to sit at the lessons with a flute in their hand. They just want some connection to music and find the experience pleasurable, so I need to have their goals reflected in my teaching approach.

Tailor Adults' Time Frames to Their Needs

It may have been a long time since some adults were in a learning situation like lessons. Give them a chance to acclimate to being "back in school." Be patient about practicing, doing homework, and buying books; it takes a while for lessons to be part of their lives. They may need help fitting practice into their daily routines, just as children do. Emphasize that steady practice brings steady improvement and that with sporadic practice they will probably get discouraged and quit.

Don't attribute all the problems an adult may have to age. They might have had the same difficulties as a child, and now you get to deal with them! Accept your student's timetable for improvement. Sometimes it is hard to change old bad habits. You *can* teach an old dog new tricks, but it just may take a little longer than teaching a puppy. Don't compare your adult students to your younger students. Appreciate each of their good qualities and let it go at that.

Many times adults progress much slower than kids. Introduce one small concept at a time and use many etudes and songs that reinforce the same technique; don't worry about making it through the book or rushing to the next level. Let them help set the standard by asking if they want to repeat a piece or move on. Get used to repeating songs and concepts and get them to focus on the process, not the product. No, it's not a Beethoven sonata, but it is the first step. Teach them to be realistic about their expectations, acknowledge each small accomplishment, and enjoy the journey along the way.

Tailor Lessons to the Adult Level

Try to use books that are designed for adults. It's hard for a serious adult to play "Hillary Hog Plays Half Notes." If you can, use music that is specifically written for adult beginners or real literature that is simple, and use familiar pieces (Für Elise anyone?). Let students be involved in the choice of music. If they have wanted to play a certain piece all their lives, work up to it, but let them try. They are not going to "lose the competition" or be laughed at, so let them live their dream even if you know the composer is rolling over in his grave.

Keep them stimulated by teaching them about all aspects of music, instead of just the piece they are performing, but don't teach "meaningless information." Do they really need to know the names of the modes or the scale of A-sharp minor? Teach only what the adult can use today; life is short.

Don't talk down to adults or speak to them as if they are children, even if their playing is basic. Don't dictate, judge, or punish them (they won't stand for it!). Do your best to be reassuring to the student and make your studio a safe haven. Adults put enough pressure on themselves without the teacher adding to their stress. Teach adults to criticize their playing and not themselves. So you missed the key signature (for the eighth time!); it doesn't mean you are a worthless person. Remind them of all their friends who can't even play an instrument and who are jealous of them.

There may be safely in numbers. Try teaching adults in group lessons or add ensembles to their regular private lessons. The pressure is off when there is a crowd, and adults more than likely will be cheerleaders and not critics as they see others with their same hopes and handicaps. Performing in front of others may be motivating for some and demoralizing for others, so you need to be flexible. Help arrange church performances, small soirées, or just informal chances to play for one another. But always give students the choice.

If you just can't understand why it is taking them so long to improve, try a new hobby or skill yourself to remember the pain, suffering, and excitement of being a beginner. Ha. It's not as easy as you remember.

HINTS FOR ADULT BEGINNERS

Be honest with your teacher about what you are looking for in lessons. Do you have particular goals, such as learning a treasured piece of music or being skilled enough to play in an ensemble? How serious are you? Can you only carve out an hour a week to practice or do you want to plow ahead as fast as possible? Let the teacher know when the workload is too light or too heavy.

When it seems like you are not improving, try keeping a music journal. Record new techniques or ideas learned to see the forward progress which is not always evident at every lesson. Have fun going back to laugh at what used to seem hard. Keep playing the old songs just for fun. Listen to good music for inspiration. Struggling with counting and fingering sometimes makes music seem more like a job than the beautiful thing it is, but it will all be worth it.

"MUSIC THERAPY"

Adults come to lessons with a bigger burden on their shoulders than do children. Life can be hectic and stressful. Jobs, family, illness, and even politics are all concerns that take time and worry. Many adults need to "unburden" themselves to the music teacher every week before they can get down to the business of playing. We sometimes begin to wonder if we should be paid as therapists as well as musicians. Communication between adults and teachers must be open. This way, adults can describe their week's practice without fear of being chastised, and know they have a sympathetic ear for their life story. Sympathetic music teachers care about the music *and* the student.

You can still use music as therapy and be sure you are fulfilling your role as a teacher too. Start and end lessons promptly. Have lesson material planned and tell the student at the beginning of the lesson what you hope to cover. Encourage adults to express themselves through emotional music instead of just talking. Spend less time on technical exercises and more on music. Use music that is easily accessible to give the student an uplifting feeling of accomplishment. Give the student some relaxing time by using part of the lesson to demonstrate or to listen to a CD, or just give up and have a cup of coffee and play a few duets. Whatever works.

PHYSICAL CHALLENGES

Many adults are in great shape physically and mentally. The comments below are for those older adults who may need a little help.

Arthritis

Many adults have trouble with arthritis. Arthritis may be a hindrance to playing music, but playing music can actually *help* arthritis. When stiffness sets in, the natural tendency is to stop moving to avoid pain. Playing an instrument can be a fun way to exercise and keep good muscle tone and flexibility.

- Pianists can try an electronic keyboard with semi-weighted keys, a keyboard with smaller keys, or a keyboard with a variable touch setting on low. Other instruments can be modified with key extensions. There is even a flute that is played vertically.
- Be sure to warm up the fingers, neck, and shoulder before starting to practice.
- Start the practice session out with slow scales to gradually stretch.

- Play in a warm room.
- Divide the practice session into five-to-ten-minute segments with small breaks in between to stretch stiff muscles.
- Wrist supports can help stabilize.
- Use a pillow to prop up an instrument, to help with neck and shoulder problems.

More Ideas for Adult Physical Limitations

- Play at a slower tempo to compensate for a decline in reaction time.
- Because it takes longer to learn and longer to retrieve information, play with music instead of memorizing.
- Hearing loss may cause adults not to hear the fine points of a performance. The teacher should speak and play loudly.
- Record the lesson on a tape recorder to help remember what was said. Sometimes ask the teacher to play sections of the piece slowly on tape so you can play along at home.
- Sit in a supportive chair, use angled chair cushions for proper posture, or even sit on an exercise ball.
- Drink lots of water or chew gum at the breaks to help with dry mouth.
- Wear glasses with a good prescription. Experiment with music stand placement to coordinate with bifocals or trifocals.
- Have plenty of light or enlarge the music.

THE BAG LADIES

Twenty-five years ago, several women starting taking lessons from me at approximately the same time. They called themselves the "BAG Ladies" because the first notes they learned were B, A, and G. The BAG Ladies took lessons for over ten years. We had many fun (food and drink intensive) recitals and saw each other through (literally) thick and thin. Now, fifteen years later, we are still close friends. I feel blessed to have brought this lively group together and brought them into the world of music, making life-long dreams come true. On my fiftieth birthday, Nancy, Margie, Linda, and Susanna, the infamous BAG Ladies, presented me with

BONNIE'S CREATIVE GUIDE FOR TEACHING BAG LADIES THE FLUTE

Up-to-date and pre-tested strategies for teaching the flute to the assortment of adults who express an interest in learning, despite their lack of talent, tenacity, tone recognition, or ability to tell time or tie their shoes.

ELEVEN EASY STEPS AND ONE CAUTION!

1. Getting off to a good start (give them cookies)
2. What to do for the hungover student

3. How to get them to practice

4. Always start with B, A, and G

5. Tuning in less than 20 minutes

6. Inspire them with concerts (by others)

7. Trios for the pigheaded, tone deaf, and sleepy

8. Challenge them to perform (bring ear plugs)

9. How to get them to buy decent flutes

10. Stickers, and what you can do with them

11. The benefits of enjoying the moments when it all actually works

Caution:

Remember you gotta work with what walks in the door!

ADULT CONCERTS

Adult students enjoy the camaraderie of other adults in the same boat. "Does she make you play scales and that Telemann sonata too?" they love to ask. Performing in groups takes the pressure off individual performers and provides a fun social outlet. My adult ensembles have called themselves everything from the BAG Ladies and the Hot Tamales (during our Mexican-themed concert) to the Haute Aires (a title the husbands readily agreed with). Every Christmas I bring my adults to a hospital and we carol with our flutes in the halls. (No one's died yet.) They have also performed at churches and a few other community events. But the most effective stimulus has been to party! We have had parties with music and food from around the world, solos from every musical period, and holiday themes (Halloween, Oktoberfest, and Christmas parties). We ply our audience with refreshments and always receive a warm reception.

As much as I enjoy the challenge of teaching young students to become "superstars," I have a special place in my studio and in my heart for my adult students. My only prerequisite for being my adult student is not the ability to play the flute, but the ability to cook, talk, laugh, and enjoy learning from me as much as I enjoying teaching and learning from them.

TWENTY-ONE

Troubleshoot Problems and Turn around Complaints

Sandy seems like a smart kid. He gets good grades in school and is attentive at his lessons. His mother comes every week to support her son. Then why does Sandy always arrive so unprepared and nervous? Does he even try to practice?

It's a mistake to assume the source of problems is laziness. Students may consistently fall short of expectations for many reasons. It's the teacher's job to find out why. Are they practicing? Are other issues interfering? Do they know how to practice? Have they set up a practice schedule? Is the home environment a hindrance?

Possible explanations for underperformers

- Does the student want to take lessons? No matter how bright the student, if lessons are not his idea of a good time, there will be little progress. Ask the tough question, "Do you *really* want to be here?"

- Does the student understand there is a problem? Perhaps the teacher has not clearly communicated expectations.

- Do the parents praise the child no matter the effort or the result? It's time to bring the parents into the lesson and let them know the standard for the age and length of time studied. If they think Johnny is wonderful, let them hear Tommy, who truly is.

- Are the teacher's goals and the student's goals different? Practicing ten minutes per day may satisfy the student who sees music lessons as another casual sport.

- Do they dislike the music, or not see the importance of scales and technical exercises? Would a change of music help? How about teaching technique through fun pieces instead of etudes?

- Is the student overwhelmed with school obligations and other activities? Be aware of students' schedules and make assignments accordingly. Wait until after soccer season to require they memorize the big piece. If students consistently have too much to do, suggest they drop an activity or the lessons.

- Is the student afraid to try? How many parents have said, "Oh, she is such a perfectionist," as we watch the little darling make mistake after mistake. But if the student truly is afraid to fail, work first on self-esteem issues. Give her the courage to believe in herself and try something out of her comfort zone. Make sure the atmosphere in the studio is welcoming and doesn't make the student fearful.

- Does the student not know how to practice? This is one of the biggest problems. Do you give him an assignment and expect him to know how to tackle it? Devote a few lessons to showing the student the steps needed to learn something from the scratch. Chapter 14 offers tips on getting the job done better and faster.

- Does the student know how to organize practice sessions to master everything during the week? The solution many times is to assign daily practice assignments. The student then does not have to plan the practice session and can put a check by each assignment.

- Is the student disorganized? This is another common problem. Help address scheduling and other time management issues to solve the problem.

- Do emotional problems interfere with concentration? If the student is upset with a boyfriend or girlfriend, worried about getting into college, or dealing with the host of other problems that can plague kids, music may have to be on the back burner. But keep in mind: these kids most need music in their life, so hang in there with them.

- Does the student understand the importance of practice? Does he see gifted athletes and musicians and know that they too put in their time?

- Is it just a stage? Beginners may need up to two years to embrace the rigors of learning music. Others may be going through a tough patch in the road.

- OK. Is the student *lazy*? Now it's the teacher's choice: Try to light a fire under the student or fire the student. Letting students know their place in the studio is not guaranteed without practice may be all the motivation they need.

Can the parents help?

- Can the student or parent provide you with a solution? Schedule a three-way conference with student and parents to brainstorm possible reasons for not practicing, and possible solutions.

- Can the parents help make it fun by playing practice games or taking the child to a concert?

- Do the parents expect the student to do too much at home? (Contrary to what my sons may tell you, this is not the case in my house.) For some students, family and church obligations may leave little time. Try to work with the parents to create a time for practice every day. Remind them they are not getting their money's worth out of lessons unless the student practices regularly. Perhaps broker a compromise that practicing gets the child out of some chores.

- Do the parents put the whole burden of practice on the young child? Do they hesitate to interfere so as to prevent practice wars? Do they expect the child to always be self-motivated? Explain to parents that they may always have to monitor the child's practice, but it is worth it.

- Do the parents provide a controlled environment and a scheduled practice time?

- Do the parents put too much pressure on the child? Do they jump on every mistake? Do they only approve of the finished product instead of the small accomplishments along the way? Help them change their tune by saying, "Practice does not make perfect, practice makes better."

- Is the child not practicing as a result of a power struggle with the parents? "*No one can make me practice! You're not the boss of me!*" If the child is struggling to prove his independence, work to separate the child's feelings about the parent and the child's feeling about music. Ask the parent to stay away from lessons and make the child only accountable to the teacher. If the child is given the choice whether to take lessons or not, he will realize he is practicing for himself, not his parents.

- Is the family life chaotic? Is there a functional adult at home to supervise? If the child does not have a sound home life, then the teacher must prioritize. What is more important? The child's performance at the lesson or your relationship as a caring adult with that child? Choose to save the child and not the concerto.

- Can the parent provide a reward system? As we've talked about in previous chapters, parents can give positive reinforcement verbally or with tangible rewards such as a new CD or an outfit for the recital. Some parents of my younger students use prize boxes with different levels of rewards that correlate with how good the lesson was.

- Instead of a structured reward system, perhaps the parents can offer intermittent reinforcement by offering a spontaneous reward after an extremely good practice session or lesson.

Consider: Is the problem with the assignment or my instruction?
If the student has put in the required practice effort and tried to be self-sufficient but *still* doesn't sound good at lessons, try to find out if the problem is with your instruction and not the student.

Determine problems with instruction by asking:

- Am I assigning too much? Is it impossible for the student to prepare scales, etudes, finger exercises, orchestra excerpts, and four solos, memorize a concerto, and perform in two chamber groups?

- Am I going too fast? Sometimes students need time for a new technique to settle in. Don't confuse the issue by introducing important new concepts every single week. Expect to review tough concepts. (I wish I had a dime for every time I have reviewed the steps for students to figure out the relative minor scale, or how to count a dotted quarter and eighth rhythm.) Keep a feeling of forward motion by assigning new pieces but at the same technique level.

- Is the student struggling with the basics? Technical concepts such as shifting, new bowing techniques, vibrato, dotted rhythms, or analyzing chords can block progress on pieces. Isolate and cement techniques before they are needed in music by using separate drills and exercises.

- Have I chosen appropriate target skills for this student? Can the student who has only been playing for a year memorize a two-page piece? Is it too much to ask a fourth grade cellist to play double stops?

- Have I been absolutely clear in my assignment and expectations? Does the student not only know *what* to practice, but what level to accomplish? Have I written performance suggestions to refer to at home?

- Are my teaching strategies effective for this student? How many ways can I say the same thing? Have I supplemented my demonstrations with explanations?
- Does my demeanor work well with the student's personality? Does the student need the warm fuzzy teacher, the fun, jazzy teacher, or more of a disciplinarian?

REEVALUATE ASSIGNMENTS AND STANDARDS

Be More Demanding

If the lessons are not going well, perhaps what the student needs is a harder assignment. What? Why would you assign a student who is limping along something even harder? For the challenge. Playing the same old assignments the same old way can be mind-numbing. Assigning a harder or longer piece may be the jump-start that's needed.

As you read before, learning to adjust goals is a necessary skill for a great teacher. Watch the student sit up straighter after the "big talk." "I think you're smart and talented, and I know you can do more. You've had it pretty easy around here for a while, but like a race horse that's been training, let's see what you can really do. I have this piece that I think you would love, but it will take a lot of work. Interested?"

Performances may provide the jump-start able students need. Even preparing to play for visiting grandparents or the neighbors can give lagging students an objective. Practicing to join a performing group can accomplish the same thing. Any goal that gives the lessons a sense of purpose will do.

Be Less Demanding

Stay attuned to the demands of your students' lives. Go easy on them during finals week and in return ask for accelerated practice later. "I understand why you couldn't practice much this week, but next week you owe me. Right?"

When students persist in saying their workload is excessive or the piece is impossible, maybe they are right, at least this time. Ask yourself if you're moving too quickly and whether it is time to change gears. Throughout this book you have learned techniques for encouraging students to higher, faster, better, new and improved performance, but here is the other side of the coin. Slowing down, even temporarily, may be what is called for. Reducing the assignment load and difficulty of the pieces will give students a feeling of success and may well give them the courage to later try harder pieces. It is better to play two pieces well than five pieces poorly. Another variation on this theme is to go back to the beginning of the book and this time require higher standards. Instead of being insulted, most students look forward to the chance to review and look successful. Give late bloomers a chance to shine.

Slow the Pace

Divide a piece into distinct sections and only assign one section at a time. This way there is a feeling of forward motion but it allows the student longer to conquer the whole piece. Give students a longer timetable to perfect a piece. If the contest is in

March, start working on the piece in June, put it "in the freezer" in October, and "thaw" it out in January so students will know they have plenty of time and will not feel stressed. Assign short- and long-term goals. Stretch a long piece out over several months while assigning shorter pieces for completion every week.

Reevaluate Assignments

Students' performance is vitally linked to the repertoire that is assigned. How many times have you heard students playing music that was way above their capabilities? Wrong notes and wrong rhythms ruin the music. Or how about the young students who play Bach and Mozart but have no insight into the greatness of these works? Sure, they may play the notes, but that's all it is—notes. There is no glory in assigning pieces that are too hard. Who cares if you are in book 8 or you play the Tchaikovsky concerto if it is bad? *Please, only assign pieces for performance that can be played well.* Promote a love and respect for the music and give the audience a break.

TURN AROUND COMPLAINTS

Even students who "love their lessons *and* their music teacher" may complain about their assignments, their workload, and especially their time commitment. If their complaints are legitimate, it may be time to back off. Many times, though, it takes a little cajoling to put them back on the sunny side of the street. I find that beginners, who aren't used to the rigors of lessons and practicing, tend to be the biggest complainers. Older students, used to the practice and lesson routine, are usually more accepting, but they still have a litany of complaints about their schedules and stress especially when they hit their junior year in high school. Try these techniques for turning your students' downbeat into an upbeat.

To counter excuses and complaints, say: "I know this week you had a big test, but last week you seemed to have a big test, too, and I'll bet *next* week there will be another. You'll have to learn how to juggle both school and music lessons or school will have to go." (Just kidding.) "I'm sure you could play it at home, but I don't live with you." (Thank goodness.) "I know you practiced, but you must prepare 120 percent so you can lose 20 percent under pressure, and still be perfect. You were 80 percent prepared." "Yes, it's a hard piece, but did you follow my suggestions and work slowly on one small section at a time? If you practice right I know that you will master it." "I wouldn't give it to you unless I thought you could do it. Have faith in yourself. Put in your best effort and I know you will be able to do it." "You think this is too much work? *I'm* really working hard at teaching you and I expect *you* to really work hard at learning. It's only fair, right?"

Let students hear their own complaints: When students whine that the piece is too hard, write down everything they say verbatim. Later, after they've mastered the piece, show them their protests. Take the list of complaints out again when they whine about the next piece, and you can both have a good laugh. My son Scott would write NCD (Never Can Do!) on his beginning piano pieces. These old markings make us laugh as he is now playing Brahms.

Use humor. When students say, "I don't want to do this exercise" or "This piece is way too hard," ask them to rephrase it with a smile. Have them say instead: "This exercise looks fun" or "I can't wait to try this four-page etude" or "This piece is easy for someone as good as I am." They will laugh and you won't have to hear their complaints.

Divide and Conquer Assignments

- When students complain the piece has "too many black notes," subdivide the rhythm (play 4/4 passages in 8/8 or 16/16) or even write out the hard parts in more beats per measure. Sixteenth notes are more easily readable than 32nd notes.
- If they protest that the piece has too many fast notes, set an upper speed limit and make them promise to play at a snail's pace all week. Trust me, they will be dying to play those black notes faster at the next lesson.
- If students argue that their piece is too long, assign only the first page. When that first page is learned well, take out the second page.
- For pieces that include difficult scales, shifting exercises, long phrases, or some other technique, concentrate on those elements in etudes so they can pick up the skill faster and thus learn the piece more quickly.
- To counteract the fear of new music that overwhelms, analyze it and show the student measures that are just scales and arpeggios, repeating patterns, and whole sections that repeat. "See, it's a shorter piece than it looks!"
- When a new etude seems insurmountable, point out all the easy places and have them learn those first. Save the tricky parts for later, when the student is already vested in the piece. "You already know half of the etude; you might as well learn those *interesting* measures now."
- When students stumble on a work that introduces several new techniques, try dividing techniques into different categories. One week only require them to work on notes and rhythm. Next week focus on evenness, articulation, dynamics, phrasing, tone and tone color, or tempo. Everything does not need to be perfect all at once. (I have to keep reminding myself of this!)
- As I've mentioned, when students think the weekly assignment is too long or have a hard time knowing how to get started, try daily assignments instead. Let them realize they don't need to practice every single thing every single day.

Use Psychology

When students feel they are not making progress, remind them of what and *how* they were performing a year ago. Praise them for the techniques they *do* excel in. "Remember last year when you could only play four notes on one bow? Now you just played a whole measure of sixteenths! Wow."

Look to future improvements. "Compare" a younger student to a more advanced one. "Lydia played the Bach Double Violin Concerto in eighth grade, and you are playing the Bach Double in eighth grade; you're going to get just as good as Lydia!" Or "I remember when Jennifer couldn't get a good sound on her clarinet for two months and she wanted to quit, but now listen to her. Your tone will be as good as Jennifer's." Ask older kids to relate to beginners their initial struggles and act as counselors and role models to the younger students.

Help students understand that mistakes are part of the learning process. There will always be that perfectionist child or perfectionist teacher who does not understand that making mistakes is OK. Actually it's OK to make lots of them, as long as we can understand what went wrong and are willing to fix it. That's life.

Separate hating the piece from hating the way they play it. When students say they hate their piece, play it for them or play a recording. Most of the time hatred of the piece is not because of the sound, but because of the difficulty. If they truly hate the piece, change it; they won't practice something they don't like.

Be sneaky. Use music to teach technique. If students hate scales or long tones, go through the back door and try giving them pieces that incorporate these techniques.

Be a Positive Role Model

If students hear you getting excited about a sonata and about music and lessons in general, your enthusiasm will rub off. This is an oft-repeated theme throughout this book, but perhaps the most important one. You reap what you sow. The positive energy you put into teaching will come back to you ten times with happy, hard-working students.

DO SOMETHING DIFFERENT

Sometimes students become complacent and begin to take their lessons for granted. If they started when they were young and studied with you for years, they may see coming to your studio as a boring old routine—nothing to worry about and nothing to get excited about. Changing the assignment, goals, or work load can do a lot to turn a student around. Vary your routines enough so that you both have something to look forward to. Shaking things up a bit keeps both you and your students on your toes.

At Lessons

Vary the Music Room
Make the music room a stimulating and dynamic place with decorations that give it a distinct personality. My music room may be somewhat visually chaotic, but it has lots of fun props and pictures. A giant Winnie the Pooh dresses according to the season. During contest time he wears a shirt, tie, and clipboard as the pretend judge, and in the summer he sports a baseball hat; his winter outfit is a muffler and umbrella. For holidays he's awfully cute in his St. Patrick's Day hat, bunny ears, or Santa hat. A Black Labrador puppy statue sitting by my music room door holds a sign that asks, "Did you practice?"

The walls in my studio are full. Above the door a sign with a pointing finger admonishes, "Be good or be gone." Another sign reads, "But I could play it at home."

There is a watercolor painting of my Zephyr flute quartet that performed with the Seattle Symphony, a puppy calendar, music cartoons, and a collage from former students. But wait, there's more. A bulletin board features pictures of all my current students, and another has pictures of past studio events. Over my piano, a picture of Bach reminds us that we have a great tradition to uphold, and on another wall is a history of music poster. On the piano my Bach, Mozart, and Beethoven action figures are ready to do everything from fighting to push-ups.

I perk up the room with fresh flowers, and on dreary Seattle days I sometimes burn a candle. (The moms think they are having a one-hour break at the spa!) At Halloween a skeleton adorns the door (the boy who practiced his fingers to the bone), an R.I.P. grave marker (the girl who would not count rests and now *rests in peace*). Yellow caution tape gilds the music stand. At Christmas, a fiber optic tree adorned with flute angels (just like us) gets us in the spirit.

Try changing the furniture arrangement or adding new paint. Be creative and add new decorations and props to make your studio a lively, happening place.

The teacher is part of the music room décor too. If you teach every day in jeans, a T-shirt, and tennis shoes, students might not get the idea that the lesson is an important event. Dress up a little to look more like the professional you are.

Vary Your Teaching Style

Challenge yourself to devise more interesting ways to present difficult material. Can you use a poster to explain and illustrate a concept? Can you listen to a CD for ideas? How about a handout or an illustrated book? What props can you use to demonstrate? I'm always on the lookout for kooky ways to get the idea across, because even though we all agree they are silly, they are memorable. Keep your students wondering what you have next up your sleeve. This is a partial list of the things that I do to enliven the lessons.

- Bake cupcakes and sing "Happy Birthday" to favorite composers.
- Let dog-lover students give my black Labrador Angie a treat after a great lesson.
- Provide rewards four times a year when I check to make sure the *Music for Life* books are updated. On Halloween they go trick-or-treating in my living room, and on Valentine's Day they get candy kisses and hearts from the teacher who loves them. At Easter time they get candy and around the Fourth of July they get a cupcake.
- Pass out handouts for technical flute subjects, but also for composer biographies and even fun cartoons and jokes.
- Use big Hershey chocolate bars as rewards for surprisingly good lessons.
- Use props. Blowing bubbles, sitting on an exercise ball, and spitting rice can enhance technical teaching.
- Make cookie bets. If a student does something amazing, such as playing sharp on a notoriously flat note or even smiling and bowing after a performance, I reward them with a dozen homemade cookies. But I get the cookies if they don't come through.
- Hand out pencils with poignant sayings such as "Practice! Practice! Practice!"

- Make copies of pictures of studio events for every student.
- Celebrate year anniversaries with a small present or cupcake.
- Share a beautiful new CD or piece of music to sight read.
- Bring out silly stuffed animals that spout, "You're a genius, how do you do it?" or a scaly dinosaur for when they are doing scales, the three-eyed Martian to remind them to watch the key signature, and the bobble-head dogs that always nod, "Yes, I practiced."
- Award special stickers for holidays and their birthdays.
- And my new favorite prop to pull out when students do something really bad? A screaming rubber chicken. That gets the point across!

Timing Is Everything

Change the Day of the Week of the Lesson

For some students Friday is the best lesson day because they have no homework to worry about. For others, Friday is the worst lesson day because they are exhausted from the week and their mind is on the weekend, not their lesson. Mondays may be good for those who spend the weekend catching up on practicing, but bad for those who spend the weekend skiing. When students sign up at the beginning of the year, help them think through their obligations in order to pick an optimum lesson day and time.

Vary the Lesson and Music

Change the order of the lesson. Try playing solos first and scales last. Pick one day where all you play is duets and solos. How about a day of improvisation or composing, or a day of reviewing old favorites? How about a lesson devoted to ensembles or sight reading? For a kick, try playing something other than classical music. Themes from movies or musicals can entertain and divert. If students are lagging, ask them to go to the music store and pick up music they think would be fun. Then surprise them by demanding higher standards on these pieces too.

Play for Fun

If it feels like the whole year revolves around contests or concerts, take time to play pieces just for fun that round out students' repertoire. Ask the student to become proficient enough on the piece to enjoy it without worrying about performance standards. What fun to learn lots of new songs without worrying about being judged. Play fun duets and solos, then move on.

Vary Parents' Participation

Parents can be a help or a hindrance. If parents always sit through the lesson, ask them not to come so you and the student can connect better one-on-one. If parents have not been present, invite them in. Encourage them to get them involved in practice at home or to attend a few lessons to give the student an audience.

Get a Pet

I will never forget one of my college voice juries in front of the entire voice faculty at the University of Washington. One of the teachers, a former opera star, came to the jury with her jewel-bedecked white poodle. As I was singing, the dog kept sniffing my shoes and skirt. It's hard to sing an aria while you are trying to kick a dog. The emotion in my voice had more to do with disgust with the dog than my feeling for the music!

That dog was distracting, but of course *my* dog, Angie, is perfect. When she hears a flute, Angie races to the top of the stairs and whines until I appear to start the lesson. With her favorite command, "Music room!" she races downstairs and bursts through the door. Her happy greetings always lift our spirits. Angie's unconditional love gives comfort and consistency and makes the music room a more welcoming and, many times, comical place. She also lets students see a more personal side of me. A dog can bring out the puppy in all of us. Of course, the dog must be very well behaved, and love children. Cats and fish may work OK too, but I don't know if I would recommend a bird—that may be too much competition for airtime!

Do Something Different
at Practice Sessions

After a while almost every student gets tired of practicing. "Back to the old treadmill," they think as they start to practice. "It's always the same old thing." Try some variety to spice up their home practice sessions.

Change Practice Requirements

Decide together on the practice time requirement. Try a practice chart if there hasn't been one. The new chart may only need to reflect scales and skill-building exercises, or it can be a record of time. Its main goal is to make students aware of their practice habits.

As suggested in previous chapters, making the practice assignment job-oriented instead of time-oriented might do the trick. If students using practice charts are still not getting the results you ask for, throw the practice charts out the window. Give precise assignments and tell your students to practice as much as it takes to complete the assignments instead of a prescribed amount every day.

Change the Practice Time of Day

If the student usually practices at nine o'clock at night, try having her practice right after school. If she practices right after school, try practicing as a break from homework later at night. If school starts later, how about an early morning practice when she is fresh?

Change the Practice Location

Try anything to break the routine. Have students practice sitting in a chair some days and standing on other days (OK, that's pretty hard for piano!). If they feel isolated in their room or down in the basement, bring them out of the dungeon. Let them feel that they are the center of attention and in a place where parents can give helpful encouragement and they can provide mini-concerts. If they have been practicing in the midst of family hour, with the TV going and kitchen smells wafting through the practice area, try a designated spot with more quiet to allow for better concentration. For a change of pace, try playing in the Tone Hospital (the bathroom) for that wonderful "singing in the shower" tone. Set up a music stand outdoors to serenade the (lucky?) neighbors.

The key to troubleshooting problems, as we have seen, is flexibility—on the part of both teacher and student. It's also clear that no one solution is the blanket answer to these trouble spots. As in everything else you do in your studio, you'll succeed when you pay careful individual attention to each student's personality, needs, problems, and unique character. There is no such thing as "one size fits all" in the world of music, so be creative!

TWENTY-TWO

Prepare Students for Performance

I don't want to play in a contest!" 13-year-old James protests. "I have to work on the same piece for months just to play it one time. I hate playing in front of a judge. What if he's mean? What if everybody's better than me? Why can't I just play my songs at home?"

James's teacher, Margaret, has doubts about contests too. Contests are too much work! The list is long—choosing pieces, ordering music, timing the selections, filling out the darned forms, rechecking the forms, asking parents to pay entry fees, and getting everything mailed before the deadline. The clerical duties alone are daunting.

And the time it takes. Will I need to teach extra lessons? Do I have to sit through rehearsals with the accompanist? Must I spend my Saturday listening to twenty kids playing book 2?

And don't forget the stress. No more relaxed lessons. Now our sole focus will be on perfecting the contest pieces on a deadline. Enforcing practice and keeping students on schedule. Trying to second guess what the judge will be looking for. Worrying about the competition. "Maybe James is right," Margaret thinks.

James and Margaret have valid concerns. Do contests force comparisons between students? Do they make less advanced students feel unworthy? Do students spend too much time playing just one or two pieces? Do contests put undue pressure on students? Will parents judge the teacher's effectiveness solely on the outcome of the contest? Are contests more trouble than they are worth?

Even though contests and public recitals have a potential downside, generally the good outweighs the bad. Let's examine both sides, starting with the positive.

WHY PARTICIPATE IN CONCERTS AND CONTESTS?

Contests allow students to:

- Work toward a goal. In a manner similar to the difference between auditing a class and taking it for a letter grade, contests force us to set our sights higher. Amazingly, even though they're focusing on a few pieces, students will attain a whole new level of expertise because of the performance preparation.

- Focus and direct their efforts. Preparing for a recital in October, a holiday concert in December, and contests in February and April provides deadlines.

- Prepare for the real world. Almost every aspect of life is competitive: sports, getting into college, and landing a job are but a few examples. As much as we want to value students and never compare them to others, life doesn't always work this way.
- Gain self-confidence from performing in public. Giving class speeches will seem easy after performing in front of a hundred people.
- Discover there is "life after death." One of the greatest qualities we can internalize is the ability to bounce back after defeat and pick up the pieces. Even so called "failures" teach perseverance and the ability to put success and disappointment into perspective.
- Gain valuable input from outside sources. It is always important to "hear many sides of the story." Judges emphasize different techniques and can sometimes point out something that has been overlooked, or can reinforce the teacher.
- Channel nervous energy into the thrill of performance. What a natural high! Performing heightens the fun of playing.
- Hear other players. Many performers are "big fish in little ponds." Hearing the performances of their peers lets students evaluate their own ability and hear the possibilities.
- Be recognized for all the effort that has gone into the preparation.
- Be the center of attention. We all love that applause!
- Give parents "proof" of the work done in lessons.
- Provide written documentation of awards for use in college applications.
- Get a new outfit and a treat afterwards (parents, take note).
- Have fun and share the wonderful gift of music that brings both the performer and audience pleasure.

USING GOALS TO PREPARE FOR PERFORMANCES

In chapter 10, "Energize Students with Goals," you learned how goal-setting can make reality happen. Instrumental technique goals (stretching yourself on your instrument), musical goals (playing beautifully), solo goals (perfecting the piece), performance goals (living through the performance and enjoying it), and outcome goals (realizing your dream) dictate how to direct energy and help measure progress.

Avoid Focusing Solely on Outcome Goals

The contest was over and the winners were being announced. ". . . And third place goes to Barbara Lang." "How wonderful!" I thought as I made my way through the crowd to congratulate my student Barbara. But Barbara's mother intercepted me, a distressed look on her face. "Third place is *not* OK," she said coldly. "We were expecting first. What happened? Why didn't she get first?" Her response shocked and dismayed me. "Barbara played beautifully and I am so proud of her. What's wrong with third place?" "In fact," I thought, "What's wrong with not placing at all?"

Goals are a good thing, right? Yes, but not always. When you set your sights only on winning you take a big risk. The danger here bears repeating. No matter how competitive a teacher or student you are, *outcome* goals will disappoint you time after time. Placing too much emphasis on the outcome may even *change* the outcome. If you *have* to win, you will worry and "psych" yourself out, and one mistake can put you into a tailspin. You've seen it happen with ice skaters and gymnasts at the Olympics. Some make a mistake, dust themselves off, and go on to win. Others are visibly shaken by their first misstep and lose their confidence, only to fall again.

Forget Perfection

Only CD performances are perfect, and they're technically enhanced. In real life, notes squeak and get missed, and we run out of bow or air. Students of mine have bolted out of competitions in despair because they missed three notes! They haven't just missed three notes; they have missed the whole point! A mistake here and there does not doom a performance.

Allow yourself to be human and make mistakes. Don't be the harsh music critic sitting on your shoulder as you play. Perfectionism doesn't result in better performance; it causes us to devalue all but the best performances. You are who you are, not how you play. Everyone makes mistakes; no one wins all the time, so *get over it.* Make it your goal to do your *personal* best, not to be *the* best. Keep the joy in your music; let it bypass your head to reach your heart.

One Day Is Not Your Whole Life

The emphasis the teacher, student, and parents put on the performance and on the preparation is a delicate balancing act. On one hand, the process of learning and enjoying music must be more important than the product. On the other hand, there are so many good musicians in the world that to be competitive requires real focus and dedication. We need to practice our hearts out, but keep in mind that what happens on contest day may be out of our control.

There are so many variables in a judged situation. The adjudicators only hear you for that moment in time. They are not aware of the progress you have made, how long you have studied, how long you have been with your current teacher, or how much effort it took to get where you are. They don't know if you're sick or couldn't sleep the night before. They didn't hear you yesterday when it was perfect at home, and they don't know if today's performance represents your best effort.

Every judge stresses certain qualities, and these may conflict with those valued by the teacher. Many years in the state competition I see three judges give opposite comments for the same technique. ("Loved your tone," "Your tone needs work.") Music isn't math. We love it because it is an art, which means that people's reactions vary, and we wouldn't want it any other way.

You also can't control the competition. You may have practiced two hours a day, but the next kid practiced for three . . . or played the judge's favorite song or had a better smile. None of us rules the universe, and we can only be responsible for ourselves.

We have no power over the judge's opinions or how well our competition performs. If someone does better and your only goal was to win, you may feel like a failure even if you played well.

Remember that *the event isn't as important as the preparation leading up to it.*

No audition should define our playing. Sometimes we don't play our best, sometimes we are *not* the best, and sometimes the adjudication is just plain crazy. Even Mozart never got a real job! Combine the judges' evaluation with your own assessment and that of your teacher. No judge is God (even though we have seen a few who acted as if they were!).

You are a winner if you answer yes to the following questions:

• Did I put in my full effort in preparing?
• Did I improve on the piece and in my playing?
• Did I learn about my instrument and music?
• Did I enjoy the process of learning and my lessons?
• Did I gain valuable experience performing?
• Did I make music and entertain the audience?

If you answer YES, the audition or competition was a success. If you answer these questions *before* the big day and give some negative answers, your disappointment will be easier to swallow and not so earth-shattering.

Rethinking the Idea of Winners and Losers

What if you don't win? Welcome to the real world of musicians who vie with many for that coveted first prize or spot in the orchestra. Are you a failure if you go home empty handed? NO!

When your performance is less than perfect, the audience will likely forget in a matter of minutes—if they even noticed at all. And in the scheme of life, if your performance is off a teeny bit, it's not going to drastically affect your future. Now, if a *neurosurgeon* is off a teeny bit, someone's future could be cut short. *We'll* still play again, but that spinal cord patient may never walk again. What if you really bomb? Take time to lick your wounds and then analyze what could have helped. Direct your thoughts to "Next time" instead of "What if." Because it didn't go as planned does not mean the process of learning was not worthwhile. Don't let your own performance or a judge's decision undermine your confidence. Anyone who puts themselves through the rigors of performance deserves to feel proud. And that applies to the teacher who prepares the students, too.

Dealing with Disappointment

Of course it is fun to bask in the glory of students and children, but as teachers and parents we need to check our own motivation. Are we living vicariously through our students? Do we see them as vehicles for our own aggrandizement? Do we get too involved and emotional over their "failures" and successes?

My husband, Don, is a non-musician. When I get too worked up over the judge's personality or scoring (and believe me, I have experienced some shockers) he has a way of letting me know it's not the end of the world or even close to it. Don (who *never* ruffles) reminds me that teachers need to be calm role models, since our students mimic our own reactions. How do we respond to a terrible experience with a judge who has not a single good word to say about the performance, whose ideas clash with ours, or who is just plain heartless? How do we teach our students to go on when they have played their very best and it's not good enough? How do we come to peace with a poor judging decision? We react with calm and put it in perspective.

When we overreact to life's adversities we make ourselves more upset. (I speak from experience.) Life is not always fair, and how the teacher reacts will breed optimism or bitterness. I have learned the hard way that it does no good to complain to the "authorities" about a judge who seems unfair, arbitrary, or even cruel. Give yourself a day to feel disappointed and then pick up and go on. Teach your students to say, "Oh, well, there is always next year." Remind them of their past successes. I have a competitive spirit and I sometimes have to remind myself along with my students that music is not a race, but a wonderful gift. We are all winners.

HOW TO PREPARE A STUDENT FOR A CONTEST OR AUDITION

You can help students enjoy the process of preparing for performance.

- Let them help choose the piece. If you force them to work on something they hate, they'll be miserable. Choose pieces that showcase students' strengths and challenge them to work.
- To avoid direct comparisons, don't assign two students in your studio the same music.
- Help students with the clerical work of forms. Insist they buy the real music (no playing from copies!).
- Offer a few extra lessons to students who need them. Decide if you want to be paid.
- If a student suffers from severe stage fright, choose an easy piece to help guarantee success.
- Give students ample time to master the material.
- If you play the piano even a little, work with students at lessons to help familiarize them with the accompaniment and to work on intonation.
- Hire a first-rate accompanist for the actual contest or concert. Arrange for ample rehearsals so students feel comfortable with the ensemble. Do not handicap students by accompanying them if you don't play like a pro.
- I've stressed it before, and I'll stress it again. Students must be *overly* prepared. Skills must be so solid they will happen automatically under pressure.
- Practice the *performance* as well as the *music*. Arrange for as many practice performances as possible before the actual contest.
- Never let students perform if you don't think their effort will be successful. Don't let them embarrass themselves or you. I have pulled students out the morning of

a contest (with a sudden attack of the flute flu!) to save us all grief and to teach them a valuable lesson.

- Attend students' competitions to give moral support and a debriefing and to learn how to teach them better in the future.
- Carefully consider whether to enter students in a competition. Some may benefit more from spending time on more repertoire and technical exercises instead of on competition material.

When students struggle:

- Give students a timetable. "By next week you must play this section with the right rhythm up to tempo. Next month you must have it memorized."
- Be realistic. If a student has played a piece for five months and only learned half, why think he can speed-learn the second half in the last two weeks?
- Let students know they may perform only when they are ready.
- Consider adjusting the program to make it more doable. Eliminate a movement, slow the tempo, or play with music instead of from memory.
- Set up an alternative performance. Play at the nursing home instead of the contest.
- Offer extra lessons or rehearsals with the accompanist.

Once your students are prepared for the big day, how can you help their best effort shine through in a good performance? The next two chapters will help students and teacher triumph over stage fright to play comfortably in concerts and auditions.

TWENTY-THREE

Conquer Stage Fright

All musicians know the signs: your knees shake, your heart is in your throat, blood pounds in your ears, and your chest feels heavy. Negative thoughts speed faster and faster: "My hands are so sweaty I'll drop my instrument. I can't breathe! I can't hear! I should have practiced more and now I'm going to make a fool of myself! Why did I ever choose to do this performance? Why didn't I remember my *deodorant*?"

Frightened Students, You're Not Alone

Are some people natural-born performers while the rest of us must suffer? True, some performers are so confident they never worry about stage fright, but for many of us, feelings of anxiety and dread can erase six months of hard practice. It's no wonder we say people *suffer* from stage *fright*. Many talented musicians undermine their chances for success when they allow anxious thoughts and feelings to overwhelm them. Help your students avoid this fate by offering them the following advice:

You *Can* Control Your Stage Fright

Sufferers, take heart. You can learn new habits to help you feel more relaxed and confident playing in front of any number of people. Some people think of stage fright as some deadly demon that appears out of nowhere to terrorize them. But stage fright is not something that happens *to* us. It's something *we* create with our own minds. Self-created and self-imposed, our fear of missing a note here or there can kick our adrenaline sky high, trigger other uncomfortable physical symptoms, and strip the joy from any performance. Stage fright is not a permanent condition you need to learn to live with; it's a behavior pattern you can change. Since it is such a universal problem, my advice will apply to both teachers and students. In this chapter I'll show you a step-by-step approach to reducing performance anxiety by preparing your music *and* your mind.

PREPARE YOUR *MUSIC*
Start Practicing NOW

"The best defense is a good offense." Most everyone has heard this saying as it refers to sports teams being prepared with a plan of attack. Since we may lose a large percentage of our ability when faced with the extra pressure of performing, musicians need a plan of attack, too. You might say we need to be prepared "130 percent." Don't be lulled into a false sense of security if your piece is good enough "most of the time," or if you can play the run on the seventh repetition. During your performance, those funny runs or difficult intervals may come back to haunt you. There's a saying in the military that when a great problem or crisis arises, you don't rise to the challenge, you fall to your level of training—so make sure you are trained well.

Plan a Training Schedule and Stick to It

We all hate that sense of panic when we realize we've fallen behind and know it will be almost impossible to catch up. Begin practicing early, or you may find yourself praying for a miracle. Like a long-distance runner, use time management to space your practicing so you won't have to cram at the end. Write out your practice goals with a daily practice schedule that allows you to achieve your goals well ahead of performance day.

PREPARE YOUR *PERFORMANCE*

Why do some students play perfectly during practice sessions, then "fall apart" during pressure situations? Chances are, they've only played their pieces in comfortable, familiar environments and have not learned to adapt to the stresses of performing before a large audience or a judge. I have a sign in my studio that reads, "But I could play it at home!" You may think you sound like James Galway or Yo-Yo Ma in the privacy of your living room, but can you recreate that superior performance in public?

Set Small Performance Goals

The path to a stunning performance can seem long. Start small and set progressively more demanding performance goals along the way. Let's say that it takes you twelve performances to go from panicky first-timer to savvy performer. Set performance goals for each of these performances—even if they start out as small as these.

- Performance ONE: Make it through the performance *alive*.
- Performance TWO: Make it through the performance alive *without fainting or tears*.
- Performance THREE: Make it through alive without fainting or tears, and be able to *remember your name* in the announcement.
- Performance FOUR: Make it through alive without fainting or tears, say your name, and correctly *pronounce the name of the piece and the composer*.
- Performance FIVE: Make it through alive without fainting or tears, say all the names correctly, and then *smile at the audience*.
- Performance SIX: Make it through alive without fainting or tears, say all the names correctly, smile at the audience, and then smile at *the judge*.
- Performance SEVEN: Make it through alive without fainting or tears, say all the names correctly, smile at the audience and at the judge, and *really mean it*.

- Performance EIGHT: Make it through alive without fainting or tears, say all the names, smile at the audience and the judge, and *look confident.*
- Performance NINE: Make it through alive without fainting or tears, say all those names, smile at the audience and the judge, look confident, and *keep playing after you make mistakes.*
- Performance TEN: Make it through alive without fainting or tears, say all those names, give the big smile, look great, keep playing after the mistakes, and *don't beat yourself up* for them.
- Performance ELEVEN: Make it through alive without fainting or tears, say all those names, smile big, look great, make the mistakes, don't worry, be happy, and then *smile and bow* at the end.
- Performance TWELVE: Make it through alive without fainting or tears, say all those names, smile big, look great, make fewer mistakes, take the bow, and know that although everything wasn't perfect, *you did your best, enjoyed the process, shared your music, and look forward to the next time.*

Practice Playing—Even for Audiences Who Can't Hear a Note!

Perform as often as you can, taking baby steps if need be. Start with concerts for stuffed animals or even a chair or music stand. Be your own audience by setting up a tape recorder or videotape. Tape yourself giving your introduction and then playing your piece. Do you sound confident? Oh, by the way, did you get a little nervous when playing in front of the unblinking eye of the video camera? Feeling anxiety when playing alone in a room with a tape recorder or video camera is proof positive that performance anxiety comes from within.

Gradually Increase Your Audience Size

Desensitize your fear of playing in front of people by building a progressively bigger audience. After your concerts for stuffed animals, progress to the family dog, siblings, parents, relatives, and unsuspecting friends and neighbors who drop by. Don't be shy about asking people to be audience members; they will appreciate hearing your music. Ask your "audience" for feedback: How did I come across?

Once you feel confident with your in-home audiences, stretch yourself.

Play for the people who have the lessons before and after you and anyone else who might be around the music room. Perform at the library, hospitals, church, or retirement homes. Grab your friends at school and perform at one another's homes, or perform in front of the band or orchestra. If you have played for an audience nine times before the big event, the tenth time will seem almost routine.

Simulate Your Performance by Role-Playing

Role-playing is practicing a situation in an environment that closely simulates the actual one. Role-playing helps students practice the *performance,* not just the music.

Reinvent the atmosphere of an audition. Take time to warm up, then take at least a ten-minute break (while you wait to be called). Next, run up and down the stairs to simulate the out-of-breath feeling of nervousness. If possible, have "judges" on hand to worry you. If you can't find live judges, play to three chairs.

Simulate your real performance as closely as possible by wearing the same clothes you will wear at the actual event. From the moment you walk through the door you must be "in character." If you stumble up to the front, giggle, wipe your sweaty hands on your clothes, drop pages of your score, sigh, or look distressed, both you and the audience will sense a potential failure. Your posture and look of confidence "set the stage" for a polished performance.

Learn how to shake hands with strangers, look them in the eye, and introduce yourself to gain that aura of self-confidence. Practice walking with your chest lifted, abdomen tight, and chin level with the floor. Performers who walk confidently onstage, make eye contact with the judge and audience, and offer a sincere smile have already begun to win them over. Acting with confidence will also make you *feel* more confident. As a bonus, just turning your lips into a smile emits endorphins that help you relax.

Tune quickly and efficiently, slowly and loudly announce your piece, take time to get ready, and then play your heart out. Acknowledge your audience with a smile and a bow. No matter how the performance went, pretend it was fun. Make your audience feel you are happy to be there—even if you have to fake it. Start the mock auditions at least two weeks before the big day, and the real audition will feel familiar and comfortable.

Know Your Performance Environment

Why do directors call for dress rehearsals? Because every chance to perform under the same conditions boosts confidence and gives insight into what may falter under pressure. Pilots and astronauts use this technique when they learn to fly using simulators. Just as pilots must become comfortable in the cockpit, as a performer you can become more comfortable in front of an audience if you know your performance environment.

If possible, visit the room you'll be playing in even if it is the day of your performance. Note the seating arrangement for the audience and the position of the stage. Notice the position of the music stand, piano, and judge's table. If possible, stand on the stage and mentally place yourself looking out to an audience. Are windows and doors to the sides or in back?

Activate all your senses. Does the room have a particular smell? Is the floor slippery? Does the floor squeak when you walk on it? Do you hear traffic noises? The more specific information you gather about your performance locale, the more successful you'll be with our next suggestion.

Performance Suggestions for *Teachers*

- Plan formal and informal recitals.
- Invite guest teachers to give master classes to students. Students often get nervous when they know a professional musician is listening to them.

• Hold a simulated contest where students play and the audience completes a grading sheet similar to those used by judges in the upcoming contest. Ask "graders" to frown and scribble notes during the performance.

• Require students to participate in a "you are the judge" master class. Each student plays, and after each performance, the other students offer one compliment and one constructive criticism.

• Require all students to perform, even those suffering from stage fright. If students are truly paralyzed, require them to at least attend the concert and invite them to play when they feel ready. Start with playing a duet with the teacher for extra support, or have the teacher sit between the student and the audience. Make sure the first recital piece is easy, to give extra insurance for success.

PREPARE YOUR *MIND*

Being prepared is more than knowing your music cold. It's about knowing how to control your body when it reacts to the stresses of performance, and training your internal voice to speak positively to yourself without judging and criticizing. Most importantly, it's about learning to stay in the moment so you can share your music and your passion with the audience. Let's tackle the self-defeating habits that can contribute to feelings of stage fright.

Forget Perfection

The only "perfect" musical performances are sitting on shelves in jewel cases. Set impeccably high standards for the practice room, but realistic ones for the performance hall. What if you do make that dreaded mistake during a performance? You could choose to berate yourself for the next two pages, causing even more mistakes. But instead of falling apart, get over it! Anticipate that the performance will not be flawless, breathe a sigh of relief, and think, "Well, that's done." Give yourself a second chance and keep going.

Work on what is wrong while reminding yourself of what is right. Keep your mistakes in perspective. Two measures can cloud our feeling of proficiency, even when the rest of the piece is spectacular. Remember, no one wants to see you fail. Giving yourself permission to fail a little relieves the pressure and allows you to stay in touch with your music.

Speak to Yourself Using Positive Self-Talk

We've said it before and we'll say it again, attitude is everything! Have you ever heard of a self-fulfilling prophecy? Just thinking about failing can make us fail. Without playing a note, you can lower your performance by saying discouraging things to yourself. Tune in to the negative messages you're sending yourself and challenge those assumptions. We get into terrible habits of putting ourselves down. If you continually say to yourself, "Everyone is better than me. I know I'll screw up!" your body will be happy to oblige. Imagine if you told yourself every day, "I am a mean and horrible person. I hate everyone and they hate me." Acting and feeling like a caring, giving human being would be against your beliefs. We become what we tell ourselves. Force yourself to use constructive self-talk and eliminate negative thinking. Talk to yourself using the kind words and the attitude you would use with an admired friend.

Imagine the "Worst"

What's the worst that could happen if your performance goes awry? You may feel embarrassed or disappointed, but it won't be life threatening. It's Brahms, not brain surgery. Your teacher and parents will still love you. The audience may not even know. A year from now you'll have forgotten about it. The bottom line is, while it may feel bad, even horrible, at the moment, in the end it will add to your experience and build character, and you will recover if you try to learn from your mistakes.

Recognize What You *Can* and *Can't* Control

You can control your *performance,* but you cannot control its *outcome.* You have no power over whether you're assigned a cranky judge, playing in a cold room, or competing against players who are years ahead of you. You can't control whether your piece appeals to the adjudicators or whether you catch a cold the day before. You only have power over what *you* will do, such as practice early and often. After the best planning and preparation, we may still end up disappointed in our performance. Life is not always fair, so be patient with yourself. Let go of what you can't change and concentrate on doing your best. Focus on the goals of improving and playing musically, not just *winning.* Worry less about what other people do or think and you'll feel a new sense of freedom.

Ignore Distractions

Performances aren't played in a vacuum. As the saying goes, "Stuff happens," and barring an earthquake, "The show must go on!" Ignoring distractions takes effort and practice. Get used to different playing conditions. Practice in every room of the house. Start with the bathroom, where the tone sounds wonderful (tone hospital) and the mirror gives valuable feedback on posture, position, and how your announcement looks. Practice in a common room with lots of commotion: people walking back and forth, the radio or TV playing, cupboards banging, someone talking and laughing on the phone.

I have attended contests where sirens wailed outside and a ballet company danced on the floor above, in rooms with temperatures soaring or freezing rooms with the wind blowing through. Sometimes piano keys stick or you hear performances in the next room. Be prepared.

Focus on Your Playing

How many times have you read a page in a dry textbook and realized you didn't remember a single word as your mind drifted? Try playing your instrument while doing math problems. How much concentration is left for the music? Our own wandering thoughts can interfere with our performance as much as they can reading a book. Learn to bring yourself back on track.

Practice your concentration. Have someone read a book out loud to you. Follow the text and repeat the words right behind them. Listening to the words spoken while you relay the previous words (like a simultaneous translator) forces you to stay focused. As you practice your instrument, make a game with yourself to see how long you can focus on the music without letting other thoughts interfere. As soon as your mind starts to drift, make a conscious effort to pull it back. Ignore extraneous thoughts as you would ignore a four-year-old trying to disturb you on stage.

To Teachers: The Recital from *Hell*

Here is a fun recital that develops concentration. Warn your students ahead of time so they won't think you have gone off the deep end! Tell them you will be doing your best to distract them while they play. Emulate the worst conditions possible in any performance to help teach your students to concentrate and continue playing through any disturbance.

Invite all students (even those not performing) to be "judges." Players are allowed to go to another room to warm up but then must sit at least ten minutes inside the room to let their instrument get cold and build their anxiety before their turn. As each student performs, I act like the mean or wacky judge and make the atmosphere as "unwelcoming" as possible. I coldly ask each student to begin, and then look bored and distracted. Then the fun begins as I create a different "torture" for each performer.

Be creative. Be the judge from hell. Get everyone involved in the act. This recital is hilarious and your students will learn to play through *anything!*

- Act bored. Look at your watch. Say "Next" and then sigh deeply.
- "What did you say?" Ask students to repeat the announcement of their name and the piece until it sounds loud and proud. Again. And again.
- Whisper during the performance. Say, "Isn't this the thirtieth violin we have heard today?" "Why does everyone have to play the violin?" "I think that last girl was better, don't you?" "I have always hated this piece." "What score did you give her?" "That dress is ugly." "She's flat . . . I was talking about her *pitch.*"
- Isn't this the Olympics? Hold up a score card for the audience to respond to.
- Scribble on a judging form. Write faster if the student makes a mistake.
- Walk by and brush the student's shoulder. Breathe down her neck.
- Sit in the judge's chair. Wiggle the chair. Wiggle your foot and your leg and your arm and your head.
- Jiggle the stand. They don't make stands like they used to.
- Play wrong notes in the accompaniment. Stop and start. Play the wrong tempo or dynamic.
- Walk past wearing a Santa hat. A pair of funny glasses. Or a fake nose.
- Invite the dog or the neighbor's three-year-old to "listen."
- Turn the cold fan on the performer. Let it rustle the music.

- Turn the heater on high. Way too close and way too high.
- Let a book or lamp crash to the floor. Oops!
- Run up and down the stairs.
- Let a stack of papers fall over the floor, and make a scene cleaning them up. Take time to shuffle them back in order.
- Throw a ball or a pillow at the performer's feet.
- Dim and brighten the lights.
- Eat crisp potato chips. Pour fizzy pop.
- Circle the student. Glare.
- Walk in and out of the room. Bang the door. Say "Excuse me" every time and smile.
- Play the piece at the same time in a different room—two measures ahead.
- Order pizza on the phone. Don't forget the anchovies.
- Have fun!

Students may counter that these things don't happen in real life (although who knows?), but their powers of concentration should be able to withstand any outside distractions as well as their powerful inner voice.

Focus on Your Music

Remember why you are doing this in the first place: because you *love* music. When stage fright rears its ugly head, plunge yourself into playing. Gain control of your wandering thoughts first with the technical aspects, including correct notes, rhythm, intonation, and tone, and then, more importantly, give yourself over to the music. If it is a calm piece, imagine playing to soothe a baby; if the piece is romantic, tell the world you are in love; and if the piece is exciting, get supercharged. You love this piece, so make your audience love it too!

Imagine Success with Visualization

Athletes and musicians alike find it beneficial to visualize performance situations and how they will respond to them. Studies have shown that basketball players, for instance, can improve their performance by only imagining shooting and making baskets. Visualization, or mental rehearsal, can also help you prepare for a successful performance.

Even if you have never visited the performance room, still try to envision it. Picture where the judges and audience will sit and where you will perform. Imagine every detail of your performance, from walking into the room, announcing your name and piece, to playing every note perfectly. When you mentally rehearse the music, play wonderfully, and always end with a standing ovation! When performance day arrives, you'll feel more confident having already "experienced" the competition.

Visualization is more than humming the song to yourself. Visualization is like watching a great movie and feeling, hearing, and seeing yourself in a perfect performance. When you practice using imagery, your body will better know what it is supposed to do. A good time to practice visualization is when lying in bed in a dark room with no distractions and right before you fall asleep. During this twilight time, your thoughts tend to stay in your subconscious and create a memory as if you had experienced it. Tip: This is also a good time to memorize material for school tests.

Visualize the good, not the bad

One of the most important aspects of visualization is imagining a positive result, not an embarrassing scenario. On the big day, while you're waiting to perform, imagine the audience clapping and feel your happiness from a job well done. Focus your energy on your feelings of confidence and competence. By banishing negative thoughts and visualizing success, you can learn to think and act like a winner. Later, we'll discuss a proven routine you can put into action that will carry you from the time you're waiting your turn until you've finished your successful performance.

Savor the Sweet Taste of Success

No, I'm not talking about eating chocolate. Get in touch with the rewards of all your hard work. As you work toward the next concert or contest, remember how your practicing allowed you to play the last piece with fun and ease. Weren't you proud of yourself? Isn't it worth all that practice to make it happen again?

Your Audience: Friend or Foe?

How many of us have gone on stage, heart pounding, asking ourselves, "What will they think when I mess up?" But do *you* sit in the audience thinking, "I can't wait until the performer makes a mistake? There's one. Great!" Of course not. You're there to enjoy the music, and you feel sorry for performers who trip up. The audience is rooting for you. They don't want to see you looking nervous or making excuses. They want to relax in the confidence of your performance, see you succeed, and enjoy themselves. The audience is not the enemy; in fact *we* are our *own* worst enemies.

Many people try to *fight* their fear by separating themselves from their audience. They might pretend the audience isn't there, or imagine them wearing their underwear or even wearing nothing at all. While the underwear trick may work for some people, I don't advise it. When you distance yourself from your audience, you focus even more on your fears. You go into your head and not into the moment. Embrace the audience by remembering your purpose and you will become "music-conscious" instead of "self-conscious." Think of sharing your music as a service to others; you'll enjoy yourself more and the audience will, too.

Tell the Audience Your Story

Imagine a minister who concentrates on the sound of his own voice instead of the message of his sermon. His congregation would lose interest quickly. The same thing happens when we focus just on our tone and technique and not on the feeling and expression we wish to convey. Communicate to the audience the beauty of the piece, not just your fingering technique.

Imagine what the composer thought when writing the piece. Picture a scene, a person, an event, even a mood or a color. Treat each piece like program music that depicts a person, place, event, conversation, or emotion. Let this picture help you share the drama with your audience.

Now that you have the screenplay, you need the actor, and that's you! Recall performers you've seen who look totally natural on stage. Picture a famous singer performing your piece on stage or in a movie. How would they sing it? Emulate their behaviors. Move past the notes to become your character and communicate your story. These stories we create focus on the feelings the music conveys, not on ourselves.

Now that you have your mind under control, what can you do for your shaking body?

TAME THE PHYSIOLOGICAL
ASPECTS OF STAGE FRIGHT

Recognize the physical sensations of stage fright and know which symptoms (such as dry mouth or sweaty hands) you're most likely to experience. Managing your emotions before these symptoms appear gives you power over them. Try these methods to minimize your body's uncomfortable responses.

- Feeling out of breath: If one of your symptoms of stage fright is feeling breathless or running out of breath, run up and down the stairs a few times to simulate that feeling during practice sessions. Then play the audition piece to learn how to control your breathing.

- Shallow breathing: Breathe in slowly and deeply for a count of five, hold it five seconds, and then breathe out slowly for five counts. Some psychologists call this "square breathing," a technique used to combat panic attacks. Repeat until your breathing feels more normal. If you play a wind or brass instrument, circle the important breaths in a color to remind yourself to breathe deeply.

- Hiccups: Try making snake sounds by hissing to control the diaphragm.

- Dry mouth: Keep hydrated. Don't eat salty foods before your performance. Be careful about drinking too much water, though, because it can replace your natural saliva. Try eating a cookie or a piece of candy to make your mouth water, or chew "Quench" gum, which keeps you hydrated. If you are desperate you can massage the sides of your throat or bite your tongue. Avoid taking cold medicine containing antihistamines, as these can dry your mouth.

- Too much saliva: Tilt your head back slightly to move the spit back. Take an antihistamine before the performance.

- Tight throat: Yawn to relax your throat. Remember that open position when it's time to play. Breathe in with an open throat and keep it open as you breathe out.

- Sweaty hands: Rub unscented deodorant on your hands. Run your hands and wrists under cold water just prior to coming onstage. Keep a loose grip on your instrument.

- Sweaty lips: Put a stamp or use lip plate grips on the instrument.
- Cold, shaky hands: Wear gloves to warm them. If you can, immerse your hands in warm water and dry them well before you play.
- The shakes: Shake out the shakes! Get blood out into your hands and away from your heart as it prepares you for fight or flight. If possible, take a short walk and breathe deeply.
- Feeling upset: Think of something funny like a pet or a joke or smile at a friend right before you play. Activating your smiling muscles elevates your mood.
- Neck and shoulder tension: Bring your shoulders up to your ears. Count to five, and then bring them all the way back down. Roll your shoulders forward, then back. Do neck circles.
- Shaky tone: Concentrate on support, deep breaths, and being in control of vibrato.
- General feelings of nervousness: Concentrate on how much you've practiced and how good you are! Acknowledge nervousness as excitement.

Try the Alexander Technique

When under the pressure of performance our bodies need more adrenaline to perform the task. The difference between tension and a peak performance is how our bodies handle that adrenaline. The Alexander Technique fosters spontaneity and creativity by helping the body move in good coordination. Simply putting the body in alignment can help overcome the tightness and tension from adrenaline and make movement help the performance.

Natural Calming Agents

Food

Bananas and turkey have been touted for their ability to calm nerves and aid sleep. The helpful ingredient they contain is tryptophan, an essential amino acid, a substance the body cannot produce naturally and must get from food. Tryptophan helps the body produce niacin, a B-vitamin, which in turn produces a remarkable chemical called serotonin that has been proven to promote feelings of well-being, calm, relaxation, confidence, and concentration. People used to take tryptophan supplements, but we've since learned that the safe way to get this amino acid is by eating whole foods. Monitor how much of these you eat before a concert, though, or you may feel like curling up for a nap or racing to the bathroom!

Biofeedback

Physical therapists can connect you to a biofeedback machine that will measure where and how much tension you are carrying in your body. With this reinforcement, you can learn to relax specific areas such as the neck and shoulders.

Meditation

Unbelievable things can happen through meditation. A friend of mine meditated (not medicated) her way through childbirth! Even if you are not a master at meditation, learn to center and relax before every performance.

A word about beta-blockers

Prescription beta-blocker pills such as Inderal are used in the treatment of high blood pressure, angina, and other symptoms of cardiovascular problems. Because they act to steady heartbeats, they have also proven useful in steadying performers' nerves. Many professional musicians use them before auditions and performances, although some report that though Inderal helped their nerves, it also made them feel more detached from the music and audience.

While beta-blockers have been shown to be effective, their misuse can be dangerous, especially in asthmatics. Taking this prescription medication is something you must discuss with your doctor. Never accept medication from a friend or relative. Relying on drugs doesn't address the real problem. The best solution is not medication but focusing on techniques to combat anxiety and self-doubt.

ANTICIPATE PERFORMANCE DAY

Star athletes begin their training months in advance of the big event; we too must train our bodies and our music to prepare for performance day.

Two Weeks before Your Performance

Be "contest ready"

If you can play the trick runs only five times correctly out of fifty repetitions, those are not good odds! If you can barely play the phrase in one breath, be assured that under pressure, you will be gasping at the end. Keep your standards high as you learn your piece. Don't allow yourself to leave a passage as "good enough." Keep going back until you can play it with at least a 90 percent success rate. Aim for a date at least two weeks prior to your performance to be "contest ready." This means playing a performance you can be proud of every time.

Prepare yourself with the "first chance" practice method

How many times have we performed and wished we could say, "Cancel that one!" and play it again? During a performance, we only get one chance. Test your preparedness with the "first chance" method. For one week, at the *beginning* of each practice session, play through the piece without stopping. Ask yourself, "Did I play at the level I'll be happy with for my performance?" Be assured that you're ready if you have five good "first chances" in a row. For every mistake you make, give yourself a "penalty" such as five minutes extra practice that night or taking one piece of candy from your reward stash. The reward if you perform it perfectly? A boost in your confidence.

Pace yourself

Athletes alternate strenuous workouts with more relaxed workouts. Likewise, musicians must learn to balance the need for improvement against the danger of burnout. Practicing hours on end does not necessarily mean improved performance if your mind is not engaged and your body is tired. Sometimes the best thing you can do to improve a piece is to take a day off. Don't practice every piece every day. Some days lighten your practice routine or don't practice at all.

Dress for success

What you wear can give people an impression of who you are. One year one of my students showed up wearing an outfit that reflected something other than "talented flute student." She walked onto the stage wearing a tight knit dress with plunging neckline, enormous hoop earrings, fishnet stockings, and strappy high heels. At the same contest, another student refused to change out of her school clothes and came dressed in an old wrinkled shirt and jeans with a hole in the knee! Thankfully the judge commented on both of their inappropriate clothing choices.

Keep in mind that you're dressing for the judge, not your friends. This is the time to be sophisticated, not trendy. I like my students to dress in distinctive colors because I think judges may be more likely to remember the girl in the red dress or the boy in the bright blue shirt than players dressed in dark, drab colors. Black pants or skirt and a white top are always appropriate, but a little boring and reminiscent of a French waiter. Other times, I recommend my students dress to reflect the piece they're to perform. A modern piece could be paired with a sophisticated outfit and the Doppler *Hungarian Fantasie* could be paired with an outfit with gypsy flair. My students' ensembles usually match each other in some way, such as all wearing blue, solid tops with floral skirts, or black skirts and red sweaters. When you know you look great, your mind will be free to concentrate on more important things—including your playing! Dressing well shows your respect for the event and the judges. Wear something that reflects how you want the audience to see you.

Leave this *clothing behind*

Regardless of your age or style of clothing, please cross certain items off your wardrobe list: wild prints and patterns, tippy high heels, short short skirts, fishnet stockings, T-shirts, tennis shoes, jeans, plunging necklines (or waistlines), and exposed bra straps; and *please,* no bare bellies! Above all, be comfortable and classy.

Continue visualizing success

In the days leading up to your performance, arrange for as many mock auditions as possible and keep visualizing yourself performing with confidence. Imagine the smiling faces and loud applause of the audience. Look forward to the event as a time to "show off" what you have learned and to play great music.

Create a routine

Practice your piece slowly, in a quiet, calm room. While you play, focus on relaxing and putting all negative thoughts and emotions aside. This will help you associate relaxation with playing your piece.

If possible, create a routine that can be duplicated on performance day. Getting up at the same time, eating the same breakfast, practicing technique in the same order, even saying a mantra ("I love performing") right before playing every day will help make performance day seem like any other. Instead of a general mantra you may also pick the two things that you hope to succeed on and make them your mantra: for instance, singing tone, strong breaths, or even vibrato, or perfect intonation. Getting in the habit of repeating your mantra right before you play will help you remember what to concentrate on and will calm you down.

Two Days before Your Performance

Practice slowly to retain your confidence. Concentrate on every aspect of playing *but speed.* For at least two nights before the concert, go to bed early and get a good night's sleep. Exercising moderately in the afternoon will help you sleep better, but exercising too close to bedtime may have an energizing effect. Confirm transportation arrangements to and from the performance hall. Double-check with friends and family you've invited to attend. Plan what to bring with you on the day of your performance. You might include a water bottle, tissues, snacks, your camera, and, of course, your music and your instrument!

While stage fright or performance anxiety will diminish, it rarely disappears completely. It can return in full force when you are not prepared for a performance. If that happens, review what you did well and what is in your power to correct, and aim to do better next time. I hope reading this chapter has inspired you to try new strategies for overcoming your fears. Continue to practice overcoming stage fright right along with practicing your instrument. When you consistently apply these methods you'll notice a growing trust and confidence in yourself. Now read on to see how all this preparation plays out at the audition.

TWENTY-FOUR

Ace the Audition

In chapter 22, "Prepare Students for Performance," and chapter 23, "Conquer Stage Fright," we talked about how to prepare for the big day. Now it's here. *What do you do?* Offer these tips to give students their best shot at success.

PLAN YOUR PERFORMANCE DAY

The contest routine starts from the minute you wake up. Or more exactly, started when you went to bed the night before. Practicing until two in the morning and then getting up at seven denies your body the energy and defenses it needs for the big day. A former student of mine thought she was totally prepared for her crucial audition at Juilliard. But on the night of the audition, she accidentally set her alarm for *p.m.* instead of *a.m.* and she awoke an hour late. A nightmare! With her stomach empty and heart pounding, she raced to her audition. She arrived in the nick of time, but feeling a lot less composed than she had planned to be. Get your sleep and set your alarm right!

The focus of the day should be the audition. If you are serious about performing well, make it the top priority of the day. This is not the day to do errands, work on taxes, or go sightseeing. The plan for the day is to keep as calm and focused as possible.

Eat Wisely

Eat a well-balanced meal. Include a mix of carbohydrate and protein. Filling up on only carbohydrates gives you instant energy but your blood sugar may plummet by the time you perform. A mix of two-thirds carbohydrate and one-third protein will give you continuous fuel. Try eating a piece of whole wheat bread and cheese, an apple with peanut butter, or a dish of yogurt and a piece of fruit. Eating a banana or turkey can help your body produce calming agents. Vocalists, be cautious of eating dairy products before your performance. Avoid caffeine and alcohol. (How do those jazz musicians do it?) Keep yourself well hydrated several hours before the event by drinking at least four cups of water in the two hours before the performance. You'll avoid being dehydrated—a major source of fatigue—and will feel more alert on stage. Schedule a pit stop before you go on.

Exercise

Our body releases adrenaline when we are nervous, but slows production of adrenaline after exercise. Exercise also releases hormones called endorphins that make us feel relaxed and happy. Take a walk or a run outside early in the day, or, if possible, before you perform. It will get you awake and ready, and will clear your mind of cobwebs. If you don't have time for a walk, step outside for a moment. To shake out jitters, some people even run in place or do jumping jacks before going on stage. Remove those high heels first!

AT THE CONCERT HALL

Arrive Early and Well-Rested

Plan on being at the performance hall at least an hour before you are to perform. This gives you a cushion of time to allow for getting lost, being stuck in traffic, finding a parking spot, or getting sick in the car (just kidding). Arrive early to allow time to size up the room, and walk a little to calm your nerves. If you've followed this advice you'll arrive with your body fueled, hydrated, and refreshed after at least two good nights' sleep and not experience the nightmare of my student Anna:

> It was finally competition day. I woke up on time, showered, dressed, and then woke my dad, who was driving me. After our breakfast it was suddenly time to go. That's when things got crazy. Who was riding with us? My mom? My sister? By the time I got my whole family into the car we were already late. Then I realized I didn't have my music! I frantically searched all over the house and by the time I found it, I had that terrible feeling in the pit of my stomach.
>
> Every red light made me crazy. I pressed my foot on the floor wishing I had the gas pedal. When I got to the contest I didn't have that precious time to warm up, that time to focus on my music, my goals, and myself. I bolted out of the car and rushed, out of breath, to the performance room. Who was to blame for my being late?
>
> When you arrive at the contest unprepared and rushed, you are already *finished*. I advise other students to tell their parents you have to be at the contest site at least a half an hour earlier than is necessary, so there are no fights in the car or trying to beat red lights!

Bring a Cheering Section

If possible, bring friends and family to give you the "home court" advantage. Encouraging students to attend each other's performances fosters support instead of competition. Even if you are on a college audition tour, it helps to know Mom or Dad is just outside rooting for you.

Begin Your Pre-performance Routine

You've practiced every nuance of your piece, dressed appropriately, and arrived on time with your music. Now what? Maintain an established routine when you arrive. This makes your waiting time more predictable and productive. Here's how to make that tedious waiting time more productive.

Make a pit stop

First, head to the bathroom and check your appearance. Smile at your reflection—you'll feel better! Make note of where the bathrooms are so you can easily run back if your nerves bring on the urge.

Scope out the performance room

If you've been visualizing the room for weeks, none of what you see should surprise you. If possible, if you haven't been to the room before, check to see where the judge sits, where the music stand is, and where the entrants wait for their turn. Notice how the entrants announce themselves. Listen to a few people if possible to understand the protocol and get a feel for the judge.

Retreat to the warm-up room

Notice that now we call it the *warm-up* room, not the *practice* room. It's too late to practice now. Now is the time to practice slow scales as though they are opera melodies, to repeat tone exercises, and to run through the piece at only half-speed. My student Lauren never practices her contest pieces right before she plays; she soothes her nerves by only playing her favorite beautiful pieces slowly. The danger in practicing the audition piece up to tempo is that any mistakes you make will cause self-doubt and anxiety. Take this time to enjoy your instrument and the music, not test yourself.

Meditate and breathe

Put down your instrument and take the time to be totally alone and become centered. Sit up straight with both feet on the floor, put your hands on your thighs, or cradle one hand with the other. With eyes half-open, relax and listen to your breathing. Don't let other thoughts protrude into your mind. Try isometrics to relax. Tense your body. Squeeze hands, shoulders and chest tight then notice the difference when you release them. Maintain that relaxed body.

Breathe in through your nose and exhale through your mouth. (Mouth breathing can be drying.) While you exhale say a mantra such as the words *Ohm,* or *sky,* or *I'm calm,* to focus on and control thoughts. Breathe in on the count of five beats, hold your breath for five, and then exhale for five. As you wait for your turn to play, keep your breathing slow, deep, and even. If you begin to feel light-headed, take more shallow breaths.

Don't let them see you sweat

Many performers believe the hardest time to control anxiety is right before we play. When you're waiting your turn, force away any negative self-talk and visualize only positive outcomes. Remember happy times and successful performances. I sometimes pass around cartoons at contests to help break the tension. Close your eyes and hear the thunderous applause of an appreciative audience. See their smiling faces as you take a gracious bow after a winning performance.

Be Prepared

One year at an important contest, I witnessed the most complete lack of preparation for performance I have ever seen. When 14-year-old Jaclyn's name was called, she remained seated, calling out "Wait a minute!" as she rummaged through her backpack for her music. Finally she pulled out a pile of photocopies and trudged up toward the stage dressed in jeans with shiny zippers running down both sides and embellished with metal hoops and studs. Wild red-streaked hair framed her face. Her top, a tie-dyed T-shirt, was adorned with several homemade beaded necklaces that swung as her sturdy hiking boots clunked to the music stand. Immediately she dropped her straggly bundle.

Sighing, she then turned to the piano to tune with her accompanist. After she tuned she shrugged, as if to say, "I guess that was good enough?" Her pianist said, "So what order are we playing these pieces in?" The order was decided and then she asked the pianist, "How fast should we play the first one?" When the girl finally played she stumbled on the runs and her body slumped along with her flute, dragging toward the floor. The saddest thing about this whole scenario was that even through the badly chosen packaging, it was obvious this girl had talent and personality. She moved her fingers quickly and sparkled when she spoke to the judge, yet I knew she would never get anywhere without the guidance of a good teacher and a trip to "charm school." Remember, you are on stage from the moment you walk in the room.

You're *On*!

You hear a name called. It's yours! Now you must make your entrance. All your planning and preparation will now begin to pay off. To avoid that feeling of "My gosh, now what?" memorize this routine that you can put into action once your name is called. Above all, take your time.

Before you play, follow these steps:

- Tune before you come on into the room.
- Take a deep breath and tell yourself, "Remember to breathe." Exhale as slowly and quietly as you can. Remember, you've practiced diligently and you're prepared.
- Rise from your chair and walk confidently toward the stage, making brief eye contact with the judge.
- Announce your name slowly and loudly. Use this time to get used to being on stage. Stand still while you talk. Don't fuss with your clothes, rock from side to side, push your hair back, or scratch yourself—anywhere!
- Make eye contact with a few people in the audience. Imagine you are playing for these few people. Some students have a ritual of smiling at their moms right before they play.
- Present yourself to the audience with confidence. They have no idea what you're thinking, and your nervousness will not show as intensely as it feels to you. Show them you are happy to be there and have a wonderful story to tell.
- Before you begin to play, quickly recheck the pitch to be sure you are in tune. Take time to get it right.
- Adjust the piano bench or music stand to the proper height. Don't hide behind the music stand; let the audience see your face. Try putting the stand down low and flattening it to make it less obtrusive.

- Take a moment to think about the first few phrases of the piece and get into character or say your rehearsed mantra ("Beautiful tone" and "dramatic dynamics."). There is no rush. Gather your thoughts and give the audience a moment of anticipation. Remember to share your passion.

Here we go!

- Breathe deeply. Especially on wind instruments, shallow breathing can lead to nervousness and bad playing. We need the oxygen for our body and fingers to perform even when we play the piano.
- Don't clutch your instrument; maintain a relaxed grip. You should feel it resting loosely but firmly in your hands.
- Keep balanced on both feet. Most people feel secure with feet about shoulder width apart and one foot slightly in front of the other. Don't tap your foot along with the music! If you must keep time, wiggle *only* a toe in your shoe. Keep your knees bent to help get a deeper sound on wind instruments and prevent fainting (that's a good thing).
- Begin playing that opening line you've memorized to perfection. Often your stage fright will disappear as you keep playing and get into your piece.
- Keep in character. It breaks the spell if you smile (or look scared!) at the audience in the middle of the piece.
- Keep an upright posture. Don't bend over when the going gets tough. Remember, you are a performer and this is all part of your act.
- Don't let the audience know your mistakes by your facial expressions. Don't grimace or sigh when something goes wrong. Even if you make a mistake, maintain a positive impression. Fake it. Move on.
- It's over: No matter how you feel you performed, don't grab your music and charge off the stage. Bow graciously; acknowledge your accompanist and the audience's applause. You did it!

PREPARING FOR COLLEGE OR PROFESSIONAL ORCHESTRA AUDITIONS

The next part of this chapter addresses the special challenges of the college or orchestra audition. I will share tips I've used to help many of my students succeed in the college and conservatory audition process. I will also draw on the advice of professional musician friends who have been on both sides of the screen. Christina, who did her undergraduate studies at the Manhattan School of Music and her graduate studies at Rice University, offers this advice about conservatory auditions:

> The auditions themselves were different from anything I had ever experienced. Every one was unique. I flew into each city a few days before the audition, and had to quickly adapt to the unfamiliar place and its weather. Though suffering from jet lag, I had to play my absolute best. And in those same two days, I had to evaluate the school to see if I wanted to spend the next four years of my life there. Quite a daunting task! I always contacted the flute professor at each school ahead of time and requested a lesson.

This was really helpful. Sure, getting into a famous conservatory is wonderful, but if the teacher is not right for you, you will be miserable. Get to know as much as you can about the school, the programs offered, and the professor, and then you will be prepared to make your choice.

What to Play for the College Audition

- Know your scales from memory.
- Play pieces you can nail, rather than reaching for something that might be too difficult technically. Play contrasting pieces that show all aspects of your technique and musicality. Though you may think they are "easy," Bach and Mozart reveal technique and musicality.
- Choose repertoire that can double for auditions at more than one school.
- If you have a choice, start out with your easiest piece to gain confidence.
- Select the piece that shows off your fantastic sound. Pay close attention to vibrato (unless you are playing the piano!).
- Study concerto and orchestra excerpts until you know them inside and out. Listen to the CD and study the orchestra score to see how your part fits in so that you can play in context. Play as if you hear the orchestra playing along with you. Ask an orchestra musician or conductor to listen to you play prior to the audition.
- Practice with the *Orchestral Musician's* CD-ROM volumes. Print out the full orchestral part and start with Beethoven. Know the whole orchestra piece and not just your excerpt. Understand how your excerpt fits into the rest of the movement.
- Use actual orchestra parts, not excerpts, which might not have all the right markings.
- If the audition will be behind a screen, practice behind one or facing away from your audience to learn how to communicate without the visual impact.

Simulate Normalcy

Auditions for orchestras and for some conservatories are unique. With a call-back system, you are never sure of when you will have to play and what you will have to play. You may draw the number to play first or to play fortieth. You may have no time to eat or no place to warm up. The whole system may give you no sense of time or normalcy. (Sounds fun, huh?) Here are some suggestions to give you an edge.

- Bring something to read or something mindless to do, like knitting, to keep your mind occupied if you have a long wait.
- Bring something light to eat and drink.
- Give yourself quiet time. Talking too much can tire the embouchure and take away from time to inwardly prepare.
- Make a connection with your audience. Remember you are on stage the moment you walk into the room.

• Be careful about how much you eat and how much water you drink. Go to the bathroom (and check your zipper!) before you go on stage.

• Check your watch before you walk out. Look around to get your bearings. Take an extra few seconds to take a few calming breaths.

• If you make a mistake in a college audition, show your maturity and concentration by going on.

• Knock 'em dead!

How to Play for Auditions

• Adjust your sound to the room. In a very dry room, play staccatos longer and add more vibrato.

• Because so many players are now so technically proficient, the key (especially with strings) may be vibrato and warmth.

• If you are playing behind a screen, go for even bigger dynamics and dynamic contrasts, as the screen deadens the sound.

• Be a human metronome.

• Fast fingers are not everything, although in some auditions it may seem that way. Tone and phrasing should count as much or more.

• Listen to CDs of the orchestra or the conductor you are auditioning for to know their tempos and what the conductor is looking for. Study the major orchestras and learn what they value. The Philadelphia Orchestra, for example, is known for its big, luscious, fat sound. The L.A. Philharmonic has its own interesting musical personality.

• If you are auditioning for a particular teacher, listen to recordings of that teacher.

• Most orchestras opt for the competitor who makes the fewest mistakes. With competition so high, you can hardly afford to make one.

• Orchestras are looking for someone to fit in. Their number one priority is rhythm, number two is pitch, and number three is sound.

• If auditioning for an assistant job, work to be able to blend your sound and vibrato with the principal player.

• Become more marketable. Know how to play all "variations" of your instrument, such as piccolo and alto flute, English horn, contrabassoon, etc.

• Orchestras are also looking for someone who is a leader and a follower. They want someone who will be part of the team. Personality counts.

• Colleges and orchestras are looking for someone who looks like they enjoy what they are doing. If you enjoy the music, the committee will too.

The (Unreal) World of Perfection

Students receive conflicting advice from teachers on how to best play an orchestra audition. Because of the intense competition for orchestra jobs, technical perfection has almost come to be the baseline. Because there is no room for error, many musicians have decided to "play it safe." They play with a safe tone to avoid a cracked note and to fit in, and they play with a safe interpretation to not offend anyone. A bad sound, out-of-tune note, or imprecise rhythm will get you eliminated in the first and second rounds of the orchestra audition.

But if everyone is perfect and everyone sounds the same, then how can they choose a winner? Some teachers advise students to exaggerate tone, dynamics, and phrasing to stand out in the crowd or even prove it is possible. Other teachers say to play it safe and play what is on the page and no more. Other teachers advise students to follow their heart and play the music as they think it should be played and hope the judge on that day agrees.

Instant Replay

After each audition, take stock of what went right and what went wrong. If the audition was not successful, what did you learn? Were you taken off-guard by the questions or format? Were there any surprises? Did you prepare well? Did stage fright rear its ugly head? Did you play less than your best because of physical problems related to travel? Or did you play your best and was your style not what the judges were looking for? Were you great, but was someone else greater? Are you being realistic about your abilities? Are you being realistic about the opportunities on your instrument and in your field? Don't let a few disappointments discourage you. Try, try again.

Some thoughts:

- Ask your friends to help you prepare for the audition. Ask for their musical advice and use them for mock auditions to help get over nerves.
- Play lots of chamber music to learn to listen to others in a group and to refine musicianship.
- Don't be so busy practicing excerpts and audition pieces that you forget to study music. Tunnel vision cuts you off from the real world of great artists, concerts, and composers.
- Music school and orchestra positions are now international competitions, with a big percentage of players coming from around the world. Recognize the odds.
- Realize that orchestra auditions may seem to have nothing to do with the actual job opening. Violinists are asked to prepare solos from *Don Juan* and *Capriccio Espagnol* to audition to play in the middle of the second violin section. A better audition would be for finalists to sit in the section on probation.
- Make sure audition tapes are high quality. Some students even record in rented cathedrals or rehearsal halls. A professional tape should not be compromised. It may cost big money but is a necessity of life in the music world.

VIEWS OF A VETERAN AUDITIONER

Lois Bliss Herbine, flutist with Orchestra 2001, has recorded for the CRI and Albany labels and for radio and television. I appreciate her sharing her experiences and philosophy with us.

"I believe the orchestral audition process has no correlation to the actual job. As an orchestral musician, when do you ever stand on stage alone, save one person sitting and listening to you at your back? Where you have no accompanying musicians? No conductor? No audience? Where else do you need to play better than the musicians performing the selections before and after you or you are out of a job?

"Students are the best candidates for this type of audition experience. They are used to having their teacher standing alongside them, judging them as they play the standard unaccompanied excerpts. They compete against other students, vying for positions and solos. Those musicians considering taking an orchestral audition would do well to prepare by taking weekly lessons and entering competitions.

"As an orchestral flutist and piccoloist, I am a team player. I match ensemble and pitch and I work with other flutists, not against them. I do play my solos like a soloist but unless I'm playing the opening to the *Prelude to l'apres-midi d'un faune* I am sensitive to the fact that my solos are always performed with someone else and I'm following the conductor. Not having the musicians there in the audition to work with, blend with, follow, or lead, then being judged for the job I am doing without them doesn't make any sense, but in this day and age it is how it's done. A sports team would not hold tryouts without seeing what the player does on the field with the other players. I'm not sure why we continue to hold auditions this way.

"In the audition there is nothing to look at, nothing to listen to, and if the judges don't ask for something differently, nothing to respond to. I personally play better for an audience than I do alone. I do get nervous playing for people who are judging me and much more for those who can't show their faces because the audition is held behind a screen. Mistakes happen because of these nerves that would never happen in performance. I liken the process to a gunfight at OK Corral. I'm standing in the center of town with my pistols drawn and I'm sure there is more than one gunfighter hiding behind the saloon gauging the right time to make their move. Since I can't see or relate to them I can't engage or disarm them. In the end, I get blown away.

"My worst audition experience started with my first exposure to a 'cattle room,' a place where all auditioners are sent to warm up together. Sometimes it's the only place made available, other times its use is offered until a private room opens up (about ten minutes prior to the audition). Since the auditioner is not given the opportunity to prepare quietly and thoughtfully, it's the prime spot to become the victim of mind games. This was such a bad experience for me that it helped me stay away from auditions for years. As I warmed up for my audition in a large room with at least a dozen other piccoloists I ran through the excerpt from the *Semiramide* Overture. This excerpt was not difficult for me, nor did I feel threatened by any of the players in the room, but I flubbed the first run-through. Concerned and a bit embarrassed, I played it again and made the same mistake. Instead of stopping and slowing the music down to correct the problem, I continued to play it in succession, getting more frantic and making the same mistake every time. Going through my head was a mixture of 'How can I be missing this? I know it cold; I don't need to slow down to get this!' and 'I hope no one here recognizes me!' At the point when I finally gave in and slowed it down to clean it up the damage had already been done. By the time I exited the room I was a bundle of nerves and had set myself up for the worst audition experience I ever had. I had pre-pared for over six months and driven a thousand miles—five minutes and twenty-eight measures later it was all over.

"The best audition experience I had was for one of the top ten American sym-phony orchestras. The preliminaries were by invitation only and were held on the stage of their largest concert hall. I was awestruck standing for the first time on this stage with the elegant crystal lighting. It was so inspiring that I pretended to play for a packed house of twenty-five hundred eager audience members instead of a committee of judges behind a screen. It was the best I had ever played for an orchestral audition, far better than the later semifinal round, when the spell was broken and I was back to a screened competition for a position. With the help of the personnel manager, the judges sought me out afterwards to speak with me. I had been eliminated after the sec-ond round, but they revealed to me that I was the top contender after the first.

"I took something else valuable home with me from this audition—the judging sheets. This is not often offered, but the auditioner should always ask for this or for a judge's personal feedback. From these sheets I learned the reasons I was elevated as well as ways to improve my performance. I've become a better performer by acting on these suggestions.

"Sometimes the judge's comments can be revealing in a different way, and we need to ask a trusted teacher or colleague to look over the comments and verify their sugges-tions. After my audition for a regional symphony orchestra fifteen years ago, one of the judges told me my opening to the Vivaldi Concerto in C Major was not 'even.' The committee was interested in hearing the opening sixteenth note passage metronomic and straight, while I was emphasizing the first of the groups, which were the melody notes, by elongation and volume. The committee did not ask me to play it differently, so I was eliminated from the onset.

"From years of experience, I've learned:

1. Even the top auditioner has room to improve.

2. No one should overlook the auditioner quickly eliminated from the start.

3. Last but not least: There are ways to have a satisfying career in music other than winning an orchestral audition."

TWENTY-FIVE

When It's Time to Say Goodbye

"Oh no, it's Tuesday." Patty's stomach tightens. "*Sharon's* lesson is today. No wonder I'm getting a headache. I can't believe how she talked to me last week! She acted liked she hated every minute of the lesson. She never practices. She can't even remember to bring her books to the lesson. If I hear her play one more piece in D major with C-naturals I am going to scream! I hope she remembers to bring the check for her last two months of lessons. Better yet, maybe she'll call in sick and mail the check!"

"What more can I do to turn her around?" Patty wonders. "I already applied the great ideas from *Music for Life,* such as teaching her practice techniques and setting goals. I followed the advice about instilling pride and respect and I looked for ways to praise her. It worked with my other students. Why not Sharon? If *Music for Life* won't help her, what will?"

Here's a *Music for Life* tip: You can't "cure" every student. Why let a poor student ruin your day, your health, and your love of teaching? Don't put up with it! When you are a good teacher, every student should work hard and be grateful for a place in your studio. When you keep students who do not live up to your standards, you devalue yourself as a teacher. Have the self-respect to only teach students worthy of your time and talents. If you dread seeing a student walk in the door, then say goodbye. You will feel incredibly liberated and rejuvenated and will be doing yourself *and* the student a favor.

SHOULD I CONSIDER "FIRING" THIS STUDENT?

Are Your Goals the Same as
Those of the Student and the Parents?

Some students want to take lessons because they have lofty goals to be principal in the orchestra, win every contest, and major in music. Others take lessons because their friends do, because they want to get good enough to play in their school group or at church, or to add another activity to their list of soccer, swimming, skiing, art, karate, chess, basketball, and underwater basket-weaving. Still others suffer through lessons only because their parents force them to. Are you willing and able to work with the student's goals, or does that mean lowering your standards?

Is the Student Practicing?

We have all had students who profess a desire to improve but are not willing to put in the time and effort. They hope that by sitting in lessons they will get better by osmosis. Every week brings excuses of homework, tests, sports events, illness, and visiting grandmothers. Be clear about how much practice is necessary to remain in your studio. Ask parents to help set up a practice schedule and monitor daily practice. There is no getting around consistent weekly practice. Even the greatest teacher cannot change a student in only one hour a week.

Is the Student Really Trying?

I've had students who make little progress yet never leave the house without practicing. They love the flute and their lessons. I would never "fire" a student who works hard unless I felt a different teacher might help the student in the long run. I feel you should reward students for effort no matter what level they attain.

Is the Student Progressing?

People learn at different speeds. Don't dismiss a student because she is not zooming through books at the same rate as others her age. If she's making consistent progress, hang in there with her.

Is the Problem Temporary?

Every student has a bad week now and then. Many have a bad month and some even a bad year, but you know they'll be able to pull themselves out of it and return. Give students a break if you know they're doing the best they can and are not getting on your nerves. Still, be clear about your standards and insist upon them when the situation allows.

Do You Have a Good Relationship with the Student and Parents?

Is there a feeling of mutual respect? We become part of some students' families and others treat us as hired help. Some don't care if their child quits, offer no support at home, and complain about every dime and every minute they spend on music. Some students are downright rude. If the family treats you like the maid or a potted palm, say, "No thanks."

Are You Performing a Function Other than Music Teacher?

Music teachers teach more than music; many children depend on them as security in the world. Some children may not be the best students, but they value their lessons and look to their teacher as a friend and role model. If the child has problems at school or at home, perhaps you need to look past the music and at the person. Never underestimate the value of friendship and music therapy.

Is It a Lost Cause?

Everyone can learn to play to some degree. Everyone can progress, but at what price? It is such a struggle for some students that the effort brings them to tears. The amount of time they need to spend to become proficient is not worth the investment for them. Each new step seems insurmountable and learning becomes stressful. Slow, patient work with these students can help, but sometimes they must realize that this may not be the perfect instrument for them or they should focus on another hobby. Maybe they need a teacher who does not pressure them. I hate to give up on these kids, but they are not enjoying themselves and get so bound up in frustration that it begins to damage their self-esteem.

Is It Worth the Money?

Firing a student may be the most difficult thing you will have to do as a teacher. Some teachers find it so emotionally wrenching that they keep all students, no matter what. Deciding to let a student go is hard, but many times it is even harder to keep going. You will be *amazed* at the freedom and happiness you find when you don't have to dread that lesson every week. Imagine the freedom and happiness the student will feel too! A bad student can use your whole day's supply of energy and patience, leaving nothing left for the rest of your students or your family. If you think it's not fair to "fire" a student, then consider the effects of this student on your physical and mental health. If you need the money, search for a replacement student or give up your daily latte.

The Process of Deciding Not to Keep a Student

If you are unhappy with a student, try these things first.

Be honest and open about your feelings. First talk privately with the student. Let her know that she is not living up to your expectations and that things need to change if she is to continue taking lessons. Be kind, yet firm. Be specific about the problem. Is it the amount of practice, low standards of performance, attitude, or missed lessons? Tell the student you don't want to talk to her parents and hope the two of you can work something out. Treat her as the master of her own destiny and ask her help in creating a new plan.

Discover the student's motivation

Does she want to continue lessons? Would she be happier with another teacher? If she has wanted to change or if taking lessons is only her parents' idea, then your decision is easy. If she is being forced into lessons, she will be relieved when you make the choice to not keep her.

Determine the student's goals and commitment

Does she want to take shorter lessons? Does she want a lighter load? Does she want to opt out of performances? Does she want to progress at a slower, less pressured rate? Not everyone can or wants to be a superstar, and that's OK. Determine the student's desires and what you are and are not willing to accept.

Ask the student whether something could be changed in the lessons

Perhaps this particular student needs a different approach. In chapter 21, "Troubleshoot Problems and Turn Around Complaints," you'll find lots of ideas on how to change the lesson, the practice, and the attitude. A simple thing such as different repertoire, fewer performances, or a lighter load can make all the difference. Sometimes finding just the right piece energizes students. Involve them in ensembles, or set up a performance opportunity.

Reiterate your practice expectations

Music lessons can be a shock to the system of a child who is used to watching TV and wasting time. Other children feel that homework and other obligations leave no free time for practice. Give new students ample time to adjust to the rigors of music lessons, but let them know that taking lessons and practice go hand in hand. Make it clear that your job is to teach, not to beg students to practice or allow them to do their practicing at lessons.

If the student wants to continue in your program, brainstorm ways to fit practice into her daily life. Ask what is possible and reasonable and make a practice pact. When the student has a good practice week and plays well, be liberal with your praise.

Teach the sudent how to practice

Many students don't know where to start. Try a daily practice chart with detailed progressive steps to learning each piece. Find tons of practice tips in chapter 14.

Set goals

Use time goals (let's get out of this book by Christmas), performance goals (sign up to play in the spring recital), and playing standards (you need to double-tongue the sixteenths, the rhythm must be precise, and the tempo at MM = 120). Many times setting concrete goals will get a student out of the doldrums.

Ask the parents for help

As much as you would like the motivation to come only from the child, sometimes we must involve the parents. Be honest with them. Perhaps they have insights into how to help their struggling child. If the situation is salvageable, enlist their help to monitor practice.

YOU'VE COME TO THE END OF THE LINE

You've tried everything and the situation looks hopeless. How do you say, "I don't want to teach you anymore"?

Step 1: Give a Warning with a Time Limit

"If you are not practicing forty minutes a day in six weeks, then I can no longer teach you." "I need four good lessons in a row to make me happy." "My students all do their homework. If you continue to ignore your homework then you will be deciding to no longer be my student. You have two weeks to make up your missing assignments." "You are on a two-month probation. At the end of the two months you will either lose your place or be doing better, and we will both be happier."

Step 2: Bring in the Parents

If you see no sign of improvement in attitude or performance, then talk to the parents *again*. Parents want to know if their time and money are going to a good cause and whether they can help turn things around.

Step 3: Carefully Monitor Progress

Use the *Music for Life* notebooks to keep an accurate record of practice time, lessons that need to be reassigned, homework finished, and the equivalent of "sticker lessons." Make sure your bias against the student doesn't cloud your perception if the student tries to turn the corner.

Step 4: Be Firm When the Grace Period Is Up

I had one student who canceled lessons or didn't show up, came late to ensemble rehearsals, and arrived to lessons unprepared. Her checks even kept bouncing! After about the sixth transgression, I had had it. I told her she was no longer my student because she didn't treat me with the courtesy of a valued teacher. Even though she begged for another chance, I remained firm because I knew things wouldn't change. I hope she treated her next teacher with more respect.

Step 5: Give Referrals

Just because you and the student were not a good match does not mean the student should quit taking lessons. Do everything possible to ensure the student keeps playing. Provide names of a couple of teachers to call whom you feel would be a good fit. For the rare rude and uncaring student that you would not wish upon your worst enemy, remain silent.

Step 6: Have a Last Lesson and Part as Friends

I feel it is important, when either you or the student have decided to part ways, to have a final lesson to say goodbye. It may seem a little uncomfortable, but it assures both of you that the lessons and the relationship have been valuable. Many times the student will bring a present and card, and I too have a card for them to read when they get home to create one last good memory.

How can both you and the student survive the breakup? Let the student save face. Many times I "place the blame" on myself by saying that I am the most demanding teacher in the universe and that my goals are different than the student's. No matter how students perform, they and their parents are people worthy of our respect. I do my best to make sure students that don't feel I am rejecting them as people, and that when we run into each other later at the movies or grocery store, we will be happy to see each other.

Step 7: Get over the Guilt

Every student will not thrive with every teacher. Firing a student may become a wake-up call and an invitation to success if the student chooses to continue with another teacher. In the long run you are actually doing them a favor.

If you have "pulled out the stops" for a student and she or he has not "gotten the bug," it is probably not your fault. As much as we hate to see a student miss the opportunity to fall in love with music, not all of them can or will. Get over it and get on with teaching the next shining star.

WHEN THE SHOE IS ON THE OTHER FOOT

It's not always the teacher who decides to call it quits. Many times it is the student who decides enough is enough. Why?

Students leave their teachers because

- They have lost interest and want to call it quits.
- They want a less demanding teacher.
- They sense a personality conflict with the teacher; the teacher may be dull and boring, irritating, too laid back, or scary.
- The teacher has expressed disappointment and they are tired of feeling like failures.
- The particular program (private/group/Suzuki) is not a good fit.
- The teacher misrepresented the program and is now asking for too much practice or performance, and the student feels pressured to progress too fast.
- They are not progressing quickly enough. The teacher does not impart enough information at each lesson and they want to be taught in a faster gear.
- They feel the teacher is "mean" because she is demanding.
- They blame the teacher for their not winning contests and awards.
- They have achieved their goals and are ready to quit.
- They don't feel valued as individuals since the teacher moves students through a pre-ordered program regardless of their abilities and goals.

Students look for new teachers who
- Fit their commitment level better.
- Offer new ideas and techniques.
- Motivate them to practice more.
- Make learning fun.
- Have big-name prestige that may help students gain entry into top schools.
- Help develop talents to a level higher than the former teacher was capable of.

Has the Student Progressed Past Your Knowledge?

Students need to move on when they feel they have outgrown your own expertise. Teachers must be careful not to limit students by their own inadequacies. It is hard to give up a really fine student, but when a student needs new challenges we must keep the student's best interests above our own.

Are You Doing Your Job?

If your idea of a good lesson is uninterrupted daydreaming about things you'd rather be doing, such as performing, eating or sleeping, then maybe it is time for *you* to quit.

If you look at the clock more than the student, something is wrong. Teachers are responsible for giving students new information at every lesson and developing their love of music. It is also the teacher's job to challenge students and encourage them to reach higher. Most students want to learn and improve. Perhaps your students are not practicing because they are uninspired. Are you putting in your time until retirement or until you make it big? No amount of practice charts, lectures, threats, or even self-discipline can replace the inner motivation of wanting to do something they love. If your students are not doing well, examine their problems and also look to yourself. If you are not really trying, how can you expect them to? If your heart is not in teaching, then find some other way to make money.

How to Respond When Your Student
Leaves You for Another Teacher

I don't know the difficult answer to this one. Handling it gracefully can be hard. One year my three top students decided they wanted to broaden their horizons, and quit within the space of three months. I was devastated. They had no specific complaints (at least that they told me), and their quitting came as a complete surprise. I'm afraid I took it all too personally and felt they hadn't appreciated the effort, education, and love I had given them. The downside of throwing your heart and soul into each student is that the more you risk, the bigger your chance of being hurt. It was hard for me to work to "get them out of diapers" and then not have the chance to see them grow up. I reacted badly, but now hope I am better able to handle "rejection." Students leave the best and the worst teachers. It happens to everyone and we need to keep our self-esteem intact and put our energies into other students. Remember that as personal as it seems, teaching is a business and life goes on.

TWENTY-SIX

Ask the Teacher

Even the best teacher faces challenges. I've been there myself and so have the music teacher friends I commiserate with. In this "advice column" for teachers' true-to-life questions, I'll offer practical solutions you can use *today*. Take heart; you're not alone.

Q: I live in a rural area with a high unemployment rate. Many of my students can barely pay for lessons and some deserving ones can't afford lessons at all. I feel bad for them but don't know how to help without becoming a charity. Besides finding a patron, what can I do to help?

A: How about getting more creative? By teaching group lessons you'll make more money per hour and the students will pay less than for a private lesson. Could you team-teach with a talented high school student or beginning teacher? They could teach three out of four lessons for a lower price. They could teach the first half hour of drills and you could teach the second half. Your "teammate" could also be the computer. The student could do one half hour of drills and another half hour with you for a lower price than the regular lesson. You might also entertain the option of trades. I have traded lessons for sewing, cooking (my favorite), yard work, painting, recording, clerical work, and babysitting. I would trade great lessons to anyone who would clean my house!

Q: Time and again my adult student arrives to his lesson at least fifteen minutes late. How can I get him to be more prompt?

A: Why not adopt the policy of many childcare centers? Charge him $5 for every minute late. I'm joking! Don't cheat yourself by allowing him to set your schedule. You're running a business. The ironclad rule: lessons start and end at the prearranged times; if you snooze, you lose. When he's late, never get around to the fun solos because of lack of time.

Q: My bright (yet lazy!) 7-year-old student has been playing the same eight-measure song for three months. When I told him he needed to cover material more quickly his father exploded. He told me my demands were ruining his son's self-esteem. "We like to give our children only positive reinforcement," he lectured me. How can I get him to understand that challenging his son is not a personal put down?

A: It sounds like this dad doesn't know what music lessons are all about. Once you can do first grade math, you should be praised, but then you need to be challenged to do second grade math. Music is the same. Try to depersonalize your comments by saying, "The standard for a second grade student who has studied this long is . . ." Perhaps ask the student to grade each lesson. "Was that a sticker lesson? What do you need to work on for next week?"

As to the self-esteem issue, it's true that students deserve our unconditional love and acceptance. Tell the student how much you like and enjoy him, but the greatest builder of self-esteem is pride in a job well done, not the empty praise of a parent or teacher.

Q: One of my teenage students treats me disrespectfully. He comes in late and never apologizes. He continually complains about having to play scales or anything that's not a real piece. He looks bored and distracted when I talk and thinks his mediocre playing is good enough. I can't get rid of him because I need the money, but I can't go on feeling like a punching bag. How can I survive?

A: You "can't" get rid of him? You *won't* get rid of him, despite his demeaning behavior. Would you consider letting him go if his behavior was 25 percent more offensive? 50 percent more offensive? Never accept behavior that demeans you as a teacher. But first let's see if you can salvage the situation.

Have you spoken to him about his rude behavior or have you suffered in silence, allowing your resentment to build and wishing you could do something creative with a roll of duct tape?

Talk to him about his negative behavior at the NEXT lesson. Start by saying, "*I want to talk to you about* . . . your behavior during lessons. *I've noticed* . . ." Describe behaviors and quote the words that offend you. "*What concerns me is* . . ." Describe the impact of his behaviors: e.g., they hinder his progress; when treated that way, you feel like a "punching bag." The ultimate impact of his disrespectful ways is that you can no longer teach him. You might save that one for later in your conversation or to be pulled out as needed.

Stress that to be successful, he must actively participate in learning and in life. It's too bad that our culture promotes a spectator mentality and leads many students to believe they must be entertained.

Perhaps he'll be surprised and say, "But my parents never complain about how I act." You may need to teach him what he hasn't learned at home. Set rules that demand respect, and be a positive role model. I tell my students: "When you enter my studio, I would like you to say hello, smile, and ask how I am. If your smile or tone of voice isn't enthusiastic enough, I will send you outside for another try. Please say goodbye and thank me for your lesson before leaving." I'm careful to follow similar rules of politeness.

Tell him, "Please reserve certain phrases (insert examples) for your friends." "When I talk, please look at me, and stop playing. Don't look at the clock and sigh or ask me how soon your lesson will be over. None of these distractions to us makes your lesson go faster."

Say, "When I assign you homework, I'm glad to hear your comments, but not your complaints. I only assign work that will improve your playing. Please say, 'This looks interesting' instead of 'This looks hard!' Say 'I'll try' instead of 'I can't do it!' If you really dislike something, let's talk about it." If you're comfortable, teach him a password: "My favorite hour of the week is here!" "There's no where else I'd rather be." I'm ready to work hard and enjoy music." Or borrow mine, "I love my teacher and my lessons!" Yes, even a sullen teenager can be taught to say this phrase. At the end of the discussion, say, "Can I count on you?" Students accept these requirements when you tell them in a kind way and explain their benefits.

Some students need more than a brush-up of their manners. If your student's underlying problem is that he resents his parents for forcing him to take lessons or that he is not a nice person, you may need to forgo the income to retain your peace of mind.

Q: My student's mother frequently asks me to drop her son off at home after the lesson. Since it is on my way I really don't mind, but I wonder if it is wise.

A: As helpful as this might be to the mom, it could be disastrous to you should there be an accident. As well as you might know and like this family, they might seize the opportunity to sue you. Even if you win the suit you will still have the time, expense, and stress of defending yourself. The best policy is to not transport students.

Q: I have a talented 10-year-old student whose parents think she is another little Mozart. They've already planned her music career to age 25. She's innately talented but lacks maturity and is just a beginner. They want to sign her up for contests she's not ready for. How do I get them more realistic about her skill and her chances?

A: Tell them that if she enters a contest and has a bad experience, she might never want to enter one again. The criterion is not how old she is or how talented. It's how well she plays right now. Ask them to close their eyes when they listen to her play and imagine they are hearing a recording. Would they buy that CD, or is part of her charm being young and cute? Insist she only play pieces she can learn to play well. Help them to look at the big picture and her future. Their priority should be to provide her with the basics and foster a positive attitude about learning and practicing, not to show her off. She'll only be young a few more years, and if she is pushed to perform without a solid base she may self-destruct when she is older.

Q: My middle school piano student is a great kid and good student, but he won't quit playing when I tell him to stop!

A: Remind him that the more he plays after you interrupt him, the less time he has to learn. After you ask him to stop, just sit there until he finally quits. Then say, "I waited so long for you to stop I can't remember what I was gong to say. I guess we will have to start back at the beginning again." You can also say, "Let's make a deal. If you stop as soon as I ask you to every time, I promise to let you play through the whole piece once without me stopping you."

Q: I have a high school student who keeps skipping lessons. At the last minute she cancels or doesn't show up at all. How can I get her to take lessons seriously?

A: It's more than irritating to be twiddling your thumbs waiting for an arrival that never comes. Every time you start a new student, clarify your attendance rules up front in a studio policy. Insist on monthly payments at the first lesson of the month. Talk to students and parents about the importance of regular lessons in their development as players.

Educate students and parents to view paying for lessons as tuition. Some parents may view you as a store and may shop when convenient and only pay for what they buy. Remind parents that this is your job and income you rely upon. How fair would it be for their boss to tell them to stay home without pay?

Q: One of my students rarely practices and balks at my directions. Now she tells me she wants to switch to another teacher who will "work her harder." Should I call the new teacher to warn her?

A: This is a sticky situation. You feel an allegiance to your fellow teacher. As a courtesy you may call the new teacher to warn her of the student's performance but in doing so your negative predictions may sabotage the student's chances for success. And unless you know the other teacher well, you'll never know to whom and to how many she'll repeat your warning. In fairness to the student, it is best to remain silent. If the new teacher calls you, then you can be more direct.

Q: I have a high school student who all but refuses to do technical work such as scales and etudes. His parents agree with him, saying that since he is not going to be a professional musician, why can't he just play the songs he loves?

A: Your first step should be to show the parents and student the connection between scales and etudes and better playing. Without them, the son will never improve enough to play the songs he loves well. Work on a compromise. How about asking for one scale each week and an etude every other week? How about using some pieces as etudes to teach specific techniques? What about holding out a favorite song as a carrot in reward for learning a difficult etude? What about letting the student pick part of the repertoire while you pick the rest?

Q: I hold recitals every six weeks. It's a lot of extra work for me but gives students the motivation to keep practicing and helps them with stage fright too. At the last recital, one of the dads told me, "I've talked to other parents and we think you give too many recitals." What should I say to him?

A: Have you told the dad the reasons you give recitals? Can you tell if his complaint is that he feels it puts too much pressure on his child? Or does he not like showing up for so many recitals? If he is adamantly against the recitals, a compromise could be for students to give a recital every six weeks at the lesson. Invite family members and set the date for the material to be concert ready.

Q: None of my students or their parents takes lessons very seriously. This town values sports above everything. How can I get them to take music more seriously?

A: Step 1: Choose the three or four students whom you think have the most potential and the most supportive parents.

Step 2: Shower them with attention: Invite them to a concert. Take them on a field trip. Place them in an ensemble. Have a music party. Take them out to lunch. Teach them the very best lessons you can.

Step 3: Make these committed students the core of your studio. Encourage them to talk to other students and their friends about how fun and rewarding their lessons are.

Step 4: Have a recital and show them off.

Step 5: Other kids will want to work to be in the "in crowd" too.

Q: One of my students is not making the grade. She rarely practices, never has all her materials, and is not prepared for contests. Her parents can't afford my regular fee. She has a very rough home life with divorced parents who feud and offer little support for the lessons she loves. What should I do?

A: You may not realize the importance of lessons in your student's life. You may be the only adult she can count on who provides a haven of stability in her unstable world. At the same time, you don't want her embarrassing herself (or you) at the contest. Commit to keeping this needy girl but put her on a different track. Don't enter her in contests but include her in your in-studio recitals. You might spend part of your lesson time talking and listening instead of playing, and that's OK.

Q: I have a very bright 8-year-old boy in his second year of lessons. He never remembers all his books and only practices right before the recital. His parents ask for extra lessons to help him catch up. When I complain to his mother, she defends him, saying, "What do you expect? He's only 8!" How can I get him more dedicated and organized?

A: In some ways his mother is right; 8-year-old boys are usually better at riding bikes than remembering books and practice. First, let's get the boy and whoever drives him to the lesson to work together. Each week put an adhesive note on the front of the book with boxes to be checked off: scale book, instrument, manuscript book, solo books.

Agree with mom that practicing is tough for 8-year-olds and that's why he really needs her help if he is to improve. Ask her to attend lessons, help with practice, and set up a reward system for steady practice. Arrange for the parents to hear other kids his age to see how he measures up.

Q: My student "cannot" remember key signatures. The repetition is driving me nuts. How can I jolt his memory?

A: Start with the basics. Explain how scales are built and how each piece is created from the key signature scale. Then drill, drill, drill in scales. Each time the student plays a piece at home or in the lesson, ask him to first play the tonic scale. When he misses a sharp or flat, ask him to follow these steps: write the sharp or flat symbol in front of the note, say the names of the notes in the measure out loud, play the measure, and then play the scale.

Once your student understands scales and key signatures, how can you make him more aware? Here's a trick I learned from my husband, Don. Don's college roommate, Jim, often appeared angry because he habitually and unconsciously grimaced. Don volunteered to help break Jim's habit by making him acutely aware of when he made the ugly face. Don's not-so-subtle biofeedback: Every time Jim scowled, Don slugged him. Jim turned out to be a fast learner!

Believe it or not, I've adapted and used Don's technique. My eighth grade student Soren, a wrestler, could never remember key signatures. I offered to good-naturedly "slug" him each time he forgot. Soren once bragged to a friend in band, "I had a really good lesson. She only slugged me three times!"

More subtle ways to increase their concentration: Put ten pennies or candies on the music stand and take one away for every key signature mistake. Write with marker pen on their hand for every mistake. Tie a scarf around an elbow that needs to be kept lifted or put a pipe cleaner on an "offending" finger. Do something goofy or surprising. Throw a stuffed animal, ring a bell, or make the student do jumping jacks. Grabbing his attention will help erase the bad habit—just ask Don.

Q: My student is chronically unprepared for recitals. When I tell him he can't play his piece unless it's in good shape he says that it is good enough. When his parents learn I'm excluding their son, they protest and say because he takes lessons he deserves to play in the recital. Besides, they've been paying good money for the lessons. Do I lower my standards for this kid?

A: Explain to your student and his parents that recitals celebrate what students have accomplished in their lessons and practice. You are acting in his best interest because you would never want him to be ashamed or embarrassed about his performance or to feel inferior in front of the kids who are prepared. Tell them your goal as a music teacher is to give students a love and a respect for music. If the parents disregard music's value by accepting their son's poor playing you will have failed in this mission. If they insist on a recital, invite a few family members for a private recital during the lesson time.

Q: I'm new to town and getting new students has been slow. A local music store contacted me to teach there. I was shocked at the cut the store takes from my lesson fees. I need students but I'm afraid to be trapped in this expensive arrangement. Should I make a deal with them or hold out for students I find on my own?

A: Teaching at the store may help you get started and build a reputation in the town, but consider negotiating something more attractive to you. Perhaps you can suggest you start at the level they request but when you have a certain number of students, their cut diminishes. Or you might ask to negotiate doing a few master classes or general seminars in trade for a reduced hourly rate. Before you sign anything, talk to other teaches at the store and get a feel for the working conditions, the ease of getting students, and of course, the rate they are paying.

Q: I have been teaching two delightful young sisters for six months. I love teaching them but the big problem is their mother, a professional vocalist. She decides what books and what parts of the lesson they should do. When I explain my decisions she overrules me. This controversy goes on during lessons and the girls are totally confused. How can I convince the mother to let me be the teacher?

A: I love parents coming to the lessons, but I'm lucky I've never had to deal with your "Helicopter Mother" problem. Speak frankly to overbearing parents at the beginning to establish who is in charge. Now six months into this pattern, you must reestablish yourself as the "Alpha Dog." Without attacking HM, talk to her in terms of benefits to her children. Say "Learning music takes a lot of trust in the teacher, and if the girls are confused as to who calls the shots, they will never trust me and be willing to let me guide them. You have chosen me as their teacher and I take my role very seriously. Through the years I have devised an effective method of teaching and ask that you have faith in my abilities and my decisions. Your girls are so lucky that their mom is a musician. You expose them to great music and are a big help to them at home practice. I may not choose music or run lessons the way you would, but this has worked well for me. No two teachers are alike and to teach them exactly your way, you would need to teach the girls yourself, and perhaps you should think about that. If you choose to have me be their teacher, I really need your support so we can work together for the sake of your lovely daughters."

Q: I live in a factory town. My students' parents naturally question my fee because most earn half as much per hour as I charge. How can I convince them I'm worth it?

A: Help parents understand two things about your job. First, the hour you spend with their child is just the tip of the iceberg of time you spend in the business of teaching. Consider the time you spend making phone calls, arranging rehearsals, buying music, giving extra lessons, preparing recitals, contests, and other events, practicing, doing bookkeeping, continuing your education, and attending professional sessions. All told, your hourly wage would pale in comparison even to theirs. They also may get sick leave, vacation pay, a savings plan, and retirement, none of which the self-employed enjoy. Second, the money they spend for music lessons is for much more than music lessons; it is for enriching their children's lives beyond measure.

Q: My students rate pieces by grade levels. They say, "I don't want to play this piece because Shirley played it in eighth grade and I'm in tenth grade."

A: Explain to students that once they leave the graded beginning books, music is music. Even professional musicians play the "easy" pieces because they are beautiful. Remind them that an eighth grader may play a piece pretty well but a tenth grader may bring more maturity and interpretation to the same piece. "I know Shirley played this piece when she was in eighth grade but I can't wait to see what *you* will do with it!"

Q: The parents of one of my students judge my effectiveness by what seat their son gets in band and his score at contests. How can I convince them there's more to music than competition?

A: "Standardized scores" may be the only way these parents know how to measure their son's progress, but we all know that subjective ratings are not always the best judge of musical development. Remind them of the odds of winning. Fifty people audition, one makes it; forty violins are in the orchestra, and only one sits first.

Involve parents in the joy of music. Help them see that music is not just a race to the top by pointing out the many dividends of learning music. Invite them to lessons, and demonstrate how he has grown. "Listen to that great tone! Do you hear how much he has improved?" Then remind parents that it takes two to tango. The best teacher in the world makes little progress with a student who is not ready, willing, and able.

Q: My student divides her time between her divorced parents' homes. Her mom supports the lessons, but not her dad. He says the trombone disturbs his peace and quiet. He also complains about having to alter his routine to drive her to lessons and rehearsals.

A: Try to bring Dad into the loop: Make sure he receives a copy or e-mail of any written communication. Invite him in and brag about his daughter. If he won't come in, send e-mails or call to update him. He'll have to come in if you arrange a special concert for Dad only. Make Christmas, Father's Day, or his birthday the excuse to "fete" him and win him over.

Your best hope is for the mother to talk to him directly. You might also enlist the daughter's help: If she explains to her father why music is important to her, and promises to mitigate the "practicing noise" by choosing the right time and place to practice, he might be more understanding.

If none of these ideas brings Dad around, you may need to ask your student to practice when he is out of the house or just do theory homework there. She may have to double up on practice at her mom's or you just may have to accept less from her due to her circumstances. Most importantly, understand how difficult this is for the child.

Q: Several of my students seem to hit a plateau and then want to quit. How can I get them to stick with it?

A: If many of your students have this problem, perhaps you have assigned music that is too hard for them too early. They need more time to understand and to develop their technique. If the student seems stuck, try some different fun music that may be at the same level but that will give a sense of forward motion. If the problem is boredom, dream up some fun lesson plans and activities.

Q: Many of my students want to take the summer off and some of them don't return in the fall. How can I keep them going throughout the year or ensure they come back?

A: Summer can be the period of most intense learning and also the most fun for students with no school obligations and plenty of time to practice. How about offering extra enrichment in the summer with group lessons, ensembles, or parties?

If they insist on taking the summer off, schedule the fall lesson time before they quit for the summer. Make the first lesson of the fall seem like graduating into a new grade by not teaching the week before, starting all new music, and measuring how the student has improved over the past year. Host a reward party and give certificates for another year of playing. On the other hand everyone needs a break, so be sure you both take time off.

Q: One of my students never practices. When I tell his parents he hasn't practiced, they contradict me. They don't realize that the piece they hear him playing at home was the one he learned three months ago.

A: If the child is middle school age or younger, it's time for more parental involvement. Invite the parents to the lesson to hear how their son plays. Be clear in your assignments and ask them to listen to his practice at least twice a week.

Q: A violin teacher in town requires his students, regardless of age, to practice three hours a day! His students win every competition. How does he do it?

A: Wow! This teacher must be successful at motivating his students to practice. How does he so consistently gain their cooperation? Here are a few explanations: He may accept only the most motivated students. His rigorous program may involve more-than-weekly lessons and frequent performances. His students may have hands-on parents who may homeschool and monitor, instruct, and support their practicing time. He may charge such a high fee only the dedicated will accept it, or he could be a fabulous motivator who inspires dedication. Somehow he's found the magic formula. Get to know him!

Q: Some of my students' parents blame me if their child doesn't win a contest in which the winner played a more "difficult" piece. They think whoever plays the hardest and fastest pieces will be the winner.

A: Any piece can be a winner. It's not the piece *but how it is played*. Show parents the wide range of former contest-winners' repertoire. Explain that you choose the piece that allows the child to have the contest be a rewarding experience.

Q: One of my high school students cries at her lessons. I don't think I am being mean or overly demanding. Her tears unnerve me. How can I help her stop?

A: Your student may be one of the estimated 15 to 20 percent of people born with a highly sensitive temperament. Highly sensitive students are more prone to intense reflection, feeling overwhelmed, and dissolving into tears at the slightest frustration. They need the security of a warm responsive teacher. Other students may cry because they're already on edge about a struggle with homework, friends, or family. Start each lesson by chatting to ensure your student is in an emotional state to learn, especially if you plan to introduce new techniques. A few laughs, a sympathetic ear, and fun music will get her off to a good start.

The next time she cries, acknowledge her emotions and then hand her a tissue. Probe a little. What is she thinking right before she cries? Is she talking negatively to herself? Students who are perfectionists by nature may feel dejected at the first wrong note. Is she feeling guilty because she hasn't practiced enough? Is she struggling with an issue at home or at school?

So her home and social life are perfect and she only breaks down at her lessons with you? Music brings out emotional responses in both teachers and students. Have you offended her or treated her harshly? Do you need to soften your tone of voice? Are you less patient when you lack sleep, are hungry, or are tired of teaching at the end of a long week? Has she mistaken your enthusiasm for anger? What words have you used to critique her? Separate your critique of her playing from her as a person. Are you finding things to compliment? Earlier praise may have been lost in a deluge of corrections.

Observe your student's body language and facial expressions. Does she frown or slump in the chair when you explain new concepts? She might feel frustrated or inadequate. Teach new techniques step by step and make sure they're solid before you move ahead. Guide your student and avoid putting her on the spot to pass or fail the "test."

When your student cries at a lesson, follow up with a phone call to ask how she is feeling and to let her know you care. To ease any embarrassment, reassure her it's OK to cry and you understand. And remember, she's a teenager! Never expect hormone-surged teenagers (or pregnant women) to keep their emotions on an even keel!

Q: I have a wonderful 14-year-old student who plays well beyond her years. She is a natural musician and her love of music is obvious to all who hear her. A big contest is coming up in two weeks and suddenly she has lost her nerve. She makes mistakes, her tone is bad, and her vibrato is shaky. The girl who loved being in the spotlight now looks embarrassed. She is more than prepared but has become her own worst enemy. What can I do to get the "old student" back?

A: The early teen years are a transition for many kids. They're forming their identities and they crave the approval of their peers. Girls especially want to blend in with the crowd (note how they all dress alike) to not be noticed. Perhaps your student feels embarrassed about the attention she received for playing so well. Is she putting undue pressure on herself to win because she's expected to win? Has she placed that pressure on herself? At fourteen she may also have a hard time juggling homework and the practice she needs to do well at the competition. She could feel all of the above!

Give her a chance to open up to you about her feelings. Reassure her that anxiety in moderation is normal and can help her focus. Some of us feel anxious anticipating the performance (pre-performance anxiety) and then are fine once we play. Anxiety before the performance increases when we are not prepared and when we expect perfection. Remind her that while competition is important, even more important is enjoying our playing. Let her know that no matter the result, she is not letting you down. Relate the ebb and flow of learning an instrument to the ebb and flow of life. Recall times in your own life where things went well and not so well. Upon looking back, none of them had any effect in the long run. Encourage her to take the long view and not focus on a single event.

Next, make her promise to practice half as much as usual. Concentrate on slow warm-ups to focus on tone and position and to help her relax. At the end of her practice she can play through her pieces but only slowly. No testing.
The next assignment will literally make her laugh. Every night of the week before the contest she must eat her favorite ice cream and watch a funny movie. This will keep her from obsessing about the contest and help her lighten up. This assignment also tells her you care more about her than about winning or losing.

Q: I am going on a three-month maternity leave in the middle of the school year. How can I ensure my students will be waiting for me when I return?

A: Make it clear to your students that you will be returning and will have expectations for them. Before you leave, schedule the next lesson so students can anticipate and look forward to your return. Give them weekly assignments and establish performance goals for your return. Try to arrange a couple of master classes, ensemble rehearsals, or rehearsals with the accompanist while you are gone.

You might invite one or two other teachers to substitute for you—with the understanding that they're not trolling for students. A new teacher in the area or a college student might welcome this opportunity. This might sound risky, but if you have established strong bonds with your students, they will remain loyal to you. Keep communications going with parents and students and let them know they can still reach you by e-mail if there is an emergency.

Q: What do I do with a student who thinks he only needs to practice ten minutes a day? How can I raise his standards?

A: With ten minutes a day he'll be an old man before he gets good! Give him measurable goals such as playing with only three mistakes or playing up to a certain tempo. Then he will be able to compare his playing to your agreed-upon criteria. You can skip the discussion of whether his ten minutes of practice a day is good enough.

Q: The mother of one of my students overheard her daughter telling a friend she didn't want to take lessons anymore. Her daughter hasn't mentioned it to the mom or me. Should her mom and I be worried?

A: Kids like to try out their independence by feeling they can quit at any time. Often they have no intention of doing so. If she enjoys her lessons and is making progress, I wouldn't worry about it.

Q: The parent of one of my students sits in on every lesson and makes negative comments to her son like "Why didn't you get that?" and "You always make that mistake!" usually followed by "I told you to practice more!" Her sour attitude spoils the lesson.

A: Nothing can tear down students' confidence faster than hearing parents berate them in exasperated tones. When parents interfere, ignore their input. Turn your attention to the student and jump in talking to take away the parent's forum. At an appropriate time remind these parents of their role as silent supporters during the lesson. Restate your rule that they must make positive comments or none at all. Ask the boy's mom, "Can the two of us work together? I'll provide specific feedback to your son about his playing and at times I'll ask you to chime in and praise him." You might say things like "Wasn't that great?" or "He's improving, isn't he?" or "Listen to that tone!" Teach parents how to make positive comments. If the student is not improving, say, "It is my job as the teacher to tell you how you are doing and it is your job to do better. You don't need your mom to tell you when you play well or not; it's *your* responsibility!"

What if you can't handle having Mom at lessons at all? Tell her you're planning a surprise and she can't come to the lesson for a month while you prepare. Whip up some cute duet or solo for the surprise. Comment on how the child has matured and done well even without her supervision at the lesson. Ask the student how he feels about his mom at the lesson. "Do you enjoy having your mom here?" If the student doesn't want her there all the time, let the request come from him. Even when parents are effectively "banned" from lessons, maintain contact with phone calls, e-mails, progress reports, and other communications.

Q: The parents of one of my students want her to take lessons every other week. I believe students need weekly lessons to progress. How do I convince them she needs weekly lessons?

A: Taking lessons every other week usually only works well with advanced students who need "coaching" to refine skills, not help with the basics. Lessons every other week are a bad idea for you because the spot you would need to reserve on your calendar every other week could be taken by a weekly student.

Why does the student want to skip lessons? Is it financial? Perhaps you can compromise with a lower fee or a shorter lesson. Does your student sincerely think that she could progress as fast with half the number of lessons or does she think coming for lessons every other week would be half the work? Explain that the amount you accomplish in each lesson equals four hours of focused practice. Without lessons every week she would need to double her practice time to compensate for missed lessons. Students usually end up practicing only the few days before the lesson. And if they do practice for two weeks without a lesson, it's hard for them to unlearn a mistake. If they have to miss a lesson, they'll have three weeks between lessons. Lessons every two weeks can lead students to be discouraged and even quit.

Q: I became good friends with the family of one of my long-term students. Her mom and I are especially close. For seven years we attended parties together, had dinner at each other's homes, and exchanged Christmas gifts. I did special things for their daughter I don't do for other students. Their daughter graduated from high school and when she left town for college, they cut all contact with me. They won't even return my phone calls! Were they just using me?

A: "Friends may come and friends may go," but letting friends go is a common lament among music teachers. When parents have treated us as extended family it hurts when they so easily move on. This is a perfect example of the conflict that can occur when we blur the lines between personal and professional relationships.

Let me offer a different way to view their decision to end your friendship. Picture yourself moving far away from your family and friends. You'd have new neighbors, make new friends, and be involved in different schools. Your life would revolve around these new circles. You'd have less time for even your closest friends now that they were long-distance ones.

Many of us have formed friendships we enjoy with other parents we see regularly for sports teams or school events. When the season ends, these "friendships of convenience" fade and we rarely or never see our friends again.

When parents no longer see you at weekly lessons, it's the same thing. Playing an instrument is still a major part of your life, but with their daughter out of town, you're no longer part of their "world." Your student's mother has turned her attention to people who still affect her every day life, such as other members of the club for "Worried mothers with daughters attending college out of state." It may sting to realize that their friendship with you was less a function of their ties to you personally than a way to support their daughter.

But imagine the full-time job it would be for *you* to remain in close contact with every doctor, pediatrician, teacher, receptionist, or store salesperson you ever knew, not to mention all of your former students. You wouldn't have time to eat!

Finally, ask yourself, "Do I regret the extra time and effort I put into this student and her family? Might I have done it anyway, as a reward in itself?" I'll bet your answer is "yes." You gave your student and her family your best and enjoyed it along the way. Appreciate friendships for the time you have them and continually build new ones to replace them.

Q: I would love a university teaching job, but they all call for experience. How can I get my foot in the door?

A: Be the best teacher you can be. Build your private studio, reach out to the community with workshops, build an interesting and ongoing website, join professional societies, and perform. Networking will win you friends who know about your strong performance and will give you references and even help look at your resume.

Q: I've heard about public school teachers losing their jobs for sexual harassment. I touch my students to show them proper position and even hug them when they do well. Do I need to be more careful?

A: Even being falsely accused of sexual harassment or misconduct can devastate a teacher's reputation and career. Britain has "solved the problem" by strictly forbidding all teachers to ever touch a child. What a sad price we all must pay for a few unscrupulous teachers. Such suspicion conflicts with the caring nature of teaching music.

To avoid having your intentions taken in the wrong way, ask students for their permission to touch them the first time. "May I touch your shoulder to show you proper posture?" Try to replace touching students by having them just look and model you. Be sure that whatever you do is completely non-threatening. Once you get to know your students, you'll be better able to judge whether a pat on their back or congratulatory squeeze to the shoulder makes them uneasy.

Piano teachers should sit on a separate chair and not on the bench next to students. When teaching in a school setting, you may need to keep the door open. If parents are in the room, you may have a little more leeway. I still hug my students, but that may be out of the question for some teachers. If you have any doubts about your actions, don't.

Q: I dearly love one of my students, but his crazy mother is driving me crazy! She wants me to counsel her son about his behavior at home. She calls, writes e-mails, and leaves notes complaining to me about her son's grades, girlfriend, and even his messy room. As if I could do something about them! I'm hearing details I don't even want to know. I hate to drop her sweet son, but I don't know how much longer I stand being put in this uncomfortable position.

A: Wow! You're such a great teacher that your student's mother believes you have psychic control of her son between lessons? As hard as it may be to deal with the mother, you know it isn't fair to punish the child for the "sins" of the parent. If your student tells you about true physical or mental abuse, suggest he make an appointment to see his school counselor or psychologist.

Could this be a normal mother/son relationship with a mom who just needs to vent? Be kind to the mom but minimize contact. Tell her that her son performs much better without her in the room. If you have caller ID, don't answer her calls and communicate only through e-mails and newsletters. At the lesson, keep your conversations focused on her son's musical performance. Redirect her if she strays to other topics by saying, "I'm sorry. That's not something I feel comfortable discussing with you. Let's talk about . . ." When you see this woman, please act friendly, and brag about her son. Flattery may help soften her complaints. She may see her interference just as concern for her son and may be looking for a sympathetic ear and the parenting help we all need.

Q: My student refuses to practice unless his mother helps. He says she catches his mistakes and he gets done faster. When he has a bad lesson he blames his mother.

A: When he performs, does he plan to have Mom in the wings ready to signal him after every mistake? Gradually wean him from his dependence on Mom. Have her help him at only the first and last practice sessions of the week. Put him in charge of checking off a daily assignment. At lessons, make him responsible for finding and fixing his own mistakes. Give him a solid basis in theory and rhythm so he has the tools to be independent.

Q: One of my students is discouraged. He started as a teen and has limited skills, but he hates playing in the "baby" books.

A: If the teen plays piano, switch him to adult beginner books. Suggest he visit the music store to pick his own music. Let him choose the genre he wants to learn, and even if it's not Beethoven, you can still find plenty of learning opportunities. Set up the computer to accompany him to make easy songs more fun.

Q: Schools in our district are letting music programs die. Is there anything we teachers can do?

A: It is our job to educate schools about the importance of music. Join the local music education coalition (www.supportmusic.com), and go to service organizations such as Rotary armed with facts and ask them to get involved. Bring students to perform at PTA and school board meetings and join the MTNA community outreach and Education for the Arts programs.

Q: I have become a successful teacher in my city and my former teacher is now acting jealous.

A: If your students are doing so well, your own teacher must have done a good job with you. Tell her! Call her, write a note, send her flowers, or take her out to lunch. Credit her ideas and phrases in your teaching and ask her advice for perplexing questions. Strengthen your bond and she may think of you as continuing her lineage instead of being a rival.

Q: I have a student who never brings all his books to the lesson, doesn't return the ones he borrows from me, and doesn't order the new ones.

A: Perhaps he is not as forgetful as he is lazy. I used to "forget" the piano books that I didn't want to play at the lesson—and my teacher believed me! If you have copies of the books at the lesson, he won't get off so easily. If this is a chronic problem, instead of playing the "forgotten" book, do "really fun" things like playing all the sharp scales or doing rhythm drills. That'll teach him!

For newly assigned material, I don't lend out my books ever, but let the student copy the first page to work on until their real music arrives. If ordering is a problem, supply the parents with contacts to music stores or buy several copies and have students reimburse you. If too much time lapses, ask parents when they ordered the book. (They'll get on the phone right away!) When the boy does remember everything, praise him liberally.

Q: I have a student who plays on at least two sports teams year round. During winter she skis five times a week. She also plays soccer, is on a swim team, does gymnastics, and now plays

Ultimate Frisbee! Is it any surprise she has little time to practice? She often has to reschedule lessons to attend games and meets and with every new sports season I need to find her a new lesson time slot. But she loves her music too. Am I wrong to accept less commitment and acquiesce to so many schedule changes?

A: If she's making progress and you both enjoy the lessons, why ask her to choose between sports and music? Tell her she's not going to zoom ahead like students who devote their time to more practice. Let her understand the choices she makes will affect her progress, but always remember that the process of learning is as important as the product. So encourage her to lead a well-balanced life and have fun along the way.

In return for your understanding, ask her to make practice time really count with concentration and careful planning. In the summer when she's out of school, ask her to double up her practice time. As to the schedule changes, make it clear that make-up lessons due to sports conflicts will be entirely up to the discretion of the teacher.

Q: I like to invite parents into my lessons, but some bring their other children and let them run wild around my house. After a lesson yesterday, I came out to a toilet that had overflowed into my family room. What can I say to them?

A: Siblings who attend lessons can distract both you and your students. If parents insist on bringing the whole crew, let them know the only room in the house available to them during lessons is your music room or a waiting room. If children need to use the restroom, a parent must accompany them. Suggest parents bring a quiet project to entertain fidgety children. Keep your own supply of crayons, paper, and books to keep them busy. If siblings continue to distract you during lessons, interrupt your teaching. Say nothing and pause until they stop. After a few lessons full of starts and stops, their parents may reconsider.

Q: A student I've taught for four years has secretly started taking lessons from another teacher. I can't believe it! Why would she do that and what should I do about it?

A: Learning from two teachers with two different styles and requirements can confuse students. Advanced players have the background to pick and choose advice, but younger students may end up being confused. Now that you know your student has been doing double-duty lessons, ask yourself what might have contributed to her decision. Does the new teacher offer in-depth training in an area in which you are not well versed? Does your student want additional coaching without leaving you? Is she trying out another teacher before leaving you? Has she decided to leave but is afraid of hurting your feelings?

Start an honest conversation about the future of her lessons. If your student says she wants to stay with both of you, explain the benefits of having one person to look to for guidance. Taking a few lessons from a new teacher to prepare for a specific event or learn a specific topic is fine. I've even heard of the original teacher attending a lesson once a month and learning along with the student. The other three lessons of the month, the original teacher "coaches" the student. Work out what will be best for the student. If you come to the conclusion that two teachers are best, then be open and cooperative with the other teacher. Please remind her that you're not afraid to discuss sensitive topics or hear bad news. No one likes to be blindsided by someone they trust.

Q: I have been asked to write a letter of recommendation for one of my students and don't know how to best describe her. What should I include?

A: Always begin the letter with an introduction as to who you are and in what capacity and for how long you have known the student. Next write about the student's musical strengths. You don't need to include an extensive list of accomplishments as these will all be listed in the student's application, but you might want to touch upon the most impressive few. Next talk about the applicant's personality. Things such as being inquisitive, open-minded, cooperative, and hard-working will let the committee know this student is ready to learn. Include concrete examples, not just adjectives. If possible, show how the qualities of this applicant match up with the requirements of the school. If you have concerns about the applicant, offer to speak on the phone with the committee personally, or tell the applicant you think it might be best if another person wrote the recommendation. Above all you want to be positive yet honest, and brief.

Q: One of my students has parents who are both professional musicians. They don't interfere during the lessons, but the way they follow every note and flinch after sour notes makes me nervous. How can I feel more comfortable around them?

A: Relax. Think of these musical parents as your supporters, not your critics. As professional musicians, they must have done their homework before choosing you for the teacher. Focus on teaching the best lesson you can, not on their reactions. Haven't you ever felt like wincing after hearing sour notes?

Incorporate music theory and history into your lessons. Involve parents at home by having them help their children learn with flash cards, supervise theory homework and practicing, and bring their child to concerts. Occasionally ask for their musical opinion about phrasing or dynamics. Invite them to echo your praise. Musical parents are a plus!

Q: My students want to stop working on pieces before they're acceptable to me. They're satisfied with getting a piece fairly good and then want to move on. How can I get them to raise their standards?

A: Create performance opportunities for your students that will motivate them to do their best. "You really want to have this sonata up to tempo for the recital in a month." Don't assign pieces that can't be perfected.

On the other hand, be careful not to beat the piece into the ground. We all know that every week spent working on a song will make it better and that students have so much to learn, but most grade school and junior high students can't work on a piece for seven or eight months. They'll get bored or start to hate the music. To keep younger students more excited, move through pieces quickly but still retain your high standards. If you wish, return to pieces later, to study at a high level.

Q: My student is the best trumpet player in his high school band. He thinks he made it to the top and has quit trying. How can I encourage him to keep working?

A: Your trumpet player has enjoyed being a big fish in a little pond. Show him a slice of the outside world. If you have any more advanced students close to his age, try to arrange their lessons back-to-back. Enter him in a competition where he will hear a judge critique him and (most likely) hear other students who play better than he does.

Encourage him to audition for a youth or All-State band or orchestra. Involve him in chamber music with students at his level and above. Help him aim for higher goals.

Q: What do you do about students who cancel because they haven't practiced all week and think the lesson will be a waste of time?

A: If you show understanding about the *occasional* bad week, students won't fear your "wrath" if they arrive unprepared. Note my emphasis on the word occasional! Explain to them that since they haven't practiced, they especially need a lesson. Use the time to explore theory and history, play technique drills, do detailed work on one of their pieces, and do some fun sight reading. When they leave, say, "It was so relaxing to have the time to do these things we can never get to in a regular lesson. Now aren't you glad you came?" Requiring parents to pay by the month regardless of how many lessons were taken will ensure steadier attendance.

Q: I have a student who says she practices regularly but I have my sincere doubts. Is there some way I can find out for sure?

A: Unless you sneak into her house or rig her practice room with a video camera, you can never be certain. Have her sight read the new assignment at the lesson and then compare it to how it returns the next week. Ask her parents to sit with her during practice, or at least be in the house to monitor. Another thing I do is to give written homework every week. With written homework you can at least tell if the student has done it. Chances are if the written homework is not done, the practice was not done either. If you really want to be sure, have her play the hard measures on your answering machine!

Q: My student literally stinks! After every lesson I have to air out the room.

A: You'll do the student a favor if you politely mention it. Boys nearing adolescence may not realize their deodorant needs have changed with their changing bodies. How about saying, "Boy, you play so hard you really work up a sweat at these lessons! You better always take a shower on lesson day!" Will he fall for that one? If that's too subtle, just tell him that he really needs to shower and wear clean clothes on lesson days. Tell him he wants to get a reputation as a fine player and not a smelly one. Good luck.

Q: My student takes half-hour lessons but is really ready for hour lessons. How do I convince him and his parents?

A: Step one: Always play the etudes and scales exercises first. Go into such depth on each assignment as to leave no time to hear all the pieces the student prepared. Every week say, "Oh my gosh, look at the time. I just can't believe the lesson is over. Well, we didn't get to your solos or duets this week or last week, so you'll have to keep practicing them."

Step two: When you have had time to really work on a piece, and the student greatly improves, rave about his progress. "It was so great to see what you could do when we really worked on the sonata in depth. You are really reaching a whole new level now. I wish we had time to do this on your other pieces."

Step three: Listen to the student beg you for longer lessons!

Step four: If by some chance they need a little extra push, explain that a half-hour lesson is really only twenty to twenty-five minutes, due to the time it takes to welcome the student and get the books ready. Thus, an extra half hour is really a half hour and a good deal for the money! Clarify that an extra half hour is not really double the homework, but just a chance to get better on the normal assignment.

Q: Two weeks ago I started teaching a 10-year-old boy who has been diagnosed with ADHD. By the time he sees me, his medication is starting to wear off. He gets distracted easily and has a hard time following my explanations from beginning to end. And the wiggling! But he's a neat kid. How can I help him?

A: Expect him to wiggle. Then try these strategies for teaching students with ADHD. Get him moving now and then. When teaching a new rhythm, have your student clap and then play it or march around the room. Halfway through the lesson, stand up and stretch and let him switch to a different chair. Ask him to listen to you and play "Follow the leader."

Be specific when you redirect his attention. He won't translate "Pay attention" into "Put that ball back in your pocket and look at me." Say, "Look at the measure I'm pointing to." Give him a checklist of things he needs to bring to his lessons. Students with ADHD need lots of repetition. Make a chart or flash cards he can easily refer to. Speak slowly and quietly. Break new techniques or pieces into chunks he can manage. If he progresses more slowly than some, teach him step by baby step. Then teach him again. Provide him with structure. Playing his music and exercises in the same order every week provides him comfort and the time to gradually learn new things. Work with his parents to support and encourage him at home. Actively look for reasons to praise him. And get out those stickers!

Q: I'm a busy mom and teach lessons in the afternoon after a full day with my two preschoolers. My schedule is tight and I rush right from their activities to my studio wearing sweats and a T-shirt. I'm wondering what other teachers wear to lessons. Are my casual clothes a problem?

A: Whether you like it or not, students and parents may judge you by your attire. Your choice of dress sets the tone for your students. Casual attire gives students the impression that lessons are a casual, carefree event. In our informal world, wearing professional clothes shows you take lessons seriously, conveys higher expectations, and helps win their respect. Your dress may vary according to where you teach. When teaching at home you can be a little more casual than in a school or business setting.

Attire is of special importance to new teachers trying to create an image of being mature and trustworthy. Dress for a look that assures students and parents of your credentials or authority. A sweater or jacket and slacks can be comfortable and professional.

Q: I have a young student who can only afford one lesson per month. One lesson a month seems almost useless to me but I guess it would be better than nothing. Any ideas?

A: You're a kind teacher to want to help this student. One lesson a month can help a highly motivated student, but for many, it may just lead to frustration all around. If group lessons, team teaching with another teacher, or doing trades for extra lessons are not feasible, try another approach. Give detailed weekly assignments and ask the parents to check off each when completed. At the end of each week have the student play into a tape recorder and then write down what needs improvement. Circle chronic problem measures and ask the student to play them to your answering machine once a week. Assign theory homework so you don't waste time doing it at the lesson. Impress upon your student that he must come to his lesson with his music prepared so you can spend your hour teaching new concepts, not correcting his mistakes.

Q: I don't give recitals because I can't afford an accompanist. My students' parents are so used to getting the extras for free they won't pay for one.

A: Have you asked the parents or are you assuming they won't pay? If you are really stuck, do you know a pianist with whom you could trade services? Perhaps the church organist would play for your students in return for you performing at a church service. Do any parents play the piano or is there a piano teacher in town with some talented students who might accompany? Have you tried Smart Music? (This great program plays the accompaniments on your computer.) How about planning a recital of only ensembles without piano accompaniment? The value of recitals to students is worth some creative thinking.

Q: My students win almost every contest but it's causing me grief! Other teachers are jealous and complain about me always "showing them up." One of them started a rumor that I have some "in" with the judges to win so often. I work hard to prepare my students and they win on their own merit. I feel uneasy being around the other teachers. How can I make them see that my students earned every single win?

A: Jealousy and competitiveness are part of the music world, but they should never lead you to feel sorry your students are winners! As proud as you are of your students, don't brag about them in public. You may be complimenting them on their hard work but other teachers will take offense.

When a student of another teacher performs well, be sure to compliment the student *and the teacher* with specific praise. "I really enjoyed hearing Susie play. She has come a long way since last year. Good work!" If you are friendly with the judge from previous encounters, save your conversations until after the contest is over.

Successful teachers may have to live with the jealousy and suspicion of teachers who feel threatened. Teachers who are insecure often blame others for their lack of success. You're a convenient target. Continue to interact with teachers in a kind and supportive way.

Q: I have a 1-year-old and would like to start teaching again after my maternity break. My problem is childcare. Would it be all right to let my son stay in the studio with me? If he became disruptive or I had to change a diaper, I could just make the lesson a little longer. Is this a good solution?

A: When parents are paying your for your time, they should know that your full attention is on *their* child, not yours. Adding extra time to the end of the lesson may seem fair to you, but will not help a busy parent's schedule. Nor is it fair to the next student, who arrives on time. Hiring a babysitter is the best solution, but if this arrangement is too expensive for you, perhaps the parents can look after your child in exchange for a discounted lesson. Another solution is to schedule students for two hours: one for the lesson, and one to baby-sit.

Q: My students don't show up for recitals. All the planning and music goes out the window when only half of the kids come.

A: Schedule recitals well in advance and make sure parents know the schedule and the expectation of attendance. If necessary, talk to each parent about the recital and say, "Can I count on you and Jenny on Saturday at three o'clock?" Tell them you have a printed program or that their daughter must be there as part of an ensemble. Make the recitals fun affairs so everyone will look forward to coming.

Q: I have two students who can play better than I do. Am I still qualified to be their teacher or should I send them to someone else?

A: Have your students outgrown your expertise or can they just move their fingers faster than you? If you are not assigning higher-level pieces because you don't know them or don't feel that you can coach your students to be the best they can be, then it is time for them to move on. However, if they are still learning from you and you are not holding them back in any way, it is not necessary that you can perform at the same level as them.

Q: I have a terrible time with transfer students. They are usually very unskilled but think they are advanced just based on the number of years they have had lessons. How can I make this transition easier?

A: During the initial phone interview describe your program and your philosophies. Do not use this session to "dig the dirt" about the first teacher. Even if the student and parents willingly changed teachers because they wanted something different, they are probably still bonded to the old teacher and you must honor this relationship.

Before the first lesson, inform them that no matter their level, you will start back at square one so you can make sure there are no holes in their knowledge and so they can learn the way you approach each subject. "I know this will be really easy for you, and you will be able to zoom through these early lessons, but I would just like to review all the basics." If students have been playing music that is too difficult, it might be wise to let them choose one piece they would like to continue working on but assign the rest in a lower-level book. "Justify" this choice by saying, "I love this book because even though the notes and rhythms may look easy, it has so much to teach about musicality." Or "Since you liked that piece, I bet you will find this one fun too" and sneak in a similar but less technical piece. Or "This book, which is probably below your level, will be good practice for sight reading." It is a tricky business to give students the feeling of forward motion even though you are really moving "backwards" to pick up the pieces. During the lessons, don't pronounce your superiority over the former teacher. If your teaching is indeed superior, the student's progress will be statement enough. It serves no purpose to make them feel bad about all the "wasted" years and money. If the student has been well taught, be sure to compliment the former teacher to the student, and, if the situation is appropriate, to the teacher.

Q: My once bright and cheerful student has recently taken a nosedive since her boyfriend broke up with her. Her grades have gone down, she's not practicing, and she comes in looking depressed and disheveled. She doesn't even like to play the duets she loved, and says, "I just don't care anymore." I've tried to cheer her up but it hasn't worked. What can I do to make her feel better?

A: Your student shows signs of depression. This is not a problem that can be solved with a kind teacher or beautiful music; she needs a trained professional. Always be there to listen but encourage her to seek out a trained specialist.

There are many teenagers who have eating disorders, cut themselves, are abused at home, or have fantasies of suicide. I had one student who had quit lessons about four years earlier call me out of the blue to say how much I meant to her and how she was going to turn her life around. The next week she shot and killed herself. Another who had quit earlier went to a therapist and was prescribed sleeping pills. She took the whole bottle. If these two girls had been still taking lessons, perhaps I could have helped them, but as teachers, we are trained as musicians and not counselors. We can help only as a friend, not as a professional. Because we may see our students more than any adult, we may have more insight, but if you sense someone has deep problems, don't try to tackle them yourself. You are responsible for notifying someone about the warning signs. So please speak to her and to her parents about getting the help she needs before it's too late.

And this brings us to the end of the "Ask the Teacher" chapter. All the problems you read about were real-life situations that my music teacher friends or I have experienced. I'm sure you recognized yourself or your students in a few of them too. If a problem continues to dog you, don't spend another day feeling disillusioned or defeated. Tackle it. Speak up if you feel hurt or angry. Don't excuse students who devalue your standards by ignoring them. End conversations with the ignorant or the arrogant. Learn to say, "I'm sorry, I have to say no." When you're fighting a losing battle, make the hard choice. Fire that apathetic student, ban the disruptive parent, and say "so long" to anyone who takes advantage of your kindnesses. Get back to enjoying the rewards of teaching! And if those rewards include trusting relationships with your students and caring for those who need and look up to you, your choice might be to bend a little, keep the needy child, and allow her to experience the joy and healing power of music. Not every problem has a simple solution or a happy ending, and as musicians and caring people we know we don't have all the answers. Life is full of problems and promise. It's a wonderful journey that requires us to learn and grow and commit to do our best.

Part 4

RUNNING YOUR
PRIVATE MUSIC STUDIO

TWENTY-SEVEN

Establish Your Private Studio and Develop a Business Plan

CHOOSING TO BECOME A PRIVATE TEACHER

You've always dreamed of being your own boss, setting your own schedule, and avoiding the daily eight-to-five grind. Your dream includes a studio filled with talented, inspired students who revere you and would rather practice than eat. Their parents are enamored with you and are happy to pay you top dollar, so grateful are they for the privilege of filling one of the treasured spots in your studio—after a two-year wait. Wait a minute . . . this is your *dream,* remember? Even dreams have tradeoffs. Before striking out on your own, carefully consider whether becoming a private teacher will be the best use of your time and talents.

Is Being a Private Music Teacher Right for You?

You want to be a private music teacher? As they say in fine restaurants, "*Excellent* choice!" Being a teacher is one of the most fun and rewarding jobs, yet even "dream" jobs present problems and can be personally and financially draining. Poor planning is the cause of most business failures. Before you open for business, do some soul-searching. Many musicians decide to teach because they love music. A more deciding factor is, do you love kids?

Is Entrepreneurship Right for You?

Being a private music teacher involves not only sharing knowledge with your adoring students, but running a business too. Some of you may shy away from the business side. "I went to music school, not business school. The highest I can count is 12/8!" Regardless of your training, you must have the qualities and drive to be a successful business owner. Answer these questions: Do you get along well with all types of people, including pushy parents, complaining students, and unkind judges? Do you have a passion for being your own boss? Do you have enough money for start-up costs? Are you willing and able to sacrifice earnings in the short term until your advertising and networking pays off? Is your family prepared to bear the financial and time burden of your new business? Are you committed to working long, irregular hours, evenings, and weekends to get a good start? Do you have the discipline to delay gratification? Are you self-motivated? A hard worker? Are your home records and files organized? Do you have the confidence to sell yourself? Are you emotionally strong? *Can you stand to hear lots of wrong notes?* If you've answered these questions with a resounding "Yes!" you're strong, you're smart, you're Super Teacher!

HOW DO YOU GET STARTED?
THE MUSIC TEACHER'S BUSINESS PLAN

Every company needs a business plan to succeed in the future. And yes, *teaching private music lessons is a business.* Your business plan should be a realistic look at your objectives and the future expectations you have for your business. In other words, *where do you want to be five years from now and how do you want to get there?* Your business plan is a working document giving you a path in the uncharted territory of being a small business owner. It can also provide a foundation for setting your prices and help in marketing. It will evolve with you. Developing your business plan can require some research, but will be worth it in the end.

Set up a logical, effective business plan and *write it down.* There's a big difference between having it in your head and committing it to paper. Building the plan forces you to do your homework and give your dream a reality check.

CHOOSING A GENERAL LOCATION

Several considerations can help you decide where your business can be the most profitable.

- Where do you want to live? In a large city? The suburbs? A small town?
- Where is there a need for teachers? Are there lots of teachers in a particular area? Are there music schools offering your same service?
- Will your students have access to other musical stimuli such as youth orchestras, concerts, visiting guest artists, or master classes? Are the band and orchestra programs in the public schools healthy?
- What is the economic health of the town and the particular neighborhood? Are people used to paying top dollar for what they perceive to be excellence? Is this a locale that values education?
- Is there opportunity for you to make money in other ways in the community, including playing or singing at a church, conducting a community ensemble, or playing gigs?
- Are there many children in the neighborhood? Is it an aging population? Are you willing to adjust your target audience?
- Is there another teacher who might recommend you?
- Is the community too small to support a music teacher of your instrument?
- Is the cost of renting or buying a home or teaching space in a particular area prohibitive? Can you charge more in a certain neighborhood?
- Can you more easily make a name for yourself in a small community?

CHOOSING A TEACHING SPACE

Will You Teach out of Your Home or Find a Separate Space in Which to Teach?

If you want to teach at home, ask yourself these questions: Do you have the right physical setup for teaching music in an environment where students will not be distracted by the business of your home—including small children, spousal interruptions, and neighborhood noises? Will you be able to present a professional setting, or will students have to climb over the laundry basket and your kids' sports equipment to get to your studio?

If you want to teach outside of the home: Are you willing to travel to students' homes? Can you charge extra for travel? Can you be assured of a professional atmosphere with enough space, quiet, and privacy? Can you trade one lesson for using a student's home for many lessons? Can you rent a space in a music store or share a space in a church or community hall and share costs with another teacher? Are there any schools that allow private teachers to take kids out of band or orchestra for lessons? Can you use the space to teach before or after school?

Advantages to teaching at home

The commute is great and you have no car and gas expenses. Your music room is a lot nicer than a rented studio. Students get a feel for you as a real person; they see your house, your family (sometimes), and your dog, and may treat you with higher standards of respect and behavior. Though you're not with your own children, you are a "presence" in the home for emergencies or casting a pall on wild parties. You can eat your meals at home and if a student cancels, you can do the dishes. Students can reach you for last-minute cancellations, and make-up lessons are easier to schedule. All your materials are at your fingertips. You have a permanent recital venue. There is no "rent" and studio expenses are tax deductible. You have much better communication with parents because you see them. *Your neighbors may love the music they hear wafting out of your house.*

Considerations when searching for a potential apartment or home

Do strict zoning laws or homeowner covenants restrict home-based businesses? Is your target market within a twenty-minute drive? Is your house easy to find and easy to access? Is there good bus service? Is the studio close to any schools? Is the neighborhood quiet? Is there ample parking for waiting parents? Is there sound insulation or separation from neighbors? Are the neighbors nice?

Advantages to teaching outside the home

You are not restricted in where you live by where you can teach. You can get more students and charge more by offering to travel to students' homes. You don't have to buy all the equipment, including stands and a piano. Rental expenses and mileage are tax deductible. You may get discounts on music supplies if you teach at a music store.

And the privacy issue: You can much more easily separate your work from the rest of your life. You don't have to designate a room in your house as a studio and your family is not disturbed by your students and your students are not disturbed by your family. You're not on public display and don't have to clean your toilets. You're not on call 24/7. *Your neighbors may hate the music they hear wafting out of your house.*

If you teach at a school, it's easier to get students because you have a built-in clientele and ensembles require no scheduling. You can teach during the day instead of just after school hours, a perfect setup for teachers with school age children. You can get students whose parents can't or won't drive them to a lesson.

But the disadvantages to teaching at a school are numerous, too. It may be harder to teach back-to-back lessons, so your free time is spent at school. The lesson times are short. School assemblies, holidays, and even fire drills can wreak havoc with your schedule. Teaching at a school may be noisy, and the practice rooms are usually small, dark, and smelly. Band or orchestra conductors may expect you to concentrate on helping students with their school music only. Students may view you just like another teacher instead of the "honored private music teacher." Students may choose to study with you because of the convenience, not because of their commitment.

Other Things to Consider
When Deciding Where to Teach

What effect will the neighbors have on your business?

A well-known violin teacher in Seattle bought a house in a lovely suburban neighborhood and spent thousands of dollars to remodel it. His refurbished home included a large studio with room for recitals and a waiting area for parents. It even had an air conditioner (in Seattle!) to mask any sound coming out of his house. Everything seemed perfect for a professionally run studio to fit into a neighborhood. But no. One of his neighbors was so upset that he was running a business at home that he made the violin teacher's life miserable. This neighbor complained to the neighborhood community organization, who then made rules targeted just at the violin teacher. The new neighborhood covenant stated that the teacher could only teach Monday through Friday, cars could not park by the sidewalk or in front of anyone else's home, only one car could be in his driveway at once so he must rent a van to transport students for recitals, no one was to stand outside and talk, and none of the students' siblings were to play in the back yard while waiting. And he was only allowed to teach twenty students per week! What a nightmare!

To make peace with your neighbors, give them peace

There is no pleasing some people, but if you develop a personal relationship with your neighbors they will be much less likely to complain. Talk to them before you move in and let them know you are a music teacher, and when new neighbors move in, inform them about your studio. Ask students to park in your driveway or where they won't block the neighbors. Keep your doors and windows closed in the summer if you have any complaints. Ask students to carpool or park in designated areas for recitals and big parties if necessary. Let neighbors know of any big recital and invite them to come. If they *do* complain, work toward compromises. If you run into trouble, the Music Teachers National Association can help with legal advice.

What are the temptations of working at home?

Just because you don't walk through the front door to get to work doesn't mean teaching should be regarded as anything less than a *real job* with real responsibilities and codes of behavior. Manage your private studio as you would manage an office and keep it organized and clean. Think of this space as separate from your home; no teaching with the TV blasting in the next room or children interrupting. Buy an answering machine and try to keep off the phone during lessons. Finally, separate home and business time: Because you teach at home does not mean you are always on call.

Your home music studio needs

- A private entrance if possible.
- A large enough space for four chairs and stands, a seating area for parents, and an available bathroom.
- Musical equipment, including music stands, a piano if possible or at least a keyboard (please don't use a cheap keyboard to teach *piano*!), a library of standard repertoire and music reference books, access to a CD player and tape recorder, a tuner, and a metronome.
- Other equipment, including a phone and answering system in the room or nearby, a full length mirror to check posture, a clock, and good lighting.
- Office supplies, including a calendar, a book to record lesson payments, an appointment book with a telephone list of students, and file folders.
- Shelves or file cabinets for music and a computer for printing out bills, forms, letters, and announcements, and for keeping track of income and expenses.
- And, if you have small children, a *babysitter*!

First Impressions: Your Studio's Appearance

Consider how you can make the music room both more visually appealing and more functional. Purchase a bookcase and filing cabinet for music and projects. Maintain a master calendar that tracks schedules, appointments, student attendance, and payments. File music alphabetically for easy access and also keep handy a computer printout of all music you own. Use file cabinets for easy-to-find handouts. (I find that using different-colored folders and paper also helps me spot what I need quickly.) In addition to the supplies you'll need to run your business, allow money in your budget for possible expenses such as decorating and remodeling, special music for beginners or ensembles, licenses or permits if necessary, insurance, and utility deposits.

Supplies for the Traveling Teacher

OK, does teaching away from home sound more appealing now? Here's what you will need:

- A dependable car and membership in AAA for emergencies.
- A cell phone.

• The same office supplies as in the studio.

• A carrying case for music.

And it never hurts to have a thermos, snack food, and lots of extra energy.

ANALYZE YOUR MARKET

Now that you have a great teaching space, how do you find great students to fill it? First research the market. If you're vying for students in a tight market, analyze what other teachers offer. What are their strengths and weaknesses in terms of availability, location, expertise, and reputation? Like a corner store trying to compete with giant retailer Wal-Mart, find a niche that will help you survive alongside more well-known teachers, or focus on a market that has not been fully served. How can you make your service unique?

What Special Services Can You Offer?

Give lessons that special touch with superior customer service. Go out of your way to meet your students' needs. Pride yourself on your personal touches, such as sending birthday cards, notes to parents, and studio letters.

Do you have something special to offer that other teachers don't? Can you give more or make it easier? Has your educational background given you specific skills that you can pass on? Do you have a music degree? A graduate degree? A teaching certificate? MTNA certification? Will your performing background influence your teaching? How long have you been teaching? Can you specialize in an area most other teachers neglect, such as adults, students with learning or physical challenges, children who speak a different language, the very young, or students who want to learn both classical and jazz? Can you offer more convenient hours or travel? Do you teach more than one instrument or incorporate piano into the curriculum? Can you offer different-length lesson times? Can you meet the needs of students at all levels? Do you have a proven track record with successful students? Do you offer enrichment that others don't, such as music theory, music history, improvisation, performance opportunities, ensembles, computer programs, spectacular recitals? *Do you provide an atmosphere of excellence?*

GETTING NEW STUDENTS
Network

Now that you have identified how special you are as a teacher, how can you let prospective students know? Broadcast your availability. Get out into the community and let everyone you meet know that you are a good teacher and are looking for students.

When my husband and I wanted to adopt a baby, we used this same approach. We wrote a letter and made a scrapbook of pictures and stories about us that we would show to anyone willing to look and asked them to spread the word. It worked and now we have our wonderful son, Scott, through the power of networking. Trust me, getting students is a lot easier than getting a baby!

Develop a network of support in your field. Find a mentor who can give you the inside story on neighborhoods in which to teach, prices other teachers charge, method books to use, and whom you can use as a sounding board for the inevitable problems that may arise.

Join local and national music societies and go to meetings, master classes, and conventions. Join professional groups such as the local chamber of commerce, service clubs, charities, or small business networking groups such as Rotary or Kiwanis. Bring the fact that you are a music teacher looking for new students into the conversation wherever you go. Don't be shy. Hand out your cards and ask people to pass them on wherever you go. Offer to contribute educational articles or information to association newsletters, trade journals, and other publications that reach your intended audience. Perform in the community and always have your cards and brochures ready. *Remaining visible is key.*

Become "Famous"

In schools

Help the band and orchestra teachers at local schools: offer to teach the beginning instrument class, give the teacher technique tricks, conduct sectionals, or take students out individually for extra help or enrichment. Arrange to teach lessons during school or at a grade school in their extended care program before or after school. Coach an ensemble, offer to accompany the choir, or help with the spring musical. Ask the band and orchestra directors if you can give a demonstration and tell the class about your teaching. Build your reputation with band and orchestra directors and keep your students' schools informed about their success.

Look at teaching adult education extension (no credit) classes offered through universities, start classes at an adult retirement facility, or become part of the homeschool system to get students you can teach during the day. Offer to teach at private schools, as they may have no other music program and would appreciate being able to offer music through the form of private lessons and ensembles. Interview at community music schools and brainstorm about classes such as improvisation, recording, sight reading, ensembles, lessons, music appreciation, music history, and music theory that you might teach.

Through your present students

Offer students incentives for referrals, such as a free lesson once the new student has paid for three months of lessons. Offer incentives for new students, such as two free lessons or free lessons during a vacation, and end with a concert for the adoring parents. Tell your students you have a few openings and ask if there is anyone in their class who would like to come observe their lesson or come to a recital. Invite students from school who don't already take lessons to play in ensembles in your studio.

Get your students performing: organize concerts on the radio and in shopping malls, school assemblies, talent shows, and community events. Arrange for students to play in the lobby before symphony concerts or children's concerts and get your name in the program. Broadcast outstanding students' accomplishments and create a buzz about your ability as a teacher. Attend concerts featuring your students, be the proud teacher, and proudly present them with flowers.

As a music specialist

Network with other teachers and let them know you are available for their "overflow." Refer students of other instruments to successful teachers who may return the favor. Host a fundraiser concert or practice-a-thon sponsored by your studio for a worthy cause and inform the media. Provide seminars of interest to parents about how to choose an instrument, how to practice, how to choose a teacher, when to start playing an instrument, the benefits of music lessons, or how parents can help their children learn. Hold the seminars in your studio or music stores, schools, the library, a bookstore, or a preschool. Submit articles to local and neighborhood papers, children's magazines, school newsletters, PTA newsletters, and teaching and music professional societies. Offer preschool groups a "field trip" to your studio. Include some hands-on activities and something each child can take home (such as a picture of them sitting at the piano, with your name and phone number on it). If you are a member of the Musicians' Union, use their services. Establish rapport with a local music store and music repair person and give them your cards. Get on the teacher referral lists for youth orchestras and schools. Offer a couple of free lessons as an auction item or a month of lessons in a raffle. Start a summer ensemble program.

The "golden rule" for getting new students:

DO NOT try to "steal" students from other teachers. Never initiate a conversation suggesting students leave their present teacher. If they want to change teachers, let them come to you. Always take the high road in your studio and in your life, and behave the way you hope other music professionals will behave to you.

Advertising and Marketing Your Business

How we wish we had an agent who could put up billboards, shake hands, and kiss babies while telling the world how wonderful we are. Sometimes being a musician feels like always waiting for someone to ask you out on a date! Unfortunately, we must do this part of business ourselves. You'll find more ways to get new students listed below. If you tried them all, you would have one hundred students but be too exhausted to teach them. Try out each idea and see if it fits your special situation, pocketbook, and personality.

Business cards

Pass these out everywhere. Your business card should be striking in color and format and professionally made. Include your name, address, phone number, e-mail address, and if you will travel to teach, and name the instrument you teach in big print. (And make sure the information is up to date: no scratched-out phone numbers!)

Flyers

Flyers can be handed out directly to potential students or posted on bulletin boards. They're cheaper than ads or brochures and thus can be broadcast more widely. If you are going to distribute your flyers to teenagers, make them flashy or even a little humorous. Target your audience by posting flyers in areas where children go. To make it easy for people to contact you, write your name, instrument, and phone number many times vertically across the very bottom of the flyer with small cuts between each entry. This way prospective clients can just tear off your vital information and make that call. The most effective way to use flyers in schools is through personal contact. After school music directors know you (and are indebted to you), you can distribute your flyers with their endorsement.

Brochures

Brochures give out more information and may include the information on your business card plus your resume, pictures, special background, or the expertise that distinguishes you from other teachers. They may also state your expectations and include a mission statement. Give brochures to your present students and send a brochure to every student who inquires about your lessons. Hand out or post cards, flyers, and brochures at grocery stores, church bulletin boards, schools, music stores, places where kids take other lessons, and even at the hairdresser.

Print advertising

Print advertising can be costly, so you may want to hold off until you see how other efforts pan out. You can try the yellow pages, but you need to have a separate business phone number, and the commitment to running the ad is one year. Newspapers are cheaper and lower-risk. Write a succinct ad and place it in the classifieds for at least three months around the beginning of the school year. It is smarter to spend your advertising budget on many smaller ads than on just a few large ones. If you live in a neighborhood with a local newspaper, try placing your ad there instead of in the *New York Times*. Church bulletins, PTSA newsletters, and high school and college newspapers are also economical choices. Make sure everything in print advertising looks professional.

Signs

A sign in your window, front yard, or car will attract people in your neighborhood.

Websites

Websites are a sophisticated way to show the world how great you are. Include smiling pictures or even video of you and your students. Your qualifications, mission statement, and studio policy give people an insight into who you are. Include endorsements from parents and other teachers, and up-to-date chronicles of your students' accomplishments. A website is also a cost-effective and timesaving way to bill your current students, keep them informed about schedules and performances, and give monthly hints, praise, or awards.

SELECTING STUDENTS

How Many Students Do You Want?

Now that your phone is ringing off the hook, you need to decide how many students you really want. The number of students you teach each week may make or break you financially, physically, and mentally, so give it some careful thought.

The advantages of having lots of students

Of course, more students mean more money. The loss of a student is not so critical to the well-being of the studio, and you can pick and choose whom you teach and charge more. It's easier to group students of like aptitude together for classes or chamber music, and recitals can be grand affairs. You have a better chance of having more outstanding students and a full studio gives the impression of a successful studio and a good teacher.

The disadvantages of having too many students

Too many students can cause problems. There is no time to regenerate between lessons. Physical problems such as sore shoulders or backs can be exacerbated with constant playing and demonstrating, or even just sitting or standing in the same position for too long. The sheer number of interpersonal relationships can make you feel as though you are living in a soap opera. Students can become numbers or just paychecks instead of people.

Time of course is also a problem, with no wiggle room for schedule changes or extracurricular activities such as ensemble practice. Your whole identity is wrapped up in your students because there's no time for yourself, your family, or your dog. One bad student can ruin your attitude for the next ten! Too many students can make you start to hate teaching.

Lesson length

Sure, you can teach more students if you teach shorter lessons, but will that give you better students or just more mediocre ones? Half-hour lessons are good for young beginners unused to focusing for a long period, but forty-five-minute or hour lessons will allow you to be a better teacher.

Focus on the Big Picture: Have Patience

It takes a while to build up a studio and a reputation. The very best way to get students is through referrals of people who have heard your students play. Keep teaching the very best lessons you can and students will come to your door and will stay with you for years. Always call or write the people who recommended you and thank them.

With all these suggestions of things to do, remember to take care of yourself. Find time to do something relaxing. Exercise, get together with friends, play music. Maybe having fewer students will give you a much-needed break.

What to Say When the Phone Rings

The initial contact on the phone has to be some sort of a sales pitch for your services as well as a screening process for the prospective student. Be sure to always return a phone inquiry that very day if possible; the caller may have a list of referrals and sign up with the first one she can reach!

Write down the features of your studio and its benefits to students so you'll be prepared for the call. Practice your script. Be welcoming and friendly and speak in layman's terms. Let the caller gain insight into your teaching techniques and personality. Express pride in your program but don't use a hard sell approach.

Find out what the caller is looking for. And as I've said before, be honest and forthcoming about the contents of your lessons, the benefits received, and also about your requirements, so there will be fewer surprises later.

Qualify Your Prospect

Parents may think they are interviewing you, but you are interviewing them too! Ask callers basic questions about the student's age, musical experience, and outside activities. Also inquire about the musical life of the family and ask how involved the parents are willing to be in the learning process and whether they have any musical goals. If the student is quitting another teacher, ask what they have they heard about your teaching and why they chose to call you.

Tell callers about your background. Include your education degrees and/or MTNA certification, your years of experience teaching, the accomplishments of your students, your goals for your students, and your excitement about teaching. If you are a new teacher emphasize your love of children and teaching. You may speak briefly about your own performing, but remember, the caller is inquiring about your teaching, not your solo career. It's got to be about *them,* not you.

Thanks, but No Thanks

I've had all these requests, but I'm not that desperate and neither are you. Reject applicants such as these:

They want you to travel to their home forty-five minutes away. (You live too far away for them to come to you.) They need to take a break from lessons during soccer and basketball seasons. (Leaving about five months of lessons, but please hold their spot.) They think private music teachers should charge as much as babysitters. (What? You don't even have to leave your house to go to work. The teenage girl down the street said she would teach for one fourth of what you are asking!) There should be no pressure to practice. (Music should always be fun. Having to practice every day takes the joy out of it.) The parents don't want to get involved. (We have to remind him about so many other things, like homework, that we just don't want to get involved in music too.) Lessons are only the parents' idea. (The child is hiding in the car!) They only want to take lessons until the audition is over or the contest won. (No pressure here.) You would be the fourth teacher in two years. (You have about as much chance for success as Henry VIII's fifth wife!) They just want to play the band music. (Or, as one parent requested of me, "Could you just teach her the band notes and not make her play B-naturals?") They never study for school and never practiced with the old teacher but heard you might be just the one to kick them into gear. (And I never listened to the former teacher when she warned me whose idea no practicing had been.) They can commit to practicing fifteen minutes a day, four days a week. (She's got so much else going on, you must understand.) They want to take lessons every other week. (That way they can afford you and the student won't have to practice so much, either.) Their only available time is Fridays at 7:30. (*You* have a social life?) They just decided in the spring of their senior year that they want to take lessons for the first time so they can audition to become a music major. (Seriously, she played like a seventh grader, but really liked band, and thought being a music major might get her a scholarship.) They want to study with you and their old teacher at the same time . . . but don't tell her. (Or, in my case, find out the hard way that the student never quit the first teacher.) The mom thinks her daughter shouldn't have to take private lessons—that's what the school is for—but since she's lagging so far behind could you teach her every other week? (She's a senior.)

Sounds Interesting, Now What?

The parent or student thinks that your system of teaching sounds wonderful and they haven't fainted over the price. The student has passed *your* "phone test" too, so what do you do now? Ask if they would like to observe a lesson, come to meet you, or have a trial lesson.

If the parent has called, it is a good idea to speak a moment with the child. Put the child at ease and say, "I am excited to meet you; your mom has told me great things about you." Assure him, "Don't worry about meeting me and playing for me. I don't care what you know when you first come, I just care what you know when you come back!"

The first lesson/interview/audition

You finally get to meet the person you may be spending the next eight years with. It feels like a blind date! Make the family feel at home with some light conversation but be sure to direct most questions and attention to the student. Use this time to interview students but also to give a mini-lesson so they can imagine themselves as your student.

This is also the time to explain your studio policies, expectations, opportunities, and calendar year. At the end of the interview, it will probably be obvious to everyone the decision that needs to be made. If you really want the student, say, "So, does this look like something you would like to do?" Or "I think we would make a great team!" If the student or I seem a little hesitant I might say, "Why don't you go home and discuss it?"

You may commit to a trial period or just assume a long-term commitment.

Establishing yourself as a teacher and choosing your students may seem like a complicated and daunting process, but it is a process that is vital to your studio and will become easier with time as you learn what to say and how to present yourself. With luck and skill, you will soon find yourself in that enviable situation of having exactly the number of students you want and need—and having the kind of students who will thrive under your tutelage.

TWENTY-EIGHT

Get Paid What You're Worth

Talking about the business aspect of music is as embarrassing to most musicians as talking about their underwear! We feel our lives should be centered on the beauty of Mozart, not ledgers and checkbooks, and that our students and parents are our friends, not employers or clients. And that's why many musicians are barely getting by. We have to remember that this is our job, and just like doctors, lawyers, and other professionals, we must be clear and up-front about the business aspect of our work. Once you have decided on your policies and parameters, you can get down to the job we all want to do: make music and enrich lives.

PRICING YOUR SERVICE AND BILLING

Pricing services is one of the biggest challenges for new teachers. Generally the best approach is to base your price on the fees charged by other teachers *of your education and experience in your area.* Teachers should exchange information about fees to maintain a high standard. You should be paid what you are worth, even if you only have a few students or if you teach out of passion for your work. If you undersell yourself you will also be underselling other teachers.

Remember that tuition does not just cover the lesson time. It also includes countless hours spent choosing music, planning lessons, preparing for and attending competitions, arranging recitals, learning new music, attending and volunteering in professional organizations; purchase of music, instruments, bookkeeping supplies and studio upkeep; convention and master class attendance, time on the phone, computer and letter writing, and on and on. (Sounds like a big job, doesn't it?) The weekly fee should also be set in consideration of the fact that independent music teachers get no paid vacations, sick days, retirement plans, or health insurance.

Contact music stores and ask what teachers who teach in their store charge. Call instrumental teachers on different instruments to ask for advice. (This way you won't be seen as a competitor.) And always keep in mind that in survey after survey of what customers want, quality and service consistently outrank price.

A business word to the wise: Consider having an annual registration fee to offset library and equipment expenses and your time spent "off duty." Think of your future and contribute to an IRA, keep a few months' salary in the bank, get in a health plan, and consider disability insurance. And marry rich!

Factors to Consider in Establishing Your Fee

The variables of location, the facility you teach in, your education, your performing and teaching experience, lesson content, and enrichment will all play into the fee you can charge. The law of supply and demand will make a huge difference too.

How do your fees compare?

Should you charge less because you are just starting to make a name for yourself? Can you charge more and appeal to a wealthier or more committed clientele because of your background or location? How does the price of your lessons compare to the fee for lessons on other instruments or voice? What about dance or karate? How much did they pay for those fancy tennis shoes?

Advice on fee structure

If you start with your fee too low, it will be very hard to gradually raise it to the level you deserve when you are more experienced. A very low price also carries with it the stigma of an assumed very low quality. "She must not be that good if she is that cheap!" On the other hand, if you are just starting out, you should not charge as much as experienced, successful teachers. No matter that you are a virtuoso player: Years of teaching make the experienced teacher "worth" more.

Should you have a sliding fee scale?

Should you keep teenagers who have had several rate increases at the same rate until they graduate from high school? Keep a student at a rate for a specific amount of time? Charge new students more? Charge more for a particular population (for instance, adults, preschool, very advanced)? Charge lower rates for hard-to-fill times, such as mornings?

Or charge a fixed rate for everyone?

I strongly recommend charging everyone the same amount. Charging different rates makes your accounting difficult and your students unhappy if they find out someone is getting cheaper lessons than they are.

Other advice for setting a fee structure

Don't give a family rate. If the parents were paying two different teachers for lessons, they would never ask for discounts. Charge more than half the hourly rate for a half-hour lesson because it is twice as hard to have two students and their "baggage" in one hour as to teach just one student. Don't give lessons every other week because your schedule will have a hole in it every other week that could be filled by a full-time student. And *don't negotiate, apologize for, or rationalize your fee.* It is what it is. If it is too much for the caller, be happy to recommend a less experienced teacher.

And then make exceptions

Be a good businessperson, but always be a generous person. Any rule may be broken. My own flute and violin teachers gave me free lessons as a struggling college student; they said some of their teachers had shown them this generosity and they were sure I would continue that tradition. In all my years of teaching, I have always had someone on reduced tuition. Help the student who really needs it and really appreciates it. If you choose to barter, keep in mind that you will almost always come out on the short end of the financial stick. Just be very sure to spell out before the service is done what the trade value is.

How Do I Charge?

The best advice I can give is to ask for payment at the beginning of the month. Not only will students cancel less (they are suddenly sick much less often!), but you will also have less bookkeeping and fewer trips to the bank, and an income and schedule you can count on. I've included many payment options from other teachers below. Figure out what works best for your schedule, personality, clientele, and pocketbook.

Payment plan options:

- Pay for the number of lessons in each month at the first lesson of the month. This is the most common method and the one I use. (There are four Tuesdays in May times $1,000.00 per lesson. $4,000.00 due at the first lesson in May. The method is real; the numbers are fantasy!)

- Pay a set fee per month no matter how many lessons there are. Some months the student will get an extra free lesson and other months the teacher will be paid for vacation and missed lessons. This method gives teachers a salary they can count on even through holidays or the summer. Some parents are very uncomfortable with this because they feel they are paying for lessons not taken, and others may like the regularity of the payment amount. (Pay $4,500.00 every month, due the first lesson of the month.)

- Use a contract for a semester. State how long the period is (usually three months), how many weeks will have lessons (including dates for vacations), the amount due, and when. (Students sign up in three-month increments. The fee is $1,000.00 per lesson with twelve lessons in this semester. $12,000.00 due the first week of the semester.)

- Bill twice per year and offer payment through PayPal.

- Bill at the end of the month for the number of lessons that were taken. This works well for musicians who must miss or reschedule lessons frequently for performances. (The fee is $1,000.00 per lesson. Four lessons were scheduled in October but only two were taken. $2,000.00 is due the last lesson in October.)

- Pay weekly with no strings attached. (The student shows up at every lesson with a check.)

- Prepay for the entire year. Some parents like the longer-length plans because they don't have to worry about writing all those checks. An installment plan can be agreed upon if paying for the entire year at once is prohibitive. The teacher likes this plan because of the simplified book-keeping, getting a lump sum that can be used for a major purchase, and committing students to a year of lessons. (The fee is not dependent on the number of lessons but is a yearly tuition fee for September through May. $35,000.00 is due in September.)

• Pay weekly in advance for the next lesson. The student pays for two lessons the first time and then pays weekly for the next lesson. This still keeps students on a pay-in-advance system without having to write one big check for the month.

How to Bill

Billing systems can be as formal or casual as the teacher deems necessary. I use no formal billing. Parents know that the fee is due the first lesson of the month as stated in my signed studio policy.

Options:

• Discuss the due date for each bill in the policy statement and expect parents to remember.

• Hand out a copy of the weekly schedule of students and the teacher's own performances for the month at the first lesson of the month. Include the monthly fee for lessons, recital fees, and money owed for music purchased.

• Mail the bill two weeks before the due date.

• Give the bill to the student at the lesson the week before it is due.

• Give each student a set of payment envelopes at the beginning of the year.

• Write the amount due in the lesson book.

• Expect the check at every lesson, negating the need for a statement.

• Allow parents to pay with credit card or PayPal.

Some teachers "inspire" students to pay in a timely manner by using rewards or consequences: a 5 percent discount if paying for the entire year, a 3 percent discount if paying by semester, or a $15.00 late fee. If students pay by the week, insist on cash at the beginning of the lesson. This inconvenience will persuade them to pay monthly by check.

Raising Your Rates

The rent just went up for the fourth time in three years, it took two days' worth of teaching to pay for the dinner out last night, and you need to spend your inheritance to fill up the gas tank. When the term "struggling artist" begins to have too much personal meaning, consider raising your rates.

When to raise your rates

When you have a waiting list. When you want to cut down on the number of students you teach. When your students are very successful, winning competitions and earning top chairs in their music groups. When you have a very big reputation. When your program offers a tremendous amount of enrichment. When prices for other children-based activities such as dance, karate, and tennis lessons have gone up. When you haven't raised your fee in three years. When your fees have not kept up with inflation. When your fee is below that of most teachers of your caliber in your area.

When not to raise your rates

When you have just had a sizeable rate increase in the past year. When your area is in an economic downturn and a fee increase would be a burden on your students.

When there is lots of competition for students. When you need every student you can get and can't afford to have one quit or turn away because of a high price. When you've bought a shiny red sports car and need the extra cash. When your students don't perform well and your heart isn't into teaching.

How and how much to raise your fees

There are two methods of raising fees. One is to raise by a small increment, a few dollars or a 5 percent or 10 percent increase every year. With this method your students are prepared for the increase and can budget it in. The other method is to have a larger increase less often. I prefer this because it makes accounting easier with round numbers (I hate to figure out what $43.75 times 5 is) and I also don't need to "break it" to the parents so often. I raise my fee about every three years.

The best time to raise your rates is at the beginning and end of the school year. You can call, e-mail, or mail a more formal letter. Here again, don't apologize for the rate increase or promise to use the extra money on students.

Extra Ways to Earn More Money through Teaching

We all know teaching music is not a get-rich-quick scheme. Try these ideas to augment your income: Charge a yearly registration fee that includes administrative and supply costs. Charge for recitals. Charge for accompanying students on the piano at recitals and contests. Teach more lessons to the same students: add ensembles, performance class, or music theory classes. Teach two lessons a week to very serious students or to those who have missed a lot of lessons in the summer. Teach more hour lessons with students: one half hour on the computer and the other half with you. Team-teach with an apprentice teacher and give him or her a percentage of the half-hour fee: the apprentice can teach basic skills for one half hour, and then the main teacher comes to the second half of the lesson. Hold a summer seminar with other teachers: offer special classes in composition, singing, ear training, ensembles, and percussion instruments.

Switch to group lessons. Many students will be happy to pay the same fee for an hour with four other students that they paid for a half-hour private lesson. I have never taught group lessons, preferring to teach on a one-to-one basis, but have heard of many other teachers who find group lessons more lucrative and more fun. Students enjoy the camaraderie and learn from each other. Consider giving group lessons instead of private lessons, once a month in addition to private lessons, or only in the summer.

Remember, what we do and who we are is valuable. Our years of training and devotion to our students need to be compensated. If you truly believe in the importance of music education, then believe in yourself and charge like any other valued professional; you will be setting a good example for your students who might want to make music their own career. You may even find that charging more will give students one more reason to take their lessons seriously and to believe you are a fantastic teacher. Whatever fee you charge, make sure you earn it. Work at being a good teacher just like you worked at being a good musician.

MAKE-UP LESSONS

Giving "make-up lessons" on how to apply lipstick and eye shadow sometimes seems easier than formulating a policy on what to do when students miss their lessons! Why can't they just always come at the right time and not bother us with rescheduling? Oh, well.

Having a regular income and schedule helps both the teacher and the student do their jobs better. Educate parents that they are paying tuition, just like that in a private school, and that tuition covers so much more than just the weekly lesson and includes all the preparation and extras we give. As in a private school, if the student misses a day of school there is no financial compensation. Inform students that the time they have selected is their time, reserved just for them. It is their decision whether to show up or not and it is not your responsibility to adjust your schedule.

Make it a little uncomfortable for students to reschedule and they won't take changing their lessons lightly. Hand out your student schedule or post it on the computer and make them responsible for making the trade. If they can't find a suitable trade, it is up to the teacher to decide if another lesson will be rescheduled. Charging at the beginning of the month also really cuts down on poor attendance, especially for those who are tempted to cancel because they didn't practice. Keep track of students who regularly try to cancel their lesson and never give refunds.

Policy *Options* and *Advice* for Make-Up Lessons

- Offer no make-up lessons.
- Offer make-up lessons if possible but only charge the student for lessons that were taken.
- Charge extra for make-up lessons. Make the charge less than a normal lesson. If you don't charge for make-up lessons you are, in effect, getting paid half as much because the student has reserved your time for two lessons.
- Only teach at the appointed time. Charge for thirty-five lessons but teach thirty-seven weeks. The last two weeks constitute make-up lessons. The teacher may not earn as much but has a hassle-free, regular schedule.
- If the student quits before the end of the month, no refund for that month will be made.
- If the teacher herself is busy or sick, the lessons will be made up.
- Charge students when you need to cancel their lesson to attend their performance. Why should you have to take a pay cut to further their educations? Their "lesson" is your presence and later commentary.
- Planned vacations will be exceptions and not paid for.
- Summer schedules are flexible. The tuition fee corresponds exactly to the number of lessons received.
- Charge for two months during the summer, guaranteeing a minimum of eight lessons, but without make-up lessons.

- Demand payment for every week there should be a lesson unless the student is on vacation the whole week. Offer make-up lessons only with twenty-four hours' advance notice.
- Offer make-up lessons if the student calls by a certain time: right after school or by nine o'clock Saturday morning.
- If there is more than one no-call/no-show lesson per semester the student is on probation.
- Give students a refund for one lesson per semester missed due to illness. No other refunds offered.
- When students miss more than a week in a row during the summer, or when students have a playing deadline or just feel they have some catching up to do, offer to give two lessons per week.
- When it's the teacher's fault: If you forget and miss the student's lesson they receive credit for that lesson, and the next lesson is also free as an apology.

Options on *When* to Offer Make-Up Lessons

- Reserve sacred off-limit lesson times. Don't give parents and students the idea you are "on call" seven days a week. Be firm about keeping parameters on your free time or you won't have any. (Note to self.) Also make it known that the lesson starts and ends at the appointed time even if the student happens to arrive ten minutes late.
- State the number of make-up lessons you will allow per month or per semester.
- Offer make-ups as soon as possible or on a specific day when all make-up lessons will be taken.
- If the lesson is missed due to illness, request that they call you as soon as they are well. If you can fit a make-up lesson into your schedule, then they get one. If not, then they forfeit their lesson fee.
- Offer make-up lessons only during a free spot that has opened up in the normal schedule that week so that teaching hours remain the same.
- Offer extra time at the beginning of the year when schedules aren't so hectic as insurance for later missed lessons.
- Put a time limit on make-up lessons. A lesson missed in October can not be made up in May but must be made up within the week, two weeks, or month.
- Offer a master class every six to eight weeks instead of a private lesson. Use the free time this opens up to give make-up lessons. Or consider the master class a make-up lesson.
- Offer special make-up lesson times, such as a four-hour block on Saturday once a month.
- Extend the next lesson longer to cover the missed lesson time.
- Offer make-ups only in the first week of January, Thanksgiving week, and spring break.
- Give extra time during the year for ensembles and count it as make-up lessons.

SHOULD YOU TEACH IN THE SUMMER?

Summer is a wonderful time to teach, not only because it pays the summer bills but because the school year pressures are gone and coming to music lessons is more relaxed. I've never had a student who complained about summer lessons when the benefits were explained. Students can get twice as much done in the summer, and in fact some of my students even have two lessons a week. When students drop out for the summer, the first month back is lost in review. There is also a good chance they won't return in the fall, having felt the "freedom" of no lessons over the summer.

But remember, everyone needs a break. Make sure to take your own vacation and be understanding of students when they take theirs. Should students take their instrument on vacation? Yes, when they visit grandma, and no when they visit Mickey and Minnie.

WHAT TO DO IF THEY DON'T PAY

Asking for Money Owed

Here's a great idea. Hire a big thug named Igor. Get the address of your student. Give Igor a kind note from you politely requesting back payments. If the student doesn't hand Igor a check and an apology, leave the rest up to Igor.

OK, OK, maybe Igor is not such a good idea. He's probably too expensive to hire anyway. What should you really do about a student who has not paid? Step one: Make sure you keep accurate records of all checks. Have a system so you don't leave the accounting to memory. A written ledger will come in handy for figuring out who has not paid, what your monthly and yearly income is, and what to tell your accountant around April 15th.

If there is any question or discrepancy, ask parents to check their records to be sure the mistake is not yours. Some teachers refuse to teach a lesson that has not been paid for. If the check doesn't arrive at the second lesson then the child sits in the music room and reads music books or does theory homework. Other teachers won't retain the student if payment is over thirty days late. I admit that I am not this strict, being a busy, forgetful parent myself, but if late payment is a pattern you must consistently follow your studio policy.

Late Payment Penalties

The credit card companies do it, why shouldn't you?
- Charge a set amount when the payment is over two weeks late.
- Charge a weekly late fee that is cumulative; every week the fee increases.
- For teachers asking for payment by the semester or more, charge a monthly fee for those who only pay by the month.
- If the payment has not been made by the time it is a month overdue, the student loses his place in your studio unless other arrangements are made.
- If the parents are really strapped for money, *consider* doing a trade or work out a payment schedule. (I guess we are nicer than Visa.)

STUDIO POLICY STATEMENT

My best piece of business advice: write and enforce a studio policy. Writing a studio policy statement forces you to think about your mission and goals in teaching and your rules for running your business. Don't expect your students to be mind readers; they must be told how to behave and how to pay. Decide on your own comfort level and make sure it is fair to both you and your students.

I had a student, Emily, who came to my house *three* times one week for coaching sessions with her ensembles, for which there was no charge. (I have since changed that policy.) But on Emily's lesson day, she cancelled to study for a test and thus missed her regular lesson. Her father docked me for the missed lesson! I mentioned that I *had* taught her for three hours already that week and he replied, "But that was just ensemble rehearsals, not a real lesson." Boy, it felt like real lessons to me! Situations like this made me start to feel used and a little resentful, but because I didn't have an official studio policy, I had no right to expect my students to know what the rules or good manners were.

Soon after that incident, I wrote the policy that you will read below. What a difference it has made! Everyone knows the rules. If they miss a lesson, they know they still must pay for it. If I give a make-up, they know I am doing them a favor. They value the extra time I put in and are more aware of how their rescheduling and missed lessons affect my business. My studio policy also states my goals so we can work together. And somehow, even though I have been doing this for thirty years, I feel more professional and more "real."

Present the idea of a studio policy as a plus for students and parents, as it defines goals and requirements and eliminates confusion. You, the parent, and the child should sign the policy and then commit yourself to following through, or it will mean nothing. If a parent complains about a required performance or payment plan, just smile sweetly and say, "Please refer to your studio policy."

The studio policy *may* include practice and behavior expectations, a visitors rule (Parents are required/encouraged/not allowed in the studio during the lesson), reasons the teacher would terminate lessons, a performance calendar, an estimate of extra costs for music, supplies, recitals, and accompanists, and a refund policy for if the student quits during a pay period.

Other money decisions that may be included in the policy statement: Do you buy music for the students and have them pay you back? Is there a registration fee to cover printed materials and administration duties? Is there an activity fee to cover the time and cost of activities outside the normal lesson, such as parties and recitals? Is there a charge for ensemble lessons? Do students pay the lesson fee when you have to cancel to attend their performance? What is the charge if you give group lessons, master classes, and theory or history classes? If you accompany your students, do you charge for that service at contests and recitals?

This is my studio policy. Feel free to use it yourself and amend it to fit your own needs.

Bonnie Blanchard's Studio Policy

Studio policies help teachers clarify to students and parents their studio goals, rules, and business policies. These policies eliminate ambiguity and can serve as both a reference guide and a springboard for discussion.

Teaching Goals for My Students

Every teacher emphasizes different aspects of learning. After many years of teaching, I have identified the skills I believe are most important in developing students who are technically proficient, love playing the flute, and embrace music in their lives. Some of these skills are measurable, others are not. I have achieved my goals when students:

- Are successful musicians, not just flute players.
- Play using proper technique with a beautiful tone.
- Play musically and know how to phrase, where to breathe, and how to express the composer's intentions and their own emotions through their playing.
- Play a wide variety of solo and ensemble repertoire.
- Learn the equivalent of first-year college music history and theory and are able to apply that knowledge to their performance and sight reading.
- Become their own teacher by applying the basics of music theory and technique, solving their own technique problems, and learning to make choices. Students will not only perform certain pieces well, they will understand them and know how to practice the steps needed to perfect them.
- Set personal, technical, and performance goals, and work toward becoming the best musicians they can possibly be.
- Enjoy their lessons and the benefits of personal relationships forged through music.
- Include music as a joyful part of their lives. They incorporate music into their lives by listening to classical music on the radio and on CDs, attending concerts, becoming passionate about their favorite pieces, sharing music with friends, playing in ensembles, and being eager to perform. My greatest wish is that their joy for music will infuse the rest of their lives.
- Apply music skills such as goal-setting and perseverance to other aspects of their lives, leading them to be more confident, happier people with a greater ability to succeed in other areas of their lives. True self-confidence is achieved through attempting important goals, overcoming challenges, and achieving goals.

Student Responsibilities

Learning a musical instrument can be one of life's greatest challenges and rewards. My job as a teacher is to share with students my knowledge, my teaching skills, and my love of music. I promise to be respectful of students, work hard to develop their skills, and be sensitive to their individual needs. Although I will maintain my status as teacher, I will also be a reliable, trusted friend. I expect my students to maintain these same high standards and responsibilities:

- Arriving promptly to lessons.
- Bringing all lesson and assignment books.

- Being prepared for lessons with diligent and sufficient practice time. A rule of thumb for most is to practice daily an amount of time equivalent to the length of the lesson (but remember that time does not always equal quality).
- During lessons and practice, always being open to new ideas, trying hard, and putting forth their very best effort.
- Buying music, sending in contest forms, and arranging rehearsals in a timely manner.
- Paying tuition promptly.
- Petting the dog (you will both enjoy it!).

Lesson Payment

Tuition for a particular month is due at the first lesson of that month. The amount owed will be the weekly charge times the number of lessons reserved for that month. For example, if lessons are on Tuesdays, then the number of Tuesdays in that month will be multiplied by the lesson price. Ensemble lessons scheduled outside a member's normal lesson time carry a $15 per person charge. This charge must be included with the regular lesson payment.

Please remember that the lesson fee is tuition. It reserves a spot in my schedule every week for that student on that day. Though the total tuition for the month is based on an hourly amount, tuition paid also includes time and effort I invest outside of lesson time.

Payment Policies

Understanding the following payment policies will help us avoid any misunderstandings or unpleasant surprises. Please observe that:

- Tuition is due at the first lesson of the month.
- A $20.00 late fee will be assessed if tuition is not paid by the third lesson of the month.
- **Tuition is due whether or not the student attends the lesson.** I plan and provide a place for students; therefore missed lessons cannot be deducted from your tuition. No refunds will be given for cancelled lessons.
- When you have **advance knowledge of a conflict,** please refer to my student schedule to **arrange a trade and then inform me** of the schedule change.
- As a courtesy, I will try to arrange a make-up lesson for students who cannot attend due to illness. Make-up lessons are scheduled on an availability basis and are not guaranteed. Please note that when little advance notice is given, a slot may not be available. I will do my best to schedule make-up lessons but cannot promise that I can fit them into my busy schedule and yours.
- If *I* must cancel a lesson due to scheduling conflicts, there will be no charge.
- These attendance rules may be relaxed in summer and during holidays, as I can be more flexible then.

Performances

Concerts, contests, recitals, and master classes can be rewarding experiences. They give students tangible goals, opportunities to learn, and a venue to share their music. I expect all students to participate in some mutually agreed upon public performances. These may include their school district solo and ensemble contest, the Seattle Flute Society Contest, the Seattle Young Artist Festival, master classes given by invited musicians, and of course, our famous Mother's Day Recital. We all work hard to do well at all these events. Please remember that while I don't expect my students to *be* the best, I expect all of them to *do* their best.

Observation

Students with involved parents are often more successful. The learning triangle of parent, student, and teacher forms a team working together. I have an "open-door" policy and encourage you to attend lessons, especially if your child is a beginner. You'll enjoy learning music theory and listening skills right along with your child. It's a 2-for-1 deal! Please feel free to call or e-mail me with any suggestions or concerns for your child.

Please acknowledge that you have received a copy of these policies and understand them.

_____ / _____

Bonnie Blanchard   Parent Signature   Date

_____

Student Signature

Being informed of these studio policies will allow us to make beautiful music together! Thank you

DEATH AND TAXES

Everything in life is uncertain except for death and taxes and students who don't practice.

Keep good records of your income and expenses. Save receipts for music and purchases, office supplies, party supplies, advertising, studio computers and sound equipment, dues to professional organizations, and convention costs. You can deduct a prorated amount for your house based on area used primarily for business and also for utilities and a second business phone. Big expenses like pianos can be depreciated. (And be sure to deduct the cost of buying this book!)

Always consult a tax advisor when you are first starting out. If you're a homeowner, ask your tax accountant whether you should take the home office deduction. Use a computer program to keep track of income and expenses during the year so tax day is not such a shock. The Internal Revenue Service has Web pages that can help your accounting at www.irs.ustreas.gov, and you should also download IRS publication 587, *Business Use of Your Home.*

YOU ARE A VALUED PROFESSIONAL

Just as you make a commitment to your students to be the best teacher possible, make a commitment to yourself to get reimbursed for the good job you are doing. You are worth it!

TWENTY-NINE

A Life in the Arts: Is It for You?

THE JOYS AND PAINS OF A MUSICIAN'S LIFE

Our group of eight musician friends talked and laughed as our lively conversation drifted to a discussion of the ups and downs of life as a self-employed musician. Louise, a music major in college, had recently changed positions, leaving the music field. "How's your new job?" I asked. "It's a great job, with a lot of advantages," Louise told us, and then added, a little wistfully, "I do love it, but I'll never feel the passion I did when I worked in music." "At least it's an eight-to-five job with benefits," said Karen, a former member of a professional quartet who worked many evenings and weekends as director of a successful teen chamber music program. Melinda, the music critic for the Seattle Times, Eileen and Page, who teach, play in two orchestras, and freelance, Mary Kay, who accompanies my students, and Nancy, an internationally known vocalist, readily agreed.

As we talked that afternoon, I realized that life is a tradeoff sometimes. Musicians enjoy rewards unsurpassed in other professions and also experience some downsides. As musicians starting out, it was perfectly normal for us not to get any money at all for our first few gigs. I pictured a comic drawing you may have seen, titled: "If other professions were treated like musicians." The illustration shows a homeowner talking to a plumber as he points to his toilet. "I need you to fix this today," the homeowner says. "I can't pay you, but I promise to give you great exposure." Every musician, at one time or another, has been taken advantage of as free entertainment, and we all know that such "exposure" doesn't pay the bills.

Even as a professional, the life of a self-employed musician can be tough. Unpredictable paychecks, unusual hours, and fierce competition are a few of the disadvantages. But don't let those discourage you. Career experts suggest we find our perfect job by first determining our passion. Here are some things to consider when making the choice to become a professional musician or teacher.

The Downside of Life as a Self-Employed Musician

- You have weird hours. Musicians typically perform at night and on weekends. Even if you're teaching, you will still need to work mainly after-school hours and on weekends.

- Your life is not your own. Teaching is not just a job that you can leave at the office. Students phone seven days a week and some assume you're always on call.

- Your paychecks fluctuate. One month you get four extra playing jobs and two new students, and then the next month is a week-long school holiday and all your students desert you for Hawaii or Disney World.

- You might need two or more jobs. If you don't have steady work, you must supplement your playing with extra jobs sometimes unrelated to music.

- You might experience dry spells. Only musicians with long-term contracts, such as symphony players, can count on seasons of steady work, and even these players don't necessarily have long-term job security. The stress of always needing to find more work leads some musicians to seek permanent, full-time positions outside of music and then play music to supplement them.

- You have to race from one job to the next, and your car may become your second home.

- Your "benefits" will not be monetary. If you're self-employed, or work part-time for many different employers, you won't be eligible for unemployment compensation and typical benefits such as sick leave or paid vacations (unless you factor vacation days into your payment schedule). You'll also have no retirement plan with matching funds, no employer-sponsored health plan or life insurance, and no automatic pay raises.

- The amount of practice, money, and work you put into music could make you a millionaire in other jobs.

- You are your own promoter, marketing department, and publicist. You can never stop "selling" yourself and your business to prospective clients. It's like perpetual dating!

- You may feel taken for granted. Some students and clients treat you like royalty while others treat you like a babysitter, a servant, or even a potted plant.

- You are your own boss.

As the joke goes: The definition of an amateur musician is someone with a day job, and the definition of a professional musician is someone whose *spouse* has a day job!

The Plus Side of Life as a Self-Employed Musician

Who can put a price on the joy of music and moments like these? The feeling of being in love when you hear or play a romantic piece. The goose bumps that appear when you hear a phenomenal composition. The pride of accomplishment when you overcome technical difficulties and finally get it. The intense communication and joy in sharing when playing with others. The sense of awe from a master's performance. The applause after a stellar performance of your own. The pride in a student's accomplishments or the warm glow when students say you changed their lives. The comfort of having a lifelong friend to turn to through better or worse, in good times and in bad, in sickness and in health, until death. . . . You understand the analogy to marriage—although love of an instrument has outlasted many spouses.

Your job is both your passion and your hobby. You work hard and make sacrifices, but how many people spend their days (OK, and nights) working with something so dear to their hearts? As a musician you bring to people inspiration and magic to entertain them, ease their aching hearts, and stir their emotions. We are so privileged!

- You can always keep learning. There is one more piece to practice, one more topic to study, something new to listen to, one more student to figure out, and one more teaching trick to learn.
- You meet wonderful, educated, creative, and inspirational people.
- You're never totally out of work. Unlike employees in "regular" jobs you can lose by being fired or laid off, musicians can multitask.
- You contribute to society. As a musician you connect to the past and give to the future of civilization.
- You can set your own hours to some extent.
- You can enjoy lifestyles of the rich and famous, at least while you're at the gig.
- You're admired by people in the community. When new people I meet ask me my profession—after they ask, "Do you play for the symphony?" or "Can you make a living doing that?"—they are intrigued by what I do. Many times I even detect a bit of jealousy.
- The pay per hour can sometimes be fairly good. Okay, it's not a doctor's or lawyer's salary, but we're dealing with music, not blood and messy divorces!
- You are your own boss. No time clocks, no performance ratings; upper management is you!
- Teaching music can touch your students in every way: Music for Life!
- You can't live without it!

Do you feel better now? Life as a musician or self-employed studio teacher can be crazy, but it can be well worth the rewards.

MAKING THE DECISION TO BECOME A PROFESSIONAL PERFORMING MUSICIAN

Remember the questions you asked yourself before determining if you were qualified to become a private music teacher? If you are considering a job as a freelance musician, consider these practical issues. Will this career provide the income and benefits you need? Is family your highest priority at this stage in your life, or is career advancement, self-fulfillment, or having free time more important? What is most significant to you in a career: money, power, stability, fulfillment, flexible hours?

If you want to perform, list all the possible jobs you could have considering your skills, personality, values, and experience. Expect keen competition. How do you measure up compared to others in your field? Are you versatile, or do you have something special to offer?

Can You Make a Living as a
Musician or Private Studio Teacher?

As in most careers, it takes time and effort to build a reputation, and it's a long way to the top. As a musician you may need to use all your skills and have several jobs. Currently I teach twenty-five students, am writing this book, and am the director and musician in five groups with Silverwood Music Ensembles. It's a job with many hats, but all are fun.

Use these ideas to compose a list of all areas in which your talent can be used:

Band musician (blues bands, jazz bands, rock bands, wedding bands); Casino, lounge, and hotel vocalist or musician; Chamber musician (playing in quartets, trios, etc.); Church choir director, soloist, or organist; Cruise liner musician; Ensemble singer; Musical theatre performer; Cabaret, classical, or concert performer; Pit orchestra musician; Private studio musician; Private teacher; Recital soloist/concerto soloist; Sacred music specialist; Studio musician; Theme park (such as Busch Gardens, Disneyland) vocalist or musician.

Other Opportunities May Await You
in the Music Community

Does the thought of being self-employed without a steady paycheck make you break out into a cold sweat? Do you love music and want it to be in your life, but need a steadier paycheck than part-time or intermittent work would give you? Do you have other talents, such as teaching or writing skills, that you'd also like to use on a professional level? Many exciting careers can provide the security you seek and allow you to merge your music skills with your other talents and training.

Here are some possibilities to get your brain ticking:

Accessory maker (of music bags, jewelry, etc.); Actor; Armed forces musician or vocalist (4,000 serve worldwide in the Army, Navy, Marine Corps, Air Force, and Coast Guard); Arranger; Booking agent; Business manager; Choral director (for community choirs, schools, theatre groups); College or university professor; Composer; Computer musician; Conductor; Early music education specialist; Elementary through high school teacher; Employee of the Public Broadcasting Service or National Public Radio; Educational outreach person for a major performing group; Ethnomusicologist; Film or CD editor; Grant writer; Government arts advocate/worker (that is, National Endowment for the Arts); Instrument maker; Instrument repair person; Instrument or sheet music sales representative; Music attorney; Movie, jingle, computer game, or ad composer; Music book author (!); Music consultant; Music copyist; Music critic; Music editor; Music promoter; Music publicist; Music researcher; Music store manager; Opera vocalist or musician; Orchestra or opera education specialist; Orchestra conductor; Performing arts manager or development specialist; Piano tuner; Radio announcer, disc jockey, or producer; Recording engineer or technician; Recreation Director; Sound reinforcement specialist (setting up sound systems for pop/rock); Staff or freelance song writer; Transcriber.

The Reality of Jobs in the Music World

Wow! There sure are a lot of jobs for musicians, but wait, there are even more musicians wanting those jobs! Imagine the thousands of music students at the thousands of colleges and conservatories around the country. Add to that the professionals with degrees searching for more work. Compound that with people coming from all around the world to get their training and make their mark. The result? Sixty string basses try out for one symphony position; one mistake and they're out of the running. The Juilliard graduate lands a one-year contract with an orchestra; when the contract expires he can't find any other work and has to sell his bassoon to make ends meet. The conservatory master's degree student earns as much money teaching as the person with no degree at all. One principal orchestra job opens up every year and two thousand people are dreaming and practicing. The volunteer community orchestra is full of conservatory graduates. The student with the doctorate finally lands the orchestra job in the small city and gets paid yearly half of what he was paying in tuition. Argh!

The Music Teacher's Responsibility

In my studio alone I have many wonderful students who would make terrific professionals. They have the talent, love, and drive to make it happen, but there are so few jobs. Am I being less than honest by pushing them and preparing them for this life?

My goal is to awaken in my students a love of music and to help them fulfill their potential. I push and prod them to become the best they can be. I will give them the skills and knowledge to become music majors if that is what they want. But I am very open about what life as a professional musician is like and their chances of ever having a music career.

It's immoral to give students with marginal talent encouragement to become music majors or professionals, and our duty as teachers is to be brutally honest with students about their chances. Most teachers need to realize that we are ultimately training *audiences,* not performers.

My musically talented and bright student Katy just finished auditioning for conservatories. Almost weekly I have counseled her to consider going to a college that offers other programs, too, and suggested she might double major. But all Katy can think about is music, music, music. Last week she finally said, "I know you keep telling me that becoming a professional musician is really tough, but you know I am going to do it anyway so you might as well accept it." I am thrilled that Katy got accepted to a major conservatory (Eastman) and will be living her dream, but at the present writing I have seven other students who are at conservatories. There are not even enough professional playing jobs for my own students!

But I and most of my other musician friends are glad of the path we have chosen. I love my job and my life as a performing musician and teacher and wouldn't trade it for anything. As long as I am truthful to my students about what life is like as a musician, it is their choice. If they want it badly enough, they will find a way.

THIRTY

Make the Teacher's Life Easier

I f you've read this far, you know that the job of the music teacher is an extraordinarily demanding one. It is deeply rewarding to teach aspiring musicians and watch them blossom, but it's also stressful, both physically and mentally. Teachers need to learn how to take care of themselves so that they can do their job well and truly enjoy what they're doing. Let's look at the many ways we can save our time, our bodies, and our sanity with a little careful planning.

IN THE STUDIO
Sitting and Standing

Just sitting or standing still for hours on end can be tiring, so try to keep moving. Changing positions is good for our bodies and also simulates real-life performances in ensembles and as soloists. Even if you have an instrument that requires sitting, take frequent breaks to stretch during the lesson. Shift positions in the chair; walk around the room. Move your arms and legs out of a static position.

Get a comfortable, ergonomic chair. If you sit next to your student, try using a revolving chair so that you are not always turning your head or twisting your body. Use a wedge-shaped cushion for back support and a comfortable cushion on the piano bench. For the ultimate in winter luxury, use a heated chair pad as I do.

The Studio

Make your "work station" efficient and convenient. Use a conductor's stand that holds a lot of music and be sure it is high enough. Put pencil holders (wire spirals or clip-on shelves) on every stand. Have a nightstand or small table close at hand to hold necessities including a tuner, a metronome, reward stickers, extra manuscript and notebook paper, a music dictionary, and a *stash of candy*. Keep a designated place for your lesson schedule, payment records, checks, and phone numbers, so you're not always scrambling. Bring a thermos for hot tea or coffee. Use a rear-view mirror on the piano if soloists are not in your direct view.

Sheet Music

Tired of all those piles on the piano, the chairs, the couch, and the floor? Is your music studio a black hole? Use file cabinets to hold music. The time you spend filing will be half of the time you spend searching. File music alphabetically by composer under such categories as etudes, solos, duets, duets with piano, trios, trios with piano, quartets, larger ensembles, pop music, and Christmas music. Compile a master list. (Use this system for CDs, too.) Reserve a special place for music that is presently being worked on so you don't have to go into the file cabinet every lesson. I have plastic folders that hang on the wall within easy reach of the piano. You can use a small box or a corner of the piano if it is reserved only for music that is needed every week. Use a file cabinet for handouts (such as biographies of composers, theory pages, studio policies, how-to-practice lists, etc.) and again have a master list. Save time by ordering music by mail, the Internet, or phone and have students buy their own music instead of buying it for them and charging them.

Designate a "lost and found" spot so students know right where to go when they are missing something. Have students mark their manuscript books and each assignment with a stiff adhesive note so they can immediately turn to their assignment and save time.

At the end of each workday or between lessons, take time to organize your studio and put everything back where it belongs. You'll thank yourself tomorrow.

Using the Computer

Ever wish you could clone yourself? Teach one student while the other learns music theory, history, rhythm drills, or ear training on the computer, and then switch. Computer games and timed drills make students more fluent and make you more money.

Order music and books online. Access information about composers and so much more on the Web. Use digital recordings and keyboards hooked up to the computer.

Tired of writing lists and other information that you can never find? Type it on the computer! Keep all contacts and appointments here.

Stay connected through the computer. Regularly send out e-mails and pictures. The computer can even be used in place of a phone dial up your students! Talk long distance through a computer microphone and save money on phone bills.

Keep your calendar on the computer and program it to remind you of things that need to be done on certain dates. Categorize your life into teaching, family, and student lists to stay organized.

Who needs a bookkeeper? Print out checks and use your computer to balance your checkbook and keep track of all expenses for tax time.

SAVING YOUR BODY
General Tips

When traveling to gigs, use a lightweight folding Manhasset stand and a suitcase with wheels to transport music.

Don't fight your instrument; keep it in good shape so it plays well. Spend the money for comfortable chin and shoulder rests, neck straps, and piano benches.

Prescriptions from "the doctor": Stand far enough away when students' playing is extremely loud or high-pitched. Investigate musician earplugs and visit an ear-nose-throat doctor to test whether you have any hearing loss. If you need reading glasses, use them (and as much as we hate to look like old schoolmarms, glasses hung around the neck save lots of time searching for them). Frequently use a metronome, tuner, and full-length mirror and let them "do the nagging" instead of using your voice.

Are you eating in the car? Is McDonald's your home away from home? Make time to eat healthy foods. Watch all that caffeine, fat, and carbohydrates. (OK, chocolate is an essential!) Do you exercise? If you are too busy to exercise, you are too busy.

I'm Always Catching Colds from My Students. How Can I Keep Well?

At least you're not sick of your students! Encourage your students to stay home when they're ill, especially in the first forty-eight hours when colds are most contagious. Offer make-up lessons if necessary. Educate students on how colds are spread through contact and in the air. Find out whether such popular remedies as the herbal supplement Airborne, taken both as a preventative and at the first sign of a cold, will work for you.

Don't touch students or their instruments. Demonstrate on your own instrument. Wipe the piano keys and doorknobs with disinfectant wipes after a sniffling student and keep your distance from "drippy" students so they're not blowing germs on you. Avoid touching your eyes, nose, and mouth.

Keep a bottle of waterless hand sanitizer in the studio for you and the students. Ask those with colds to use it at the beginning of their lessons. Advise them to cough into their shoulder, not their hands. Keep a supply of tissues available.

Set a good example. When you're sick, cancel lessons so you can take care of yourself and avoid contaminating others. Rest in bed, treat your symptoms, and increase your fluid intake. Eat right, sleep well, exercise. Keep yourself strong so you'll be less vulnerable to illness. Only your body's own defenses can combat a cold.

SAVING TIME AND BEING MORE EFFICIENT

When your schedule is crammed, schedule a couple of nights where you work late or get up earlier a few mornings to get things back on track. This works especially well for parents with children. You can get twice as much done before the kids get up or after they go to bed.

Keep a daily "to do" list and check it to prioritize. Keep a separate list for long-term projects. (Sometimes just writing it down puts it in perspective.) Try to handle papers only once. As soon as the mail comes in, stand over the waste paper basket. File papers right away so you don't have to keep moving those piles around your desk.

Stay off the phone as much as possible; use e-mail instead. Keep parents informed with a newsletter. Do mass e-mails or mass mailings instead of talking to students and families individually about upcoming events.

Hire students to do drudge work such as filing and mending music. Ask parents for help with small secretarial and phoning jobs. Most parents are happy to help you out when they see how hard you are working for their child.

Assign scheduling responsibility to your students when they need to trade lessons or have ensemble rehearsal.

Cut down on rehearsals by letting students rehearse on their own for ensembles and privately with the accompanist. Rotate using students' lessons for ensemble time instead of adding extra rehearsals for ensembles. Only attend very special concerts.

No time to practice? Squeeze in scales and etudes before, after, and in between students. Play duets, sometimes play etudes along with the student, and demonstrate. When a student is late or cancels, use that bonus time to practice. Consider bringing your instrument along on vacation.

How Do I Balance a Full Teaching Schedule, Performing, and a Family?

We all have many demands competing for our time, and if we're not careful, we'll shortchange ourselves or someone else. Learn how to prioritize, delegate, and "just say no." Write your priorities down on paper and budget your time accordingly. If personal practice is at the top, or family time, budget time for it. (And to my friends who are reading this book, yes, I will have more free time once this book is published, once my children have graduated from high school, . . . and when pigs fly.)

Suggestions to Make Your Family Life More Balanced

Your schedule

If possible, teach during the day if you have school-age children. Taking kids out of band or orchestra for private lessons at a school provides this opportunity. Ask students who call at ten o'clock on Friday night to call back during the "workday." Keep your family apprised of your daily schedule so they know when they can count on you. Save weekends for family activities, and take family vacations and leave music student worries behind. Practice your instrument when your children are napping or at school. (Drummers and trombonists, do your best!)

If you can afford it, hire a cleaning service. It is really more time-efficient to teach a couple of extra hours and earn the money to pay someone to clean for four hours. Or better yet, just get your kids to do it!

Family life

Involve your children in their own music lessons so they understand your commitment to the tradition of music. And even if it's the last thing you feel like doing after a long teaching day, help your children with their practice if they want you to. Invite your family to performances so they can share in your pride of accomplishment.

Try to teach in a private room away from family activities so they don't have to tiptoe around and interrupt lessons. Hire a babysitter so young children don't interrupt lessons.

Don't compare your children to your students, even if these students are talented, well-behaved children with perfect 4.0 grade point averages. Remember, like a grandparent, you only see students at their best.

Marry someone who understands the importance of what you do, not just the amount of money you make. (Thank you, Don!)

If you had a lousy day teaching, try not to take it out on your family. Take a big breath, take five minutes away by yourself, and then change your attitude. (I do admit my husband has been known to ask the last student of the day, "How was your lesson? Because if it was bad, she'll take it out on me!" He's just kidding. Isn't he?)

Remember that being a part-time teacher is really a full-time job. Don't take on too many other responsibilities because you or your family feel you only work part-time. Above all, remember that your first priority is to your family. Make time every week to share laughter, fun, and love. (And don't spend all your time writing a book!)

Dinner

End your teaching day at a normal dinner time so you can have a family dinner together. Numerous studies have proven the benefits to children of a family meal, including mentally and physically healthier children and even reduced substance abuse risk. Make dinners during the day so they're ready to pop in the oven as soon as the last student leaves. Cook dinners in large enough quantities to freeze and defrost for those crazy days. Ask for help from family members and use time-saving tools such as quick packaged dinners, pizza, or take-out food, but don't fall into the trap of family members heating up their own dinners and retreating to their own corners of the house.

Analyze your work day

Would working different hours help you feel more energized? How about putting Saturday students during the week so you can have a weekend? Conversely, if your weekdays seem to stretch from morning to midnight, consider shifting a couple of your students to a weekend day. Can you teach at "odd hours," such as first thing in the morning, or teach adults during school time so the evening can be freer? Can you start earlier or teach with no breaks to end earlier? If you travel to teach, are you wasting time between lessons or could you set up a home studio to eliminate commute time?

SAVING YOUR SANITY

Make the Lessons Pleasant for Yourself as well as Your Students

Small treats in the lesson can help sustain you through hours of teaching. Keep hydrated with bottled plain or sparkling water. Get a thermos with a pump top for easy access to tea or coffee. Eat a handful of almonds or—my personal favorite—have some chocolate chips handy when you need to be sweetened up after that exasperating student. Make the room pleasant and *clean.* Keep it a comfortable temperature. Burn a candle. Buy yourself flowers. How about a comic calendar with a joke a day? And remember to only teach the students you are happy to see walk in the door.

Gain Perspective

You love music, but music can't be your whole life. We all need short breaks to rejuvenate our enthusiasm. Take a vacation (and the music convention doesn't count). Go out with friends and don't talk about students or other musicians. Have another hobby. *Get a life.*

When teaching seems like an overwhelming job, talk to people in other professions. Do they love their jobs all the time? Your job has some stresses, but so do all jobs. Are you feeling burned out as a result of teaching or of other aspects of your life?

Keep some distance between yourself and your students by not being too involved in their personal lives or caring more than they care. Be happy for their successes but don't let their "failures" get you down. Do your very best, but don't beat yourself up when it doesn't work.

Realize the impact you have on students' lives. Take the responsibility of teaching them seriously, but don't make it your whole life, or you will end up demanding too much of your students and of yourself. This book is about being a hard-working, dedicated teacher, but it must also be about balance. As much as it might seem like life and death sometimes, it's not. It's not worth it if it's not fun. Keep healthy and happy for yourself and your students so you can all have *Music for Life.*

FOR FURTHER READING

BOOKS ON MUSIC PERFORMANCE

Bruser, Madeline. *The Art of Practicing: A Guide to Making Music from the Heart.* New York: Bell Tower, 1997.

Green, Barry. *The Mastery of Music: Ten Pathways to True Artistry.* New York: Broadway Books, a division of Random House, 2003.

———, with W. Timothy Gallwey. *The Inner Game of Music.* Garden City, N.Y.: Anchor/Doubleday, 1986.

Greene, Don. *Audition Success: An Olympic Sports Psychologist Teaches Performing Artists How to Win.* New York: Routledge, 2001.

———. *Performance Success: Performing Your Best under Pressure.* New York: Routledge, 2002.

Havas, Kató. *Stage Fright: Its Causes and Cures, with Special Reference to Violin Playing.* London: Bosworth, 1973.

O'Reilly, Sally. *String Rhythms for Classroom or Individual Study.* San Diego: Kjos, 1992.

Ristad, Eloise. *A Soprano on Her Head: Right-Side-Up Reflections on Life and Other Performances.* Moab, Utah: Real People Press, 1982.

BOOKS ON SIGHT READING

Ayola, Edward L. *Winning Rhythms: A Winning Approach to Rhythm Skill Development for All Ages and All Instruments.* San Diego, Calif.: Neil A. Kjos, Jr., 1985.

Bona, Pasquale. *Complete Method for Rhythmical Articulation.* New York: Carl Fisher, 1961.

Ely, Richard. *Accuracy in Rhythm for All Instruments: 55 Studies in Duet Form.* Century City, Calif.: Wimbledon Music, 1980.

O'Reilly, Sally. *String Rhythms: For Classroom or Individual Study.* San Diego, Calif.: Neil A. Kjos Co., 1992.

Richman, Howard. *Super Sight-Reading Secrets: An Innovative, Step-by-Step Program for Keyboard Players of All Levels.* 3rd rev. ed. Tarzana, Calif.: Sound Feelings, 1986.

BOOKS ON TEACHING MUSIC

Baker-Jordan, Martha. *Practical Piano Pedagogy: The Definitive Text for Piano Teachers and Pedagogy Students.* Miami: Warner Bros., 2004.

Beeching, Angela Myles. *Beyond Talent: Creating a Successful Career in Music.* Oxford: Oxford University Press, 2005.

Bernstein, Seymour. *With Your Own Two Hands: Self-Discovery through Music.* New York: Schirmer, 1981.

Boytim, Joan Frey. *The Private Voice Studio Handbook: A Practical Guide to All Aspects of Teaching.* Milwaukee: Hal Leonard, 2003.

Cannel, Ward, and Fred Marx. *How to Play the Piano despite Years of Lessons: What Music Is and How to Make It at Home.* Garden City, N.Y.: Doubleday, 1976.

Clark, Frances. *Questions and Answers: Practical Solutions and Suggestions Given to Questions Commonly Asked by Piano Teachers.* Northfield, Ill.: The Instrumentalist, 1992.

Cutietta, Robert A. *Raising Musical Kids: A Guide for Parents.* Oxford: Oxford University Press, 2001.

Elliott, David James. *Music Matters: A New Philosophy of Music Education.* New York: Oxford University Press, 1995.

Gordon, Stewart. *Mastering the Art of Performance: A Primer for Musicians.* New York: Oxford University Press, 2006.

Holt, John. *Never Too Late: My Musical Life Story.* Reading, Mass.: Addison-Wesley, 1991.

Horvath, Janet. *Playing Less Hurt: An Injury Prevention Guide for Musicians.* Rev. ed. Minneapolis: J. Horvath, 2004.

Johnston, Philip. *The Practice Revolution.* Canberra, Australia: PracticeSpot Press, 2002.

————, and David Sutton. *Not until You've Done Your Practice.* Pearce, Australia: Future Perfect, 2000.

Jordan, James. *The Musician's Walk: An Ethical Labyrinth.* Chicago: GIA Publications, 2006.

Jourdain, Robert. *Music, the Brain, and Ecstasy: How Music Captures Our Imagination.* New York: W. Morrow, 1997.

Judy, Stephanie. *Making Music for the Joy of It: Enhancing Creativity, Skills, and Musical Confidence.* Los Angeles: J. P. Tarcher, 1990.

Machover, Wilma, and Marienne Uszler. *Sound Choices: Guiding Your Child's Musical Experiences.* New York: Oxford University Press, 1996.

Marsalis, Wynton. *Marsalis on Music.* New York: Norton, 1995.

Richards, Cynthia. *How to Get Your Child to Practice without Resorting to Violence.* Provo, Utah: Advance Publications, 1985.

Sand, Barbara Lourie. *Teaching Genius: Dorothy DeLay and the Making of a Musician.* Portland: Amadeus, 2000.

Shockley, Rebecca. *Mapping Music: For Faster Learning and Secure Memory—A Guide for Teachers and Students.* Middleton, Wisc.: A-R Editions, 2001.

BOOKS ON THE MUSIC BUSINESS

Butler, Mimi. *The Complete Guide to Making More Money in the Private Music Studio.* Haddonfield, N.J.: Mimi Butler, 2002.

————. *The Complete Guide to Running a Private Music Studio.* Haddonfield, N.J.: Mimi Butler, 2001.

Newsam, David R., and Barbara Sprague Newsam. *Making Money Teaching Music.* Cincinnati: Writers' Digest Books, 1995.

BOOKS ON MUSIC

Barber, David. *Bach, Beethoven and the Boys.* Toronto: Sound and Vision, 1996.

Kogan, Judith. *Nothing But the Best: The Struggle for Perfection at The Juilliard School.* New York: Limelight Editions, 1989.

Krull, Kathleen. *Lives of the Musician: Good Times, Bad Times (and What the Neighbors Thought).* San Diego: Harcourt Brace and Co., 1993.

Pogue, David, and Scott Speck. *Classical Music for Dummies.* Foster City, Calif.: IDG Books Worldwide, 1997.

Stanley, John. *Classical Music: The Great Composers and Their Masterworks.* Birkenhead, Auckland, New Zealand: Reed Consumer Books, 2004.

INSPIRATIONAL BOOKS

Blanchard, Kenneth. *The One Minute Manager.* New York: HarperCollins, 1982.

Blanchard, Ken, Susan Fowler, and Laurence Hawkins. *Self-Leadership and the One Minute Manager: Increasing Effectiveness through Situational Self-Leadership.* New York: W. Morrow, 2005.

Carnegie, Dale. *How to Enjoy Your Life and Your Job.* London: Cedar, 1989.

————. *How to Win Friends and Influence People.* London: Vermillion, 2006.

Covey, Sean. *The Seven Habits of Highly Effective Teens: The Ultimate Teenage Success Guide.* New York: Simon and Schuster, 1998.

Covey, Stephan. *The Seven Habits of Highly Effective People: Restoring the Character Ethic.* New York: Simon and Schuster, 1989.

Lowndes, Leil. *How to Talk to Anyone: Ninety-Two Little Tricks for Big Success in Relationships.* Chicago: Contemporary Books, 2003.

McGinnis, Alan Loy. *Bringing Out the Best in People: How to Enjoy Helping Others Excel.* Minneapolis: Augsberg, 1985.

McGraw, Phil. *Family First: Your Step-by-Step Plan for Creating a Phenomenal Family.* New York: Free Press, 2004.

Peale, Norman Vincent. *The Power of Positive Thinking.* Running Press, 2002.

Scott, Steven K. *Simple Steps to Impossible Dreams: The Fifteen Power Secrets of the World's Most Successful People.* New York: Simon and Schuster, 1998.

Urban, Hal. *Positive Words, Powerful Results: Simple Ways to Honor, Affirm, and Celebrate Life.* New York: Simon and Schuster, 2004.

PERIODICALS

American Music Teacher, the official journal of the Music Teachers National Association

Clavier magazine

Flute Talk magazine

The Flutist Quarterly, the official magazine of the National Flute Association

The Instrumentalist magazine

Windplayer magazine

INDEX

ABOUT THE AUTHORS

BONNIE BLANCHARD has long been respected in the Seattle area as a versatile free-lance musician and a dynamic instructor of award-winning students. She holds music and teaching degrees from the University of Washington. She began playing flute when she was 19, and later engaged in a series of private lessons on piano, violin, viola, voice, and flute.

A flute instructor for thirty years, Bonnie has had the opportunity to work with many of the world's greatest flutists and teachers. Her creative ideas and unbridled enthusiasm for teaching have consistently produced students who win top awards in local and national contests and earn college and conservatory scholarships. Her students excel at their instrument *and* love what they are doing. The rapport Bonnie cultivates with her students and her unique teaching techniques create musicians who develop the skill and the lifelong love of music that help them achieve in other areas of their lives.

Bonnie is founder of the popular Silverwood Music Ensembles (www.silverwood music.com) and is featured on the Silverwood compact disc *Here Comes the Bride,* used by brides all over the country. Silverwood has performed in the Northwest's top venues and performed for the Boeing Company, Microsoft, the World Trade Organization delegates, and President Bill Clinton.

Bonnie lives in Seattle with her "tone deaf" but supportive husband and their two sons, who each play piano and a stringed instrument. Most of the time they accept her special blend of motivation and humor as the result of genuine concern for their talent and potential.

CYNTHIA BLANCHARD ACREE is author of *The Gulf between Us: Love and Terror in Desert Storm.* Her dual memoir was featured as a "Today's Best Nonfiction" excerpt in *Reader's Digest.* Her presentations around the country have included appearances on ABC's *20/20,* NBC's *Today,* CNN, FOX, C-Span 2's Book TV, and National Public Radio.

Cynthia graduated magna cum laude with a bachelor's degree in psychology from the University of Washington, where she also earned a Master of Science degree in psychology. An author, writing consultant, editor, and dynamic speaker, she has developed and presented scores of programs on topics including public speaking, motivation, and goal-setting. Her "Writing for Results" workshops draw on her nearly three decades of experience helping people to strengthen their writing skills and their confidence.

Cynthia has performed in choral groups in Washington, Virginia, Georgia, and Florida, and now sings with the North San Diego County Concert Chorale. She lives in Oceanside, California, with her husband and their two boys, who play violin and trombone. Her sons have given her the opportunity to field-test suggestions for how to get kids to practice.